Plan To Protect®
ISBN: 978-1-4866-2277-1
All rights reserved.
2022

Plan to Protect®
117 Ringwood Drive
Unit 11
Stouffville, ON
L4A 8C1

Tel: 905-642-4693
Toll Free: 1-877-455-3555
Email: info@plantoprotect.com
Website: www.plantoprotect.com

Plan to Protect®
A Safeguarding Guide for
Children, Youth and Adults
Church Edition

Published by Word Alive Press
119 De Baets St.
Winnipeg, MB Canada R2J 3R9
www.wordalivepress.ca

All rights reserved with the exception that permission is granted to the purchaser of this manual a single license use for your local church. No part of this book may be transmitted in any form or by any means, electronic or mechanical, or any part posted on the internet, without written permission from Plan to Protect®. Permission is granted to the purchaser and/or bearer of this published work a single party license of the registered trademark "Plan to Protect®." This use of the single third party license is restricted to organizations that credit the majority of their abuse prevention policy to the Plan to Protect® manual. The registered trademark symbol must accompany the phrase Plan to Protect®. For more information on use please visit our website www.plantoprotect.com

Scripture quotations marked NLT are taken from the Holy Bible, New Living Translation®, copyright © 1996, 2004, 2015 by Tyndale House Foundation. Used by permission of Tyndale House Publishers, Carol Stream, Illinois 60188. All rights reserved. Scripture quotations marked NIV are taken from The Holy Bible, New International Version® NIV®, Copyright © 1973, 1978, 1984, 2011 by Biblica, Inc. TM Used by permission. All rights reserved worldwide. Scripture quotations taken from the (NASB®) New American Standard Bible®, Copyright © 1960, 1971, 1977, 1995, 2020 by The Lockman Foundation. Used by permission. All rights reserved. www.lockman.org

The development, preparation and publication of this work has been undertaken with great care. However, the publisher, editors, employees and agents of Plan to Protect® are not responsible for any errors contained herein or for consequences that may ensue from use of materials or information contained in this work. This manual is not a policy, but rather a plan to establish policy. It is only as current as the date of the publication and does not reflect subsequent changes in law. This manual is distributed with the understanding that it does not constitute legal advice.

Organizations are strongly encouraged to seek legal counsel as well as counsel from their insurance company who can give written opinion concerning the specifics of their particular situation when establishing a policy. With regard to case studies, identities and circumstances of information discussed herein have been changed to protect confidentiality.

Cover Design: Eilleen Navarro

Congratulations on your purchase of Plan to Protect®
A Safeguarding Guide for Children, Youth and Adults (Church Edition).

Besides purchasing the paper version of this manual, we are happy to make available to you a downloadable copy of the Appendices from the manual for your use. Simply use the code listed below when visiting our website. Once you have downloaded it to your computer, you can customize the documents to reflect your policies and add them right on to your policy document.

How to access the free download:

1. Visit www.plantoprotect.com

2. Click on the link for Downloads (at the very bottom of the home page)

3. Click on the picture of the newest edition of the manual for churches.

4. The Username and Password are both (including the dashes): **C&m22-mvrf-101020**

5. Download the file and save onto your computer.

While you are visiting our website, we encourage you to take a few moments to:
- View a complimentary webinar on tips for successful implementation of Plan to Protect®;
- Read our extended list of FAQ's and articles; and
- Acquaint yourself with our many tools, resources and training options.

Plan to Protect® provides the HIGHEST STANDARD for safeguarding and abuse prevention for churches and community organizations serving the vulnerable sector in North America and around the world. The HIGHEST STANDARD that you will find in the manual meets the insurance company demands for abuse coverage and will demonstrate your duty of care.

Plan to Protect® was first written with a deep desire to provide protection for the vulnerable sector and the church. Please join us in helping to inspire others to see that Plan to Protect® is not just something we have to do in order to do ministry, rather it is a ministry in itself.

Thank you for investing in this resource and the protection of children, youth and adults within the church. We encourage you to check out our other training, tools and resources to help you achieve a high standard of protection. We invite you to become a member of Plan to Protect®!

Plan to Protect®

- A Letter from Plan to Protect®
- Call to Action
- A Safe Ministry: A Partnership
- Document Terms
- Table of Contents

A Letter from Plan to Protect®

Twenty-five years ago (1996), we entered the race to combat abuse within churches. At the time, incidents of abuse were hitting the headlines, and insurance companies were excluding abuse from insurance policies. Victims started publishing stories of their lived experiences of abuse, including abuse by clergy. Churches and denominations scrambled to write protection protocols.

That race became a marathon; the marathon has now become an integral part of church ministry. There are many reasons why churches join the race. For some it is to avoid liability, for others it is to meet the requirements of insurance companies, and for others it is because they are resolving to do better after an incident of abuse has occurred.

Twenty-five years ago, it started as a labour of love and a deep desire to protect children by Carol Rice Wiebe under the direction and mandate of The Christian and Missionary Alliance in Canada. However, no one wants to run a marathon on their own. Over the years, Jane Cushing Cates and I joined the marathon, along with Wayne L. Bernakevitch (McDougall Gauley LLP), Ken Hall (Robertson Hall Insurance), Adrian Miedema (Dentons) and individuals who we have consulted and highly respect.

Fifteen years ago (2007), under the name Winning Kids Inc., a small group of people, including Carol, Jane and me, started the company with the blessing of The Christian and Missionary Alliance in Canada. We desired to create a social enterprise, missional in focus. We were then, and continue to be committed to providing the HIGHEST STANDARD of abuse prevention and protection to organizations serving the vulnerable sector. Each year we have expanded our reach ... beyond churches, beyond Canada, beyond protecting children. Thank you for helping us make a difference. As a company, we have witnessed the hand of God providing for us and protecting us through difficult times. Our staff have made tremendous sacrifices, for which I am incredibly grateful.

Today over 16 denominations and 15,000+ churches have partnered with Plan to Protect® with a shared goal to encourage the church and our communities to achieve a high standard of protection. For so many of our clients and members Plan to Protect® has become a ministry of safety! It has become a ministry to Children, Youth, and Adults. Plan to Protect® has become a ministry to Parents, Ministry Personnel, and offenders. It has become a ministry to victim-survivors of abuse.

It has been our privilege to run this marathon, influence the Church in Canada, protect the vulnerable, and speak on behalf of victim-survivors of abuse.

This newest and updated version of Plan to Protect® represents 25 years of research, consulting, and a collection of best practices in safeguarding from many, many voices. In this newest manual we have incorporated the voices of victim-survivors of abuse. Also new to this manual are protection procedures for ministering to adults, including the elderly, new immigrants, and those with disabilities. I wish to thank everyone that has contributed to this newest work. I am especially grateful for Charlie Smith-Brake, Victoria Bissell, Milina Endresen, Eilleen Navarro, Danielle Escuadro, Maria Tropiano, Heather Bewley, Sandra Dalziel, and Elisa Do for your efforts to complete this manual with me. A big thank you to the team of Word Alive Press for partnering with us to publish the manual.

As you run this marathon with us, may you too embrace Plan to Protect® as a ministry within your churches. Remember you don't have to run this race alone, we are here to help you achieve the HIGHEST STANDARD of safeguarding.

On behalf of Plan to Protect®,

Melodie Bissell, MDiv, DMin
Editor

Plan to Protect® the company was incorporated in 2006 under the name Winning Kids Inc. We started the company with a desire to be a social enterprise committed to providing the HIGHEST STANDARD of abuse prevention and protection to organizations serving the vulnerable sector.

Our clients are primarily not-for-profit charities and churches. We have priced our services with these clients in mind and with a desire to honour and provide a competitive wage to our team members.

As a business committed to a social cause of preventing abuse and the protection of Children, Youth, and Adults we invest any profits earned each year back into the company to further develop new services for our clients. Our revenue sources are primarily through the sale of our resources, memberships, consulting, and training. Thank you for helping us make a difference.

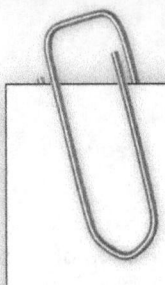

Call To Action

"Shhh...don't tell." Sometimes the whisper was harsh and threatening. At other times it felt comforting - similar to the soothing of a little one who has just been hurt. Either way, the message was clear: this is a secret. Don't you dare tell anyone. He didn't need to worry. I would never tell. I didn't even have the language yet to put into words my awful secret. On top of that, who would ever believe an over-sensitive little girl over the dynamic, well-loved church leader?

In the same basement where he taught my youth group the Scriptures is where he stole my innocence. Not knowing what to do with the horrifying experiences, I buried them deep as if they never happened. That seemed so much better than the ramifications of revealing the truth. The anxiety of my secret caused migraines, stomach pain and deep fear. For years, I would sit in church and try to block the dirty images of what happened to me by a youth leader. I would inwardly cringe at the dark threats I still heard in my heart. For some relief of the anxiety, I would self-harm and even at times wish for death.

I am amazed and grateful that the place of my greatest wounding - the Church - is also where I found my deepest healing. Decades later when I could no longer hide, and the wounds refused to allow me to function normally, I released my secret to my pastor. He believed me. He apologized on behalf of the Church and spiritual authority. He helped me to find a counsellor and to receive prayer ministry. He treated me with the respect I thought I didn't deserve. I suspect my scarred soul will forever remember and hurt, but now peace prevails and I can function normally without festering wounds torturing me. I know an intimacy with my Healer, the Lord Jesus, because the Church listened, believed, and did everything they possibly could to help me.

Most of us are familiar with the well-known quote, "It takes a village to raise a child." I believe it also takes a village to protect a child. This is the job of the whole Church. Despite what happened to me, I love the Church and serve it in a full-time capacity. It breaks my heart to hear and see how "open" the Church feels to predators, but I have hope for the present and future of the Church because of Plan to Protect®. Things are not as they used to be because sexual abuse has become acceptable to talk about, and we work hard to prevent and protect. We know what to do if allegations are made. The Church must become a safe place for the vulnerable, and this will only happen as the whole body of Christ takes action.

Please, Church, protect the vulnerable and victims among us.

Rachel*

*Pseudonym

A Safe Ministry: A Partnership

"God desires His Church to relish in His glory, share His glory among the nations, and reflect His glory in word and deed. The Church is a body made in His image, sent on His mission, to be His glory." [1]

What role can a local church, and the universal Church have in the lives of the vulnerable sector?

What role can the Church have in reflecting the Father heart of God?

What role can a local church have in creating an environment where victim-survivors discover safety and healing from the abuse they encountered in the past?

What role can a local church have in demonstrating grace and discipline in the life of an offender?
These are questions that we encourage the universal Church to consider, and every local church to answer, if they are serious about safety for the Children in their midst and also for Adults who were harmed as children.

Throughout history, God has chosen to use His people, the Church, to carry forward His story and mission to the world, including those who suffer and are oppressed. One way for the Church to do this is by embracing a ministry of protection, a ministry of safety, a ministry of healing. It is good and correct to be reminded that the Church aspires to be a place where healing can occur and where God will be glorified. God has chosen both His Word and the Church to be His vehicle of this message of healing and hope.

What does a safe ministry look like? A safe ministry is one where leadership clearly states their commitment to protecting the vulnerable, establishes boundaries for engagement with those who are weak, and passionately shares the vision of safety from pulpits and during training sessions. A safe ministry is one where leaders clearly state their commitment to protection of the vulnerable. A safe ministry calls for investments of time, resources and effort to screen individuals who wish to be placed in a position of trust among the vulnerable sector.

A safe ministry uses tough love when individuals refuse to adhere to policies and procedures. It does not focus on the minimum necessary to prevent legal recourse, but rather, it brings glory to God by reaching for the highest standard of abuse prevention and protection of those created in God's image.

A safe ministry doesn't stop there though. A safe ministry recognizes that everyone is on a lifelong journey of healing. For some it means finding an empty seat in a small group for victim-survivors of abuse, having an opportunity to share stories of hurt and abuse, inviting others to enter into their lament and exploring and walking along the lifelong journey of healing. A safe ministry exudes hope and openness to being on the journey, not in having arrived at the end – for all followers, not just those who have been hurt.

A safe ministry is one where sin and wrongdoing can be disclosed, exposed and reported while caring for the victim and the offender, reminding all that God is sovereign and is ultimately in control even when we are required by law to report abuse.

---

1 (The Passion and Practices of Missional Churches, 2004)

Finally, a safe ministry holds offenders accountable for their actions; recognizing there are long-term consequences for their past choices. They can be welcomed, but strict boundaries and accountability need to be established and adhered to. Often in our work, we see a safe ministry begin with one person who has a heart to help protect those that are vulnerable. We love those instigators who start to make changes, but it takes more than one safe person to achieve a high standard of protection - it takes a commitment throughout the community to build a safe ministry. Becoming a safe ministry is making a clear statement that you will answer the call to partnership and establish a covenant of care between leadership, front line ministry personnel, parents, church members, children, youth and vulnerable adults.

Document Terms

Plan to Protect® is designed to assist local church leaders in developing clear policies and procedures that will help protect our Children, Youth, Ministry Personnel and our churches. Our churches are comprised of small, medium and large churches who will use different structures and different ministry titles. Therefore, for the purpose of this resource tool, the following titles have been selected.

Church
An individual church congregation.

Church Leadership
Referring to the Church Board of Elders, deacons, ministers and senior staff.

Designated Screening Personnel
The individual or individuals designated and trained to screen prospective Ministry Personnel. Tasks include processing applications, reference checks, conducting face-to-face interviews and maintaining ministry personnel files.

Due Diligence
The compliance and documentation required to demonstrate that Church Leadership have reasonably done everything in their power to prevent abuse from occurring.

Duty of Care
The concept of duty of care identifies the relationship that exists between two persons (e.g., two individuals, an individual and a church) and establishes the obligations that one owes the other, in particular the obligation to exercise reasonable care with respect to the interests of the other, including protection from harm. The duty of care arises from the common law, as well as municipal, provincial, federal and international statutes.

Ministry Leads
Individuals who have successfully completed the recruitment and screening process and who have been given the responsibility to give direction to programs or ministries for Children or Youth. The term includes volunteers and all full-time, short-term or contract staff members receiving stipend or salary.

Ministry Personnel
An individual who has successfully completed the recruitment and screening procedures of Plan to Protect® and is now deemed to be a person who can be put in a position of trust with Children and Youth. Ministry Personnel include screened volunteers, full-time, short-term or contract staff and pastoral staff whether or not they receive a stipend/salary.

Ministry Personnel File
A file kept on each prospective Ministry Personnel which includes the ministry application form, record of police records check, record of reference checks, spiritual gift evaluation (if available), past areas of service and record of the interview by the Ministry Lead.

Occasional Observers
Individuals who visit and observe a ministry program on rare occasions. This term includes Parents assisting their own Children. Occasional observers do not need to be screened and trained, however, their access to minors will be limited and they will never be placed in a position of trust with Children who are not their own. That means that they will not be asked to assume responsibility for Children and they will not be allowed or asked to take Children to the washroom.

Parent
Refers to the natural or adoptive Parent(s) or Legal Guardian(s) of a Child or Youth.

Plan to Protect® Committee
A group of people responsible for the coordination, screening and placement of approved Ministry Personnel into the ministries of the church. In any given local church, this committee may be named differently and may assume additional responsibilities.

Position of Trust
The role wherein Parents and/or Guardians have entrusted their Children or Youth to your care.

Prospective Ministry Personnel
Students or Adults associated with the church congregation either by membership or regular attendance as an adherent, and awaiting approval by the Plan to Protect® team or Church Leadership for service.

Plan to Protect™

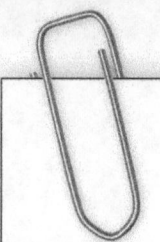

Table of Contents

A Letter from Plan to Protect®	4
Call To Action	6
A Safe Ministry: A Partnership	7
Document Terms	9
PROTECT THROUGH AWARENESS	15
Introduction to Awareness	16
A Letter from Rev. David Hearn	18
Understanding Child Abuse	19
Understanding Adult Abuse	21
Recognizing the Predator	24
Who is a Safe Person?	26
Understanding the Church's Responsibility	29
The Spiritual and Moral Responsibility of the Church	29
The Civil and Legal Liability of the Church	31
Understanding Legal Perspectives	32
Understanding Insurance Industry Standards	34
The Responsibility of the Board	35
PROTECT THROUGH IMPLEMENTATION	38
Implementing Plan to Protect®	39
Plan to Protect® Committee	42
PROTECT THROUGH RECRUITMENT AND SCREENING	44
Introduction	45
Human Rights and Discrimination	49
Recruitment and Screening Process	51
Qualifications for Ministry	54
Ministry Application Form	57
Reference Checks	59
Interview	61
Criminal Record Checks	63
Screening of Youth	66
Red Flags and Disqualifiers	67
Plan to Protect® Training	69
Code of Conduct and Covenant of Care	71
Approval Process	73
PROTECT THROUGH DOCUMENTATION MANAGEMENT	74
Introduction	75
Plan to Protect® Program Maintenance	78
Documentation	79
Documentation Storage and Retention	81
Personal Information and Privacy	83

PROTECT THROUGH TRAINING — 85
Introduction to Training — 86
Types of Training — 89
Vibrant and Creative Training — 91
Qualified Trainers — 92
Plan to Protect® Training Resources — 95
Tips for Trainers — 99
Restrictions and Parameters for Training — 100

PROTECT THROUGH PROGRAM DEVELOPMENT — 101
General Protection Procedures — 102
Introduction — 103
Administrative Policies — 106
Planning for Safety — 107
Supervision of Ministry Personnel — 108
Lifestyle — 109
Ministry Personnel Identification — 111
Registration and Compliance with PIPEDA — 112
Attendance — 114
Outside User Groups — 115
Misconduct and Accountability — 117
Disciplinary Action of Ministry Personnel — 119
Personal Interactions — 123
Occasional Observers — 124
Bullying — 125
    Harassment and Discrimination — 128
Discipline and Classroom Management — 131
Contacting Opportunities — 134
    Counselling and Pastoral Care — 135
    Gift Giving — 137
Dating — 139
Home Visits — 140
Hospital and Nursing Home Visits — 143
Disabilities and Personal Support Workers — 145
Gender Identity — 147
Health and Safety — 150
Health and Safety Guidelines — 151
    Severe Allergies — 155
    Immunizations — 157
    Drugs and Alcohol — 158
Inclement Weather Conditions — 160
Missing Person — 161
Lockdown Guidelines — 165
Fire and Emergency Evacuation — 168
Technology Concerns — 170
Online Forums and Gatherings — 171
Social Media — 174
Internet and Computer Use — 176
Photography and Video Recording — 178
Facility Precautions — 180
Modifying Your Facility — 181
Security Systems and Cameras — 183
High Risk Activities — 185
High Risk Activities — 186

Transportation	187
Off-Site Event Planning	190
Off-Site Event Planning: Shared Activities	192
Off-Site Event Planning: Home Groups	194
Special Events and Overnight Policies	196
Shower and Locker Room Guidelines	198
Overnight Trips and Housing	199
Billeting and Hosting	201
Child Protection Procedures	**203**
Introduction	204
Checklist of General Protection Procedures	205
Staff to Student Ratios	208
Proper Display of Affection	209
Child-to-Child Sexual Play or Abuse	210
Washroom Guidelines	212
Receiving and Releasing Children	214
Youth Protection Procedures	**216**
Introduction	217
Checklist of General Protection Procedures	218
Physical Contact	221
Staff to Student Ratio	222
Mentoring	223
Youth-to-Youth Sexual Activity	226
Youth Ministry Issues	228
Adult Protection Procedures	**233**
Introduction	234
Checklist of General Protection Procedures	235
Physical Contact	238
New Immigrant and Refugee Settlement	239
Personal Care	242
Mentoring Adults and Pastoral Care	243
Shelters, Recovery and Rehabilitation Ministries	245
Violence and Harassment	247
Financial Aid	250
REPORTING AND RESPONSE	**251**
Introduction	252
Reporting Abuse	**253**
Hearing of an Allegation or Suspicion of Child Abuse	256
Reporting Child Abuse	258
Hearing an Allegation or Suspicion of Abuse Against an Adult	261
Reporting and Responding to an Allegation of Abuse or Harassment Against an Adult	263
Assessing and Investigating an Allegation or Suspicion of Abuse	266
Protecting Confidentiality and Dignity of the Victim and the Accused	268
Spiritual Abuse	270
Whistleblower Policy	273
Response to Abuse	**275**
Spiritual Response and Counsel for the Victim	278
Biblical Response and Discipline for the Accused or Convicted	280
Media Relations	282
Ongoing Investigation	284
Offender's Policy	285
Conclusion	288
APPENDICES AND BIBLIOGRAPHY	**290**

Protect Through Awareness

- Introduction to Awareness
- A Letter from Rev. David Hearn
- Understanding Child Abuse
- Understanding Adult Abuse
- Recognizing the Predataor
- Who is A Safe Person?
- Understanding the Church's Responsibility
  - The Spiritual and Moral Responsibility of the Church
  - The Civil and Legal Liability of the Church
- Understanding Legal Perspectives
- Understanding Insurance Industry Standards
- The Responsibility of the Board

Introduction to Awareness

Understanding the Need

We are called by God to care for those who are afflicted and needy, to tend to broken hearts and to release the captives. Our congregations are made up of individuals that have experienced different forms of trauma in their lives including those that have been abused.

The scope of the problem is indeed enormous. According to the Canadian Community Health Survey-Mental Health conducted in 2012, 32% of Canadian adults reported that they had experienced some form of abuse before the age of 16:[1]

26% had experienced physical abuse;
10% had experienced sexual abuse; and
8% had experienced exposure to intimate partner violence.

More recently, a Canadian statistical profile in 2016 estimates that approximately 54,900 children and youth aged 17 and younger had reported violent crimes to the police. Children, youth and vulnerable adults represented around 16% of victims of violent crime, and about 16,200 of those individuals were victims of family violence[2]. To get a clearer understanding of the scope of the problem within your community, you may wish to further research information related to your province or territory.

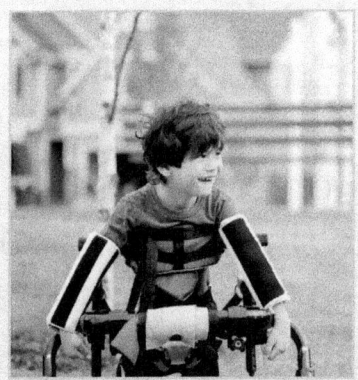

---

1 (Child abuse and mental disorders in Canada. Canadian Medical Association Journal, 186(9), E324-E332.)

Furthermore, abuse is an issue that requires attention on a global scale. As reported by the World Health Organization (WHO) in 2020, about 120 million girls and young women under 20 years of age have suffered some form of forced sexual contact. In addition, about 300 million children, or 3 in 4 children, aged 2-4 years suffer physical and/or psychological violence regularly from their parents and caregivers. Consequences of child maltreatment can cause lifelong implications, affecting children's physical and mental health as well as broader social and occupational outcomes[3].

Victims are being abused by family members and caregivers, people they know and trust. Some of these people are people who they not only trust but who speak to them of faith, God, salvation, sin, redemption, punishment, etc. These individuals are also found to be abusing victims behind the walls of churches, Christian schools, and Missions. As a result of the abuse, many are leaving the church and their faith, or at the least, questioning their faith and a God who would allow this to happen.

Local church leaders have a spiritual, moral, and legal responsibility to provide a secure environment for children, youth, and vulnerable adults. We also have a duty to care for our staff members and volunteers, to prevent wrongful allegations of abuse. As we raise the awareness of abuse within our churches, we demonstrate our commitment to the protection of the vulnerable. May we never lose sight of the fact that abuse is a criminal offence as well as a violation of human conscience and dignity. It is a violation of God's moral law within the trusted context of relationship.

The emotional, physical and spiritual trauma to victims, the destructive consequences for abusers and the devastating effects on the credibility of the church ministry and the name of Christ, make it essential that the church take all appropriate steps to aid in the prevention of abuse. When we embrace a ministry of protection, we bring hope and healing to the abused. We also provide a safe place with a goal of mitigating the risk of abuse. Our loving obedience to God to care for the afflicted and needy is also transformative in our lives as we reflect the Father heart of God.

Let's plan to protect through awareness!

---

2 (Juristat, Canadian Centre for Justice Statistics, Statistics Canada, Catalogue no. 85-002-X)
3 (World Health Organization. (2020). Child Maltreatment. Retrieved from: https://www.who.int/news-room/fact-sheets/detail/child-maltreatment)

A Letter from Rev. David Hearn

The other day I held my granddaughter in my arms and told her how precious she is. I reminded her of how much God loves her and how much I love her too. She cuddled close, and I could feel her relax as she felt safe in my arms. One of the clear priorities of churches across Canada is to establish a safe place for everyone. A place where they can be loved, affirmed, and able to dream about all that God has for them. In a world with much uncertainty, chaos, and fear, the church offers an invaluable gift to the next generation, and more, to the most vulnerable when it establishes a healthy and safe environment for individuals to thrive. However, as a leader in the church for over 40 years, I have witnessed the reality that many churches are not as safe as they think they are.

With the desire to create a strong community, churches promote trust, vulnerability, and freedom; these are amazing virtues, but if they are not careful those same churches can neglect or minimize wisdom, accountability, and discernment. An atmosphere that is designed to be safe can quickly become ripe for predators. This may sound harsh, but my family personally experienced the pain and consequences of trusting without boundaries in the context of a local church.

> I urge all church leaders to step up and ensure that Plan to Protect® is a normal part of their church ministry.

I have been so impressed with the Plan to Protect® training, protocols, and uncompromising focus on keeping children and young people safe without dismantling healthy community. The material is well researched, user-friendly, and highly transferable. It not only educates but provides clear procedures to follow, and effective accountability for those who work in a position of trust and leadership. The church cannot compromise on this. It is not optional. I urge all church leaders to step up and ensure that Plan to Protect® is a normal part of their church ministry. Then you will be able to look into the eyes of every individual under your care and feel confident that they can relax, knowing they are safe and able to thrive.

Reverend David Hearn

Understanding Child Abuse

"Canadian authorities estimate that the incidence of child abuse and neglect in Canada parallels that of the United States. At least one in three girls and one in seven boys are sexually abused by the time they reach the age of 18. In the vast majority of cases, sexual abusers are known to their victims. More than half of all sexual abuse occurs within the family. Offenders come from all economic, ethnic, racial and educational backgrounds and religious traditions. They may be respected members of the community, church or synagogue."[1]

Critical to a clear understanding of abuse, is becoming familiar with the definitions used when referring to it. As definitions vary from province to province, you may want to contact the Department of Social Services or your local law enforcement agency to obtain the proper definitions used in your region.

"Child abuse refers to an act committed by a parent, caregiver or person in a position of trust (even though he/she may not care for the child on a daily basis) which is not accidental and which harms or threatens to harm a child's physical or mental health, or a child's welfare."[2]

Abuse is primarily categorized as being physical, sexual, emotional, or involving neglect.

> Offenders come from all economic, ethnic, racial and educational backgrounds and religious traditions. They may be respected members of the community, church or synagogue.

- **Physical Abuse:** "Physical abuse is any deliberate physical force or action that results, or could result, in injury to a child. It can include punching, slapping, beating, shaking, burning, biting or throwing a child. It is different than what is considered reasonable discipline."[3]

- **Sexual Abuse:** "Sexual abuse occurs when a child is used for the sexual gratification of an adult or an older child. It can take many forms. This includes sexual intercourse, exposing a child's private areas, indecent phone calls, fondling for sexual pleasure, allowing a child to look at or perform pornographic pictures or videos. Coercion (physical, psychological or emotional) is intrinsic to sexual abuse. It is against the law to touch a child for a sexual purpose, to encourage or force a child to touch another person in a sexual way or to tell a child to touch him or herself for an adult's or older child's sexual purpose."[4] "Child sexual abuse exploits and harms children by involving them in sexual behavior for which they are unprepared, to which they cannot consent, and from which they are unable to protect themselves."[5]

---

1 (Faith Trust Institute, 2006)
2 (Ibid.)
3 (The Children's Aid Society of London and Middlesex, 2006)
4 (Ibid.)
5 (Thornburg Melton, 1998, 13-4)

- **Emotional abuse:** "Emotional abuse is a pattern of behaviour that attacks a child's emotional development and sense of self worth. It includes excessive, aggressive, or unreasonable demands that place expectations on a child beyond his or her capacity. Emotional abuse includes constant criticizing, teasing, belittling, insulting, rejecting, ignoring or isolating the child. It also includes failure by the parent or caregiver to provide their children with love, emotional support and guidance."[6]

- **Neglect:** "Neglect is the failure to meet a child's basic need for food, clothing, shelter, sleep, medical attention, education and protection from harm. This can occur when parents do not know about appropriate care for children, when they cannot adequately supervise their children or when they are unable to plan ahead."[7]

While our previous versions of Plan to Protect® specifically addressed abuse directed towards Children and Youth, we have now expanded our call to safeguarding for the whole church. We encourage you to update your policies, procedures and training to reflect this context. That begins with defining abuse of Adults. See page 21 for definitions of adult abuse.

> "Facts do not cease to exist because they are ignored."
> Aldous Huxley - Brave New World

---

6 (The Children's Aid Society of London and Middlesex 2006)
7 (Ibid.)

Understanding Adult Abuse

When we speak of abuse against Adults, the topic is complex. What makes one vulnerable?

According to Brene Brown, "To feel is to be vulnerable, believing that vulnerability is weakness is believing that feeling is weakness. And like it or not, we are emotional beings: What most of us fail to understand, and what took me a decade of research to learn, is that vulnerability is the cradle of the emotions and experiences that we crave. Vulnerability is the birthplace of love, belonging, and joy."[1]

According to Brene's quote, we are all vulnerable. We are created in God's image, and He created us to feel deeply, to experience emotions, and to crave loving and nurturing relationships. However, too often relationships that God designed to be beautiful, wholesome and good, are anything but that.

Unfortunately, often at the most vulnerable points in our lives, we may be abused and harmed by others. It does not mean we are weak, rather that someone abused their position of power to cause harm. The harm committed by others can injure us physically, emotionally, mentally, and spiritually.

When we began to expand Plan to Protect® to include Adults, we initially thought of the vulnerability of the elderly and those with special needs. We then saw the need to protect those who are newcomers to Canada, the influx of refugees to our country. More recently we have heard of the stories of fallen leaders that we once looked up to. Their misconduct was directed primarily to women whom they harmed spiritually, physically and emotionally. Their abuses of power deeply harmed the church. The list of fallen leaders is long and unfortunately new names are added to the list annually.

How do we combat and respond to abuse against Adults?

We begin (as always) by gaining insight and knowledge and awareness of the abuse of power, influence, authority and control. When that power is used to harm an individual and to injure another, it is considered abuse.

Vulnerable Adult/elder abuse is the mistreatment of an elderly person or Vulnerable Adult by someone he or she should be able to rely on ... a spouse, a Child, another family member, a friend or a paid caregiver.

Abuse of Vulnerable Adults is sometimes described as misuse of power and a violation of trust. Elder/Vulnerable Adult abuse can take place in the home, in other residential settings, or in the community.

Most - if not all - of these forms of abuse are considered crimes.

Emotional and Psychological Abuse
Psychological Abuse is the systemic destruction of a person's self-esteem or sense of safety, often occurring in relationships where there are differences in power and control.[2] It includes threats of harm or abandonment, humiliation, deprivation of contact, isolation and other psychologically abusive tactics and behaviours. A variety of terms are used interchangeably with psychological abuse, including emotional abuse, verbal abuse, mental cruelty, intimate terrorism, and psychological aggression. Also, when the abuse occurs in a residential care setting, it is often called systemic or institutional abuse.[3]

Spiritual abuse would be deemed a form of psychological abuse. See also spiritual abuse on page 270.

---

1 (Brown, B., 2012)
2 (Follingstad, D. & DeHart, D., 2000)
3 (Doherty, D. & Berglund, D., 2008)

"Emotional and Psychological abuse is any action, verbal or non-verbal, that lessens a person's sense of identity, dignity and self-worth."[4]

It includes excessive, aggressive or unreasonable demands that place expectations on someone beyond his or her capacity. It includes constant criticizing, teasing, belittling, insulting, rejecting, ignoring or isolating, threats of withdrawal of services or of institutionalization.

Financial Abuse
Financial abuse is the illegal or unauthorized use of someone else's money or property. It includes pressuring someone for money or property.[5]

In the case of an elderly person, or an individual without cognitive capacity, "financial abuse is the misuse of an individual's funds and assets without that person's knowledge and/or full consent, or in the case of an older Adult who is not mentally capable, not in that person's best interest."[6]

Examples of financial abuse can include pressuring, forcing or tricking an individual into:
- Lending or giving away money, property or possessions
- Selling or moving from their home
- Making or changing a will or power of attorney
- Signing legal or financial documents that they don't understand
- Working for little or no money, including caring for Children or Grandchildren
- Making a purchase one does not want or need
- Providing food and shelter to others without being paid

Neglect
Neglect is not meeting the basic needs of the individual that is dependent on you.
1. **Active (intentional) neglect:** the deliberate withholding of care or the basic necessities of life from an older Adult/Vulnerable Adult for whom one is caring.
2. **Passive (unintentional) neglect:** the failure to provide proper care to an older Adult/Vulnerable Adult due to lack of knowledge, experience or ability, or due to being unaware of how to access local services.

Neglect can be:
- Withholding care or denying access to necessary services (home care, nursing) or medical attention
- Leaving a person in an unsafe place
- Improper use of medication – over/under medicating
- Not providing food or liquids, proper clothing or hygiene
- Failure to assist with activities of daily living
- Abandonment
- Denial of a senior's basic rights[7]

Physical Abuse/Assault
"Physical abuse is any act of violence or rough handling that may or may not result in physical injury but causes physical discomfort or pain. Physical abuse can be: punching, kicking, shoving, shacking, hitting, slapping, poking, burning, pulling hair, biting, pinching, arm twisting, spitting at someone, confining or restraining a person inappropriately."[8]

"This may include the inappropriate and/or unwarranted use of physical or chemical restraints."[9]

---

4 (Elder Abuse Ontario, 2018)
5 (Federal/Provincial/Territorial Ministers Responsible for Seniors Forum, 2010)
6 (Government of Ontario, n.d.)
7 (Elder Abuse Ontario, 2018)
8 (Ibid.)
9 (Government of Ontario, n.d.)

A person commits an assault when[10]:
i. Without the consent of another person, they apply force intentionally to another person, directly or indirectly;
ii. They attempt or threaten, by an act or a gesture, to apply force to another person, if they have, or cause that other person to believe on reasonable grounds that they have, present ability to effect their purpose; or
iii. While openly wearing or carrying a weapon or an imitation thereof, they accost or impede another person or begs.

Sexual Abuse and Misconduct

Sexual abuse, often also known as sexual misconduct, is defined as an act or assault of a sexual nature that violates the sexual integrity of the victim. The Supreme Court of Canada held that the act of sexual assault does not depend solely on contact with any specific part of the human anatomy but rather the act of a sexual nature that violates the sexual integrity of the victim. When investigating sexual abuse, there are certain relevant factors that the police will consider[11]:

- The part of the body touched
- The nature of the contact
- The situation in which the contact occurred
- The words and gestures accompanying the act
- All other circumstances surrounding the act
- Any threats that may or may not be accompanied by force

In the case of an elderly person or a person without cognitive capacity, sexual abuse occurs "without that person's full knowledge and consent; it includes coercing an older person through force, trickery, threats or other means into unwanted sexual activity. Sexual abuse also includes sexual contact with seniors who are unable to grant consent and unwanted sexual contact between service providers and their clients."[12]

In the case where there is abuse of power of authority involving sexual activity, this too would constitute as sexual misconduct or sexual abuse.

See also harassment on page 128.

Spiritual Abuse

Spiritual Abuse is the use of spiritual or religious language and/or beliefs to unduly influence and exert control over individuals, exploiting them for the apparent benefit of the organization or those in positions of greater authority.

Ending violence against the elderly, individuals with special needs, new immigrants, women and men requires coherent policies and programs that emphasize valuing the dignity of all, gender equality as non-negotiable and the transformation of social and cultural norms. Sustainable development, peace and security can only be achieved when caring and respectful relations among women, men, boys and girls become the norm.

All human beings are susceptible to abuse one way or another. How then does one best face and respond to their own vulnerability to danger and harm? We believe it is by one's ability to resist or flee physical or emotional danger. However, for too many, that is not possible. Is it not then critical to have a community that will stand in solidarity with the vulnerable, for that community to be watchful and bold, for that community to be proactive to prevent abuse from occurring, and for that community to be swift in responding to abuse? May this be our communities of faith!

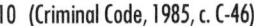
10 (Criminal Code, 1985, c. C-46)
11 (Edmonton Police Service, n.d.)
12 (Elder Abuse Ontario, 2018)

Recognizing the Predator

*"The heart is more deceitful than all else
And is desperately sick;
Who can understand it?"*
Jeremiah 17:9 (NASB)

As a child, I (Melodie) was spared twice from a predator. One day I was walking the distance of 15 houses down the street from my friend Susan's home. A car followed me slowly. A man rolled down his window and invited me into his car. Frightened, I ran the remaining few meters to the sanctuary of my home. The second time I was walking through a ravine with a friend when a man, who I had never seen before, exposed himself to us. Both of these incidences involved complete strangers.

However, most abuse does not happen at the hands of a stranger, instead it is committed by a family member, friend or caregiver.

"She was my teacher."
"He was a friend of our teenage son!"
"He was a gentleman who rented a room from us."
"She was our babysitter."
"She was my youth pastor."
"He was my father."
"He was a priest."

The stories we hear are rarely about strangers. In most cases, the abuser was someone well known to the victim.

We must use sound judgment and wisdom in raising our Children, without living in constant fear and paranoia.

Who is the predator? Only she or he, and God knows — until the silence is broken.

However, there are some signs that will help us identify a predator of Children or Youth:

- They find opportunity to engage with Children, Youth and Vulnerable Adults outside of regularly scheduled programs;
- They choose to spend more time with, or have a preference for Children over Adults;
- They have few friends with individuals of their own age;
- They pay elevated attention to Children that are in single-parent relationships, or are needy and often on their own;

- They are very touchy with Children and young people;
- They have trouble keeping a job, or change locations and residences often;
- They may have a failed marriage (or may be in a marriage but it is used as a cover up or façade);
- They volunteer or work in roles where they will have access to Children (this will allow them to groom or build relationships with Children);
- They lack social boundaries;
- They give gifts and personal compliments to Children and young people;
- They tickle and play fight with Children;
- They offer to babysit Children or find opportunities to take Youth on overnight and off-site trips; and
- They text or engage in social media outside of program.

Warning signs are not evidence that someone is a predator. Rather, they have been recognized as being common among known predators.

According to GRACE, "Many sex offenders find faith communities and Christians easy to manipulate. Dr. Anna Salter documented how one convicted sex offender (who was himself a minister) shared, 'I consider church people easy to fool… they have a trust that comes from being Christians… they seem to want to believe in the good that exists in all people…' Offenders often have lifelong patterns of manipulation and deception. Child protection expert Victor Vieth states it this way, 'Men and women who sexually abuse children are also master liars who manipulate not only their victims, but also parents, churches, and communities into believing their crimes are not particularly egregious or are even the fault of the victim.'"[1]

Warning signs are not evidence that someone is a predator. Rather, they have been recognized as being common among known predators. If there is a combination of these characteristics, be alert and watchful.

Abuse of the vulnerable by family members often happens when a family member or guardian is either:
Hungry
Angry
Lonely
Tired.

We do not need to live in fear and paranoia. However, don't ignore warning signs and your gut feelings that something might be wrong. Discernment is a gift and God uses this discernment to help us protect the church and those in our care.

---

1 (https://www.netgrace.org/resources/2019/9/4/known-offenders-five-things-to-know)

Who is a Safe Person?

One of the significant discoveries during the semi-structured interviews I (Melodie) conducted while doing research[1] for my Doctorate of Ministry was when I asked the participants (all victim-survivors of child sexual abuse) what constituted a safe person and what represented an unsafe person as part of their spiritual healing. Each of the participants defined a safe person as someone they felt they could entrust with their story of abuse.

Each participant described for me what constituted a safe person. In each interview, the safe person was described as a counsellor, friend, or pastor. It was not a family member. Surprisingly, all but two of the participants had not shared their stories initially, if ever, with their immediate family members. For most of the participants the abuse was not disclosed until years after it occurred. Still, half of the participants have only shared their story with a small handful of people.

The following description of a safe person is a compilation of the words used to describe someone that my participants deemed safe enough to hold their story. In most of the interviews, the victim-survivors disclosed their experiences of abuse at a time in their lives when they were experiencing tremendous pain and suffering, and experiencing the adverse outcomes of abuse; e.g., self-injury, night terrors, eating disorders, broken relationships, isolation, and shame.

During the interviews, participants shared several times, "A safe person has time for me."

With a safe person, there is no question as to whether or not the abuse occurred, "they respond to my story," and are "patient" as I share it.

Participants described a safe person as someone who listens with their whole body. "They sit present with me" and are "not too quick to speak," but when they do, they voice the words and sentiment, "I believe you!" or "I am so sorry that happened to you." "A safe person is generous with their listening, generous with their time." One participant indicated that a safe person acknowledges that every abuse story is unique, although there may be similar overtones among stories, and that the listener should be careful to not assume similarities. Once they listen to the story, they don't sensationalize the story or retell it elsewhere. They recognize that the story they have been told is one they should carry carefully and that the victim-survivor may have chosen very carefully the words they used in telling their story.

> "A safe person has time for me."

A safe person does not have all the answers, but they remind the victim that they have a choice about whether they let the abuse define who they

---

[1] (The Experience of Spiritual Healing Among Adult Victim-Survivors of Child Sexual Abuse: A Phenomenological Study, by Melodie Bissell)

are, or whether they live by who God says they are. One participant voiced that the safest people in her life planted seeds of hope that she did not have to be defined by her abuse; instead, help was available and they encouraged her to go for professional counselling and helped make that happen. A safe person does not make decisions on behalf of the victim - instead, they make a suggestion, leaving the decision to the victim and empowering them to be an agent of their own healing.

"A safe person maintains a healthy distance from me, but they are present in my life. They are humble and demonstrate accountability, for they will ask permission to advocate on my behalf, or if they can share my story with others. By this, they demonstrate that they are accountable to others in their personal lives, they themselves should be openly a part of an accountability group."

"One of the safest people I ever met got down on one knee, looked me in the eye and said, 'I am so sorry on behalf of men.'"

"When I finally felt safe enough to tell my story, my safe person did not focus on my behaviour; instead, they planted seeds of hope in my life that I could find hope and healing."

"A safe person gently, patiently, humbly points me in a different direction where I can find healing. The safe people in my own life did not question or shame me when I was angry with God, could not pray, or even didn't want to be in church. They took time to discover what, if anything triggered the memories of my abuse and encouraged me to discover positive coping strategies."

"They affirm, affirm, affirm the progress I have made."

"A safe person is gentle natured, comes across sincere and genuine. I can see the sadness in their eyes, but I don't feel they pity me."

"They are willing to be a whistleblower and report abuse and advocate on my behalf. The safe people in my life speak the truth but are wise and guarded when they speak up." The cost of safety is never too much – they disclose abuse, even if there is a cost to themselves or the organization. This was voiced by more than one of my participants. They speak up for injustice and call for change.

"The safe people in my life are still present in my life, they hold my story, but I don't feel that this defines our relationship."

"They have walked with me through the deep valley in my life and during my healing journey."

"A safe person always treats us [referring to victim-survivors] as though we are on an equal footing as them – like they can learn from and be supported by us as much as we can learn from and be supported by them. They are not above us or wiser than us."

Both men and women were described as safe people. Fifty percent of the participants said they felt safer with women, the other fifty percent said they had first shared their experience of abuse with a man. "A safe person accepts you as an equal and acknowledges all of your being."

> "When I finally felt safe enough to tell my story, my safe person did not focus on my behaviour; instead, they planted seeds of hope in my life that I could find hope and healing."

Alternatively, an unsafe person according to my participants exerts power, control, and judgment. They are proud, distrustful, defensive, critical, and impatient. An unsafe person blames, shames, and tries to "control the narrative instead of being in a posture of listening and learning." "The unsafe people in my life want to silence me." An unsafe person is not accountable to others.

I heard the same experience shared by two of the participants. "I shared my story of abuse at a women's retreat, and after speaking, an older woman came up and said to me, 'No one wants to hear their pastor's wife tell that much detail of their lives. That is a story you shouldn't tell anyone.'"

In another setting, "I was told not to share my story, as the congregation was not ready to hear it."

An unsafe person "will try to silence you and is dismissive."

"To me, an unsafe person defines me as a troublemaker and encourages me to move on. They take no responsibility for what happened to me."

"An unsafe person treats us [meaning victims] as a child, not the adults we have become."

"An unsafe person seems to have a preoccupation with sex and wants all the details of the abuse."

"I went from one counsellor to another counsellor. I sought out counsellors both within the church and within Christian colleges. It seems that over and over, I had the same experience, the counsellors wanted to know all about my sexual experiences and history. It seems that so many Christian men have a fixation on sexual details. I would not go back to them."

An unsafe person is an accuser. They would ask "what I did, or what I wore, or what part I played in the abuse. I was young, and I was a child."

Understanding the Church's Responsibility

> All organizations must address the risks that are inherent in their operations, especially those that deal with children, and must take all reasonable steps to reduce those risks.

"All organizations must address the risks that are inherent in their operations, especially those that deal with children, and must take all reasonable steps to reduce those risks. Further, child abuse and sexual abuse policies are often required in order for insurance to be obtained. However, this should be standard practice and driven by compassion for victims, and a sense of responsibility to society at large. Child abuse is a crime which is an especially grave crime when it is occasioned under the apparent auspices of a church, charity or non-profit organization, and through the conduct of a priest, counselor or other employee who is placed in a position of authority over children."[1]

"Churches can be vulnerable places because they are places of trust, often lack the necessary screening for volunteers and provide opportunity for predators to be in contact with children."[2]

"Churches are a natural target for sexual predators. They have large numbers of children; a shortage of willing workers, and a culture of trust that assumes no Christian could be suspect of such exploitation."[3]

For this reason, it is essential that the church develop, "clear policies and procedures that will serve to protect not only the Children, Youth and Vulnerable Adults, but also those who work with them and the church as a whole."[4]

A. The Spiritual and Moral Responsibility of the Church

> Churches are a natural target for sexual predators. They have large numbers of children; a shortage of willing workers, and a culture of trust that assumes no Christian could

In the church, we recognize that we are a reflection of God's love to those in our care and we take our responsibility seriously.

Micah 6:8 presents this challenge: "He has shown you, O mortal, what is good. And what does the LORD require of you? To act justly and to love mercy and to walk humbly with your God." (NIV)

"Micah suggests that the Lord requires three things of us:
- **To act justly** – We must work for justice, seeking to promote the truth and to speak out on behalf of the vulnerable.
- **To love mercy** – Compassion needs to be the bedrock of all our work.
- **To walk humbly with our God** – Our personal and professional lives need to be marked by humility and righteousness.

---

1 (White 2005)
2 (McCormick and Mitchell 1999)
3 (Harvey 2002)
4 (McCormick and Mitchell 1999)

> "If anyone causes one of these little ones --those who believe in me--to stumble, it would be better for them to have a large millstone hung around their neck and to be drowned in the depths of the sea."
> (Matthew 18:6, NIV)

We all make mistakes and need to be prepared to admit it. We need to recognize our limitations, but with that to do our best to act with integrity. Above all, we mustn't be afraid to engage in these difficult areas, trusting in a God who walks with us as encourager, friend and guide."[5]

God's word outlines our spiritual responsibility to Children, Youth and Vulnerable Adults:

- "If anyone causes one of these little ones—those who believe in me—to stumble, it would be better for them to have a large millstone hung around their neck and to be drowned in the depths of the sea." (Matthew 18:6, NIV)

- "People were bringing little children to Jesus for him to place his hands on them, but the disciples rebuked them. When Jesus saw this, he was indignant. He said to them, 'Let the little children come to me, and do not hinder them, for the kingdom of God belongs to such as these. Truly I tell you, anyone who will not receive the kingdom of God like a little child will never enter it.' And he took the children in his arms, placed his hands on them and blessed them." (Mark 10:13 – 16, NIV)

- "Reject every kind of evil." (I Thessalonians 5:22, NIV)

- "But among you there must not be even a hint of sexual immorality ... because these are improper for God's holy people." (Ephesians 5:3, NIV)

- "Brothers and sisters, if someone is caught in sin, you who live by the Spirit should restore that person gently. ... Carry each other's burdens, and in this way you will fulfill the law of Christ." (Galatians 6:1 – 2, NIV)

- "For we are taking pains to do what is right, not only in the eyes of the Lord but also in the eyes of man." (II Corinthians 8:21, NIV)

The guidelines in this manual are written to help churches as they work toward fulfilling their responsibilities to provide a safe and nurturing environment for Children, Youth and Adults. In partnership with parents, we, as a church, seek to provide quality care and instruction to the family and in this way, promote spiritual growth at every age level. Plan to Protect® is designed to assist Church Leaders in their recruitment of Ministry Personnel and, to the greatest extent possible, provide for the safety of those served as well as those who serve.

Church Leaders are strongly encouraged to follow these guidelines and procedures and view them as " ... a necessary component of church ministry and overall church health."[6] Individual churches need to customize these policies and develop additional guidelines appropriate to their local church setting and in keeping with the laws of their province.

---

5 (Sidebotham 2004)
6 (Zarra 1997, 22)

B. The Civil and Legal Liability of the Church

Ensuring that your church is a safe place for Children is not just a good idea, it is a legal requirement. Churches have a legal responsibility to ensure that a plan for protection is in place, and insurance companies now require this same level of diligence in order to provide financial coverage.

> Ensuring that your church is a safe place for Children is not just a good idea, it is a legal requirement.

Disclaimer:

The development, preparation and publication of this work has been undertaken with great care. However, the publisher, editors, employees and agents of Plan to Protect® are not responsible for any errors contained herein or for consequences that may ensue from use of materials or information contained in this work. This manual is not a policy, but rather a plan to establish policy. It is only as current as the date of the publication and does not reflect subsequent changes in law. This manual is distributed with the understanding that it does not constitute legal advice.

Organizations are strongly encouraged to seek legal counsel as well as counsel from their insurance company who can give written opinion concerning the specifics of their particular situation when establishing a policy. With regard to case studies, identities and circumstances of information discussed herein have been changed to protect confidentiality.

Understanding Legal Perspectives

There are five legal concepts that we believe every church should take into consideration when it comes to safeguarding.

The first, and most important is our legal "duty to report child abuse." Each Province and Territory has its own legislation, but the common components in each Province's legislation is the duty of every person in Canada to report to child protection services if you believe a Child is in need of protection. We are all mandated to report child abuse. The legislation also requires that it be a direct duty to report, an immediate duty to report, and an on-going duty to report.

The second legal concept is "duty of care." As mentioned earlier, the role of safeguarding falls on all of us. The concept of duty of care identifies the relationship that exists between two persons (e.g., two individuals, an individual and an organization) and establishes the obligations that one owes the other, in particular the obligation to exercise reasonable care with respect to the interests of the other, including protection from harm.

The third legal concept is "standard of care." Standard of care is by necessity a flexible standard, determined by speculating on what an average and reasonable person would do, or not do, in the same circumstance. The second and third concepts relate to a person's responsibility to care for the person's 'neighbours', failure of which can result in having to pay damages to the 'neighbour'.

> Church leadership can be held vicariously liable for the actions of their agents.

The fourth legal concept is "vicarious liability." If a court finds that your group could have done more to ensure the safety of the people in your programs, you may be found vicariously liable for the actions of a member of the clergy, a lay person, or a volunteer. Your best protection against vicarious liability is screening.[1]

Vicarious liability is an extension of the first and second concepts based on common-law precedent that enables victims to hold one party responsible for the actions of another, based on their relationship to each other. Church Leadership can be held vicariously liable for the actions of their agents – an example being a bus driver or an entertainer. Vicarious liability extends to the work of volunteers in non-profit organizations and can be imposed even though the wrongful act may be contrary to the desires and policies of the non-profit organization. Should an allegation of abuse make it to the courts, in their legal decisions, the court will determine if the church exerted sufficient control over their operations.

So, because churches will be held vicariously liable for the acts of its Ministry Personnel, whether they be paid or volunteer, the church should take great care to ensure that they have proper hiring and screening processes in place and an ongoing plan for supervision of its Ministry Personnel.

---

1 (Volunteer Canada 2006)

This leads us to the final concept, "Due Diligence." The compliance and documentation required to demonstrate that Church Leadership have reasonably done everything in their power to prevent abuse from occurring. It is imperative that each church understand that the lack of a preventative protection plan has legal implications, and they need to be proactive in their approach to establish safety policies that comply with legal standards. To ensure that you have done due diligence and have protected yourself from liability, call a lawyer for written opinion on your policy and consult your insurance company representative. Your policy should represent an understanding of your legal responsibilities and an awareness of statutory reporting requirements for your province. After seeking legal counsel, Church Leadership should review and adopt established guidelines as official church policy.

Understanding Insurance Industry Standards

Lawsuits for abuse are something every church and Board want to avoid. Insurance protection to cover the risk of abuse is sometimes neglected, misunderstood, or rendered invalid due to a lack of following required policies, procedures, training, and screening measures. The harsh reality is that any church that serves Children, Youth and Vulnerable Adults is at risk for actual or alleged abuse claims, whether insured or not.

It is important to understand that not all insurance companies provide abuse liability coverage. In fact, there are now only a handful of companies in Canada that even offer abuse coverage for churches or charities. Those few insurers that do provide protection require the implementation and maintenance of effective abuse prevention plans with respect to any programs, ministries, and events involving minors or Vulnerable Adults. It is highly recommended that the church maintain a continuous record of occurrence-form Abuse Liability coverage, to avoid any gaps in protection (with a minimum coverage of $2,000,000).

There is a high duty of care required both by civil courts in a lawsuit and by insurers for purposes of abuse liability coverage eligibility, including the supervision of workers, whether paid or volunteer. Churches and charities should check with their insurance provider for specific details about eligibility requirements and coverage.

Following is a 7-point checklist for abuse prevention from Robertson Hall Insurance, a leading insurance provider for churches and charities in Canada. This checklist has been acknowledged by experts as containing essential elements in establishing and upholding effective abuse prevention plans, and is required by most or all insurance companies to qualify for abuse liability insurance coverage:

- ☐ Statement of Policy
- ☐ Definition of abuse – physical, sexual, emotional and neglect
- ☐ Screening of Ministry Personnel
- ☐ Operational procedures
- ☐ Premises modifications or alterations
- ☐ Training for all workers
- ☐ Responding to all allegations of suspected abuse

"Churches are natural targets for sexual predators. They have large numbers of children, a shortage of willing workers, and a culture of trust that no Christian could be suspect of such exploitation… What is needed is a healthy suspicion of human frailty, our own as well as others."
Ken Hall, President, Robertson Hall Insurance

We want to prevent abuse, avoid unnecessary lawsuits, and protect against the need to ever make a liability claim that could drag your church through the courts for years and affect your reputation with the communities you serve. We want to do the best job possible, by ensuring effective policies, procedures, screening, and training of your workers. We want to stop abuse before it ever happens. And we want to prevent false allegations against your Ministry Personnel. With Plan to Protect®, we can help your church or charity accomplish these things and bring the risk of abuse liability to a minimum.

The Responsibility of the Board

In most churches and not-for-profits, the Board is the highest functioning authority of the church. The duty of the Board is the governance of the church, simply meaning the scope of a Board's responsibilities.

The Board should provide effective governance when developing and implementing a plan to protect the vulnerable sector, including having clear and compelling documents concerning the church's structure, operations, and beliefs consistent with safeguarding Children, Youth, and Vulnerable Adults.

In Canada, the standard of care calls for the Board and Church Leadership to oversee the protection as appropriate to their organizational structure. In the past, volunteers of children's ministry or the Children's Pastor were often responsible for Plan to Protect®. Since Board members are ultimately responsible for governing the church, delegate the oversight to a sub-committee of the Board.

We have also learned that insurance companies require that under the direction of the Board that policies be developed, approved, implemented, and periodically reviewed.

Under the direction of the Board, an audit should be conducted by having an independent internal or third-party auditor (individual or committee) appointed by your Board (or congregation) to review and survey your various programs, ministries and departments and to report back to your Board members to ensure compliance with your church's own stated written abuse prevention plan and to verify that your actual operations are in compliance with your policies and procedures. Your Board (or congregation) should ratify an internal abuse prevention audit protocol to be conducted on an ongoing annual or bi-annual basis which reflects the size, scope and nature of your organization's particular Children's and Youth ministries, programs and events.

Finally, we are reminded by Ken Hall, Robertson Hall Insurance, just because a Youth Pastor or Youth Ministry Leader has an enthusiastic idea for a new or unusual program or event doesn't mean that your Board of Directors should always go along with approval and their blessing. Not every idea is one that furthers your core ministry objectives and some often come with a very high price in terms of the potential for injury, abuse, and negative publicity in the community. This could highly impact your local reputation if it is not done properly, especially without accountability and full knowledge of the risks to your Ministry Personnel and those in your care.

For example, if a proposed activity and the way it is managed conflicts with sound abuse prevention procedures or safety standards, it should be a "red flag" causing your Board members or Ministry Leaders to further investigate, review your abuse prevention plan and make reasonable inquiries with your insurance provider and any other professionals appropriate to the proposed activity, for their advice. As you "proceed with caution" and before you give the "green light" to new programs and events, consider the following questions with respect to maintaining sound abuse prevention and screening guidelines for your Children's and Youth ministries:
- Level of access by your workers to vulnerable persons in their care, on or off-premises.
- Degree of trust inherent in the volunteer or employment position.
- Your potential liability for another organization's lack of care in a joint ministry or co-sponsored event.
- Restriction of potential isolation of a Ministry Personnel being left alone with a minor.
- Inherent risk associated with the particular activity or event.

The answers to these questions should guide the Board in determining whether new or unusual events and programs can be managed safely within the parameters of your existing abuse prevention policies and procedures. Unfortunately, in trying to "get ministry done" or in co-sponsoring events with other organizations wherein proper screening and procedures fall through the cracks, some churches and charities have placed the minors in their care in harmful situations and exposed themselves to unnecessary legal liability.

The following are motions for the Board to consider approving:

Motion #1: I move to establish a sub-committee of the Board to oversee the development and implementation of Plan to Protect® for safeguarding Children, Youth, and Vulnerable Adults within the church.

This sub-committee should be made up of no less than three people and should include representation from leaders within the church, those who work with Children, Parents, and other church stakeholders, a Pastor, and a member of the Board. The sub-committee must ensure that you meet your insurance company's requirements to qualify for abuse coverage and the standard of care followed by other similar organizations that serve the vulnerable sector. Once the sub-committee is in place, the first phase of responsibility is the development/updating of policies, procedures and forms that reflect all segments of your vulnerable sector. The second phase would be the screening and training of Ministry Personnel.

The third phase ensures that all documents relating to the vulnerable sector are retained and stored securely.

Motion #2: I move that the safeguarding policies and procedures of the church that the Board will have final approval of, include the following:
- Commitment to providing a safe environment.
- Declaration of zero tolerance for abuse, harassment, or neglect.
- Purpose statement being the prevention of harm to the Children, Youth and Vulnerable Adults and the protection of Ministry Personnel from false or wrongful allegations.
- Definitions of abuse.
- Robust screening and training of Ministry Personnel including obtaining police record checks.
- Requirement for documented procedures including but not limited to registration, attendance, documentation management, appropriate touch and washroom guidelines.
- Elevated precautions for high-risk activities, including off-site trips, social media, photography, mission trips, cell groups, retreats and conferences.
- Prohibited activities.
- Health and safety.
- Reporting and response of incidents of abuse.

Motion #3: I move that we become a member of Plan to Protect® to have access to updates to the Plan to Protect® manual, access to their professional development, training and resources, and to draw on their expertise and consult for issues that arise.

Motion #4: I move that once a year we add to our annual calendar the formation of an ad hoc sub-committee of the Board to conduct a yearly audit of our Plan to Protect® policies. The responsibility of this sub-committee is to audit the compliance of the policies and procedures and to submit a follow-up report to the Board as to their findings and recommendations for changes to the policies or follow-up of areas of non-compliance.

Motion #5: I move that the Plan to Protect® policies and procedures be reviewed every year and updated as needed.

Motion #6: I move to establish a policy that clearly states the parameters and restrictions for individuals who come to the church who are known convicted sex offenders.

Motion #7: I move that the Board establish and lead a sub-committee of no less than three people to establish a crisis management plan if and when a critical incident occurs, such as an incident that could potentially bring harm or disgrace to the church or our reputation within the community, such as abuse, fatal or severe injury, embezzlement, etc.

Motion #8: I move that the [name of the role, i.e., Lead Pastor, Chair of the Board] be the designated spokesperson for the church to media. In their absence, the [name of position, i.e., Lead Pastor, Chair of the Board] be the second person to be the designated spokesperson for the church. No one else should talk to media.

Motion #9: I move that the church prioritize and adopt the best practices for data retention, back-up, data storage, privacy, including compliance with applicable statutes.

Motion #10: I move the approval of the Plan to Protect® Policies and Procedures that have been customized for our church ministries, programs and events. Policies that are in keeping with a high standard of safeguarding, legal requirements and insurance requirements.

Finally, the Board should be aware of any prior abuse allegations that may help current leadership understand the importance of safeguarding standards and measures.

The church should reflect a commitment to healthy governance through a Board that regularly meets to address governance matters, is committed to governance training, and with Directors who each actively participate in Board meetings. The Board will maintain a commitment to overall good governance and has legal and spiritual documents in place, including a Constitution, Bylaws, Statement of Faith and Beliefs, Code of Conduct, and Lifestyle Statement(s) that relate to their Biblical definition of marriage, sexuality, gender identity, etc.

> "One of the continuing challenges in ministry and care to your organization's congregation and community is the danger of placing convenience ahead of safety. There is a huge cost in lives, innocence, and reputation, in getting ministry done at all costs when it comes to the potential for increasing the opportunity for abuse.
>
> 'How do you forgive the people who are supposed to protect you?'
>
> This danger is not one of commission. The last thing on earth ever intended is that these programs and ministries could or would result in harm. Rather it is the danger of omission — especially over time - of taking shortcuts and making exceptions to sound abuse prevention, screening, and accountability measures that must be kept in place for the protection of both the vulnerable and their own workers, such as leaving a minor alone with one adult.
>
> As insurance providers to over 7,500 churches and Christian ministries across Canada, we continue to see claims and lawsuits resulting from entirely preventable sexual and physical abuse taking place in organizations that lack the right balance between doing ministry, and maintaining a high standard of care. We are sadly closing in on 100 abuse claims involving clients, a centenary milestone I never imagined happening among the sincere and well-intentioned organizations we serve.
>
> Tragically, we have recently had two entirely preventable abuse claims in faith charity clients. One involved an organization whose leaders allowed a teacher to interact one-on-one outside of regular programs and at their home, even though it was against their own prevention plan protocol. The other was a church that permitted a youth pastor to "mentor" teenagers alone, on and off-premises. Does it really matter whether the resulting lifetime emotional and spiritual scars suffered by a child and the damage to an organization's reputation caused from such abuse and breach of trust in the name of Christian ministry was the result of commission or omission? Thank you for your organization's commitment to the vigilant protection of the most vulnerable in your care!"

- Kenneth A. Hall
President, Robertson Hall Insurance, Inc.

Protect Through Implementation

- Implementing Plan To Protect®
- Plan To Protect® Committee

Implementing Plan to Protect®

Having sound, well-worded policies and procedures is an essential first step to being safe. Putting those policies and procedures into practice in a concrete manner with the right team is the next crucial step. Our vision with this version of Plan to Protect® is to give you the tools necessary to identify risks, develop policies and create processes to address those concerns, to equip your team members, and ultimately to provide you with a framework for implementing a safeguarding ministry for your church. The following few pages will guide you as you begin the process of implementing and maintaining Plan to Protect®.

Step One: Read the manual

Carefully read through this manual, and become familiar with the templates and appendices. Mark up the texts, policies, reasoning, and implementation plans. Find out how your province defines abuse, and what laws there are and what your responsibility is within those frameworks.

Step Two: Establish a committee

Identify the key leaders who understand the importance of a protection plan for your church. Together you will draft policies, recruit and screen volunteers, train volunteers and staff, and implement a protection plan for your church. Safeguarding is an ongoing process with many elements, having a solid team with a united vision is crucial.

Step Three: Assess your procedures and policies

Take a look at each of your programs to consider whether they pose a significant risk. A risk assessment should identify: 1) programs and activities that engage the vulnerable sector, 2) programs and activities that pose a risk that needs to be mitigated by safeguarding policies and procedures, and 3) programs and activities that pose a high risk that should be altered to reduce their inherent risk.

The sample Risk Assessment (Appendix 1) gives you a series of questions that you can ask of a given program or activity, to assess the level of risk. Don't hesitate to reach out to us to help you assess the risks within your church.

Step Four: Assess your needs

Identify what your insurance company is requiring you to have in place to qualify for abuse coverage. The manual will help you identify common risks that churches face and will help you identify potential policies and procedures that may be needed for your context and ministries. This will help determine which of your programs and activities should fall under your Plan to Protect®.

Step Five: Establish a budget

There are a number of costs that will be incurred in implementing a safeguarding policy, and having a budget up front will help to alleviate some surprises that come along the way. When budgeting, you'll want to consider:

- Staffing costs and allocation of time.
- Professional development for your administrators, leaders and trainers.
- Membership with Plan to Protect® - both as a way to reduce your other costs with membership discounts as well

as taking advantage of our email and phone support. (Check out the Plan to Protect® membership options at www.plantoprotect.com).
- o Criminal Record Checks – Prices vary by police department and third party providers (Check out the Plan to Protect® ScreeningCanada services at www.plantoprotect.com).
- o Training costs (Check out the Plan to Protect® training options at www.plantoprotectschool.com).
- o Information Management Systems.

Step Six: Draft your policies and procedures

Customizing your policies and procedures is the next step. This is an important step, policies help communicate your commitment to protection and help to establish important boundaries for your leaders, staff, volunteers, and the people you serve. Procedures ensure your Ministry Personnel are all following the policies and are on the same page. You are not alone in writing this, reach out to us – we offer tools to help you write your policies, or we can even take care of that step for you.

Step Seven: Secure policy approval

Once you have written your policies, get feedback from the Committee you established, from Plan to Protect®, and from those that will be using these policies. Make revisions based on their feedback. Compare your policies to your insurer's requirements to make sure you are compliant. Have your legal council review the policies. Finally, have your Board review your policies and approve a Motion to formally approve them. This should be added to the Board Minutes.

Step Eight: Screen volunteers and staff

Good practices for recruitment and screening start with having someone (or a group of someones) whose task is to properly oversee all elements of the recruitment and screening process. This doesn't need to be an organization leader, but it does need to be someone who has been given the authority to ensure that proper processes are followed. The screening chapter in the manual will help you determine the steps to be taken. The documentation chapter will guide you on what and how to maintain the documentation needed to demonstrate your due diligence through each step of the process.

Step Nine: Train Ministry Personnel on abuse awareness, prevention and protection

Now is the time for your Ministry Personnel to receive an initial orientation training. They should attend this course prior to being placed in a position of trust. Then, every year they should attend annual Refresher training. Depending on the size of your church and the skills of your trainers, you might decide to provide regular training sessions for all new volunteers, you might decide to host a yearly orientation, or you might have everyone take their training online with Plan to Protect®. All options have their own benefits.

Step Ten: Prepare your program areas

Implementing all your protection policies and processes is a big job. Do a walk through of your building and ministry locations to identify ways to reduce the risk of abuse, injury and harm. Common safety precautions include locking doors and storage areas when they are not being used, ensuring there are clear sight lines into the classroom, installing proper lighting inside and outside of the building, restricting access to only caregivers in the nursery and toddler classrooms and retrofitting your building for accessibility. Also ensure that there is good signage for evacuation, first aid kits, Plan to Protect® policy manual, and incident report forms.

Step Eleven: Prepare your documentation management system

We strongly recommend you keep all documentation relevant to Children, Youth and Vulnerable Adults, and relevant to those that work in a Position of Trust permanently. All documentation should be securely locked, and old documentation should be kept separate from your current paperwork. Copies can be kept electronically, with protocols in place to ensure documents are protected and unalterable. See the Protect Through Documentation Management section of this manual for more details.

Step Twelve: Maintain your Plan to Protect® on an ongoing basis

Weekly
Set aside approximately 15-30 minutes to review your attendance records, ratios and Incident Reports. If time permits, compare the attendance records against your Registration Forms. Make sure you have Registration Forms for each Child who has attended your programs. Ensure that after each program day, all attendance sheets, sign-in/sign-out, Incident Reports and all other forms are reviewed by the Ministry Personnel and are filed in the secured locked cabinet or locked office and are kept permanently.

Monthly
Set aside approximately one hour to compare your volunteer and staff duty roster against your Master List of screened workers. Also ensure your Letters of Informed Consent communicate the risks associated with the activities that you have scheduled to do.

Annually
Set aside approximately one day to audit/test your procedures against your Plan to Protect® policies, update your templates and forms, and to schedule your Plan to Protect® Orientation and Refresher trainings. Make sure these training dates are put on the Master Schedule and communicated to the volunteers.

Every 1-3 Years
Review your policies to ensure they are current and up to date. Amend your policies as needed.

Every 3 Years
Update Criminal Record Checks.

On an ongoing basis
Make sure your Trainers and Administrators maintain their certification. Certifications for Administrators and Trainers expire every three years. Recertification is essential to ensure you are using updated resources and training materials and that you are providing proper training content.

Plan to Protect® Committee

Policy

1. A Plan to Protect® committee will oversee the implementation of Plan to Protect® including, but not limited to, the screening and training of all Ministry Personnel. On the committee, the following portfolios will be assigned:
   1. Chair
   2. Administration
   3. Screening
   4. Training
   5. Liaison with the Board
   6. Members at Large

2. The Plan to Protect® committee reports to the Board and will provide an annual report to the Board and congregation. The report must include the following:
   1. Members of the Plan to Protect® Committee
   2. Number of active Ministry Personnel screened and trained serving in a Position of Trust
   3. Status of abuse insurance coverage
   4. Number of Trainings held
   5. Date and findings of the annual audit
   6. Highlights of the past year
   7. Professional development completed
   8. Goals for the upcoming year
   9. Items of praise and prayer requests

Plan

- ◯ Committee Terms of Reference have been developed.
- ◯ The committee roles have been identified.
- ◯ Position descriptions for committee members have been developed.
- ◯ Committee members have been recruited and trained.

Protection

It is not realistic to believe that one individual can handle the full implementation of Plan to Protect® across a church given that you are striving to protect children, youth, and vulnerable adults, as well as ministry personnel from wrongful allegations of abuse. It is the responsibility of everyone within the church to help contribute to meeting a high standard of protection. Too often we hear that Plan to Protect® is delegated to just one person to manage.

This often creates tension among different departments within the church and raises the risk that aspects of implementation and maintenance of the plan fall through the cracks. It also does not recognize the different skills and gifts needed to successfully implement the plan. Therefore, we recommend that a committee be appointed to report to the Board of Directors. Recruited committee members should receive professional development for their specific roles.

See the Training section of the manual for suggested professional development courses.

The terms and references for a committee include:
- To stay abreast of best practices of abuse prevention and safety for our context;
- To coach and train Ministry Leads on the necessary steps to ensure implementation of the policies and procedures;
- To screen and maintain the screening requirements of all Ministry Personnel (paid and unpaid) that will be placed in a Position of Trust;
- To provide initial orientation training and annual refresher trainings of all Ministry Personnel (paid and unpaid) that will be placed in a Position of Trust;
- In partnership with the administrative staff ensure the management of documentation is in order to protect the stakeholders of the church;
- To address questions and concerns that arise in relation to the Plan to Protect® policies;
- To coach Ministry Leads on implementing Plan to Protect® within their departments;
- To maintain the procedures and forms incorporated in the policy handbook;
- To conduct an annual audit of the policies and report back to the Board the findings of the audit;
- To alert the Board of needed policy revisions and updates, and potentially draft and recommend amendments to the policies; and
- To prepare an annual report on the outcomes of the abuse prevention and safety initiatives of the church.

> It is the responsibility of everyone within the church to help contribute to meeting a high standard of protection.

Committee Make-up:

Depending on the size of your church, the following is a recommended committee size:

- **Chair (1)** - Call meetings, write annual report, meet with Board and Ministry Personnel as needed, assist with policy development and audits, in partnership with Pastoral Staff and Administrative Staff update and review forms, assist with trainings, and coach team members.
- **Board of Directors (1 or 2)** - Liaison with Board and assist with serving Pastors and Chair in dealing with difficult issues that arise from opposition or screening.
- **Administrators (2)** - Ministry Personnel who have strong administrative skills or gifts (setting up the screening files, managing the master list of screened Ministry Personnel, processing police record checks).
- **Screeners (2)** - Volunteers who have strong discernment gifts or experience in interviewing/screening staff (in partnership with Pastoral Staff, they conduct interviews, check references, etc.).
- **Members at Large (2)** – Individuals serving in Children's ministry or Youth ministry.
- **Trainers (2)** – Ministry Personnel who have strong communication skill and influence, willing to be certified as a trainer. Estimated 4-8 trainings per year.

Recommendations:
The committee need not meet often, rather, you may find it adequate to initially meet two to three times for the development of the policy prior to the approval of the policy by the Board.

Once the policy is approved, the team will meet quarterly to report on the progress of the individual's responsibilities. Remember, sitting on the committee is not the extent of an individual's involvement as each role on the committee will be assigned a portfolio which will require active involvement either in administration, screening or training.

Protect Through Recruitment and Screening

- Introduction
- Case Study
- Human Rights and Discrimination
- A. Recruitment and Screening Process
- B. Qualifications for Ministry
- C. Ministry Application Form
- D. Reference Checks
- E. Interview
- F. Criminal Record Checks
- G. Criminal Screening of Youth
- H. Red Flags and Disqualifiers
- I. Plan to Protect® Training
- J. Code of Conduct and Covenant of Care
- K. Approval Process

Introduction

Plan to Protect® is not about us not trusting you, it is about our community trusting us!

The pastor that we first heard voice these words nailed it! We don't screen individuals because we don't trust them, rather we want to demonstrate and communicate to parents, family members, and our community that we value the protection of Children, Youth and Vulnerable Adults.

For many of us, it is difficult to even imagine that abuse could happen within the context of a church.

However, child abusers build their whole lives around lying and taking their time to groom their next victim. They put on the persona of being an upstanding person, eager to serve, while manoeuvering themselves into a position to get access to the vulnerable.

It takes a skilled person to identify someone that is positioning themselves to abuse Children. You might think it would be easy to identify an abuser, but the success of offenders and pedophiles gaining access is high.

> **We want to demonstrate and communicate to Parents, family members, and our community that we value the protection of Children, Youth and Vulnerable Adults.**

The first step in screening is to overcome what has hindered us in the past from screening. Some of those hindrances may be ignorance or denial that abuse could happen within a church setting. We may all find it difficult to believe that someone is living a double life; worshiping on Sunday and struggling with habitual addictions or attraction to Children or pornography behind closed doors. Another hindrance is the role of forgiveness of past wrongs and crimes, asking "Shouldn't we just forgive them and believe that it won't happen again?" These are all good issues for the leadership of the church to discuss. We do encourage you to establish policy and procedures around screening.

The two most prevalent hindrances we hear are:

Fear that it will scare volunteers away
Screening is a process that helps match people with volunteer and employment positions while improving the quality and safety of the programs and services offered in communities. One way that you demonstrate you care for your Ministry Personnel is through screening and training.

The benefits of screening are:
- *People's skills and experience are better matched to the needs and opportunities of organizations.*
- *The quality and safety of programs in communities are improved.*
- *The risks and liabilities for people and organizations are reduced.*

Screening helps churches find the right roles for their candidates. The screening process takes into account the skills, experience and qualifications needed for a role. Through the process, Church Leaders learn about the applicant's interests and goals.

At the same time, screening improves the quality and safety of our communities. Screening policies help to communicate the responsibilities of both church and the people.

Screening practices play a role in fulfilling a church's moral, legal, spiritual and ethical responsibilities to the people it reaches. This includes members, participants, employees and volunteers. This obligation is even greater when the church is working with vulnerable people, including children, youth, people with disabilities and the elderly.

Need for volunteers
Another reason for our vulnerability to predators is that we provide increased opportunities for people to volunteer to help with our Children. Our ministry model within the last 200 years has changed: we now separate the Children from their families in church, relegating them often to the basement for age-appropriate lessons. Over the last decade we have also moved to a rotation-based teaching model where we need double or triple the number of workers we did in the past.

We would encourage you to conduct a role risk assessment and screen and train everyone that will be engaging and interacting with Children, Youth and Adults in a Position of Trust or in a leadership role. If you are entrusting an individual to serve on behalf of the church, recognize there is a risk involved in allowing this person to develop a relationship with the vulnerable sector.

One of the most important steps in protection against abuse is implementing a process of screening that is consistent across the different departments of your church. Using a multifaceted screening process of a written application, interviews, reference checks, and background screening will ensure consistency and thoroughness in verifying if the candidate has the character, competence and chemistry to work within a team setting.

We have provided you with the tools to screen your candidates. We encourage you to invest in the professional development of those that will be screening the candidates providing them advanced screening training to recognize red flag indicators. Check out our Plan to Protect® Administrator/Leader Certification Training Level One and Level Two at **www.plantoprotectschool.com**.

Case Study

Recruitment and Screening Process

Dan was excited to begin the screening process for all the volunteers of First Street Church. The board had approved the policies and now it was time to gather applications, references, criminal record checks, codes of conduct and training certificates for each person. Dan loved doing organizational tasks like this. He had created a checklist to keep track of each volunteer's screening steps, organized an excel spreadsheet, photocopied all the necessary paperwork and was ready to get started.

The problem was that around every turn Dan was faced with another challenge.

Mr. and Mrs. Green, an elderly couple who had been attending the church for over 30 years, couldn't figure out how to do the online training from Plan to Protect®. Not only did they not have emails, which they needed to sign up, but their computer didn't seem to have sound enabled.

Rodrigue, a new immigrant to Canada, was too nervous to go to the police station to get his Criminal Record check.

Susy's references were always too busy to respond to Dan's calls or wouldn't return his messages.

Deanna was nervous about taking the child safety training because she was a victim survivor of child abuse and was afraid that the training would be triggering.

And John was flat out refusing to do any of the screening steps at all.

Dan had no idea that all these challenges would arise and wasn't sure how to handle them. But he knew that all of them could be overcome…He would just have to take it a step at a time to demonstrate care.

Case Study continued ...

> *Questions to Answer:*
>
> - *How can Dan overcome these challenges?*
>
> - *How can Dan communicate the importance of screening?*

Hindsight is 20/20:

Screening your volunteers can be one of the biggest challenges you face in implementing Plan to Protect®. However, it is one of the most important steps in demonstrating your duty to care for the vulnerable and to demonstrate your care for your volunteers. If anyone refuses to be screened, that may be an indicator they know they will not pass the steps of screening. Don't let your guard down!

Human Rights and Discrimination

Policy

1. The church is committed to treating people fairly, with respect and dignity, when hiring and recruiting, in accordance with applicable provincial human rights law.
2. Ministry Personnel will conduct their hiring and recruiting practices in line with applicable provincial human rights laws.
3. Ministry Personnel will avoid asking questions that violate applicable provincial human rights legislation in interviews and when checking references.
4. The church will be transparent about how applicable provincial human rights law permits religious organizations in certain circumstances to give preference in hiring persons or to hire only persons who are members of the same religious group or meet a creed-based qualification.

Plan

- ○ Applicable provincial human rights laws are considered and complied with when determining whether creed-based or Biblical-based preferences apply in recruitment and hiring decisions.

- ○ A transparent and fair system allows applicants to know when there will be preference given in hiring persons who are members of the same religious group or meet a creed-based qualification, or when only persons who are members of the same religious group or meet a creed-based qualification will be hired.

- ○ Legal counsel has been consulted regarding hiring practices.

Protect Through Recruitment and Screening

Protection

Canadian human rights law differs from province to province, so make sure you have looked at your province's human rights laws and more specifically, the law on discrimination, hiring and exemptions before applying any exemptions permitting creed-based or Biblical-based preferences in hiring and recruitment. In general, the Supreme Court of Canada has upheld the right for religious and creed-based organizations to prefer hiring persons or to only hire persons who identify with a particular creed. However, the fact that an organization is religious is not on its own sufficient reason to require a successful job applicant to identify with a particular creed.

Specifically, organizations will need to show that they meet specific requirements in order for the exemption permitting creed-based or Biblical-based preferential hiring to apply. For example, in Ontario, in order for an exemption permitting creed-based or Biblical-based hiring to apply: an organization must be religious, show that it is primarily engaged in serving Christians, and that the requirement to be Christian is reasonable and a bona fide occupational requirement because of the nature of the role. Each province has its own framework which will have its own nuances.

The reason to have a human rights, discrimination and harassment policy to address the recruitment process is to allow clear and transparent guidelines from organization leaders down to its daily staff. Situations where there are job requirements or responsibilities with respect to lifestyle or religious identity should be obvious to all who apply. Conversely, while an employee or volunteer may disagree with the lifestyle or religious identity of another, this does not give them the right to harass or otherwise discriminate against that person (where not permitted by any exemption in human rights law).

Having a policy against discriminatory hiring practices does not remove the right from a church or other religious organization to make decisions in hiring based on their beliefs and creed, so long as the church meets the requirements to qualify for an exemption, and is consistent and transparent in its decisions. It is always best to consult your legal counsel.

A. Recruitment and Screening Process

Policy

1. All ministry departments engaging the vulnerable sector must adhere to the recruitment and screening process.
2. Church Leadership and/or the Ministry Lead determine if an individual is a suitable or potential candidate for ministry.
3. Prospective Ministry Personnel are to submit to the recruitment and screening process managed by the Ministry Lead. Individuals will submit and complete the following:
   a. Ministry Application Form (Appendix 3),
   b. Adhere to six month waiting period,
   c. Sign Statement of Faith,
   d. Face-to-face interview,
   e. Reference checks,
   f. Police records check,
   g. Training, and
   h. Final approval from Church Leadership.
4. Ministry Personnel must complete the recruitment and screening process prior to being placed in a Position of Trust.
5. Ministry Personnel who serve Children, Youth and Adults must have a personnel file kept with church records. These files are to be kept permanently.

Plan

- ◯ A recruitment and screening process has been established.
- ◯ Ministry Lead has been appointed to oversee the recruitment and screening process.
- ◯ Roles have been identified for ministry personnel.
- ◯ Initial approval of prospective ministry personnel has been given by Church Leadership.
- ◯ Up to date records have been prepared on individuals regarding their recruitment and screening status.
- ◯ Strategies have been created on how to monitor limited access to children.
- ◯ Prospective ministry personnel have completed screening process.
- ◯ Final approval of ministry personnel has been given by Church Leadership.
- ◯ Plans have been made to keep ministry personnel files permanently.

Protection

"As a volunteer in my parish, I understand that screening is not about me – it's about the ministry I'm involved in and the level of risk associated with that ministry."[1] *Plan to Protect®* has been developed to assist the church in their recruitment and screening of ministry leaders and, to the greatest extent possible, provide protection strategies for all age levels as well as those who serve.

"All organizations that provide programs to vulnerable people, whether run by staff or volunteers, have a responsibility to appropriately screen their volunteers. This responsibility is moral, legal, and spiritual; it is not only the right thing to do but it is legally required under the 'Duty of Care' concept. 'Duty of Care' is the legal principle that identifies the obligations of individuals and organizations to take reasonable measures to care for and protect their participants. Groups need to understand that Canadian courts will uphold their responsibilities with regard to screening in the context of their 'Duty of Care.'"[2]

A recruitment and screening process is critical in protecting the church from legal action should a case of abuse occur. The church that will be protected from liability will be the church that can show evidence that it has policies and procedures in place and that it has taken reasonable and ongoing action to systematically recruit, screen and supervise ministry personnel.

A recruitment and screening process is a set of procedures to outline how, when and where ministry leads are to screen ministry personnel. A good screening process would include where application forms are available, who to submit completed documents to, how personal information will be stored, who will conduct interviews and reference checks. It would also include the steps to take if a criminal record check came back flagged or not clear. This process will ensure consistency across the church.

Church leadership need to assign the responsibility for the recruitment and screening process to the ministry lead. Names of prospective ministry personnel are initially cleared by church leadership and the process is set in motion. Those given the responsibility to screen ministry personnel should sign a confidentiality agreement.

When prospective ministry personnel are approached about the opportunity to serve with children, youth and adults, a dialogue begins. An individual's gifts, passions and time commitments are matched to ministry job descriptions and expectations. Opportunities may involve teaching, leading large group events, working with small groups, managing organizational details or assisting in support roles. Some ministry positions allow you to work alone while others give you the opportunity to work alongside others as a leader, assistant or team player. All positions that involve contact with children, youth or adults or where the individual is deemed to be in a position of trust, must be screened.

---

1 (Screening in Faith, Volunteer Canada, 2006)
2 (Volunteer Canada, 2006)

protection continued...

Individuals serving in the following roles should be screened and trained under Plan to Protect®: Ministers, lay pastors, administration and office staff, counselors, cell group leaders, those serving children, youth and adults (including nursery workers, Sunday school teachers and helpers, VBS workers, child care workers, young people helping in the nursery), Board members (including trustees, elders, deacons and council members), and custodians.

Prospective ministry personnel need to be educated on the need and importance of a protection program and the steps involved in the process. The recruitment and screening process involves completing the ministry application form, adhering to the six-month waiting period, understanding and signing the denomination's Statement of Faith, having a face-to-face interview, submitting references to be checked, completing a police records check, attending a training session and receiving final approval from church leadership.

The standard of care we recommend is that the recruitment and screening steps will be completed prior to ministry personnel being placed in a position of trust. The screening process must be completed within three months of beginning service and all ministry settings will have two leaders in place who are fully screened and trained. We understand that the recruitment and screening process is extensive, however, as we will say again and again, this process protects our children, our youth, our ministry personnel and our churches.

Protect Through Recruitment and Screening

B. Qualifications for Ministry

Policy

1. A minimum six-month waiting period prior to serving is required for individuals wanting to work in ministries serving the vulnerable sector. All prospective Ministry Personnel will have regularly attended the church for the previous six months.
   - Exceptions can be made in circumstances where the Ministry Personnel have transferred from another church of the same denomination in which they have been long-time members and are ministry workers in good standing or they are being employed by the church. In these circumstances, reference checks must be received from at least three individuals, including one from their previous minister or children's ministry director.[1]

2. Ministry Personnel serving in a Position of Trust or leadership are members or adherents in good standing who support the doctrines, direction and by-laws or constitution of the church.

3. Individuals that have been accused, or convicted, or are under the suspicion of crimes against Children and/or Youth, or who have been convicted of violent crimes will not have any involvement in ministries or programs where Children or Youth participate until such time as they have been found innocent or the accusation has been found unsubstantiated.

Plan

- ○ The minimum six-month waiting period has been adhered to before placement of Ministry Personnel.

- ○ The screening process has been used to determine suitability of prospective Ministry Personnel for ministry positions.

---

[1] (Abuse Prevention Newsletter 2005, 7)

Protection

"Many volunteers are put in positions of trust with no questions asked. We all know how it happens: the organization was overburdened, no one could process the volunteer; or the volunteer was a friend of a parent – no need to go through the usual process. The reasons for accepting a volunteer without any kind of screening are often rooted in the best of intentions. ... As a result, the general belief that 'it won't happen to us' pervades these communities."[2] "In the long run, the easier process is not the safest. Screening is not meant to be invasive, it is meant to be preventative."[3]

"Screening is a ... process designed to identify any person – whether paid or unpaid, volunteer or staff – who may harm vulnerable people or groups. By ensuring good screening practices, groups can create and maintain a safe environment for volunteers, clients, members and the organization."[4]

We believe these three qualifications for ministry are essential:

• **Six Month Waiting Period**

Insurance providers consistently say that, from an abuse prevention standpoint, the single most important procedure in screening workers, apart from criminal records checks, is a six-month waiting period from the time an individual starts to regularly attend and participate in a church to the time when they are allowed to take on any role in a position of trust.[5]

These steps provide church leaders an opportunity to know the person. There are three important aspects of recruitment: character, competence and chemistry. This six-month waiting period provides an opportunity to gain insight into all three.

If the individual transferred from a church under the same denomination or they are applying for a staff position, you could waive this requirement of the six months with additional references, including from their most recent church experience.

• **Ministry Application Form**

As required on the Ministry Application Form, ministry personnel are asked to consider seriously the commitment they are making to the church.

• **No Prior Accusations or Convictions Regarding Abuse**

We recommend that those accused or convicted of abuse be directed to ministries that do not involve direct contact with children, youth or vulnerable adults. Legal counsel strongly cautions against the broadcasting of untruths as churches may then be faced with defamation lawsuits.

2 (Volunteer Canada 2006)
3 (Zarra 1997, 21-2)
4 (Volunteer Canada 2006)
5 (Abuse Prevention Newsletter 2005, 7)

Protection continued...

- **Grandparenting existing volunteers**

When updating or creating a recruitment process, some churches will run into a situation where they already have ministry personnel in place with partial screening, and sometimes these volunteers will have been acting in trusted positions for years with no screening!

Documentation is important and demonstrates our due diligence. We should be compiling a file for each volunteer with a history of their activity with the church and the steps we have taken to screen them. However, we understand that going back and screening existing volunteers that are in good standing with the church can be a burden for existing volunteers and for your screening team. Therefore, the Board may choose to make a motion to grandparent in existing personnel and waive some of the initial screening requirements for those individuals. If the Board so chooses, you can waive the need to interview and check references, as they are already well known in the church. With that said, we strongly recommend that you still require a criminal record screening and Plan to Protect® Orientation training for these individuals. These screening steps should also be updated on the same schedule as other ministry personnel. If you choose to do this, you can add the following statement into your policies. Update the dates in brackets as detailed. We do not recommend this for individuals that are new to the church or individuals that have not previously volunteered or served at the church. Checking references and interviews are requirements of the insurance company to qualify for abuse coverage. The grandparenting clause only works for existing ministry personnel that are in good standing with the church.

For ministry personnel who have been serving before the implementation of a full screening and training process, consider using the following: "Current and active ministry personnel who have been serving at our church as of the implementation of this policy will be grand-parented into the screening process as it relates to interviews and reference checks. Current and active ministry personnel must be in good standing with the church. They are required to have current Criminal Record Checks on file that have been completed on behalf of the church (not dated more than three years ago) and are required to attend a Plan to Protect® Orientation Training. All current and active ministry personnel must have their screening and training up to date within three months of the implementation of this policy."

C. Ministry Application Form

Policy

1. Prospective Ministry Personnel are to complete a Ministry Application Form. (Appendix 3) Student leaders are to complete the Ministry Application Form for Youth Working with Children. (Appendix 4)
    a. A verifiable witnessed signature is required for the protection of all parties.
    b. Individuals who transfer from another congregation unknown to the Church Leadership must include contact information or a reference from a pastoral staff member of their previous church.
    c. In accordance with PIPEDA[1] regulations, the Ministry Application Forms must include the reason for which the information is being collected.

2. Ministry Application Forms are to be kept confidential and available only to the Ministry Lead, Church Leadership and/or the Plan to Protect® team.
    a. Ministry Application Forms are to be kept in a secure location.
    b. Ministry Application Forms are to be kept on file permanently.

[1] (Different Provinces have different names for their privacy laws, BC & AB (PIPA) in QC [Respecting the Protection of Personal Information in the Private Sector])

Plan

- ☐ Ministry Application Form has been customized.
- ☐ Ministry Application Form for Youth Working with Children has been customized.
- ☐ Ministry Application Forms have been checked.
- ☐ Plans have been made to keep Ministry Applications Forms on file permanently.

Protection

Properly screening prospective ministry personnel is the first line of defence in protecting the vulnerable sector. We recognize that completing a Ministry Application Form may be uncomfortable for some individuals, however, it is important to keep the bigger picture in mind as we attempt to protect those in our church who are vulnerable. In our desire to reduce the risk of abuse within our church ministries, we believe the information gathered is necessary to protect our children, youth, vulnerable adults and ministry personnel.

"The introduction of federal and provincial privacy legislation (such as PIPEDA[1]) aimed at regulating the collection, use and storage of financial, health and other sensitive personal information has created a great deal of confusion about the length of time that the contents of files for paid and unpaid personnel should be kept. One of the key purposes of screening personnel is to demonstrate that the organization and its leaders have demonstrated reasonable due diligence when placing individuals in positions of trust. Since sexual and physical abuse claims and lawsuits often only arise many years, or even decades, after alleged incidents take place, the only way organizations can defend themselves effectively in a future lawsuit is with documentation. Therefore these records should be kept permanently! However, to satisfy the provisions of privacy legislation and the reasonable and prudent expectations of common law, we recommend the following:

- Disclose the reasons for collecting and storing this information on each application.
- Protect sensitive material in a locked and secure location to ensure confidentiality and to avoid misplacing or allowing the wrongful abstraction of documents."[2]
- Ensure that the church's privacy officer or a member of the Plan to Protect® team is appointed to oversee the security of the documents.

In general, Canadian law protects people from discrimination. This area of law, known as human rights law, deals with people's right to equal treatment without discrimination and the accommodation of their differences. Ensure that your policies, procedures and forms (including your recruitment and screening forms) are consistent with national and provincial/territorial Human Rights Codes, The Freedom of Information and Protection of Privacy Act, and provincial/territorial employment standards legislation.

2 (Abuse Prevention Newsletter 2005, 6-7)

D. Reference Checks

policy

1. Designated Screening Personnel will conduct a minimum of two reference checks on all prospective Ministry Personnel. (Appendix 5)
   a. Prospective Ministry Personnel must sign a liability release before reference checks are conducted.[1]
   b. Be sure that the references provided fit within the acceptable categories for Adults and for Youth who work with Children.
   c. Reference checks are conducted by telephone to confirm the suitability and appointment of prospective Ministry Personnel.

plan

- ○ An individual has been designated to conduct phone reference checks. (Appendix 5)
- ○ Notes have been taken on all references, and are dated and signed.
- ○ Red flag responses have been identified.
- ○ Plans have been made to keep reference checks on file permanently.

Protection

On the application form, prospective ministry personnel are to provide three references and sign a liability release before reference checks are conducted. Encourage individuals to give "references drawn from a broad cross-section of individuals who've known the applicant for many years and in many settings — personal, educational and professional."[2] "If available, the best references are from other churches or charities where the applicant has worked with minors."[3]

For adult leaders, references cannot come from relatives but can be obtained from a pastor, employer, close friend or teacher. Student leaders who work with children may have references from relatives, but must also include references from their youth pastor, employer or teacher.

1 (Cobble, Hammer, Klipowicz 2003, 21)
2 (Crislip 2006)
3 (Cobble, Hammer, Klipowicz 2003, 21)

Protection continued...

At least two of the references should be contacted by phone with records kept of the calls made, the date of the calls and a summary of the referral's comments. All reference checks will remain confidential. The person making the calls will be checking on the person's work habits, moral qualities and overall character in working with children, youth and adults, and must ask specifically if there is any reason or cause why this individual should not be left alone to care for a child, youth or vulnerable person.

It has been suggested that reference forms or letters be used for reference checks. The legal advice we have received cautions us that these references could be negotiated or prepared by the prospective ministry personnel with the individual giving the reference simply signing the letter. For this reason phone call reference checks are preferable. However, should you be unable to make contact with references by phone, a sample Ministry Personnel Reference Form has been supplied. (Appendix 7)

"The single most important factor for contributing to resiliency in children was a consistent long-term relationship with a significant adult or adults."

- Dr. Virginia Patterson
Helping Children Follow Jesus Conference

E. Interview

Policy

1. Face-to-face interviews will be conducted by the Ministry Lead or an individual approved by Church Leadership. (Appendix 8)

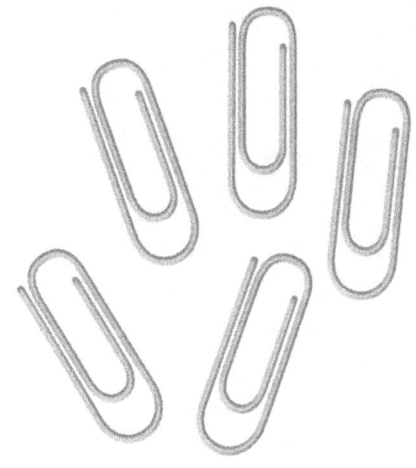

Plan

○ An individual has been designated to conduct interviews.

○ Face-to-face interviews have been conducted with all prospective Ministry Personnel. (Appendix 8)

○ Notes have been taken during all interviews, and are dated and signed.

○ Red flag responses have been identified on interview questions.

○ Plans have been made to keep interview notes on file permanently.

Protect Through Recruitment and Screening

Protection

The interview provides an opportunity for church leaders and prospective ministry personnel to dialogue together on ministry expectations and the necessity for the compliance to protection policies. "We want to do a better job at protecting ourselves, our participants and others involved in our work."[1]

Using the Ministry Personnel Interview Form (Appendix 8), have the candidate describe their spiritual journey, discuss their gifts, abilities and desires for ministry and clarify specific job descriptions. The interviewer will use this time to " … watch for inconsistencies of data, discrepancies of chronologies, … and any past or pending criminal or civil court cases. Particular attention should be paid to those applicants who are recent attendees or newer members."[2]

Please note that "According to the 2006 Annual Church and Charity Law Seminar, interviews should be done in person. No exceptions should be made for any employee or volunteer regardless of their position or length of tenure with the non-profit organization."[3]

Notes will be taken during the interview and will be dated and signed. Recommendations or concerns will be passed on to the *Plan to Protect®* team or ministry lead.

---

1 (Volunteer Canada 2006)
2 (Zarra 1997, 54)
3 (Annual Church and Charity Law Seminar 2006)

F. Criminal Record Checks

Policy

1. The Screening Committee must identify the criminal record checks available within their region.

2. Criminal record checks must be conducted on all Ministry Personnel serving the vulnerable sector.
   a. Criminal record checks are to be renewed every three years.
   b. Criminal record checks are to be conducted on all Ministry Personnel 18 years of age and older and are to be kept on file permanently.

3. If a prospective Ministry Personnel has had a history with the Child Welfare Agency, a request may be made by the Church Leadership for the individual to sign consent for a child welfare check.

Plan

- ◯ The most comprehensive screening practices have been identified and employed.

- ◯ Plans have been made to require criminal record check renewals every three (3) years on all ministry personnel 18 years of age and older.

- ◯ Criminal record check renewals take place annually for irregular or seasonal ministry personnel.

- ◯ Ensure that any previous history with the Child Welfare Agency has been identified through the screening process.

- ◯ Plans have been made to keep all criminal screening checks on file permanently.

Protection

"The request that you consent to a police records check does not mean that the organization does not trust you or has concerns about you. It means the position you are applying for is considered to have a heightened risk and the organization is managing that risk appropriately. … police records checks signal, in a very public way, that the organization is concerned about the safety of its clients."[1]

" … Criminal record checks do perform three critical and necessary roles in any effective abuse prevention plan by:

1. Identifying those who are not suitable for a position of trust by virtue of the nature of past criminal convictions and by raising a 'red flag' for individuals who refuse to submit to a check.

2. Demonstrating due diligence by the organization and its leaders, thereby making a legal defense possible in the event of an abuse claim and civil damage lawsuit."[2]

3. Help organizations assign personnel to specific roles, i.e., if someone has a DUI on their record, they should not be driving the church van.

As you study Canadian provincial laws on screening, the one caveat all provinces have in common is that 'the best interests of the child' be the standard for screening practices. "While not all provinces impose an affirmative duty to screen through their child protection laws, there is everywhere an implied duty to carry out effective screening in order to protect children, and screening is routinely conducted as a matter of policy."[3] Although provincial law is varied and open to interpretation, the insurance industry is clear. Police records checks and formal abuse prevention plans are now required to qualify for abuse liability protection from insurance companies that provide such coverage. For individual 'Provincial Acts on Child Abuse', see Appendix 39.

"Criminal record checks, vulnerable sector screening and child abuse registry screening all have limitations. Until Canada has a truly national criminal record and child abuse data base shared by all municipal, provincial, and federal jurisdictions, convicted pedophiles will continue to slip between the cracks."[4]

Criminal screening checks throughout Canada basically fall into one of three categories: police records checks, pardoned sexual crimes, and local police notes. All three database searches make up a vulnerable sector check. In some provinces you can also access child welfare checks, these contain unproved and unsubstantiated allegations or events, or tell of instances where a child needed protection from an incident involving the person applying to volunteer. In order to gain a complete perspective, insurance companies believe that " … churches should pursue the most comprehensive scan available in their municipality."[5]

---

1 (Taking the First Step, Volunteer Canada 2006, 5)
2 (Abuse Prevention Newsletter 2005, 6)
3 (Provincial Laws and Screening, Volunteer Canada 2003, 6)
4 (Abuse Prevention Newsletter 2005, 6)
5 (Abuse Prevention Newsletter 2005, 6)

Protection continued...

From our understanding and research Canada no longer grants pardons for sexual crimes against children.

We recommend that for a complete picture on prospective ministry personnel, comprehensive police records checks be pursued every three years for those age 18 and older serving in positions of trust along with permission asked to pursue a child welfare check where available. Police records checks should be conducted for all paid staff, board members and ministry personnel serving in positions of trust. All positions that involve contact with children or where the individual is deemed by the child to be in a position of trust must be screened. It is preferable to keep originals on file, however, if the prospective ministry personnel provides you with a photocopy of the police records check, the ministry lead must view the original and sign and date the photocopy of the police records check.

Plan to Protect® provides Enhanced Criminal Record Checks on our Plan to Protect® ScreeningCanada platform. Within hours you can request a criminal record check online for a candidate and have the criminal record check processed. For information contact info@plantoprotect.com.

> "Plan to Protect® is not about us not trusting our people... it is more about our community trusting us!"
>
> Pastor Andrew Holm

G. Screening of Youth

Policy

1. Minors who apply to work and volunteer shall complete the same screening requirements as Adult Personnel with the following exceptions:
    a. No Criminal Record Check is required for applicants under the age of 18. When an active Youth volunteer turns 18, they will submit a Criminal Record Check within 3 months to continue volunteering.

Plan

- Youth volunteer ages are tracked, and Criminal Record Checks are conducted shortly after they turn 18.

Protection

In past years, Criminal Record Checks have been provided to all applicants, and to third-party screening companies, even where the individual was underage. With the Youth Criminal Justice Act amendments in 2019, the RCMP has clarified that no record checks be conducted for anyone under 18 for employment purposes, except for federal departments. This change has slowly been rolled out by police departments throughout Canada, and fewer and fewer departments will now conduct these checks. We recommend that organizations that previously conducted checks for individuals 16 and over update their policies and ensure the checks are conducted shortly after these ministry personnel turn 18.

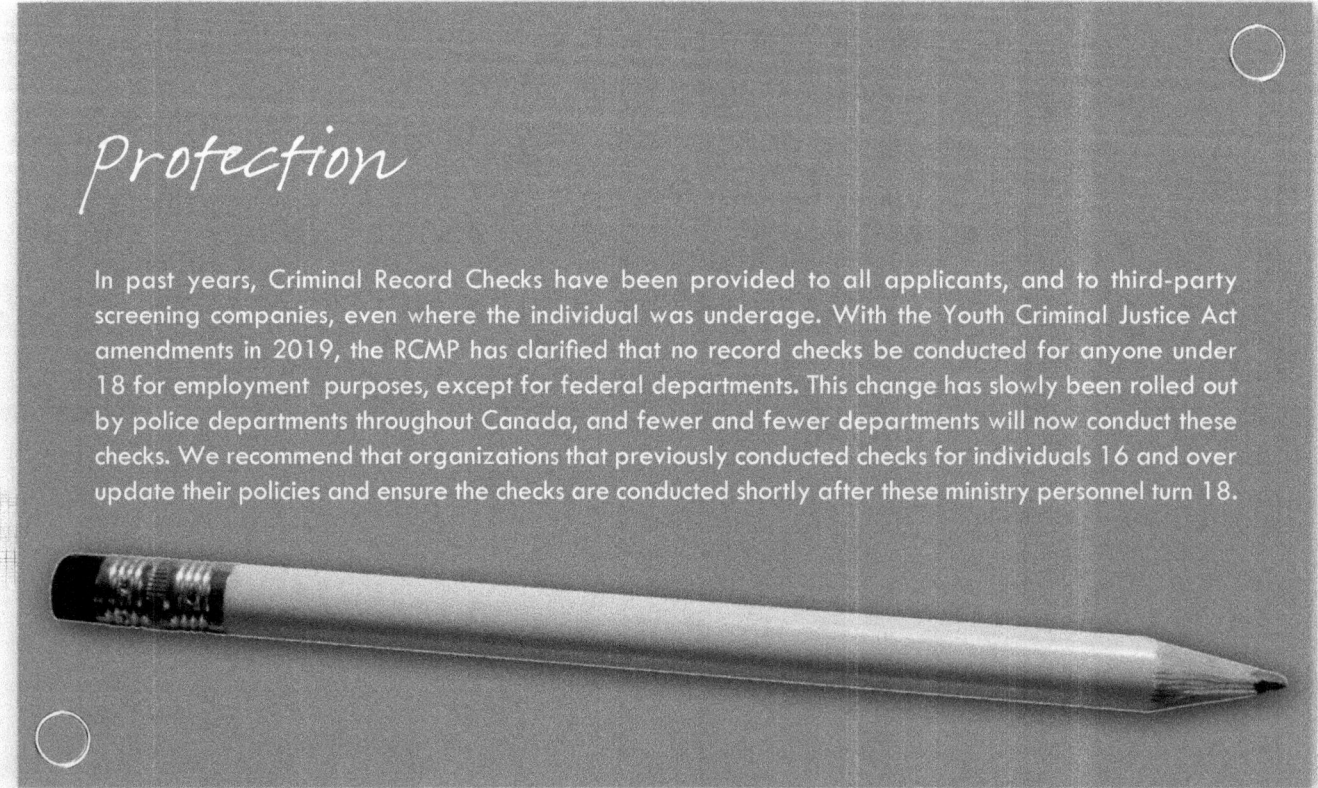

H. Red Flags and Disqualifiers

Policy

1. Screening Personnel are to be trained on identifying red flags during the screening process.
2. During the screening process, Screening Personnel are to be alert to any red flags that may disqualify prospective Ministry Personnel from working with the vulnerable sector. When a red flag is identified, Screening Personnel are to bring the red flag to the attention of the Lead Pastor or their delegate.
3. Screening Personnel are to keep information confidential and information regarding red flags and disqualifiers will only be shared on a need to know basis.
4. The following red flags are to be automatic disqualifiers:
   a. Any convictions of crimes against Children, Youth or Vulnerable Adults or violent crimes, including but not limited to:
      - Child abuse, sexual or otherwise
      - Abduction, murder, or manslaughter
      - Incest
      - Rape
      - Sexual assault
   b. Violent crimes wherein a weapon was used
5. The Lead Pastor and the Board are to make a decision to disqualify or not to disqualify someone from a Position of Trust due to one or more red flags. Depending on the severity of the red flag, the decision may be made in conjunction with legal counsel and the insurance company. Their decision, reasoning, and steps taken to mitigate any potential risks are to be documented and kept permanently. No exceptions are to be made for convictions that fall under automatic disqualifiers.
6. Documentation is to be maintained permanently for all prospective Ministry Personnel applying to be Ministry Personnel. If someone does not qualify for a Position of Trust, the reason for disqualifying the candidate is to be kept confidential but is to be included on their personnel record which is to be kept under lock and key.

plan

- Personnel responsible for screening have been trained to identify red flags.

- A process has been established to deal with red flags and disqualifiers, including but not limited to when it is appropriate to seek legal counsel.

- The Board has designated individuals responsible for managing and communicating with candidates who do not qualify to be placed in a position of trust, and any follow-up reconciliation processes that need to be followed.

Protection

Red flags may include information that is gleaned from the application, interview, reference checks or criminal background check that raises concerns that this individual may not be suited to have access to the vulnerable sector. Red flags may be based on someone's prior immoral or unlawful acts. A red flag may be identified when you are checking references and you receive one strong reference and one very weak, concerning reference. A red flag may be someone admitting to a moral failure, or addiction to pornography. A red flag includes convictions on the candidate's police record check or a history with Child and Family Services.

Based on your church's Statement of Beliefs, Code of Conduct and the position the candidate is applying for, these may not only be red flags but disqualifiers.

When evaluating someone's history and suitability for working with the vulnerable sector, consider the following if they have a conviction or history that does not automatically disqualify them but where red flags appear:

- The candidate's employment history since the negative history or other information;
- Circumstances surrounding the conviction(s) or negative history;
- The relevance of the conviction(s) or history to the duties and responsibilities of working with the vulnerable sector;
- Age at which the conviction(s) or negative history occurred;
- Length of time since the conviction(s) or negative history occurred;
- Whether there are multiple indicators that point to an ongoing pattern of behaviour;
- The level of interaction and responsibility they will have with the vulnerable sector;
- Evidence of rehabilitation;
- The position in which you are placing them in;
- Evaluation of current spiritual fitness; and
- Any other mitigating circumstances.

Churches should seek legal counsel if disqualifying candidates for reasons that fall under human rights law.

I. Plan to Protect® Training

Policy

1. An initial Orientation training on abuse prevention education is required for all Ministry Personnel serving with Children, Youth and Adults. This applies to all employees, Board Members, Screening Personnel, Leaders and Volunteers, and anyone else in a Position of Trust.

2. Training must be conducted by a qualified trainer. The training must include a review of the Plan to Protect® Policy and all safeguarding procedures. Ministry Personnel are to be educated about their obligation to report suspected abuse and on how to recognize and identify the symptoms of abuse and molestation.

3. All Ministry Personnel are required to attend Orientation training prior to placement. All Ministry Personnel are required to attend annual Refresher training sessions thereafter.

4. Attendance is to be taken at all training events and noted in the Ministry Personnel file for each individual present. All Ministry Personnel must sign an agreement form (Appendix 3a) confirming they have read, understood and are willing to comply with the Plan to Protect® policies and procedures.

Plan

- ○ A budget has been established for training ministry personnel.
- ○ Qualified training personnel have been designated and equipped.
- ○ Both Plan to Protect® Orientation and Refresher Training are made available on an annual basis or more frequently.
- ○ Training dates and locations are set and advertised well in advance.
- ○ Plans have been made for attendance to be taken at training and noted in ministry personnel files, which are to be kept permanently.
- ○ A plan has been developed for ministry personnel who cannot attend training.

Protect Through Recruitment and Screening

Protection

Ministry personnel who work with children, youth and vulnerable adults must be trained and equipped to understand your programs and any issues they may encounter. The screening and training process must include instructions on safety and child abuse prevention. "In addition to providing an opportunity to hand out written information such as manual and handbooks, and answer questions, orientation and training events give the organization a chance to track a volunteer during their probationary placement. Refusal to attend, or constant excuses for not attending may signal that something could be wrong."[1]

To qualify for abuse coverage, insurance companies require that a qualified trainer provide the training on abuse prevention. In this manual we have suggested tips and resources for training your ministry personnel. The initial Orientation training is a two-hour session. Refresher courses are to be conducted annually, reviewing policies and noting any changes that have occurred in policies or procedures.

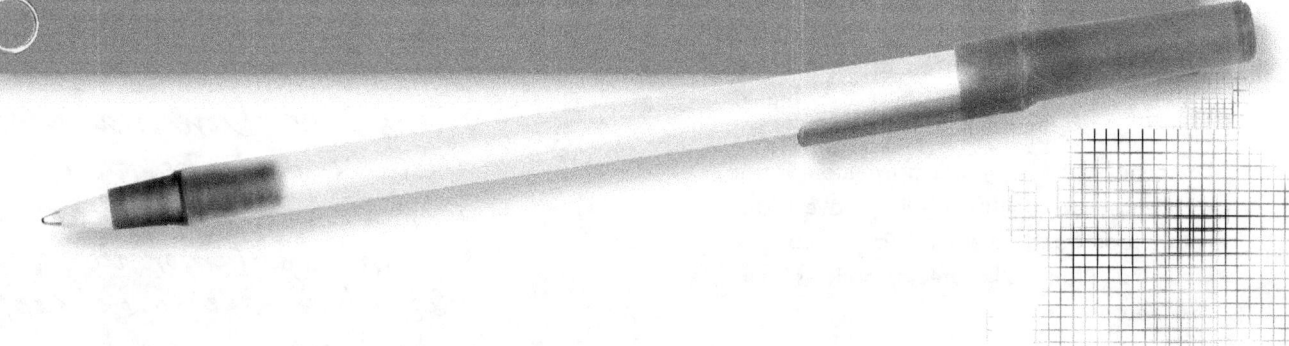

---

1 (Best Practice Guidelines for Screening Volunteers, Public Safety Canada
https://www.publicsafety.gc.ca/cnt/rsrcs/pblctns/bpg-scrng-vls/index-en.aspx#a11m)

J. Code of Conduct and Covenant of Care

Policy

1. Upon completion of screening and training, Ministry Personnel must sign a Covenant of Care and Code of Conduct attesting that they will abide by the Plan to Protect® policies, procedures and training.
2. The Covenant of Care and Code of Conduct is to be signed on an annual basis.

Plan

- ○ The Covenant of Care and Code of Conduct have been written.
- ○ The Covenant of Care and Code of Conduct are included in the application process.
- ○ At the conclusion of Orientation Training and Refresher Training attendees sign the Covenant of Care and Code of Conduct.
- ○ All signed documents are added to Ministry Personnel files.

Protection

A covenant of care encourages discussions of mutual care that both parties owe each other. A well-constructed covenant of care will communicate the steps the church has taken to demonstrate they care for ministry personnel. The document affirms that ministry personnel are a valuable part of accomplishing the vision and mission of the church.

Protection continued...

We conducted a survey among hundreds of ministry personnel, the common means wherein a church can demonstrate their duty of care is:

- clearly communicating policies and procedures,
- providing training and resources needed for service,
- maintaining reasonable ratios among ministry personnel and minors,
- providing feedback through ministry personnel reviews,
- having abuse insurance coverage in place,
- holding people accountable for their actions,
- demonstrating transparency and trust.

On the other hand, church leaders voiced that ministry personnel can demonstrate they care for the church by:

- adhering to policies, procedures, and the Code of Conduct,
- attending training sessions,
- attending services and growing in their faith,
- showing up on time,
- being accountable,
- completing incident report forms,
- communicating concerns and anything out of the ordinary,
- and trusting their leaders.

The best place to communicate this mutual duty of care is in position descriptions and in the Covenant of Care and Code of Conduct.

A well-written Code of Conduct clarifies a church's mission, values and principles, linking them with the duty of care. A code encourages discussions of ethics and compliance, empowering ministry personnel to handle ethical dilemmas they encounter during their service. A code is important because it clearly lays out the rules for behaviour and provides the groundwork for a pre-emptive warning if a disciplinary step is called for.

Your Covenant of Care and Code of Conduct should be reflective of your Statement of Faith and Beliefs.

Ministry personnel are a role-model to children, youth and vulnerable adults, and a valued ambassador for the church at all times - on and off the road, when delivering programming, and when relaxing after hours. Professional conduct is extremely important as ministry personnel actions directly affect a church's reputation.

The Covenant of Care and Code of Conduct should be signed on an annual basis.

K. Approval Process

Policy

1. The Board is to appoint an individual that is to approve candidates that have completed the screening process.

2. All Ministry Personnel are to be approved by Church Leadership upon completion of recruitment and screening process.

   a. Approval must be signed and dated.

3. The recruitment and screening process must be completed within a three month period of time

   a. Workers in process of completing the recruitment and screening process are not to be placed in a Position of Trust.

   b. Access to Children are to be limited until final approval is received.

Plan

○ Up to date records have been prepared on individuals regarding their recruitment and screening status.

○ Workers in process of completing the recruitment and screening process have not been placed in Positions of Trust.

Protection

Ministry personnel are to receive final approval from the church leadership and the Plan to Protect® Team. For accountability purposes, this should be a different person than who conducted all the screening steps. Records of this approval are to be signed, dated and kept in the ministry personnel file. Approved ministry personnel will have completed a recruitment and screening process that includes completing a Ministry Application Form, adhering to the six-month waiting period, understanding and signing the denomination's Statement of Faith, having a face-to-face interview, submitting references to be checked, completing a police records check, attending a training session and receiving final approval from church leadership and the Plan to Protect® team.

Those individuals who are serving but who have not yet completed the recruitment and screening process must submit and complete all requirements within a three month period of time. In the meantime, their access to children will be limited and they are not to be placed in a position of trust. If their service is required, they will be placed in ministry settings with approved ministry personnel. Only approved ministry personnel will accompany children to the washroom and assume the responsibility for their care.

Protect Through Documentation Management

- Introduction
- Case Study
A. Plan To Protect® Program Maintenance
B. Documentation
C. Documentation Storage and Retention
D. Personal Information and Privacy

Introduction

We may be buried alive in paperwork!

How do you balance the amount of paperwork required to demonstrate your activities knowing there is no statute of limitations in Canada for abuse against a minor?

The best means within a court of law of demonstrating your duty of care and the steps you have taken to mitigate injury, harm and abuse is to document your activity. This includes screening and training records, the registration and attendance of participants, permission forms and waivers, incident and accident records, etc., etc., etc.

We are committed to helping you establish, implement and maintain a plan to protect the participants in your programs, your Ministry Personnel and your church. You do not need to recreate the wheel, rather, we are providing you all the tools and training you need to establish your plan. Once you establish your plan, there are systems to implement and maintain your plan. Along with Plan to Protect® our network of members and partners can assist you in finding solutions to fit your budget, size and staffing (or lack thereof).

> "We are committed to helping you establish, implement and maintain a plan to protect the participants in your programs, your Ministry Personnel and your church."

If you have ever watched the television show of Judge Judy, you would know that one of her favourite sayings was "Show me the paperwork!" This chapter will help you be prepared to be able to produce the paperwork when needed. Maintaining good documentation is a means of securing informed consent and demonstrating accountability and due diligence in preventing injury, harm and abuse.

Note: The best practices found in the documentation module of the manual are not stand-alone policies and procedures. This section of the manual is supplementary material to be used with other (equally important) sections of this manual, including Recruitment and Screening, Training, General Protection Procedures, Child, Youth and Adult Protection Procedures, and Reporting and Response.

Case Study

Plan to Protect® Program Maintenance

This was a nightmare. You never thought this would happen, but someone has accused a volunteer in your church of sexual abuse and has taken your church to court. How could this possibly have happened?

Everyone knew Samuel and loved him. Samuel had been volunteering at your church for years and it was so hard to imagine he was even capable of committing these horrible acts. Of course, you hoped it couldn't be true that he had abused someone 10 years ago, but if it was, you wanted to do everything you could to help the victim get the help they needed.

As soon as the allegation had been made, Samuel had been asked to step back from volunteering. This way, the police could do their investigation, you could protect the students, and Samuel and his family could take a break as this had been very traumatic for everyone involved.

Now that this case was headed before the courts, it was your responsibility to gather all the necessary documentation to provide to your lawyers. First, you got a copy of your policies and your insurance documents. Thankfully your church was really good at updating its policies, so it was easy to find all the documentation right where it was supposed to be. Then you grabbed your incident reports and suspected abuse report forms. Flipping through them, you couldn't find any incident reports or suspected abuse report forms which involved Samuel or the child in question. Next, you pulled attendance records from the year that the accused abuse had occurred. Thankfully, all of your documentation had been backed up electronically – so it was easy to find exactly what you were looking for. Finally, you grabbed Samuel's thick volunteer folder. In Samuel's file you found his application, references, notes from an interview that was done with him, and multiple criminal record checks which had come back clear every three years. You also find a copy of his Plan to Protect® training certificates for every year he has been volunteering at the church. Wow, it was nice to know everything had been done and it was all where it was supposed to be.

Flipping through the meticulously kept attendance records, you were surprised to see that the child in question hadn't even been in attendance on any of the days the accused abuse had supposedly happened. Finally, looking at Samuel's volunteer folder you noticed something else... Samuel has only been volunteering at your church for nine years, but the accusation had been for 10 years ago.

Ultimately, you know it's not up to you to make a determination of what happened or what didn't happen. But gathering all the paperwork, you're able to pass it on to the church's legal team and it does make you feel a little better knowing everything was right where it belonged. You are so grateful that there was a history of good documentation management as it seemed to support the fact that the church did everything they could. You whisper a prayer that this was the case.

Case Study continued …

> *Questions to Answer:*
>
> - *If this case study occurred in your church, would you be as successful in pulling together the same documentation?*

Hindsight is 20/20:

Maintaining good documentation is the key to demonstrating due diligence!

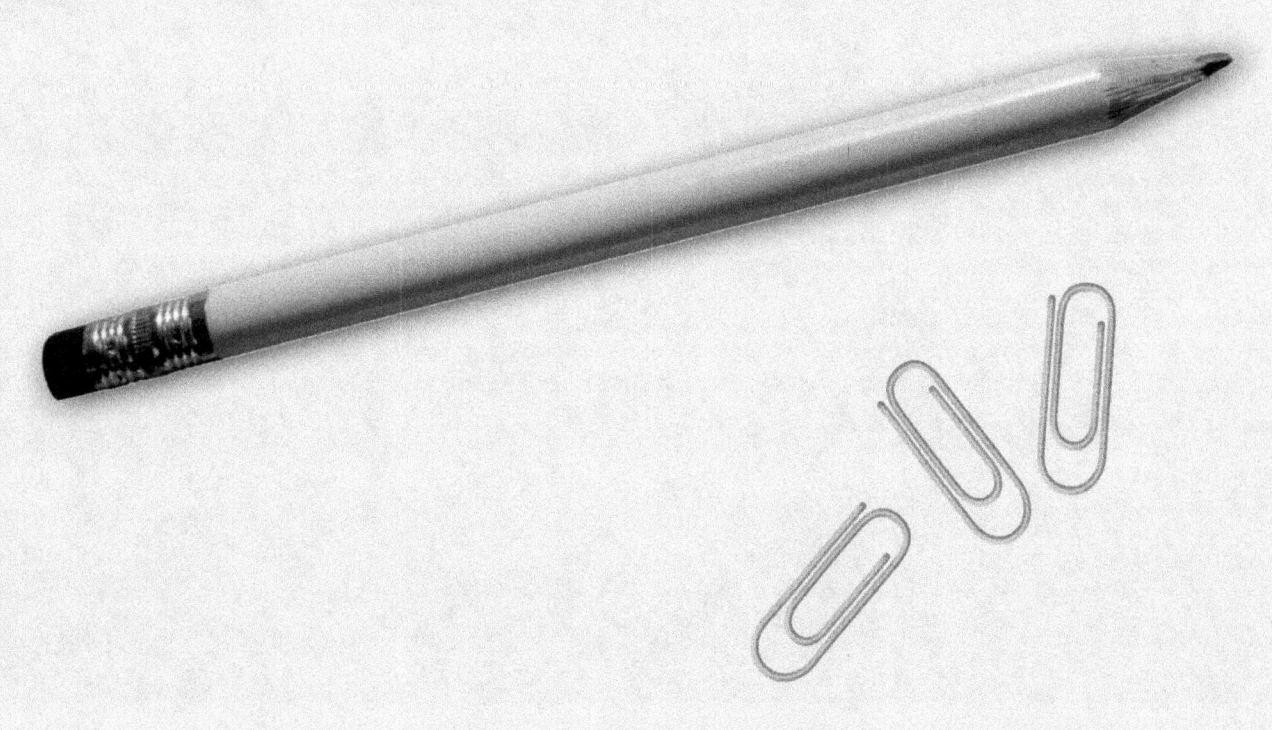

A. Plan to Protect® Program Maintenance

Policy

1. A strategy for program maintenance will be developed and reviewed at the beginning of each ministry year to ensure training, the updating of files and the physical environment are compliant with policy.

Plan

○ An annual strategy has been determined for program maintenance.

○ A system has been determined by Church Leadership as to how the review will be conducted.

Protection

The task of implementing Plan to Protect® into the life of the church is an ongoing process. You will update your policies as you discover gaps or strategies that just aren't working. You must train prospective ministry personnel at the beginning of each ministry year and re-educate existing ministry personnel annually. You need to walk through your facilities and look at classrooms, windows, toys and equipment from a safety and security perspective.

Your filing system needs to be reviewed annually with notations made on training, annual renewals and police record check updates. "Once the person is no longer a volunteer, or leaves the church, all confidential forms and documents should be placed in a sealed envelope and retained in a locked file. If an allegation of abuse should occur in the future, and some charges surface decades later, the church will need these documents to demonstrate that it engaged in reasonable care in the selection of the volunteer."[1]

Every church is now required to have a privacy officer. Perhaps our churches could be encouraged to appoint a Plan to Protect® officer who is not the children's pastor or the youth pastor, but someone charged with the responsibility of asking and finding out the answer to the following questions on an annual basis.

- Has each department trained its workers with Plan to Protect®?
- Are the policies printed and available?
- Do sufficient materials exist for training and information?
- Are workers following the required policies and procedures?
- What obstacles exist in complying with the policies?
- Do we have adequate abuse coverage insurance in place?

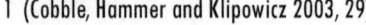
1 (Cobble, Hammer and Klipowicz 2003, 29)

B. Documentation

Policy

1. Registration Forms, Attendance Records, and Letters of Informed Consent must be collected and kept on file.

2. Incident Reports must be written and submitted on all accidents and injuries.

3. Suspected Abuse Report Forms must be written for all suspicions, allegations and disclosures of abuse.

4. Documentation on screening and involvement of Ministry Personnel will be compiled in Ministry Personnel files.

5. All documents will be scanned, saved as a PDF or saved on the cloud in a secure format that cannot be easily manipulated. A secure backup of documentation will be retained, and files will not be overwritten.

6. Documentation mentioned within this policy must be retained permanently.

Plan

- Forms are used to collect relevant personal information and documentation such as Registration Forms, Letters of Informed Consent, Attendance Sheets, Personnel Application Forms, Incident Reports, Suspected Abuse Report Forms, etc.

- Documentation is retained in a secure space which is only accessible to designated individuals.

- Ministry Personnel with access to documentation have signed a Confidentiality Agreement.

- Documents are scanned and backed up to a secure platform.

- Documents are maintained permanently.

Protection

There is no statute of limitations on child abuse in Canada, meaning that a claim of child abuse can occur at any point in time, regardless of how long it has been since the incident(s) occurred. For this reason, Plan to Protect® stands with insurance companies by requiring the permanent retention of key documentation to ensure the protection of the individual from whom the information had been collected, the organization, and the personnel employed at the organization.

An organization demonstrates due diligence by taking all reasonable precautions to prevent injuries or incidents in the workplace. While one component is maintaining and implementing policies and procedures, another component is maintaining documentation - including personnel files, incident reports, training records, and so forth. Maintaining this level of due diligence not only provides protection for the organization, but for the employees, volunteers and all persons served.

Under Provincial and Federal Privacy legislation, organizations hold responsibilities for limiting use and disclosure of personal information that has been collected, and for retaining the personal information for the duration which fulfills the purpose of its collection. The Office of the Privacy Commissioner of Canada outlines these responsibilities as follows:

- Unless someone consents otherwise—or unless doing so is required by law—your organization may use or disclose personal information only for the identified purposes for which it was collected. Keep personal information only as long as it is needed to serve those purposes.
- Know what personal information you have, where it is, and what you are doing with it.
- Obtain fresh consent if you intend to use or disclose personal information for a new purpose.
- Collect, use or disclose personal information only for purposes that a reasonable person would consider appropriate in the circumstances.
- Put the guidelines and procedures in place for retaining and destroying personal information.
- Keep personal information used to make a decision about a person for a reasonable time period. This may be useful in the event an individual seeks access to the information in order to pursue redress.
- Destroy, erase or anonymize any personal information that your organization no longer needs.[1]

---

1 (Office of the Privacy Commissioner of Canada, 2019)

C. Documentation Storage and Retention

Policy

1. As there is no statute of limitations for child abuse in Canada, and extended statute of limitations for crimes and personal injury related to Vulnerable Adults in Canada, all documentation pertaining to program activities involving Children, Youth and Vulnerable Adults shall be kept and stored permanently following the church's document retention procedures, and in compliance with the areas below.
2. Wherever possible, forms must be legible, include the date, location and full names of everyone present or involved, and include any explanatory notes which provide context. The individual who completed a form must be identifiable.
3. This policy applies to all documentation created and gathered in relation to Children, Youth and Vulnerable Adults. The documentation to be retained includes, but is not limited to:
   a. All documentation gathered during Recruitment, Screening, Training of Ministry Personnel
   b. Ministry Personnel files
   c. Files created during the planning, supervision, and implementation of program activities
   d. Insurance policies
   e. Registration Forms
   f. Attendance Forms
   g. Disciplinary memos of Ministry Personnel
   h. Letters of Informed Consent (Releases and Waivers)
   i. Transportation records
   j. Rental agreements
   k. Incident Forms
   l. Suspected Abuse Forms
   m. Any follow-up or additional information attached to such forms as is necessary to provide a clear picture of the church's activities, participants, and supervision

Documentation storage and backup
1. All documents and files pertaining to the church's activities, participants and supervision will be stored in a locked cabinet accessible only to authorized Ministry Personnel. A backup will be maintained, containing copies of all documents.
2. Physical backup will take place off-site, in a fire and water resistant location.
3. Backups of all documents will be made weekly, and added to the physical back-up on a monthly basis.
4. An online backup of all files will be maintained, hosted on a server located off-site.
5. Online storage will be password protected and secure (preferably encrypted). All information stored on the server will be done in an unalterable format (i.e., PDF or password protected) where possible, and the ability to delete items be removed.
6. Scans of all documents will be made weekly, and added to the online storage on a monthly basis. Where possible, use software that tracks all changes to stored information.

Access to archived documentation
1. Archived documentation may be needed from time to time, to verify someone's past history, for audit purposes, or to ensure accuracy. In all cases where the archived, stored information must be accessed, care will be taken to adhere to a transparent process. Individuals accessing archived files must have a clear, articulated reason, and always do so under the supervision of at least one other authorized Ministry Personnel.

plan

- ○ All documents and files pertaining to the church's activities, participants and supervision have been stored in a locked cabinet accessible only to authorized ministry personnel.

- ○ Physical backups of documents have been made weekly and added to the physical storage on a monthly basis.

- ○ Scans of documents have been made weekly and added to the online storage on a monthly basis.

Protection

Demonstrate due diligence by keeping documentation on file. There is a lot of misunderstanding about the length of time documentation should be kept. Unlike financial records which should be kept for seven years, in Canada there is no time limit (called a statute of limitations) on bringing criminal charges for sexual assault against children — meaning you can swear a criminal complaint and file charges at any point in your lifetime.

Current and past documentation may be used to provide detailed information in the future - to show the organization's compliance with safeguarding policies, to provide additional details to incident reviews, and to show steps taken to increase safety of stakeholders. Therefore for the protection of the organization, and to be able to demonstrate that you fulfilled your duty of care and due diligence in protecting those under your care, documentation should be kept permanently.

D. Personal Information and Privacy

Policy

1. The protection of personal information is all of our responsibility. Therefore, it is the responsibility of everyone serving to ensure that personal information provided is kept confidential according to this policy.

2. All Ministry Personnel that have access to personal information must sign a Confidentiality Agreement.

3. The collection of personal information is limited to what is necessary for the identified purposes and will be collected by fair and lawful means. Personal information must only be used and disclosed for the purposes for which it was collected, except with consent or as required by law. It will be retained only as long as it is necessary to fulfill those purposes. In most cases, information that relate to minors and Ministry Personnel serving with minors will be retained permanently as there is no statute of limitations on child abuse in Canada.

4. Personal information must be as accurate, complete and up-to-date as is necessary. Personal information must be protected by adequate safeguards. Information about a church's privacy policies and practices must be readily available to individuals upon request.

5. An individual has the right of access to personal information about themselves and has the right to seek correction. Both these rights are subject to some exceptions as specified in each statute. The church must provide the means for an individual to challenge their compliance with the above principles. Please refer anyone requestion information to the Church Office Administrator.

Plan

- ○ Forms used to collect relevant personal information and documentation state the purpose of the data collection.

- ○ Documentation is maintained in a secure space, only accessible to designated individuals.

- ○ Ministry Personnel with access to documentation have signed a Confidentiality Agreement.

- ○ Documents are scanned and backed up to a secure platform.

Protection

The federal Personal Information Protection and Electronic Documents Act (PIPEDA), and the Personal Information Protection Act (PIPA) share the same explicitly stated purpose: To govern the collection, use and disclosure of personal information by private sector organizations in a manner that recognizes both the right of the individual to have their personal information protected and the need of organizations to collect, use and disclose personal information for purposes that a reasonable person would consider appropriate. At the time of publishing this version of Plan to Protect®, these Acts are primarily intended for commercial activities. However, the Acts do reflect best practices in safeguarding the personal information of an individual.

An important principle with these federal and provincial laws is that an organization may collect, use or disclose personal information only for a purpose that a reasonable person would consider appropriate in the circumstances.

Organizations hold responsibilities for limiting use and disclosure of personal information that has been collected, and retaining the personal information for the duration which fulfills the purpose of its collection.

We encourage you to consider a broad purpose for collecting personal information including the opportunity to promote other programs and activities in the future and to nurture relationships with participants and their families.

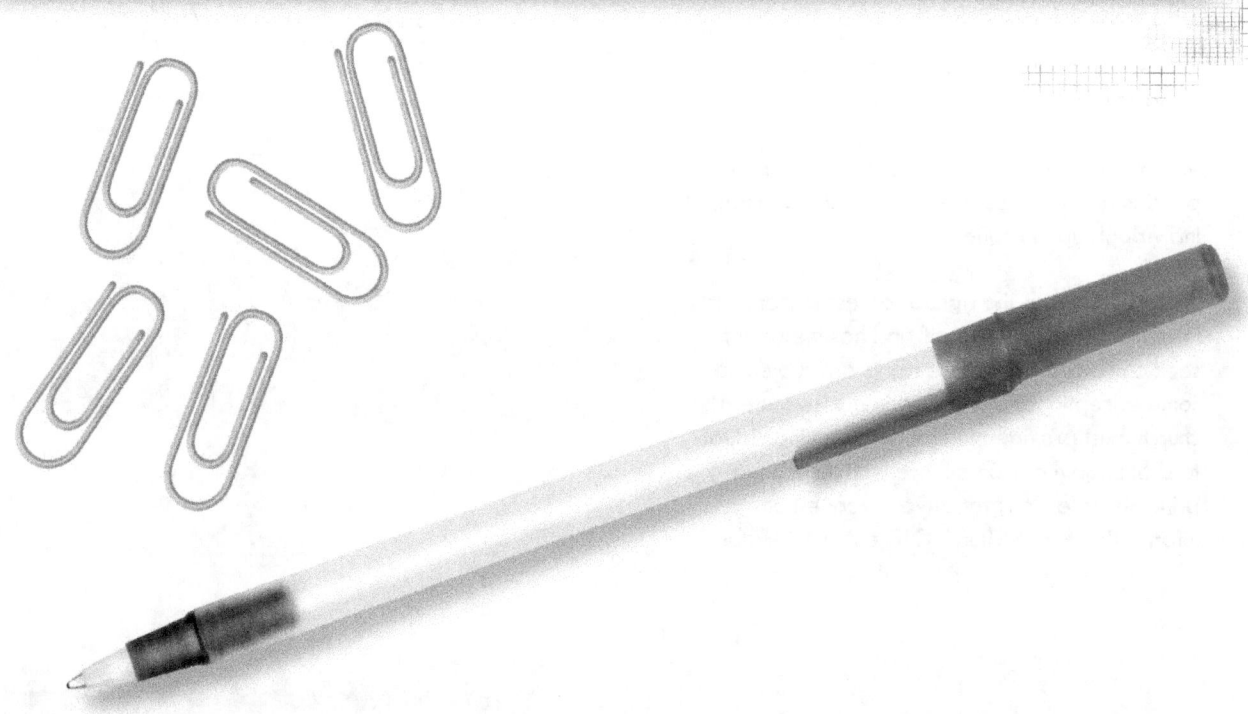

Protect Through Training

- Introduction To Training
- Case Study
- Types of Training
    a. Orientation Training
    b. Refresher Training
- Vibrant and Creative Training
- Qualified Trainers
- Plan to Protect® Training Resources
    Certification Training Programs
    Orientation and Refresher Training
    Special Interest Training
    Youth Training
- Tips for Trainers
- Restrictions and Parameters for Training

Introduction to Training

Preventing abuse and protecting the vulnerable is a skill that needs to be taught. Policies need to be implemented and people can only do what they've learned.

We are passionate about good training. Watching people develop a passion for creating safe and just communities, and enabling them to share that with others, brings us great joy. But we understand that for many people training can become just another item to check off to fulfill insurance requirements. Let's be clear: preventing abuse is not an option. Training is critical. Insurance companies require Ministry Personnel to be trained in abuse prevention, and for that training to be refreshed to qualify for abuse coverage.

In this section we'll provide resources, tips and strategies for doing training at your church. We've also provided an overview of different training services Plan to Protect® offers. The goal is to make sure that everyone in your church is on the same page, and we want to make sure everyone enjoys the process it takes to get there. Abuse is serious and heartbreaking, but teaching about the awareness and prevalence of abuse, the need to report and to respond to abuse appropriately, and how to prevent abuse can be a transformative experience.

> "Watching people develop a passion for creating safe and just communities, and enabling them to share that with others, brings us great joy."

"A good education is a foundation for a better future."
- Elizabeth Warren

Case Study

Training

Your church has been doing Plan to Protect® for over seven years now and you finally feel like you are figuring things out. You have policies which have been officially approved by your Board, and all your Ministry Personnel are now fully screened.

As the designated certified Trainer, you've created a yearly training schedule for Orientation and Refresher trainings and it's working well. Your Ministry Personnel are getting on board and enjoying the annual Refresher trainings as you have come up with new creative methods to deliver the training.

This evening you have a Refresher training and you're all prepared. You've printed off your teaching notes, photocopied the worksheets for your participants, and you even managed to get volunteers to sign up to bring snacks. You've checked and your PowerPoint is all ready to go. The room is being set up and the tech team has set up the projector, screen and microphone. Check, check, check, ready to go!

Hours later you've finished the training and it went better than expected. There was a great discussion during the case studies, and attendees asked thought provoking questions at the end of the presentation. While cleaning up, you notice your list of participants who had signed up to attend and notice that Leslie, who had offered to bring snacks, didn't come.

At church the next week, you spot Leslie and approach her to let her know you missed her at the training and ask if everything is okay. Leslie shares with you she hasn't been to your Refresher Training for the last four years. Each year she signs up and offers to make a snack, but something inevitably comes up, so she doesn't attend. She figured that since you've never said anything it didn't matter. You go back to your training records and sure enough, each year she signs up but never shows up. Oh no! You thought you were in perfect compliance with your policy and insurance requirements, but it turns out that not only has Leslie missed the other trainings for the past four years, but some other volunteers have also missed a training here or there.

Case Study continued ...

Questions to Answer:

- How important is it that your trainer is a qualified trainer?

- What are the benefits of doing annual Refresher training?

- What risks does your church face if volunteers miss annual training?

- What are you going to do moving forward to make sure you're adhering to your policies and insurance requirements as it relates to training?

Hindsight is 20/20:

Training is one of the most important steps you can take to achieve a high standard of protection. Identifying why Leslie is not attending training along with providing different options for training will help you realize 100% compliance.

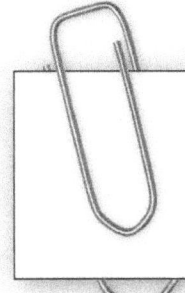

Types of Training

There are two main kinds of training your Ministry Personnel need: Orientation and Refresher Training.

a. Orientation Training

Overview: One of the first steps in protecting your organization is through abuse prevention training. Initial Orientation Training equips you and your team to recognize the different types of abuse as well as implement and maintain policies and procedures to protect vulnerable persons in your church and community. Our Plan to Protect® Orientation training satisfies the insurance requirements to qualify for abuse coverage for initial abuse prevention training, helps remove obstacles to organizational accountability and keeps both caregivers and vulnerable individuals safe.

The initial Orientation training should include:
- Awareness
    - What is abuse? How prevalent is it? Why is abuse prevention and vulnerable sector protection important? Why are we doing this?
- Prevention
    - How can we prevent abuse from happening in the first place? How can we prevent/minimize false allegations?
    - Best practices on preventing abuse.
    - Introduction of abuse prevention policies and procedures for vulnerable sector protection.
    - How can we mitigate abuse, injury and harm during high risk activities?
- Protection
    - How can we protect those who are hurting? What are the different types of abuse? How can we recognize indicators of abuse? How do we report it if we think someone vulnerable is being abused?
    - Legal guidelines for responding to and reporting child abuse.
    - How to respond if there is a disclosure of abuse against an adult.
    - Steps to follow if an allegation, suspicion or disclosure of abuse occurs.

Initial Orientation training should take approximately two hours and should be customized for your specific context.

It is not necessary for someone to redo the Orientation training. However, if you are following progressive steps of discipline and you believe they need to redo training – this may be an opportunity for them to redo the Orientation training. If someone leaves your church for a long period of time or if their role changes significantly, (i.e., moving from Children's Programming to Refugee Sponsorship Team), you may want them to redo the Orientation training.

b. Refresher Training

Overview: The Refresher training covers the same topics as the Orientation training, but as a refresher, review and an opportunity to update individuals on revisions, new policies and updates to procedures. Many insurance policies require Refresher training annually in order to maintain your abuse coverage. Even if your policy doesn't specifically mandate yearly updates, we strongly recommend annual training. Laws and policies change. Stay up-to-date on those developments and modify your training to reflect new developments. Refresher training gives your Ministry Personnel the chance to recall what they know and learn about current and emerging topics related to abuse prevention.

The annual Refresher training should also include elements of awareness, prevention and protection.

This training should take approximately one hour and should be customized for your specific context.

Plan to Protect® recommends annual Refresher training, and insurance companies require it to qualify for abuse coverage. However, it does not need to be the same every year. We recommend utilizing creative methods and videos to change up training while still ensuring your training includes an awareness, protection and prevention section.

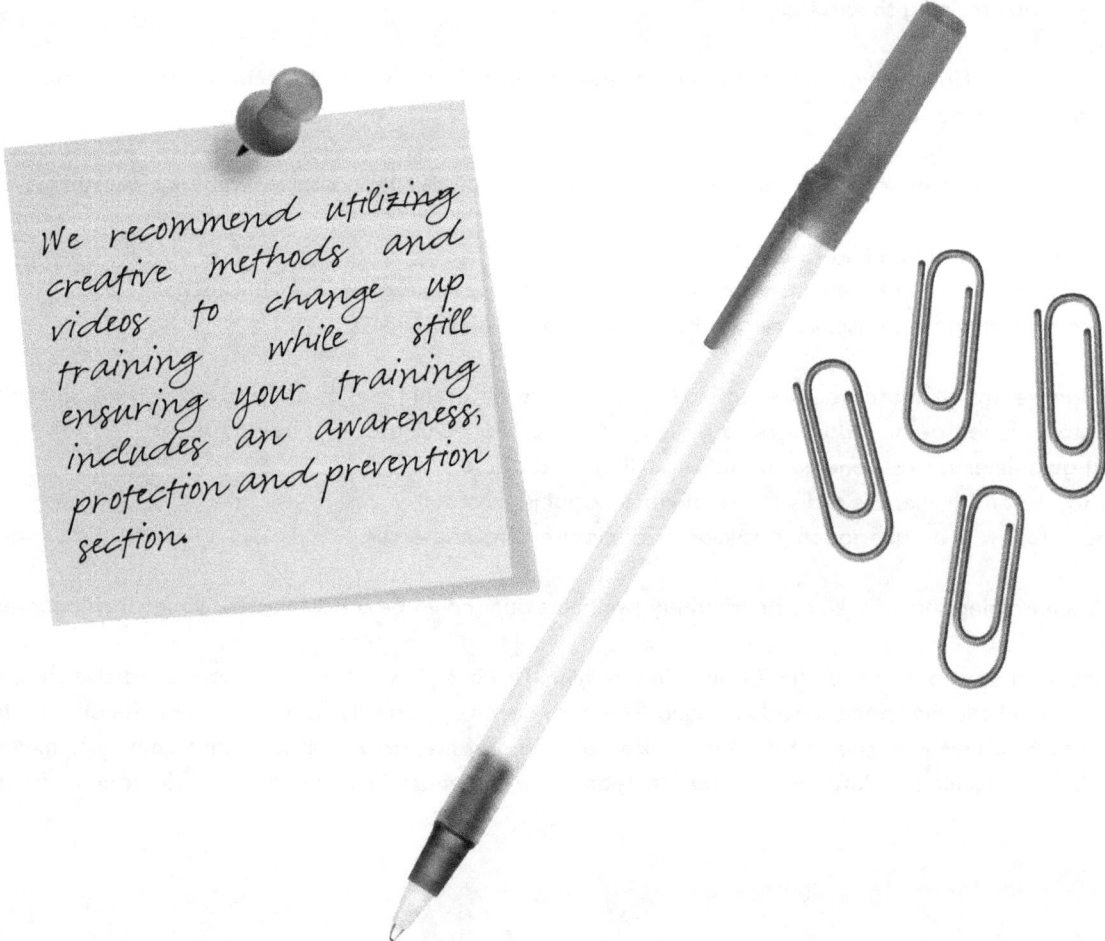

Vibrant and Creative Training

"The mediocre teacher tells. The good teacher explains. The superior teacher demonstrates. The great teacher inspires."
– William Arthur Ward

Preventing abuse and protecting the vulnerable is a skill that needs to be taught. Policies need to be implemented, and people can only act on what they've learned. Insurance companies require Ministry Personnel to be trained in abuse prevention, and for that training to be refreshed annually in order to qualify for abuse coverage.

Training does not need to be boring. It should include more than reading a policy or listening to a lecture. The goal is to make sure that everyone in a church is on the same page, and we want to make sure everyone enjoys the process it takes to get there. Abuse is serious and heartbreaking. However, we aim to make learning about abuse prevention a beneficial and enjoyable experience.

We don't know what we don't know. In order to gain greater understanding and to strengthen your knowledge, focus on specific topics. Recognizing everyone has different learning styles and modalities, your training sessions could include small group discussions, games, activities and times for questions and answers.

Qualified trainers are highly encouraged to utilize creative methods of training to engage Ministry Personnel and to keep training new and engaging for different learning styles and interests. Creative methods can include discussions, videos, scenarios, games, puzzles, etc. Sharing stories and examples can also help enhance the interactivity of training. Trainers can use their own examples and stories, utilize case studies found in the Plan to Protect® manual or on the Plan to Protect® blog and podcast, or can research ideas and stories to share. Plan to Protect® Train the Trainer Certification courses are designed to aid in the qualification process and to equip the Trainer with Plan to Protect® PowerPoints, teaching notes, student notes and extensive creative method ideas for both initial Orientation training and Refresher training.

Qualified Trainers

Anyone can do training…but, should it really be just anybody?

Insurance companies require (and Plan to Protect® recommends) that initial Orientation training and annual Refresher training be taught by qualified instructors.

But what does it really mean to be 'qualified for the job'? Often we are looking for someone who is "officially recognized as being trained to perform a particular job," that is to say, someone who is certified.

A "Qualified instructor means individuals whose training and experience adequately prepare them to carry out specified training assignments."[1]

Similarly, the Occupational Safety and Health Association (OSHA) states that qualified means "one who, by possession of a recognized degree, certificate, or professional standing, or who by extensive knowledge, training, and experience, has successfully demonstrated his ability to solve or resolve problems relating to the subject matter … ."[2]

But, why do they need to be qualified?

An unqualified (or under-qualified) trainer could put your church at risk by training incorrect reporting laws or providing inadequate prevention guidelines while failing to motivate and inspire Ministry Personnel. They may also come short of training up to insurance requirements and result in misleading declarations.

Is the person doing training at your church qualified? Could they potentially be putting your church at risk?

Here are 10 telltale warning signs your trainer might not be qualified for the job:

1. They are not certified or have received no additional instruction. One of the main things that makes someone 'qualified,' is that they have received additional training and have special expertise to be able to do the training. It's also important to keep in mind that they should be training on awareness, protection and prevention. For example, while a social worker or a lawyer may be knowledgeable on reporting guidelines and the definitions and indicators of abuse, are they also knowledgeable on preventing abuse? Are they knowledgeable on how to be a good trainer and communicator?

2. They are not inspiring. One of the worst things an unqualified trainer can do is leave participants feeling disgruntled, frustrated or wanting to quit because their training lacks inspiration and motivation. Abuse prevention isn't just something we have to do, it's something we have the privilege of doing. Is your trainer able to communicate that?

3. They give incorrect reporting guidelines. Every province and territory in Canada has mandatory reporting guidelines requiring everyone to report child abuse. Some individuals have an elevated professional duty to report. If your trainer is telling people not to report abuse or to first report to Leadership, so that Leadership can determine if a report is required, they are contradicting or impeding the law.

---

1 (Law Insider) https://www.lawinsider.com/dictionary/qualified-instructor
2 https://www.osha.gov/laws-regs/regulations/standardnumber/1926/1926.32

4. They act like a controlling drill sergeant just giving a list of things you should and shouldn't do. Maya Angelou once said, "Love recognizes no barriers. It jumps hurdles, leaps fences, penetrates walls to arrive at its destination full of hope." While abuse prevention typically does include a list of things Ministry Personnel should and shouldn't do, that shouldn't and doesn't need to be the focus of the training. Training should focus on the big picture – love and hope.

5. They act like training is a waste of time. Your trainer is the first line of defence for why we should do safeguarding – they should communicate passionately the purpose of training. Bad attitudes are highly contagious.

6. The training is way too short or way too long. Your insurance company may require (and Plan to Protect® recommends) initial Orientation training providing a thorough understanding of abuse prevention. At Plan to Protect® this is a two hour training and annual Refresher training is approximately one hour in length. If you're having drive-through training or long drawn-out lectures, your trainer might not be 'qualified' for the job – either they're not covering enough information or they're unable to be concise.

7. They are oblivious to the prevalence of abuse. A trainer who is completely unaware of the prevalence of abuse and acts like it won't happen or has never happened is completely missing the point and could be unintentionally hurting or re-victimizing victim-survivors of abuse within your church.

8. They are unable to problem-solve or to come up with solutions to scenarios or to answer questions. Qualified trainers are able to solve and resolve problems. A trainer who raises more questions than they answer and who is unable to problem solve participant's scenarios and questions may not be considered 'qualified.'

9. They are stuck in the 1990s. Adult learners thrive on relevant, applicable, up-to-date information. Training that is full of old, out-of-date statistics does absolutely nothing to inspire. Training that disregards relevant societal changes also fails to prepare participants for the reality of their roles (for example: Is your trainer still telling people only women can take children to the washroom? This is not up to date on human right legislation and may be placing your church in jeopardy!)

10. The training is boring, fails to use creative methods, and fails to engage the participants. One of the main reasons participants often dread training is because it is boring. Just because we're talking about abuse prevention and vulnerable sector protection doesn't mean it needs to be dull and dry. Qualified trainers are able to engage their audience through with creative methods and have something for each type of learner (visual, auditory, hands-on).

So, with that in mind, how do you become 'qualified' for the job?
If organizations, such as OSHA, agree that a qualified person needs to have received training and experience in that industry – both formal training and years of experience – training is obviously the key.

Organizations like Plan to Protect® offer certification for trainers, which provides both the training and experience that would help someone become qualified. Individuals with certain degrees may also have the necessary qualifications.

'Qualified' means that they are trained, equipped, and competent. Someone has taken the time to recognize and affirm that they are up to the task and can vouch for them!

When determining whether or not someone is 'qualified' or when investing in certified training in order to qualify, look for programs that include some kind of practicum component or coaching. This will demonstrate the person has received critical instruction on abuse awareness, protection and prevention; appropriate legal requirements;

feedback to strengthen their training, and that they have demonstrated the necessary competency to be able to do training.

We also recommend that certification is renewed regularly with a requirement for the certification to be kept up-to-date. This will provide peace of mind that the training meets legal and insurance requirements.

So, while anyone can conduct training ... it really shouldn't be just anybody. Let's raise the bar on protection and abuse prevention training. As Maya Angelou once said, "do the best you can, until you know better. Then, when you know better, do better."

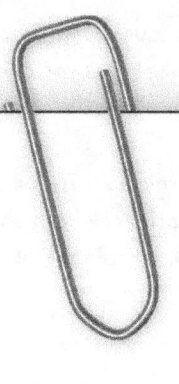

"Love recognizes no barriers. It jumps hurdles, leaps fences, penetrates walls to arrive at its destination full of hope."
- Maya Angelou

Plan to Protect® Training Resources

Looking for help training your personnel? The following training courses and options have been designed to support your training needs.

Certification Training Programs

Plan to Protect® Administrator/Leader

Overview: Become the Plan to Protect® administrator/leader in your organization. Learn how to run, implement and maintain a strong abuse prevention program.

This course includes:
- Plan to Protect® 101
- Reporting and Response
- Recruitment and Screening
- Customizing Policies
- Documentation Management

Available On-Site and Online.
This course is foundational for any person or church just beginning to implement Plan to Protect®.

Plan to Protect® Train the Trainer

Overview: Become equipped and qualified to train your own teams in abuse prevention.

This course includes:
- Training Adults and Youth
- Training resources including PowerPoints, Teaching Notes and Creative Methods
- A demonstration of a Plan to Protect® Orientation training

Available On-Site and Online.
This course is recommended for churches that already have developed customized policies for their church and desire to have a qualified trainer as part of their team.

Plan to Protect® Crisis Response and Management

Overview: Developed for Board members and Church Leadership. This course helps you learn how to respond to and manage a crisis. As Barrie Doyle (Crisis Consultant) states, "It's not if, but when, a crisis occurs."

This course includes:
- How to prepare for a crisis before it happens
- How to respond when first hearing about a crisis
- How to deal with the media
- What to do after the crisis has occurred

Available Online.

Orientation and Refresher Training

Need help providing initial Orientation training or annual Refresher training, which meets insurance requirements, for your personnel? Plan to Protect® provides training available on-site, online or as a live webinar. All courses include awareness, protection and prevention.

On-site Orientation or Refresher Training
Would you like to gather your whole team for training? Plan to Protect® has certified, qualified national trainers who may be available to provide on-site Orientation or Refresher training in your location. The training will include best practices and can be customized to your location and policy.

Orientation Training Courses – 2.5 hours
Refresher Training Courses – 1.5 hours

Online Orientation or Refresher Training
Would you like to have your personnel complete training at their own pace and on their own schedule? Plan to Protect® has online Orientation and Refresher training available. Modules include videos, case studies, discussion boards and quizzes. Participants receive a certificate upon completion.

We have courses geared for those serving among different age groups and settings:
- Plan to Protect® For Those Who Work with Children 0-12 (Orientation and Refresher)
- Plan to Protect® For Those Who Work with Youth 13-18 (Orientation and Refresher)
- Plan to Protect® For Those Who Work with Children and Youth 0-18 (Orientation and Refresher)
- Plan to Protect® For Those Who Work with Children, Youth and Vulnerable Adults (Orientation and Refresher)
- Plan to Protect® For Those Who Work with Vulnerable Adults (Orientation and Refresher)
- Plan to Protect® For Leaders (Orientation and Refresher)
- Plan to Protect® For International Workers – Short Term (Orientation and Refresher)
- Plan to Protect® For International Workers Leaders - Short Term (Orientation and Refresher)
- Plan to Protect® For International Workers – Long Term (Orientation and Refresher)
- Plan to Protect® For International Workers Leaders – Long Term (Orientation and Refresher)
- Plan to Protect® For Those Who Work with Refugees and New Immigrants (Orientation)
- Plan to Protect® For Online Engagement (Orientation)
- Plan to Protect® For Camps (Orientation)
- Plan to Protect® For Psychotherapists and Counsellors (Orientation)
- Plan to Protect® For Transportation (Orientation)

The length of each course varies.

Do you wish to provide customized online training for your church? Online training customized for your church is available for large churches, denominations and unique contexts. Reach out to training@plantoprotect.com to request additional information.

Live On-site and Webinar Training
Plan to Protect® provides live on-site and webinar Orientation and Refresher training. Join people from across Canada and the United States for monthly webinars. We also offer private customized training upon request.

Orientation Courses – 2.5 hours
Refresher Courses – 1.5 hours

Special Interest Training

Looking for additional training and professional development for yourself or your team on a variety of different topics related to vulnerable sector protection? Check out our Special Interest training available on-site, and through online recordings and live webinars where we do a deeper dive into topics of interest, i.e., off-site trips, self-injury, substance abuse, dealing with difficult Parents. Special Interest training may also be used for professional development for Ministry Personnel that have received a disciplinary step for breaching a policy, i.e., social media, transportation, sexual harrassment.

New topics are added monthly. Churches may also request specific topics for on-site or webinar training.

Topics range from:
- Child and Youth Specific (i.e., appropriate discipline, bullying, drugs and alcohol, Child to Child abuse, helping Teens in crisis, technology and internet safety, mentoring and counselling, etc.)
- Adult Specific (i.e., Caring for survivors of Abuse, Elder Abuse, Hospital and home visits, and Vulnerable Women, etc.)
- Health and Safety
- Mental Health Initiatives (i.e., depression, eating disorders, suicide, self-injury and cutting, etc.)
- Faith (i.e., spiritual abuse, small group safety, etc.)
- Disability Initiatives (i.e., AODA, interacting with Parents and Caregivers, involving Ministry Personnel with disabilities and special needs, risks, etc.)
- Diversity and Inclusion (i.e., Human Rights and gender identity/expression, racial diversity and inclusion, etc.)
- Plan to Protect® Administration (i.e., electronic documentation, hidden risks, policy overhaul, screening, training, premise modifications, registration and sign in, smart justice, supervision, etc.)
- Ministry Personnel (i.e., disciplinary actions, duty of care for Volunteers, etc.)
- Organization specific (i.e., Plan to Protect® for camps, schools, transportation companies, sports, etc.)

Visit **www.plantoprotectschool.com** for more information.

Youth Training

Plan to Protect® recommends training Youth Ministry Personnel (specifically those 12-16 years of age) separately from Adults. Check out our 'Be a Superhero' Youth training!

Why should Youth be trained separately?
- Learning Styles:
  - Young people have different learning styles than Adults. Providing training specific to the audience will allow a qualified trainer to speak their unique learning style.
- Attention Spans:
  - Depending on the age of the Youth you are training, they may have a shorter attention span than an Adult.
- Content:
  - With Youth Personnel you'll want to be more cautious about the examples and scenarios you provide in order to make sure they are both age appropriate and sensitive.
  - While it is important to go through indicators of abuse with Adults, it is not necessary with Youth because they are still vulnerable, and we do not want them to either act out or hide possible indicators of abuse.
- Roles and Responsibilities:
  - Typically, Youth Personnel will only be serving under direct leadership and supervision of Adults. Since your Youth Personnel have different roles and responsibilities than Adults, it can be helpful to train them separately so you can speak to their specific duties.

Can you train your Youth Personnel at the same time as your Adult Personnel? As much as possible, train the two audiences separately. However, yes, they could be trained together. This does depend on several factors: the age and maturity of the student as well as if their parents/guardians are comfortable with them joining the Adult training. A qualified trainer would need to be aware of this and do their best to be sensitive to the fact that Youth are present.

What are people saying about Plan to Protect®?

> "This was an excellent course! It gave me all the necessary skills for training the volunteers in my organization in an engaging and effective manner. I highly recommend this course for trainers of all organizations that need a 'Plan to Protect'!"
>
> – Jean Leslie
> Madoc Baptist Church, Madoc, ON

> "If you care for the vulnerable sector, then this is for you, it is an excellent support and guidance to deliver your trainings in a fun and engaging method."
>
> – Maria Esperanza Sztrimbely

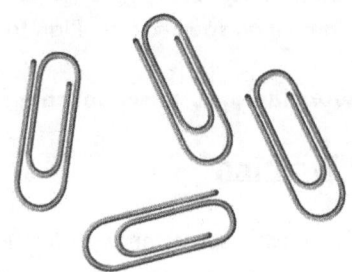

> "Plan to Protect® specializes in training and they do a good job of it to help their clients to do a good job of it. You can't go wrong, for it is time and money well spent."
>
> – Fr. Raymond Lillis
> Society of St. Pius X

Tips for Trainers

- Schedule your training dates well in advance, selecting a variety of days of the week and times in order to provide options that work for your audience.
- Remind your Ministry Personnel of upcoming training.
- Within your training, cast a vision for why you are doing Plan to Protect® by sharing stories, case studies, examples and your vision/mission.
- Stay up-to-date by following Plan to Protect® on social media, listening to the Plan to Protect® podcast with Melodie Bissell (available on YouTube and Apple Podcasts), signing up for the monthly newsletter, creating news alerts, or by attending monthly special interest webinars and podcasts.
- Some great ways to encourage your Ministry Personnel to continue following the policies after the training are posting reminders, utilizing Hall Monitors, reviewing policies and procedures often, providing supervision and resources and utilizing progressive steps of discipline if necessary.
- When recruiting Ministry Personnel, let them know that annual training is required so they know what to expect.
- Keep your training from feeling redundant or repetitive by changing it up, utilizing creative methods, incorporating new case studies, and making sure your training and certification are up-to-date.
- If possible, train Ministry Personnel by department so you can make it practical and applicable to their specific roles.
- If you only have one or two staff members who need Orientation training, consider utilizing Plan to Protect® online training so you don't have to do training for such a small group.
- If Ministry Personnel refuse to come to training, try to cast a vision so they understand why it's important. If that doesn't work, ask why they are hesitant to attend – this might help you speak to their specific concerns. Perhaps offering a different delivery method (i.e., online training through Plan to Protect®) might help. Ultimately, however, if someone absolutely refuses to attend training, we recommend removing that individual from Positions of Trust with the vulnerable sector.
- Professionals such as teachers, social workers, police officers, lawyers, etc. should still attend training. Professionals should still attend training as your training should be customized to your unique policies and context.
- When preparing for and delivering training, be aware that there may be victim-survivors attending your training. Being sensitive to your audience can include providing a trigger warning at the beginning of your training, praying for individuals, or offering an alternative delivery method (i.e., Plan to Protect® online training).
- Providing resources for Ministry Personnel can be a great way for them to take what they've learned with them. Examples of resources include My Plan to Protect® Pocket Guide (available books include Children, Youth, Vulnerable Adults, Disability Initiatives) and/or the Plan to Protect® app (available on Apple or Android devices).

Restrictions and Parameters for Training

- Purchasing a Plan to Protect® manual includes a license to use the resources in this manual to develop a policy and training for your church. However, copyright guidelines and the accompanying license for use prohibit any content from the Plan to Protect® manual to be shared with other organizations or to be posted on the internet.

- Please note the license to use Plan to Protect® resources included with this manual does not give you permission to develop or create online training for your organization, to train on an online platform, or to videotape your training and put it up on video hosting platforms. Organizations that are interested in purchasing extended licenses are encouraged to reach out to Plan to Protect® directly at **training@plantoprotect.com**.

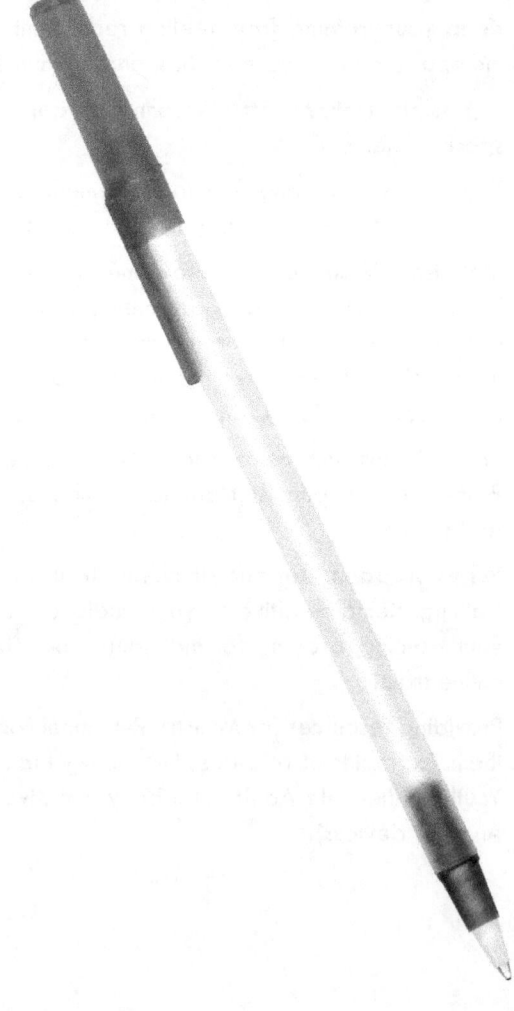

Protect Through Program Development

General Protection Procedures

- Introduction
- Case Study
- Administrative Policies
- Personal Interactions
- Health and Safety
- Technology Concerns
- Facility Precautions
- High Risk Activities

Introduction

We secure our homes. We secure our phones. We secure our vehicles. We secure our computers. We secure our passwords. We secure our bank accounts. We deal with security and safety issues every day of our lives. Why wouldn't we want to do all that we can to secure our Children, Youth and Vulnerable Adults, those that are created in God's image.

The primary way that churches can demonstrate that they value people is by putting policies, procedures and screening in place. Policies and procedures ensure that everyone is on the same page and moving in the same direction when it comes to mitigating risk and protecting the vulnerable. The policies and procedures you establish for your church will communicate the parameters for interaction with Children, Youth and Vulnerable adults. As the general procedures are followed, your Ministry Personnel demonstrate they care not only for the participants in your program but also their care for the Church.

The policy statements and best practices in this section can be applied to every program and activity you engage with the vulnerable sector. Once an individual has been screened and trained and given the green light to be placed in a Position of Trust, these best practices should be adhered to.

These general procedures are built on the five principles for reducing the risk of injury, harm and abuse:

- When RISK increases, supervision should also increase;
- RISK increases as isolation increases;
- RISK increases as accountability and adherence to policies decrease;
- RISK increases when there is an imbalance of power, authority, influence and control between a potential abuser and potential victim; and
- The key to demonstrating due diligence in mitigating RISK is by retaining documentation.

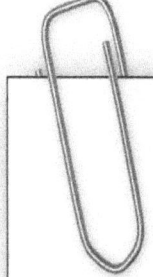

Note: *The best practices found in General Protection Procedures are not stand-alone policies and procedures. This section of the manual is supplementary material to be used with other (as important) sections of this manual, including Recruitment and Screening, Training, Age Specific Procedures (Child, Youth and Vulnerable Adult Protection Procedures), and Reporting and Response.*

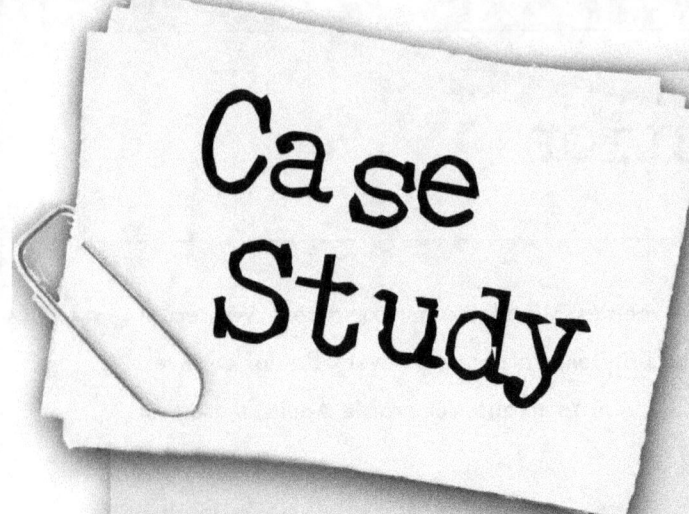

Case Study

General Protection Guidelines

Every year your Youth group heads out on an epic camping trip in the woods. A group of teenagers and leaders venture into the forest for three days and three nights. Their overnight fun includes hiking, boating, rock climbing, and sleeping in tents under the stars. Your church has been doing the camp out for years and it has always been a highlight for the teens and leaders. Every year kids' lives are transformed as they share testimonies around the campfire and sing worship songs in the beautiful nature.

This year was like any other year. Thirty kids signed up and you had six leaders all ready to go with the kids. Permission forms were signed, sleeping bags were rolled up and the school bus was packed to the brim with kids, leaders, and duffle bags.

The bus headed off ready to take the crew into the woods… the problem was that this year, unlike years past, there had been abnormally heavy rain in the days leading up to the trip. When the bus got to the little bridge which spanned a river, the bus driver realized the bridge had been completely covered with water and mud and there was no way to get through. The only way to get to the campsite was now completely obstructed.

Unsure of what to do, the Youth Group Leaders gathered and tried to come up with a back up plan. While you are meeting and figuring out if there is another way to get to the campgrounds or if you should just turn around and go home, one of the kids in the group comes up with a suggestion. What if everyone grabbed their bags, held them over their heads, and you all waded through the river to the other side. The water doesn't look that crazy right now, and it can't be above anyone's waist. All of the kids and the other leaders think this is a great idea. This way they could still do the camping trip and they wouldn't have to head home… but this wasn't part of the plan.

Case Study continued ...

> *Questions to Answer:*
> - *What do you do?*
> - *What risks do you currently face?*
> - *How could this situation be mitigated?*

Hindsight is 20/20:

It is not possible to avoid all risks, but many are avoidable! Parents have signed a Letter of Informed Consent for the retreat. The consent included releasing, and waiving the church of any liability – however, was the risk of fording a river ever considered?

Administrative Policies

A. Planning for Safety
B. Supervision of Ministry Personnel
C. Lifestyle
D. Ministry Personnel Identification
E. Registration and Compliance with PIPEDA
F. Attendance
G. Outside User Groups
H. Misconduct and Accountability
I. Disciplinary Action of Ministry Personnel

A. Planning for Safety

Policy

1. All Ministry Personnel must ensure a safe environment in their planning and evaluating of activities.

2. Safety precautions must be posted and highly visible for Children, Youth and Vulnerable Adults.

Plan

- ◯ Planning teams for events have been trained to ensure there is always a safe environment.

- ◯ Safety precautions have been posted and are highly visible for Children, Youth and Vulnerable Adults.

- ◯ Ministry personnel have been trained to identify and avoid risks.

Protection

It is no surprise that incorporating activities such as horseplay, climbing on each other or forms of roughhousing will increase the risk of an accident occurring during programming. However, accidents that arise from activities of higher risk can become the subject of a lawsuit for the church, particularly if the proper precautions have not been taken to avoid these risks.

Just because a parent has filled out a release form does not mean that a lawsuit cannot arise; if you are supervising, "negligence" can be a very scary word and should be avoided.

Release forms do not mean that a parent has consented to ministry personnel to act negligently during the course of programming. Consider the following scenario:

A child breaks his arm when playing basketball. His parents do not have a problem with it because they are huge supporters of the youth program. However, they make an insurance claim to pay for the additional costs of healthcare and recovery. Even though the family may not take legal action, the insurance companies involved may dispute the claims and not honour the policy. Or, they may debate whose insurance policy is responsible. It may also affect your ability to secure insurance coverage in the future and your premiums may increase.

Reduce YOUR risk!

B. Supervision of Ministry Personnel

Policy

1. For the protection of our Children, Youth and Vulnerable Adults, supervision of all Ministry Personnel will be intentional and will take place through formal and informal visits to classrooms and programs by a Ministry Lead or a Pastor.

Plan

- ○ A process has been developed for supervising ministry personnel.
- ○ Classroom windows provide clear lines of visibility, or classroom doors remain open.

Protection

An important step to providing a safe environment for children, youth and vulnerable adults is to ensure proper supervision of ministry personnel. This can include processes such as "spot-checking caregivers; randomly asking caregivers how many children are present; observing caregivers to ensure that they are following established procedures; and reviewing program policies on a regular basis, including presenting caregivers with hypothetical scenarios to test their response."[1]

"Supervision of ministry workers should … promote trust, accountability, and leader-worker rapport. This can be accomplished through a team-oriented approach in which leaders and workers strive toward the same goal. One way leaders can promote teamwork is to maintain high visibility, which facilitates communication and builds a sense of teamwork and trust. High visibility also fosters accountability. It is healthy for workers to be responsible to provide quality ministry."[2]

In order to refute false accusations, supervision must be intentional. The courts will look for a systematic process by which the organization supervises its personnel.

---

1 (Government of Alberta, n.d.)
2 (Zarra 1997, 65)

C. Lifestyle

Policy

1. For the protection of everyone, Ministry Personnel are to be committed to maintaining a consistent spiritual life including prayer, Bible reading, attendance at relevant events, planning meetings and worship services.

2. Ministry Personnel are to be role models of integrity at all times. Ministry Personnel are to refrain from activities that are illegal or could be considered morally and biblically questionable.

Plan

- ○ Ministry personnel have been recruited and screened in accordance with policies outlined in the 'Recruitment and Screening' section of Plan to Protect®.

- ○ Lifestyle requirements and spiritual expectations have been clearly communicated to ministry personnel.

Protection

The example we are as ministry personnel is far more critical than we think. Whether we know it or not, we are a role model to others by the life we live and our walk with God. In Titus 2:7-8 (NIV), we read, "In everything set them an example by doing what is good. In your teaching show integrity, seriousness and soundness of speech that cannot be condemned, so that those who oppose you may be ashamed because they have nothing bad to say about us." People will often make judgement or value calls based on what they see in the lives of people around them. In church ministry, the clear modeling of this is more than a statement of our values. It speaks clearly of the values of our church, our ministry and those of Christ.

When we rally the troops to live for God and are demonstrating these things well in our lives, young people can make a real impact on their world. Likewise, if ministry personnel involve themselves in questionable or borderline behaviours, young people will silently watch and, engage in similar behaviours with even more energy. An example: a leader drives like a madman when their car is full of students, it is fun and they look cool. However, when those students get their driver's licences, how will they drive when their car is full of other students?

If ministry personnel involve themselves in questionable or borderline behaviours and keep them private, then their personal integrity will be challenged.

General Protection Procedures

Protection continued...

How does this impact safeguarding?

What you teach with your life, attitudes, values, and behaviour will communicate far beyond what you teach with you mouth. We need to be thinking safely on a long-term basis as well as on a short-term basis.

And whatever you do, whether in word or deed, do it all in the name of the Lord Jesus, giving thanks to God the Father through him. (Colossians 3:17, NIV)

Since we are doing everything we can to provide a safe environment, the more work we do up-front in screening prospective ministry personnel to ensure their own spiritual consistency and growth, and solidifying like-mindedness on the team, the more confident we are in each leader's individual role and the potential risk involved. Knowing the spiritual heart and active lifestyle consistency of each volunteer will reduce the potential risk of something horrible happening.

D. Ministry Personnel Identification

Policy

1. Ministry Personnel are clearly identified with a nametag or approved clothing which identifies them to Parents, Children and Newcomers.

Plan

- Ministry personnel have been provided with identification nametags or approved clothing.

Protection

Every local church, regardless of its size, recognizes the need to maintain safety and security. Parents gain confidence in a program when they can look into a classroom and readily identify who is serving. Therefore, we recommend that all ministry personnel wear a nametag or approved clothing that identifies them to parents, children and newcomers. Some churches have developed photo name badges for their leaders, others have designed t-shirts, fleece jackets or hoodies to make their leaders readily identifiable.

E. Registration and Compliance with PIPEDA*

Policy

1. At the beginning of every ministry year, all program participants are to submit completed Registration and Medical Consent Forms, (Appendix 15) signed by their Parent. These forms are to be photocopied and originals maintained and filed permanently. The photocopies should be taken on all off-site trips and outings in case emergency medical assistance is required and the Parent cannot be notified.

2. The Registration and Medical Consent Form will not replace specific Letter of Informed Consent Forms for activities that involve an elevated risk or for overnight trips.

3. The inclusion of 'liability shields' on permission forms has been considered for activities that involve a level of risk. (Appendix 17)

4. A release and permission statement will be included on all Registration Forms releasing the church from unforeseen and accidental damages.

    I/We, the parents or guardians named above, authorize the Ministry Personnel of _____ Church to sign a consent for medical treatment and to authorize any physician or hospital to provide medical assessment, treatment or procedures for the participant named above.

    I/We, named above, undertake and agree to indemnify and hold blameless the Ministry Personnel, _____ Church, its pastors and Board from and against any loss, damage or injury suffered by the participant as a result of being part of the activities of the _____ Church as well as of any medical treatment authorized by the supervising individuals representing the church. This consent and authorization is effective only when participating in or traveling to events of the _____ Church.

5. A statement will be included on all Registration Forms which stipulates the purpose and extent for collecting personal information.

Purposes and Extent:
_____ Church is collecting and retaining this personal information for the purpose of enrolling your Child in our programs, to assign the Student to the appropriate classes, to develop and nurture ongoing relationships with you and your Child, and to inform you of program updates and upcoming opportunities at our church. This information will be maintained permanently as it is a requirement of our insurance company and legal counsel. If you wish _____ Church to limit the information collected, or to view your Child's information, please contact us.

*Different provinces have different names for their privacy laws, BC & AB (PIPA) in QC (Respecting the Protection of Personal Information in the Private Sector)

plan

- Registration and Medical Consent Forms have been distributed, completed and filed on an annual basis.
- Processes have been developed for new attendees mid-year to complete forms.
- Ensure that photocopies of 'Registration and Medical Consent Forms' accompany ministry personnel on all off-site trips.
- Specific event consent forms and liability shields have been developed and distributed for activities with elevated risk and overnight trips.
- All forms have been developed in compliance with PIPEDA and kept on file permanently.
- Periodic spot checks and confirmation have been done to ensure parent's signature is genuine.

protection

We live in an information era where information is used and misused. Privacy laws were developed for the protection of individuals against abuse. As we try to work with the realities of ministry while students are in our care and the need for protection for the church, we have developed these policies for the registration of students.

In Canada, there is no statute of limitation on child abuse. Therefore, in keeping with PIPEDA and our legal responsibilities, we are required to keep records permanently and have legitimate reason to do so.

Registration forms need to be available at the beginning of every program year, and also at every event for new attendees. Begin to train your families that when they bring a visiting student with them, they should have the family complete the permission or release form. If that is not possible for that event, the parent bringing the student would be considered the guardian for the evening and a registration form would be sent home with the student.

Registration forms really are a ministry tool to help you understand the family while allowing you to become aware of an individual's needs, special needs or any custody arrangements. Legal counsel recommends periodic spot checks and confirmation with parents that consent forms received have in fact been signed by the parents.

A separate Letter of Informed Consent must be used for every high risk and off-site event and activity.

General Protection Procedures

F. Attendance

Policy

1. Attendance must be taken each time a classroom or program is in session. These attendance records are kept on file permanently.

2. A record will be kept of Ministry Personnel on duty in each classroom or program. This record will be maintained with the record of attendance and kept on file permanently.

3. Attendance records must include the date, time, and classroom and everyone present (including visitors) during the program.

Plan

- ○ Attendance records have been taken at weekend and week-day programming.

- ○ Plans have been made to retain all on-duty ministry personnel attendance records.

- ○ Plans have been made to keep all attendance records on file permanently.

Protection

As a ministry, we should know who comes through our doors. We know their names, their birth dates, their birth order, their parents and information about each child's individual and unique needs. We can track when they come, how often they come and by doing so, understand a bit about their journey with God. Taking attendance isn't just taking attendance — it can be used to touch the lives of the children God brings our way.

Again, the taking of attendance is important for safety and security reasons — not only for attendees, but for the ministry personnel who serve them. Be sure that attendance sheets are accessible at all times and available in cases of emergency. Maintaining attendance records permanently can be a cumbersome task. There are excellent information management systems now available to capture registration and attendance. Many of these solutions are very affordable for churches.

G. Outside User Groups (Renters and Service Providers)

Policy

For the church to be a safe space for all users, the following policies apply to all groups who use the space, whether they have a connection to the church or not:

1. All Service Providers, Visitors* and Renters must sign-in upon arrival at the front desk and sign-out when they leave. The individual's name, the date and the time is to be clearly noted. This information is to be kept on file in the Activity Log for that day and kept permanently.

   *Note: This does not apply to individuals joining public events as attendees.

2. If Service Providers are onsite when programming is happening for Children, Youth or Vulnerable Adults, the Service Providers are to be clearly identified with a uniform or a nametag and are to always be accompanied and supervised by Ministry Personnel.

3. The criteria for Renters or outside user groups to use the church's facility include:

   a. Renters must complete a Rental Agreement which must be approved by the Board or by a Ministry Lead.

   b. Renters must provide a certificate of insurance, with no less than $2,000,000 Commercial General Liability coverage and the church be named as additional insured.

   c. Renters must provide evidence that they have a strong abuse prevention policy and protocol in place*, including but not limited to screening and training of staff and volunteers, and minors may not be left unsupervised.

   d. They must abide by the following for all activities where Children, Youth or Vulnerable Adults are present:

      i. Two Screened Workers providing oversight; or

      ii. One Screened Worker providing oversight where Parents accompany their Children, or Caregivers accompany Vulnerable Adults.

   *Note 2: If these individuals and groups lack an Abuse Prevention Policy, we are not to provide them with one, rather, we will refer them to Plan to Protect® to secure their own copy of the *Plan to Protect*® **manual.**

4. In the case that the church partners with other churches, agencies or community groups for the delivery of a joint activity or event with Children, Youth or Vulnerable Adults in attendance, Church Leadership requires that their insurance agent be consulted during the planning stage, to determine risks, insurance coverage and shared liability. A Ministry Lead is required to obtain written opinion from the insurance agent acknowledging the status of insurance coverage for these joint activities.

plan

- All groups who use the church's facilities have been made aware of these policies.
- Sign-in sheets are kept permanently.
- A Rental Agreement has been approved by the Board or Ministry Leads.
- Renters have provided a certificate of insurance and evidence of a strong abuse prevention policy and protocol.
- An insurance agent has been consulted during the planning stage of joint events.

Protection

Many churches rent or share their buildings with other organizations. This provides an opportunity to serve the community, and it often also provides an extra source of revenue.

If a church decides to allow the rental or use of their facilities by an outside group, organization or individual, it is extremely important to maintain arm's length from the renter, to transfer the responsibility for legal liability to the tenant and to verify that the tenant has the resources to back up the legal responsibility for their potential negligence in the supervision and operations of their activities at the host premises. This transfer of risk fulfills the stewardship responsibilities of the host organization's Board members in the preservation and efficient use of the organization's property and resources and avoids unnecessarily placing the host facility in a position of sole legal responsibility for negligence of or by the tenant organization's leaders and volunteers. It also satisfies the principle of accountability; that leaders should only assume responsibility when they also exert full authority and control.

Insurance and liability should also be taken into consideration when planning a joint event with another church or any other organization.

H. Misconduct and Accountability

Policy

1. Ministry Personnel are to refrain from all forms of misconduct.

2. It is the responsibility of the Board, Lead Pastor and Ministry Leads to hold each other and their direct reports accountable. Every member of a church must be accountable for their actions that could impact the reputation of the church, no one is exempt. This flows both up and down in in reporting concerns. For example: Ministry Personnel are to be supervised and held accountable by Ministry Leads, Ministry Leads are to be supervised and held accountable by Staff Members, Staff Members are to be supervised and held accountable by the Lead Pastor, and the Lead Pastor is to be supervised and held accountable by the Board as a collective body.

3. As a community of faith, we reserve the right and freedom to bring to the attention of individuals and Church Leadership anything we believe is compromising their integrity, walk with God, or could bring harm to the reputation of the church and cause of Christ. If a person does not feel safe to confront the individual (i.e., in the case of abusive behaviour), we urge them to follow the whistleblower policy (See Whistleblower Policy on page 273).

4. Individuals with concerns must follow Matthew 18 when confronting an individual unless they feel unsafe to do so. Matthew 18 calls for individuals to confront the individual alone first, and if they do not feel that the concern has been taken seriously, they are to bring in another. In the case of the church, they must then bring in the individual's Supervisor, followed by the Church Board.

5. When traveling, Ministry Personnel are to avoid meetings in hotel rooms of another individual other than an immediate family member.

6. With reasonable cause, Church Leadership reserves the right to look at staff computers, cell phones, and tablets that are primarily used for ministry purposes. This includes but is not limited to photographs and communication. Upon request, these devices must be turned over immediately. Staff Members must provide their passwords for their primary ministry electronic devices to the Office Administrator upon request.

7. All petty cash and expenses must be accounted for.

8. If a person is involved in a situation where a boundary is violated, or something occurs that is out of the ordinary or could be misinterpreted, or where such a violation or occurrence is alleged, he or she must immediately report it and discuss it with a Supervisor. If the Ministry Lead is unwilling, unable, or unavailable for discussion, he or she must seek out a Board Member or the Pastor to discuss the issue.

plan

- ○ All ministry personnel have someone they are accountable to.
- ○ Those in positions of leadership demonstrate accountability, transparency, and integrity.
- ○ Travel arrangements are made and demonstrate accountability and caution.
- ○ Passwords are maintained.
- ○ Expenses are accounted for.
- ○ A Whistleblower policy is also put in place.

protection

Over the years we have read heartbreaking stories of fallen leaders. May we learn from these situations, so we don't repeat history, by establishing parameters and holding ministry personnel accountable for their actions.

There is also wisdom that we can learn from leaders that have taken steps to be humble and accountable for their actions. The world can laugh at Christian leaders that don't compromise; however, their tips demonstrate integrity and humility on their behalf recognizing that they too could easily fall.

Those tips include:
- Policies and best practices should avoid gender specific language due to same-sex attractions;
- Avoid traveling alone (take separate flights, stay in separate hotels, or ask for separate floors for hotel rooms);
- Travel with your spouse whenever possible;
- Request that the concierge check your hotel room prior to entry;
- Dine with others in large groups; and
- Report to your supervisor any incidents or propositions that have been made to you

These suggestions provide insight and wisdom for Board members, when putting policies (parameters) in place to protect the reputation of the ministry, pastoral staff and the cause of Christ.

Not having an accountability and transparency policy in place does not protect the church from vicarious liability. Boards and leaders should not only put these policies in place, they should also ensure compliance and exercise the rights provided if the need arises.

I. Disciplinary Action of Ministry Personnel

Policy

When a Policy or Procedure of the church has not been adhered to, the following progressive disciplinary actions are to be taken, depending on the given nature of the offence. Serious offences such as physical or sexual abuse, assault or theft will have zero tolerance (See steps 3 and 4).

Step 1 - Verbal Warning

1. Ministry Personnel are to be given a verbal warning regarding the unacceptable behaviour or action.

2. Ministry Personnel are to be given an explanation of when and how the undesirable behaviour or action took place. This will include the reason as to why the behaviour or action was unacceptable, such as a reminder of relevant policy or training.

3. Ministry Personnel are to be given an opportunity to explain the situation and their actions. This is an opportunity to give their side of the story.

4. Ministry Personnel are to be given a description of desirable or acceptable behaviour or actions.

5. Ministry Personnel are to be reminded that they signed a Covenant of Care affirming they would abide by the Policy and Procedures of the church. A copy of this may be given to them.

6. Ministry Personnel are to be informed of further disciplinary steps that will be taken if unacceptable behaviour continues.

7. Ministry Personnel are to be notified that a note will be added to their file with a record of the verbal warning.

Step 2 - Written Warning

1. Ministry Personnel are to be given a written warning regarding unacceptable behaviour or action in the event that the behaviour or action had either been discussed in a previous verbal warning or the behaviour or action was considerably severe in nature.

2. MInistry Personnel are to be given an explanation of when and how the undesirable behaviour or action took place. This will include the reason why the behaviour or action was unacceptable.

3. Ministry Personnel are to be given an opportunity to explain the situation and their actions. This is an opportunity to give their side of the story.

4. Ministry Personnel are to be given a description of the desirable or acceptable behaviour or actions.

5. Ministry Personnel are to be provided with a copy of the written warning and another will be placed in their Ministry Personnel file and shared with a Ministry Lead or Pastor.

Policy continued...

6. Ministry Personnel are to be reminded that they signed a Covenant of Care affirming they would abide by the Policy and Procedures of the church. A copy of this should be given to them.

7. Ministry Personnel are to sign the document as proof of receipt.

8. Ministry Personnel are to be notified that future infractions will be addressed with further progressive disciplinary actions up to and including termination.

9. At this point it is recommended that the individual take additional professional development training in the area of the infraction or attend Plan to Protect® Orientation or Refresher Training again. See www.plantoprotectschool.com.

Step 3 - Suspension

1. Ministry Personnel are to be given written documentation regarding the suspension in relation to the unacceptable behaviour or action, in the event that the behaviour or action had either been discussed in a previous verbal or written warning, or the behaviour or action was considerably severe in nature.

2. Documentation must include information on the offence, the length and terms of the suspension and why the individual has been suspended.

3. Ministry Personnel are to be given an explanation of when and how the undesirable behaviour or action took place. This will include the reason why the behaviour or action was unacceptable.

4. Ministry Personnel are to be given a description of the desirable or acceptable behaviour or actions.

5. Ministry Personnel are to be provided a copy of the suspension documentation and another copy will be placed in their Ministry Personnel file.

6. Ministry Personnel are to sign the document as proof of receipt.

7. Ministry Personnel are to be notified that future infractions will be addressed with further progressive disciplinary actions up to and including termination.

8. Church Leadership are to be notified that an individual has been suspended.

9. During the suspension, the individual may be required to take additional professional development training in the area of the infraction and re-attend Plan to Protect® Abuse Prevention Orientation or Refresher Training. See www.plantoprotectschool.com.

PLEASE NOTE: Ministry Personnel suspended due to suspicions or allegations of abuse may have no contact with vulnerable individuals and may not be placed in a Position of Trust during their suspension. The suspension will **NOT** be overturned unless they have been cleared of any and all allegations or suspicions of abuse.

Where applicable, legal counsel, an insurance company representative, and Child and Family Services must be consulted prior to termination and reinstatement.

Policy continued...

Step 4 - Termination

1. Church Leadership must be consulted and notified prior to termination of any Ministry Personnel.

2. Ministry Personnel are to be given written documentation regarding the termination and the breach of policy or process, or inappropriate behaviour or action leading to and justifying the termination.

3. Documentation must include information on the offence and any previous disciplinary steps documented.

4. Ministry Personnel are to be given a description of when and how the unacceptable behaviour or action took place. This will include the reason why the behaviour or action was unacceptable.

5. Ministry Personnel are to be given a description of desirable or acceptable behaviour or actions.

6. Ministry Personnel are to be provided with a copy of the termination notice and another copy will be placed in the Ministry Personnel's file. Ministry Personnel file documentation is to be kept permanently, even after termination.

7. Ministry Personnel are to be escorted from the location while maintaining the dignity of the terminated Ministry Personnel.

8. Where possible, the reasons for dismissal are to be kept confidential.

9. At Church Leadership's discretion, the individual may be encouraged to attend services, bring their Children to programs, and participate in community events held at the church.

Plan

- ○ Ministry Personnel have been made aware of the steps of progressive discipline.

- ○ A Covenant of Care has been prepared and signed by Ministry Personnel.

- ○ Verbal and Written warnings, Suspensions and Terminations have been permanently kept in Ministry Personnel's files.

- ○ Appropriate and inappropriate behaviour is regularly and clearly communicated to Ministry Personnel and reviewed annually during abuse prevention training.

General Protection Procedures

Protection

An important principle to remember is that risk increases as accountability decreases. Having a plan for progressive discipline is a way to hold staff accountable and keep those in your care safe.

Disciplinary action protects not only the vulnerable sector, but also your organization. It ensures that ministry personnel are following established procedures and complying with policy, avoiding any actions for which the organization could be held vicariously liable.

This policy has four stages of discipline:

1. Verbal warnings for minor concerns or for failing to follow safeguarding procedures, but not actively putting someone at risk - Some examples of reasons for verbal warnings include: Not completing an incident report or attendance sheet, tickling a child, or being alone in a classroom with a child with the door shut.

2. Written warnings for inappropriate behaviour that puts the organization, it's ministry personnel or clients, or it's ability to conduct ongoing programs at risk - Some examples of reasons for written warnings are: An inappropriate or rude interaction with a youth or a parent, a raised voice, inappropriate jokes or comments, prolonged hugging or touching, an incident of harassment or bullying, or driving alone in a vehicle with youth without parental written permission.

3. Suspensions for situations where serious breaches occur, and time is needed for an investigation to confirm whether further inappropriate behaviour took place - Some examples of reasons for suspensions are: Following any suspicion or allegation of abuse being reported, sending inappropriate text messages, meeting a child or youth alone without permission and knowledge of church leadership or parents, inappropriate touching, or a revelation of ongoing harassment, discrimination or bullying.

4. Termination for situations where an individual has greatly broken the trust of the organization or where they have failed to comply with policy after multiple disciplinary actions - Some examples of reasons for termination are: Convictions of abuse, physical or sexual assault, theft, and repeated unsuccessful attempts at other forms of discipline. In cases of abuse, sexual harassment, abuse of power and influence and sexual misconduct, the person should be terminated and not asked to submit their resignation. Termination demonstrates that you are prioritizing the needs of the victim in their healing process.

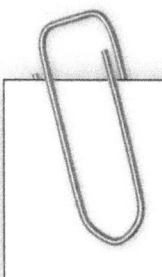

Personal Interactions

A. Occasional Observers
B. Bullying
   a. Harassment and Discrimination
C. Discipline and Classroom Management
D. Contacting Opportunities
   a. Counselling
E. Gift Giving
F. Dating
G. Home Visits
H. Hospital and Nursing Home Visits
I. Disabilities and Personal Support Workers
J. Gender Identity

A. Occasional Observers

Policy

1. Occasional Observers who join a class will have their attendance recorded and kept on file with the classroom attendance for that day. Visitors do not need to be screened or trained. Visitors will be clearly identified as guests and should be coached on proper protocols for guests. Since they have not been screened and approved, they will not be placed in a Position of Trust with Children who are not their own. Occasional Observers should not be regular attenders in a classroom.

Plan

- ○ Communication plan for coaching Occasional Observers has been put in place.
- ○ Occasional Observers have been provided with nametags.
- ○ Attendance of Occasional Observers has been recorded and filed.

Protection

Parents are welcome to work with us as we minister to their children. Particularly as preschoolers learn to trust others, there will be occasions when separation becomes an issue and that little one wants Mom or Dad to be with them in class. We want to encourage parents to work with us in this process; when they do, they must be screened and trained.

Parents who come just to help settle their child into the classroom for one or two Sundays, do not need to be screened and trained.

Similarly, there may also be occasions where people from other congregations want to come and observe a ministry in action. These are occasional observers in our classrooms.

Our protection needs to extend to those who are occasional observers in our work with the vulnerable sector. We will communicate a welcome to them, but advise both them and the ministry personnel that they are not to be placed in a position of trust with children who are not their own. That means that they will not be asked to assume responsibility for children and they will not be allowed or asked to take children to the washroom. Occasional observers will be given some type of visitor identification that, in the eyes of the child, differentiates them from ministry personnel. The names of the occasional observers will be recorded along with the classroom attendance for that day.

B. Bullying

Policy

1. Our Children, Youth, Vulnerable Adults, and Ministry Personnel have a right to a caring, respectful and safe church environment. An anti-bullying policy will therefore be in effect at all times and will be clearly communicated and enforced among participants and Ministry Personnel. All Ministry Personnel will take action to prevent bullying, teach against it, and assist and support Children, Youth and Vulnerable Adults who are being bullied. Bullying in any form will not be tolerated.

2. Bullying is defined as unwanted, aggressive behaviour that involves a real or perceived power imbalance and is repeated or has the potential to be repeated.

    Types of Bullying:
    a. Verbal Bullying
    b. Social Bullying
    c. Physical Bullying
    d. Cyber Bullying
    e. Racial Bullying
    f. Homophobic Bullying
    g. Sexual Harassment

3. Any incidents, reports or suspicions of bullying will be acknowledged, reviewed and dealt with appropriately and immediately. All incidents, reports or suspicions of bullying must be reported immediately to the Ministry Lead.

4. Appropriate action will take place based on the situation. Possible action may include, but is not limited to:
    a. Completing an Incident Report (Appendix 18) after each incident;
    b. Notifying both sets of Parents after each individual incident;
    c. Providing a warning that bullying will not be tolerated;
    d. Suspension for one day/event if bullying persists;
    e. Suspension for three days/events after next incident;
    f. Prohibiting the bullies from participating in programs if the bullying does not stop;
    g. If necessary and appropriate, contacting and consulting with police.

5. All attempts will be made to work towards change of behaviour with the person who is bullying. Counseling and support will be recommended and if possible provided for the victim of bullying.

Plan

- ○ All Ministry Personnel, Children and Youth are aware of the anti-bullying policy.
- ○ Any reports of bullying have been recorded on an Incident Report (Appendix 18) and reported to the Ministry Lead.
- ○ Both sets of parents have been notified.
- ○ Warning has been made that bullying will not be tolerated.
- ○ Individual has been suspended for one day/event.
- ○ Individual has been suspended for three days/events.
- ○ Bullies have been prohibited from participating.
- ○ Police have been consulted if bullying persists following these measures.

Protection

Bullying is a risk present in all organizations, whether it be amongst the children and youth participating in programming or amongst the ministry personnel.

"The longer a child is bullied, the more likely they are to develop physical, emotional, and psychological scars that can last a lifetime. Bullying can be devastating, leaving children withdrawn, shy, and insecure. Kids frequently suffer stomach aches, headaches, panic attacks, and nightmares. They can become unable to sleep – or may sleep too much. They often do poorly in school due to loss of focus and confidence or erratic attendance as they try to escape bullies. When unrelenting, bullying can lead children to take their own lives. Bullying also hurts bystanders, who may become fearful that they will also be victimized. Bullies who learn they can get away with aggression and violence sometimes carry this behaviour into adulthood, having a greater likelihood that they can become a sexual predator or otherwise engage in criminal activity."[1]

Bullying within an organization happens more often than we think, and often goes unreported by victims for a number of reasons, including:
- The assumption that adults rarely intervene
- Fear of being retaliated against or seen as a "tattletale"
- Lack of recognition of all types of bullying
- Feelings of shame and fear

"The perception that adults don't act may lead students to conclude that adults don't care, or that there are different standards for adults' behavior than for young people. In the workplace, shoving co-workers in the hallway would not be tolerated. Yet many adults believe that young people need to "work out" bullying problems like these on their own. This belief may promote a "code of silence" about abusive behavior. A logical consequence would be the failure of students to report other dangers, such as knowledge about a weapon at school."[2]

Churches are challenged to take seriously the reality of bullying and harassment within a church setting and provide individuals with the protection that they need to participate in a safe environment. Church leaders should demonstrate an openness for those that are being bullied to report wrongdoing, while all ministry personnel should have the knowledge to be able to spot bullying. All community members should be empowered to be a whistleblower and to take a stand for the betterment of their own lives and the lives of others. This anti-bullying culture can be demonstrated in your church; you just have to provide the right action plan to make it happen.

---

1 (Bullying Canada, 2020)
2 (Committee for Children, 2016)

a. Harassment and Discrimination

Policy

1. Our church is committed to fostering an environment that is free of discrimination and harassment and one in which all individuals are treated with respect and dignity. Every attendee of our church community has a right to equal treatment with respect to the receipt of services and facilities without discrimination or harassment based on the following prohibited grounds: race, ancestry, place of origin, colour, ethnic origin, citizenship, creed, sex, sexual orientation, age, marital status, family status, or disability.

2. A right to freedom from discrimination and harassment is also applicable where someone is treated unequally because she/he is in a relationship, association or dealing with a person or persons identified by one of the prohibited grounds of discrimination.

3. Every attendee of our church community, especially screened Ministry Personnel, is responsible for creating an environment which is free of discrimination and harassment. Those found to have engaged in such conduct will be subject to discipline.

4. Individuals who have committed an act of harassment will be subject to progressive steps of discipline. Acts of sexual harassment will result in immediate suspension and if an investigation finds that it was found to be substantiated, will result in immediate termination.

Plan

- 'Harassment and Discrimination' guidelines have been clearly communicated and posted in the Children and Youth departments as well as in volunteer manuals and training.

- Church Leadership has determined proper disciplinary procedures and clear written guidelines of these procedures have been provided.

Protection

Harassing and discriminatory behaviours are offensive, degrading and illegal.

Harassment can be physical, sexual, verbal and visual against an individual or a group. This can take place between children, adult to child and adult to adult. Whether intentional or unintentional, harassment demonstrates a lack of respect for the dignity and character of the individual whom it targets. Since the person may be in a vulnerable position such as a child (18 years or under), developmentally challenged or a ministry personnel, there is no requirement that he or she formally object to the behaviour before it is considered a violation.

The defining feature is that the behaviour is unwanted by the recipient (except in the case of children who cannot consent, by virtue of their age) and unwarranted by the relationship and also would be regarded as such by any reasonable person. People in positions of trust and authority have a particular obligation to ensure that they do not use their powers to harass. Genuine authority is based on respect.

Harassment, victimization, and bullying may include:
- derogatory name calling
- comments that are known, or ought to be reasonably known, to be unwelcome
- reprisals or threats of reprisals
- derisory remarks, verbal abuse, insults and threats
- ridicule or belittling of an individual
- display of offensive materials such as racist or sexist pictures
- offensive verbal or practical jokes
- offensive graffiti or insignia
- display or electronic transmission of offensive material
- physical attack consisting of hitting, punching, pulling someone's clothing or hair, which is unwanted by an individual

Sexual harassment can be direct, implied, obvious or subtle. Sexual harassment is uninvited and unwanted sexual attention and other verbal, visual or physical conduct of a sexual nature by a person who knows or ought to know that it is unwelcome. In the case where children are the victims, they are not required to verbalize that the contact is unwanted. Sexual behaviour of any nature towards children by an adult in a care-giving capacity or role of authority is a criminal offense and will be treated accordingly.

General Protection Procedures

Protection continued...

Sexual harassment may include:
- sexually demeaning comments, sexually explicit statements, questions, slurs, sexually oriented jokes, anecdotes or insults
- inappropriate comments about clothing or physical appearance or repeated requests for social engagements in cases where a professional relationship exists
- suggestive or obscene letters, notes or invitations
- leering, gestures, display of sexually suggestive objects or pictures, cartoons or posters
- sexist remarks, requests for sexual favours, sexual advances or demands either verbal, physical or by communication including electronics
- sexual assault, fondling, touching, brushing, and kissing
- continuing to express sexual interest after being informed that the interest is unwelcome
- making reprisals, or threats of reprisals following negative response to sexual advances or following a sexual harassment complaint
- submission to or toleration of sexual harassment is an explicit or implicit term or condition of any services, benefits or programs sponsored by the church

A single incident of sufficient severity may constitute sexual harassment. In determining whether a specific act or pattern of behaviour violates this policy, the circumstances surrounding the conduct will be considered in conjunction with the definition of sexual harassment. A determination will be made from the perspective of a "reasonable person" of the same sex and the victim.

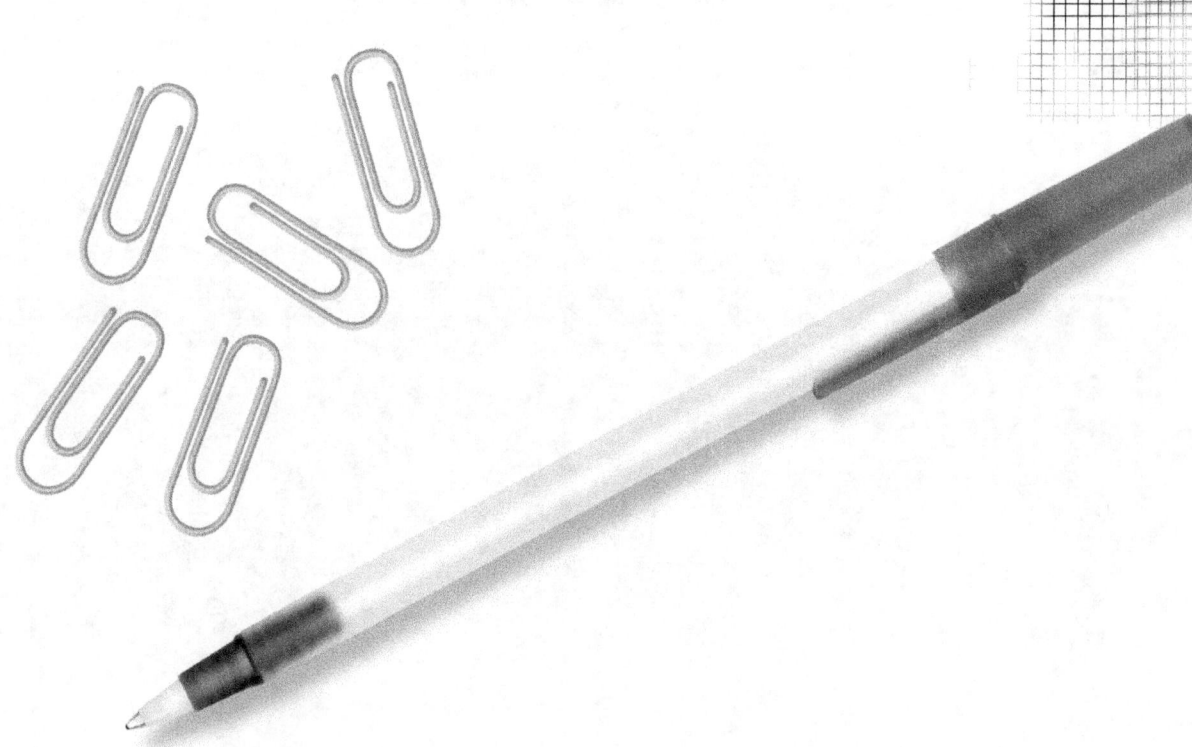

C. Discipline and Classroom Management

Policy

1. The following forms of punishment are not permitted:
    a. Corporal punishment of a Child or Youth by Ministry Personnel;
    b. Deliberate harsh or degrading measures that would humiliate a Child or Youth, or undermine their self-respect;
    c. Depriving a Child or Youth of their basic needs;
    d. Locking or confining a Child or Youth in a room separate from others.

2. All discipline and group management are to be conducted in a loving and caring environment. All attempts are to be made to prevent discipline problems from arising and to avoid the need for remedial discipline. All attempts to provide discipline are to adhere to the following:

    Preventative Discipline:
    a. Create a loving, caring atmosphere.
    b. To gain respect, you must grant respect.
    c. Model self-discipline and structure in your own life.
    d. Prepare exciting and interesting activities with short transitions in-between.
    e. Arrange your environment in an age-appropriate way and for learning.
    f. Establish and communicate realistic expectations for the Children and Youth.
    g. Be sure the activities that you provide are meaningful and age-appropriate.
    h. Be fair and consistent with all Children and Youth.
    i. Be sure your focus is on positive actions and reward positive behaviour.
    j. Be aware of Children and Youth with special needs and bring their needs to the attention of the Ministry Lead.

    Remedial Discipline:
    a. Deal with problems individually.
    b. Explain to the Child or Youth why the behaviour is unacceptable and instruct them how to do it correctly.
    c. Redirect the Child or Youth to positive action.
    d. Explain the consequences of unacceptable behaviour by defining the correct way to behave as well as the result of the wrong behaviour.
    e. Offer choices that are acceptable to both you and the Child or Youth.

3. Group rules are to be established to clearly communicate the expectations required of Children and Youth. Some suggested rules are:
    a. One voice talking at a time, and always use inside voices.
    b. Use good manners.

Policy continued...

    c. Respect each other.
    d. Quiet hands get answered.
    e. Obey directions the first time.
    f. Keep your hands and feet to yourself.
    g. Be friendly.

4. Ministry Personnel must complete an Incident Report form when an individual is removed from a program or activity or if a Child is returned to their Parents. The Incident Report Form must include the behaviour that resulted in the discipline step, the steps taken and the expected outcome prior to returning.

Plan

- Ministry personnel are educated in the discipline steps that are appropriate to use with children and youth.
- Classroom expectations have been clearly communicated to the children and youth.
- Group rules have been established.
- Incident Reports are being used.

Protection

Churches are striving to be able to provide a safe, positive, and productive environment for all persons attending. Within programs, classroom management is a concern to allow these programs to run efficiently. To enforce classroom rules, organizations are encouraged to abide by preventative and remedial discipline, determining "appropriate consequences and/or supports to help students improve their behaviour, while taking into account their individual circumstances. The goal is to help prevent inappropriate student behaviour from happening again."[1]

A practice that Plan to Protect® recommends is to follow the 5 R's:

1. **Reward** good behaviour. Immediate praise and recognition for positive actions are effective ways to encourage more of the same. Inform parents when a child does well or shows improvements.

2. **Remind** students of proper classroom behaviour. Remind them of the classroom rules and what is expected.

3. **Redirect** students. Move them to a different situation or area. Separate children from others when they are having difficulty behaving.

4. **Remove** students from the group using a time-out chair within the classroom and in view of screened adults. After an explanation of the inappropriate behaviour, give them several minutes to sit alone (a quick tool to use is: a child's age should equal their time-out minutes). When children have settled, invite them to rejoin the group. The teacher should complete an incident report form and report the action to their supervisor.

[1] (Ontario Ministry of Education, 2009)

Protection continued...

5. **Return** troubled students to their parents. If steps 1 through 4 fail to change behaviour, a child should be taken to a parent for the remainder of the class. After class, the teacher will explain the problem to the parents and reassure the child that they are welcome to join the class next time. The teacher should complete an incident report form and report the action to their supervisor.[2]

People with learning disabilities have a particular need of help both with learning skills and with unlearning problem behaviours, and particular methods exist to supply this need. Behavioural management has much in common with teaching and management methods in general but includes some special features. Many of these recommendations apply to both children and adults with special needs, although naturally the context in each case will differ.

It is important to emphasize at the outset that there is no one method that should be prescribed for any one problem. The first essential is to study the individual concerned - his or her likes and dislikes, circumstances, idiosyncratic behaviour patterns, history, family set-up, and so on. Remember to show respect and demonstrate dignity at all times.

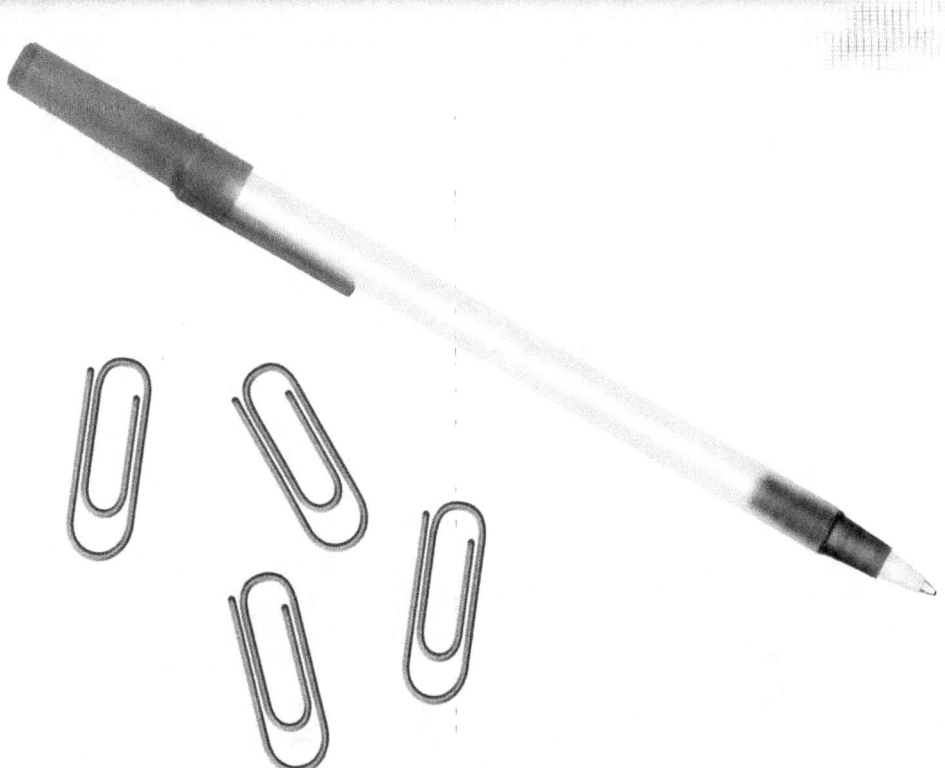

1 (Parker et al., 2002, p. 27-8)

D. Contacting Opportunities

Policy

1. Ministry Personnel may meet with Children, Youth and Vulnerable Adults only during the parameters of ministry programming.

2. Ministry Personnel are to avoid any activity that would involve being isolated with a Child, Youth or Vulnerable Adult and are only to meet in group settings.

3. Any requests for exceptions to this policy must be submitted in writing to Church Leadership. Permission must be granted in writing by both Church Leadership and Parents for each event utilizing an Letter of Informed Consent.

Plan

○ Contacting opportunities with Children, Youth and Vulnerable Adults are being conducted in small group settings and within the parameters of ministry programming.

Protection

To qualify for abuse coverage, insurance companies require that church leadership establish parameters for engaging with the vulnerable sector. Any exceptions to this should be approved by church leadership and with written permission from the parents.

On occasion, ministry personnel will be asked to follow up with students in their class through social media, phone calls, correspondence, or home or hospital visits. Separate policy and procedural statements have been written for these situations.

If a court finds that the church could have done more to ensure the safety of the people in your programs, the church may be found 'vicariously liable' for the actions of a member of the clergy, a layperson or a volunteer. Your best protection against vicarious liability is screening and establishing parameters for engaging with and contacting those that you serve.

a. Counselling and Pastoral Care

Policy

1. Ministry Personnel are prohibited to counsel the vulnerable sector unless the counselling is approved by the Board, and then only by professional counsellors with appropriate insurance in place.
2. Pastors and Board members may engage in pastoral care but must refer clients to a professional counsellor if they show signs of being affected by the following, or if they require or request specific counselling to deal with any of the following:
   a. suicidal ideation,
   b. signs of mental illness,
   c. gender dysphoria,
   d. self-injury
   e. working through a history of substance abuse, or
   f. past trauma.
3. Pastoral care and counselling must be done in a church office during church office hours, when another Ministry Personnel is also on-site.

Plan

- ○ A proposal for a counselling ministry has been submitted for Board approval.
- ○ The appropriate insurance for professional counselling has been secured.
- ○ The church's insurance agent has confirmed that the church is insured for non-professional counselling.
- ○ All counselling personnel have been screened and trained (including Plan to Protect® Orientation and Refresher training).
- ○ Letters of Informed Consent have been prepared.

Protection

Within any church there are individuals experiencing great pain and in need of a counsellor. In some cases they may have experienced trauma that is severe.

The types of counselling offered by churches and Christian charitable organizations can be divided into two broad categories. The first category is "professional" counselling which can generally be defined as instruction, advice or guidance provided by individuals by virtue of their specialized training, education or membership in an accredited professional association. Professional liability is based on the legal principles which require that professionals, relative to others, be subject to a higher duty of care consistent with their specialized skill or knowledge. Examples of professional religious counsellors include ordained ministers, therapists, psychologists, guidance counsellors, etc., whether or not fees are charged.

The second category is "non-professional" counselling, which can roughly be defined as general instruction, advice or guidance of a religious nature provided by individuals who have certain recognized responsibilities, but who have no specialized training or qualifications. The only legal liability posed by this counselling is based on general legal principles that infer the existence of a standard duty of care required of any person in a position of responsibility, to act as any reasonable and prudent person would act in order to avoid harm or injury to another. Examples of non-professional religious counselling include elders, lay persons, youth leaders, teachers, volunteer counsellors, peer counsellors, cell group leaders and certain employees, etc.

Most General Liability policies contain an exclusion for "professional" services. This standard exclusion has the effect of withdrawing any coverage for counselling services deemed to be professional in nature. With respect to non-professional counselling activities there may exist a degree of coverage in a General Liability wording, as long as there are no other applicable exclusions (however it is preferable to maintain a policy that spells out the degree of coverage for such activities).

Counselling liability issues include such interrelated grounds for negligence as professional malpractice, abuse of authority, physical and sexual abuse, emotional abuse, harassment, exceeding qualifications, failing to refer cases requiring specialized psychological or medical care to qualified professionals, as well as issues of confidentiality and the legal responsibility to report criminal acts.

Some churches have a professional counsellor on staff and carry professional insurance for that individual. If not, it is best to refer individuals to a professional counsellor that has the malpractice insurance in place. We recommend that churches limit their ministry to pastoral care and refer individuals in need of trauma care to a professional.

A great counsellor is someone who can use compassion, empathy, respect and authenticity to form a genuine, trusting relationship with their clients in a safe setting. Once you refer someone to a professional counsellor, check in often with the individual to provide additional support and pastoral care.[1]

---

1 (Robertson Hall, Facing the Risk of Counselling Liability)

E. Gift Giving

Policy

1. The church requires that all Ministry Personnel demonstrate our commitment to treating all individuals impartially. Ministry Personnel will demonstrate the highest standards of ethics and conduct in all matters when dealing with:

    a. Children, Youth and Vulnerable Adults

    b. All vendors and suppliers, both existing and potential

    c. Employees, Volunteers and prospective Ministry Personnel

    d. Any individual or organization with whom they come into contact

To demonstrate our commitment to these standards and behaviour, all Ministry Personnel must abide by the following gift giving policy requirements:

2. Ministry Personnel are to refrain from giving gifts to Children, Youth or Vulnerable Adults unless the gift is given to everyone in a class or group setting and is in no means in exchange for services or favours.

3. No gifts of any kind, that are offered by vendors, suppliers, Parents, potential employees or volunteers, potential vendors and suppliers, or any other individual or organization – no matter the value – will be accepted by Ministry Personnel at any time, on or off the work premises if it is given as a means to receive benefit or a bribe including any business courtesy offered. This could include a product discount or any other benefit if the benefit is not extended to all Ministry Personnel, i.e., sale, special accommodation, registration spot, etc.

4. Exempted from this policy are gifts such as t-shirts, pens, trade show bags and all other tchotchkes that employees or volunteers obtain, as a member of the public, at events such as conferences, training events, seminars and trade shows, that are offered equally to all members of the public attending the event. This includes:

    a. Food, beverages, and tchotchkes provided at events, exhibitor trade show floor locations, press events, and parties funded by conference or event sponsors.

    b. Cards, thank you notes, certificates, or other written forms of thanks and recognition.

    c. Food, beverages, moderately priced meals and tickets to local events that are supplied by and also attended by current customers, partners, and vendors or suppliers in the interest of building positive business relationships.

5. When a gift is offered, and it does not fall under the exceptions policy, Ministry Personnel are required to professionally inform vendors, potential vendors and others of this policy and the reasons the church has adopted the policy.

6. Ministry Personnel will request that vendors respect our policy and not purchase and deliver any gift for our employees, a department, an office, or the church, at any time, for any reason.

7. Certain gifts given to or received by Ministry Personnel may be appropriate given a context or situation outside of the scope of this policy. Church Leadership may make a written exemption to this policy detailing the reasoning and scope of their decision for any gift.

plan

○ All Ministry Personnel are aware of the gift giving policy and its exceptions.

○ Church Leadership has systems in place to be notified in the event that this policy has been breached, and to determine when exemptions are applicable.

Protection

In the context of safeguarding, we should recognize that gift giving is often a red flag, associated as the potential first step towards child abuse and sexual harassment. Gift giving falls under the risk of grooming, "a method used by offenders that involves building trust with a child, and the adults around them, in an effort to gain access to and control the child. Offenders groom children to manipulate them into becoming a cooperative participant, reducing the likelihood of the child telling and increasing the likelihood the child will repeatedly return to the offender."[1]

By implementing a 'no gift-giving' policy, you are preventing predators from utilizing gifts or treats to build trust with a vulnerable person.

See also *Financial Aid Policy* under *Adult Protection Procedures*

---

1 (Cybertip.ca, 2019)

F. Dating

Policy

1. Ministry Personnel may not pursue a dating, emotional, or physically intimate relationship with a minor, or someone in a ministry in which they serve.
2. Ministry Personnel are to immediately self-disclose to the Board any and all intimate (psychological or sexual) relationships that begin.

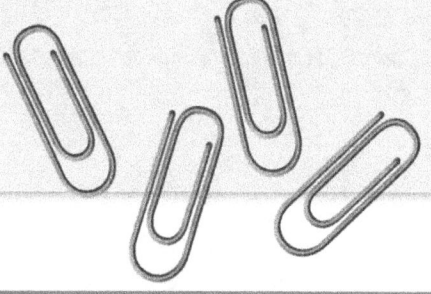

Plan

- A 'no dating' policy has been strictly enforced among ministry personnel and students.

Protection

Never. Never is the only necessary word here. Even if a relationship is to happen in the future, it is never appropriate between a leader and an individual or congregant. Often, spiritual leadership can lead towards a spiritual intimacy that can be misread and misinterpreted. It often easily leads towards other intimacies.

Leaders in youth ministry are most likely over the age of majority. Students in our ministries are most likely under the age of majority. Any physical contact between the two is not only inappropriate, but illegal, AND, not only that, but emotional, mental and physical intimacy with a minor holds HUGE risk for legal action.

As we are spiritual leaders and people who care and listen, crushes and attraction are very common. This is not a valid foundation for an intimate relationship in a dating sense. Leaders must be aware and strong; giving in to crushes and attractions is like walking on thin ice.

This constitutes an abuse of power, authority, influence and control!

G. Home Visits

Policy

1. Ministry Personnel must secure permission in writing from the Ministry Lead to visit individuals that are deemed Vulnerable Adults in their home.

2. Ministry Personnel are never to visit a Child in a home without a Parent present at all times.

3. Ministry Personnel are to maintain and submit monthly communication/visitation logs.

4. Ministry Personnel are to abide by the church's visitation procedures in order to protect both parties in these situations - the visitor and the visited.

Plan

- ○ Procedures for protecting ministry personnel and the people they are visiting have been drafted and communicated.

- ○ Ministry personnel have been provided with monthly communication/visitation logs.

Protection

There are a variety of reasons and circumstances that make meeting people in their own homes a necessary part of the ministry. When visiting shut-ins, providing meals, or responding to pastoral care needs, it is often necessary and desirable to go to someone's home.

However, visiting people in their own homes presents its own set of challenges. Homes, by their nature, are private environments. Because a person tends to be more comfortable and relaxed in their own environment, this increased degree of relaxation may, in fact, make them more vulnerable. Also, because the person being visited is better able to control the situation in their own environment, they may hold a higher degree of power than the visiting ministry personnel. Ministry personnel should be aware that they are potential victims of abuse when visiting someone's home and should take the necessary steps to protect themselves.

Protection continued...

When drafting visitation procedures, consider incorporating some of the following recommendations:

1. Always arrange the visit in advance. Establish a starting time and approximate ending time, as well as a clear purpose for the visit so that the individual knows exactly what to expect.

2. When possible, travel with another screened ministry personnel, or arrange to visit the home when a caregiver is present. If that is not possible, make another person (secretary, spouse, colleague) aware of where you are going and when you can be expected to return.

3. Be respectful of people's time and do not overstay your welcome. When visiting a shut-in or someone who is ill, be particularly conscious of how they are feeling and avoid over-tiring them.

4. Keep the pastoral care purpose of your visit in mind at all times. Do not attempt to unduly persuade or influence the person, particularly if they seem confused. Avoid offering advice about medication or medical treatment, and avoid arguing with or agitating the person you are visiting. Maintain conversations that are uplifting and encouraging.

5. Stay in the most public area of the home - the living room, family room, or kitchen. Avoid entering a person's bedroom unless a third party is present in the home, and preferably only when the person is infirmed or bedridden.

6. Choose a seat at a comfortable distance from the person you are talking to, avoid sitting next to them on a couch or sofa. Do not invite or initiate any unwanted or inappropriate physical contact. If bedridden, do not sit on the individual's bed.

7. Visitors must never engage in any form of sexual impropriety with those whom they are visiting. Sexual impropriety includes, but is not limited to, all forms of overt or covert seductive speech, gestures and behaviour as well as explicit sexual contact.

8. Do not agree to meet anyone in their own home if you sense your own personal safety may be compromised, or if you feel that there is the potential that a boundary may be crossed. If a person whom you don't know well asks for a meeting and you are at all suspicious, arrange to meet them at the church, a coffee shop, or a local restaurant until you know them better.

9. When first arriving at a person's home, assess the situation for anything that may be out of the ordinary. Do not continue if the person is inappropriately dressed, under the influence of alcohol or drugs, or if a person or animal acts in a threatening or aggressive manner and if the animal is not properly restrained. Politely excuse yourself and schedule an alternative day, time or location.

General Protection Procedures

Protection continued...

10. If the person acts strangely, says or does things that make you feel unsafe or uncomfortable, or initiates inappropriate physical contact, tell them to stop and re-establish and maintain appropriate boundaries. If the behaviour continues, excuse yourself, document what happened, and report it to your supervisor. Do not stay in a potentially dangerous or compromising situation.

11. If driving a person to appointments or errands is part of the stated ministry, drivers must hold a valid driver's license and insurance. Seat belts must be available for all passengers. Drivers must not have any alcohol or drugs in their system when driving. If possible, driving ministries should be team ministries to avoid being alone in a car with a vulnerable person.

12. Visitors must treat all confidential information and communications obtained while visiting as strictly confidential and should not disclose them to anyone except where required by law or where given written consent by the individual(s) involved. When discussing the confidential details of a particular situation with a supervisor, the identity of the people involved must be protected.

13. Except where the stated purpose of the visit is stewardship, it is best not to accept gifts or donations when making in-home visits. Encourage the person to make their donation by mailing it directly to the organization. If the person insists on giving you a financial gift while you are there, provide a temporary written receipt on a piece of paper including the date, name of donor, purpose of donation and amount. Duplicate receipts must be retained. All cheques are to be made payable to the church. Explain that the church will issue an official receipt at the appropriate time.

14. Encourage people to speak with their family and financial and legal advisors before making significant contributions in order to avoid allegations of undue influence or abuse of trust. Such encouragement must be recorded in an appropriate file.

15. Be aware of signs that a person may not be caring for oneself as they may require additional resources to assist them. Signs of personal neglect include but are not limited to: a decrease in personal hygiene, wearing the same clothes all the time, particularly if they are stained or soiled, and periods of confusion, disorientation, or loss of memory. Document this information.

16. If you become concerned about the wellbeing of a person whom you are visiting, speak to the ministry lead about trying to initiate contact with a family member in order to discuss the situation and recommend possible courses of action.

H. Hospital and Nursing Home Visits

Policy

1. There must be at least two (2) unrelated Ministry Personnel at all events and for all visitation to hospitals and nursing centres, or the door must remain open with family members, nursing staff, or caregivers nearby or present.

2. When visiting Children or Youth in a hospital, a Parent or family member should be present, or visitation must be done with Parental permission and in teams of two Screened Adults. The door must remain open.

3. When visiting Vulnerable Adults in hospitals and nursing centres, a Family Member or Personal Caregiver must also be present or visitation must be conducted in teams of two Screened Adults. In hospitals and nursing centers, visitation must be conducted in teams of two or the door must be left open.

4. Ministry Personnel must avoid scenarios where they are left alone in a hospital room or nursing home room.

Plan

- Ministry Personnel check with a nurse or other staff of the institution to ensure the individual is able to receive visitors.

- At least two unrelated Ministry Personnel are present for all visits.

- Visitations in hospitals or nursing centres are done with a family member or personal caregiver present.

- Ministry Personnel do not attempt to help with personal care or using the washroom, but instead seek the help of a nurse or personal support worker.

- Ministry Personnel are aware of other risk factors present in the environment.

Protection

Disappointing as it may be, vulnerable adults and the elderly are often targets of abuse from the very people who were set out to protect them. In 2021, through systematic reviews and meta-analyses, the World Health Organization found that rates of elder abuse are high in institutions such as nursing homes and long-term care facilities. 64.2%, or about two in three, of staff reported that they have committed abuse in the past year. This includes psychological, physical, and financial abuse, as well as neglect and sexual abuse.

Knowing this, it is especially important for ministry personnel to adhere to policies during visits. Even with the best intentions, visits mean letting an individual other than hospital and nursing home staff come in close contact when individuals are ill, weak or recovering from an illness. Their immune systems are often compromised. Ministry personnel should not visit if they are ill or have any flu type symptoms.

Visits should provide positive psychological benefits for both parties, and only by ensuring protective precautions are put in place can we make them successful.

Furthermore, ministry personnel can also keep an eye out for other potential risk factors during a visit. As noted above, vulnerable adults and the elderly often experience abuse from those who are supposed to be taking care of them. Therefore, not only should ministry personnel be screened and conduct visits in the presence of a family member or personal caregiver, it would also be beneficial for ministry personnel to be aware of risk factors for potential abuse.

For example, being in a shared living situation is a risk factor for many elderly folks. The dependency between a vulnerable person and another individual can result in financial stress. This could be a possible motive for abuse. If ministry personnel are aware of the risks, in addition to companionship and comfort, visits can also be preventative against elder abuse.

I. Disabilities and Personal Support Workers

Policy

1. On Registration Forms, Parents and Caregivers are encouraged to list known disabilities. Upon registration, Ministry Leads are to determine how best to provide inclusive programming for individuals with disabilities. Ratios will be adjusted to provide additional support needed.

2. Ministry Personnel are to receive training on accessibility for individuals with disabilities.

3. If the church is unable to provide accommodations and support for individuals with disabilities, personal support workers may accompany the individual to the program.

4. All personal support workers shall comply with the church's screening and training process prior to taking responsibility over any individual.

5. If a personal support worker is personally hired and screened by a Child or Youth's Parents then the Parents will provide a signed form identifying the support worker as a private hire and provide copies of the criminal record check and references conducted.

6. A personal support worker who is not hired or screened by the church may only take responsibility over the individual they were hired to support, but may not supervise any other participants in a program, activity, or event.

7. All documentation regarding personal support workers and their screening procedures will be kept on file permanently.

Plan

- ○ Parents and Caregivers are encouraged to share known disabilities when registering their loved ones into programs and events.

- ○ All personal support workers accompanying program participants have undergone screening.

- ○ Ministry Personnel have received training in accessibility and disabilities.

- ○ Where a support worker's screening has been conducted by a parent, the support worker will only take responsibility for that specific person and no other.

- ○ Support worker information forms including details about reasons for why the support worker is needed are signed and kept on file permanently.

Protection

Providing inclusive programs for individuals with disabilities is a rich experience for everyone involved. Many churches provide a welcoming community for individuals with disabilities. Not all disabilities are visible. Some disabilities require assistive devices and elevated attention and care, therefore, adjust your ratios to accommodate this need.

We encourage you to recruit individuals to provide necessary additional attention to these unique participants. If you do not have ministry personnel qualified to provide the attention and care needed, a family may be able to provide personal support workers. Therefore, those with disabilities may be accompanied by a parent, guardian or personal support worker. Personal support workers work with other health care professionals to provide various services for the elderly, disabled and ill. They may work in private homes or health care facilities. They help with patient care in many ways including infection control and administering medication. Since these individuals spend long periods of time in contact with people with disabilities to provide needed care, they are not considered occasional observers and must complete appropriate screening procedures. This is especially important in the case of protecting children and youth with disabilities as they can be more vulnerable due to an inability to express themselves.

If a personal support worker was not screened by the church but instead personally hired by a parent or caregiver, then the church should ensure that the worker does not provide oversight for any other individuals in the program. The support worker should only be responsible for the individual for whom they have been hired to care. It is still recommended that the church screens and trains all support workers regardless and keeps documentation permanently on file.

In the appendices, you will find additional resources for assessing the needs of individuals with disabilities.

J. Gender Identity

Policy

1. In the beginning, God created humans as relational beings, the inherent design of male and female reflecting God's image. Sexuality, our maleness and femaleness, is a dimension of our embodied existence. Sexual difference and complementarity are thus good features of our identity. While identity, fulfillment, and the path to human flourishing are founded on a relationship with the Creator, in Genesis we learn that God made sex an expression of intimacy, love, and self-giving, to be experienced between one man and one woman in a lifelong covenant.

2. Given the inherent dignity of all persons, the church will not tolerate the harassment, discrimination or any language of hate or loathing towards those who hold a differing view on human sexuality. Ministry Personnel and members of the church must treat all persons, regardless of gender, belief or sexuality, with respect and compassion. It is our desire to create a place of welcome and grace, and we are committed to creating a safe environment for all individuals. In light of this commitment, the church will take every reasonable step to ensure that its learning, working and living environments are maintained free from harassment and discrimination.

3. Every individual has a right to equitable treatment without discrimination with respect to accessing the activities or facilities of the church. No person shall be asked or required to 'prove' their gender (e.g., by providing a doctor's note, identity documents, etc.) in order to gain access to these opportunities.

4. Everyone who associates with the church community is encouraged to communicate using respectful, gender-inclusive language. Those who identify as a gender other than their biological sex should confirm with the church the name(s) and pronoun(s) by which they prefer to be referred. Everyone within the church community is encouraged to respect these preferences in their communication.

5. Intentionally addressing anyone within the church community by the incorrect name or gender pronoun is considered by the church to be a form of harassment and discrimination. Inadvertent slips or honest mistakes are not covered by this provision, but intentional and persistent refusal to acknowledge or use an individual's preferred or changed name or pronoun is unacceptable.

6. Disclosing the gender status of an individual associated with the church community without explicit and directly expressed consent or in the absence of a "need to know" circumstance is generally known as "outing". Outing in any form is not supported by the leadership of the church as it is recognized as a form of harassment that puts the individual's physical, emotional and psychological safety at risk.

7. The church will make reasonable efforts to ensure that all members of the church community can use washrooms with safety, privacy and dignity, regardless of their gender identity or gender expression.

8. Individuals within the church community have the right to express legitimate concerns about human rights violations they may experience in their interaction and engagement at the church without fear of reprisal. On the other hand, complaints made in bad faith are strongly discouraged since any accusation or complaint of harassment or discrimination is a matter that can cause considerable hardship to the person who is the subject of the complaint.

9. If individuals associated with the church community request counselling or guidance concerning Gender Dysphoria or Gender Identity Disorder, all Ministry Personnel and congregants are to notify a Pastor who will arrange for appropriate counselling.

Plan

- The church has made available a universal washroom that can be used by anyone in the congregation.

- Individuals are not asked to prove their gender when changing information on church documents.

- Individuals are given the opportunity to share their preferred pronoun(s), in which members of the church will respect and address them by.

Protection

Definitions of Gender Issues Terminology:

Gender Identity: is a category of social identity and refers to an individual's identification as male, female, or occasionally, some category other than male or female. It is one's deeply held core sense of being male, female, some of both or neither, and does not always correspond with biological sex.

Gender Dysphoria: involves conflict between a person's physical or assigned gender and the gender with which he/she/they identify. People with gender dysphoria may be very uncomfortable with the gender they were assigned, sometimes described as being uncomfortable with the expected roles of their assigned gender.[1]

https://www.psychiatry.org/patients-families/gender-dysphoria/what-is-gender-dysphoria

Protection continued...

Gender dysphoria is not the same as gender nonconformity, which refers to behaviours not matching the gender norms or stereotypes of the gender assigned at birth. Examples of gender nonconformity (also referred to as gender expansiveness or gender creativity) include girls behaving and dressing in ways more socially expected of boys or occasional cross-dressing in adult men. Gender nonconformity is not a mental disorder. Gender dysphoria is also not the same as being gay or lesbian.

The 2000's are radically different from the 1900's in regard to human rights and freedoms. In June of 2017, a Bill was passed "with both gender identity and gender expression being federally protected grounds in the Canadian Human Rights Act and the Criminal Code of Canada."[2] This means that, like other protected grounds outlined under the Canadian Charter of Rights and Freedoms, sexual orientation began to include gender expression and identity, as the right to "live free without fear of discrimination, violence or exclusion, and to be fully included and embraced in all facets of Canadian society."[3]

Although this is protected under Canadian federal law, individuals that identify as LGBTQ2I are still widely discriminated against:

- "16% of Canadian hate crimes in 2013 were motivated by hatred of sexual orientation;
- 20% of homeless youth identify as LGBTQ2I;
- 70% of trans youth in Canada have experienced discrimination because of gender identity;
- 36% of trans youth report being physically threatened or injured at school;
- In 2016, the number of discrimination complaints the CHRC received related to sexual orientation (52) was the highest in nearly a decade;
- 69% of trans youth (19-25 years old) have seriously considered suicide at some point in their lives;
- 70% of trans youth report experiencing sexual harassment."[3]

With this change in legislation, and the inherent risks for these children and youth, churches are presented with the responsibility to provide safeguards to ensure that transgendered persons are free to live and participate without discrimination and harassment from peers, superiors, colleagues, etc.

---

1 (American Psychiatric Association, n.d.)
2 (Canadian Aids Society, 2017)
3 (Canadian Human Rights Commission, n.d.)

Health and Safety

A. Health and Safety Guidelines
    a. Severe Allergies
    b. Immunizations
    c. Drugs and Alcohol
B. Inclement Weather Conditions
C. Missing Person
D. Lockdown Guidelines
E. Fire and Emergency Evacuation

A. Health and Safety Guidelines

1. Ministry Leads and Ministry Personnel are encouraged to be certified and trained in first aid.
2. The names and contact information of individuals who are certified in first aid are to be posted in the Children's and Youth program areas for easy access, with a Master List maintained by the Office Manager.
3. Ministry Leads must be informed of any individual(s) having severe allergies. The information is to be posted in the Children's and Youth departments for easy access and Ministry Personnel who have the individual(s) in their care must be informed.
4. The cleaning and sanitation of toys and table surfaces must be done after each use.

Illness:

1. An individual who is ill and could therefore expose others to illness are not to be received into the program room. Factors to consider are:
   a. Fever, unusual fatigue, irritability, coughing, sneezing, runny nose and eyes, vomiting, diarrhea, inflamed mouth and throat
   b. Individuals showing signs of a contagious illness such as viruses, pink eye, measles, chickenpox, or any other communicable disease that could be spread by touch or by coming in close proximity

Medications:

1. Ministry Personnel are not to give or apply any medications (i.e., Tylenol, Polysporin, vitamins, etc.) without written authorization from a physician and Church Leadership.
2. Any prescription medication must be brought in the original container with the doctor's prescription, dosage and date clearly printed on the label. Parents must fill out a medication form and sign dosage instructions. Medication must be presented to the Ministry Lead or designate on duty in the Child's room and handed over at sign-in. (Appendices 15 and 16)
3. When medication is brought for a Child, the medication is to be kept in a locked box in the cupboard or refrigerator. This also applies to non-prescription substances such as tobacco and cigarettes brought by Youth to events.
4. Dosage times must be recorded in the daily journal or Attendance Form for all staff to see.
5. At dosage time, the Ministry Lead or designated health worker must double check the medication form and instructions, dispense medication to the Child and sign the form noting the amount and time medication was given.
6. In the extreme case where EpiPens and puffers are needed for allergies or asthma, written instructions are to be provided by the Parent to the Ministry Lead. Requests should be written, signed, dated and filed permanently.
7. Topical medications for diaper changing purposes are to be used only when instructed and provided by the Parent.

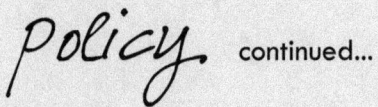 continued...

Dealing with Cuts or Injuries Involving Blood:

1. Universal precautions must be used when administering any kind of first aid. (Appendix 12)
2. Blood pathogen policies are to be posted in classrooms.
3. When an individual is injured, they are to be separated from others. The area where the injury occurred or where any blood may have dropped on the floor or toys is also to be isolated.
4. Ministry Personnel need to ensure that no other individuals have had contact with any of the blood from the cut or injury.
5. Non-latex gloves are to be used when bandaging the injury, avoiding contact with mouth, ears and eyes.
6. Extreme care must be taken in cleaning up all blood and bloody bandages and the safe and secure removal of waste and disposal of gloves to a secure waste removal container.
7. Hands are to be washed carefully with sterilizing soap available in the first aid kit.
8. When ministering to individuals with HIV or AIDS, specific guidelines for the education and care of these individuals are to be developed and followed (Appendix 14).

Emergencies:

1. Emergency and evacuation procedures are to be reviewed semi-annually by the Pastor and the Board. These procedures are to be posted in a visible place in each classroom stating the planned route of escape to the nearest exit.
2. Pastors, in communication with the Ministry Lead, are to arrange for annual fire and evacuation drills.
3. A first aid kit must be kept in each classroom with Ministry Personnel being educated on the kit's contents.
4. In addition to the first aid kits in each room, a master first aid kit must be available to the church's building and in any church-owned vehicle.
5. Each kit must contain a pair of disposable non-latex gloves, disinfectant towelettes, two or three 4" x 4" gauze pads for blood absorption, small scissors and bandages.
6. A Parent must be contacted when an injury, accident or medical emergency occurs that involve their Child. Incident reports are to be completed for any and all accidents (Appendix 18). Injuries are to be reported to the Ministry Lead.

plan

- Ministry Leads or Personnel have been encouraged to be trained and certified in first aid.

- Contact information for those trained and certified in first aid have been clearly posted.

- Severe allergies have been posted.

- Schedules have been developed for cleaning and sanitizing toys and table surfaces.

- First aid kits with required items have been made available in each classroom and vehicle.

- Master first aid kits have been made available in the church and in each church-owned vehicle.

- Blood pathogen policies have been posted in the classrooms.

- A secure waste removal container has been clearly marked and made available for emergencies.

- Plans have been made for annual emergency evacuation drills.

- Incident Report Forms have been made accessible to all ministry personnel.

Protection

"Health promotion program planning and evaluation includes everything from assessing needs, setting goals and objectives, planning activities, implementation and measuring outcomes. Effective program planning and evaluation ensures that your program is meeting its objectives and having an impact on the health of the population."[1]

Accidents happen, whether we like it or not. But as an organization, it is your duty to ensure the health and safety of the vulnerable population you serve through effective program planning and risk assessments.

Save the Children International has identified seven areas in which unnecessary risks to the health and safety of those in your program may exist: Lack of adequate risk assessment; poorly designed programs; programs designed and implemented without the full participation and agreement of children and communities; programs implemented in 'unsafe' environments; delivery of program through 'unsafe' partners; lack of adequate monitoring; and policy initiatives which do not consider adequate precautionary measures to be taken.[2]

It is in these areas that organizations need to ensure there are no gaps with the way that specific risks are assessed and addressed through the policies and the implementation. Although kids will get sick and hurt themselves, your role as an organization is to be prepared and to think through your programming and plans ahead of time.

---

1 (Public Health Ontario, 2020)
2 (Save the Children International, n.d.)

a. Severe Allergies

Policy

1. Parents and Caregivers are responsible for notifying the church of any known allergies which their Children have. This information is to be noted on their Registration Form.

2. Upon permission of Parents, the notification of severe allergies are to be posted in the Child's classroom for high visibility, including a picture of the Child, a list of his or her allergies and typical signs of reaction. Ministry Personnel assigned to care for the Child must be made aware of the allergy and the treatment required if a reaction occurs.

3. In recognition of individuals with severe nut allergies, we are to promote a nut-free environment, where no nut products should be served.

Plan

- ○ Allergy information is collected on the Registration Form.

- ○ Ministry Leads have consulted parents about posting severe allergies in classrooms.

- ○ Individuals responsible for the care of children with severe allergies have been notified and educated on the allergy and its treatment.

- ○ Ministry Personnel have been made aware of the severe allergy policy, and the restrictions regarding food and snack preparation.

Protection

Health professionals warn that individuals who provide care and supervision to children are to be educated that when a child has an allergic reaction, there is no time to wait for help. The child will be unable to self-administer the medication due to the severity of the symptoms; any ministry personnel present will have to administer the EpiPen immediately when a child has an allergic reaction.

For supporting information see 'Health and Safety Guidelines' on page 151.

Peanut-Free Policy

For churches committed to having a peanut-free facility and are moving towards having as few peanut products in the church as possible, the following guidelines may be considered as policy. However, it should be noted, churches are public buildings; it is not always possible to prevent all peanut-products from entering the facility. Parents of children and individuals with peanut allergies should be aware that it is not a 100% nut-free environment.

1. No peanut products or ingredients will be used in the church kitchen or in any snacks served to children and youth, or sold in snack machines. Parents, ministry personnel, and kitchen volunteers will be informed not to bring or use any snacks or ingredients containing peanuts to church facilities at any time.
2. The church who wants to implement a peanut-free policy for their facility, could educate their congregation through announcements, signage and in the bulletins.

For additional information, see Food Allergy Canada at **https://foodallergycanada.ca/allergies/peanut/** as this website provides more information on educating your congregation, suggestions for peanut-free products, and ideas on implementing your policy.

Scent-Free Policy

In the last few years there has been an increase in allergies to strong perfumes and scents. At the discretion of church leadership, a scent-free policy may be considered.

1. In recognition of individuals with asthma, allergies and severe environmental and chemical sensitivities, our church is striving to provide a scent-free building. People are asked to refrain from wearing fragrances and scented personal care products while in our facilities. This includes perfumes, colognes, aftershave and scented hair products.[1]

---

1 (Springridge Mennonite Church, Alberta)

b. Immunizations

Policy

1. It is the responsibility of the church and Ministry Personnel to demonstrate their care for the families they serve to ensure those providing care are vaccinated.
2. All Children, Youth and Ministry Personnel should stay current with their immunizations as recommended or mandated by Health Canada and the Public Health Agency of Canada and Province.
3. It is the responsibility of the Parent to ensure immunizations are current and to notify the church if there are immunization exemptions.
4. At such time that the church is alerted to the requirement of an immunization, a written notice will be sent home.

Plan

- ◯ Federal and provincial requirements for immunizations have been researched.
- ◯ Ministry Personnel have been informed of any required vaccinations.
- ◯ Parents have been encouraged to ensure their children are up to date on their immunizations.
- ◯ Records are kept for those that have filed immunization exemptions.

Protection

Some provinces across Canada have immunization legislation for diphtheria, tetanus, polio, measles, mumps, and rubella.

Due to recent pandemics, Federal and Provincial governments recommend vaccinations to prevent the spread of disease, and new legislation may be drafted in the future.

Although it varies by province, some Child Care operators are required to collect each registrant's immunization records to ensure that they are up-to-date before admitting the registrant into the program. This information can be found on your province's Immunization Schedule. It is also often required that those working with children are to be vaccinated "according to the recommendation made by the local medical officer of health… Parents who choose not to have their child vaccinated or staff who choose not to be vaccinated may submit an exemption for religious or philosophical reasons. Exemptions must be documented using approved ministry forms."[1] These forms should be kept on the child's file or the employee's personnel file.

---

1 (Toronto Public Health, 2019)

c. Drugs and Alcohol

Policy

1. The legalization of cannabis does not change the church's legal obligation to provide a safe workplace and programs. Ministry Personnel are not to be impaired while serving or working at the church.

2. During employment or volunteer service, the church has zero tolerance for the possession and/or consumption of illegal drugs and misuse of alcohol at any time.

3. Ministry Personnel will take action to prevent the abuse of drugs and alcohol, teach against it, and promote a safe environment for everyone.

4. The church will take steps to ensure individuals who are impaired or whose ability to work is affected by consuming substances such as alcohol and drugs, including cannabis, are removed from the premises, unless accommodation has been provided for medicinal use.

5. Individuals under the influence of drugs or alcohol will be escorted off the premises as they may pose a risk to other individuals. Children and Youth removed in this way will be separated from others until their Parents arrive to collect them. Any time an individual is removed from the premises due to drugs or alcohol, an Incident Form must be completed and a report made to the Ministry Lead.

6. Ministry Personnel cannot possess or consume alcohol or cannabis during program hours or at any time during hours of service, unless prescribed by a physician, as outlined in this policy.

7. Ministry Personnel may not possess or consume alcohol or drugs (legal or non-legal) where minors are present or where Ministry Personnel are responsible for the supervision and oversight of minors.

8. If minors are found to be in the possession of alcohol or non-medicinal drugs, it will be confiscated and reported to the police. The police should be asked if they would like the items turned over or destroyed. An Incident Report must be completed and Parents notified.

9. All Ministry Personnel working with Children, Youth and Vulnerable Adults are required to notify their Ministry Lead of their use of prescription and non-prescription medication which may produce side effects causing them to be under the influence of the medication or left impaired by the medication. If such medication is prescribed, Ministry Personnel may be required to provide relevant documentation by a physician. The church reserves the right to verify with a physician (either with such Ministry Personnel's own physician or an independent medical examination) that Ministry Personnel can safely continue to perform their duties. If the church determines from the examination or medical information that the Ministry Personnel is unable to safely perform his or her duties, the church will not grant continued service in ministry for the period of time that the Ministry Personnel remains impaired. The church is committed to respecting the privacy of Ministry Personnel, and Children, Youth and Vulnerable Adults.

10. Ministry Personnel that travel on behalf of the church are expected to conduct themselves in a professional and positive manner at all times. Irresponsible consumption of alcohol or cannabis at any time during employment, volunteer service or engagement with the church may result in immediate termination. Therefore, Ministry Personnel should exercise responsible alcohol and drug consumption when off-site, including after working hours. Any consumption should be conducted in a way that does not impede Ministry Personnel's

Policy continued...

capacity or ability to respond competently to situations that arise and in a way that does not negatively impact the reputation of the church. Ministry Personnel are prohibited from wearing church uniforms when purchasing or consuming alcoholic beverages, or while smoking or purchasing cigarettes or cannabis.

11. Ministry Personnel whose duties include driving must not be under the influence of any drugs or alcohol while operating a motor vehicle. It is important for church drivers and the passengers to be fully functional and alert when operating or driving in a motor vehicle. When church drivers are transporting other members of the church or any Children, Youth or Vulnerable Adults on behalf of the church in commercial vehicles, such as a rented vehicle, or in their own vehicles, there is a zero alcohol and cannabis consumption policy for those drivers for a full 24 hours prior to the scheduled time of departure.

Plan

- Restrictions regarding drug and alcohol use have been communicated to both Ministry Personnel and attending Youth.
- Any substance found in the possession of Children and Youth has been confiscated and turned over to the police, followed by completing an Incident Report.
- Ministry Personnel report to Church Leadership if taking medication that may affect their ability to act in a Position of Trust.

Protection

With the legalization of marijuana in Canada, this drug has become more accessible for not only those of majority age, but to our children and youth as well. Although there are many illicit drugs circulating among the younger generation, "they use alcohol and cannabis (marijuana) more than any other substances. ... Using alcohol or drugs can affect young people's general health, physical growth, and emotional and social development. It can also change how well they make decisions, how well they think, and how quickly they can react. And using alcohol or drugs can make it hard for young people to control their actions. For some young people, alcohol or drug use may turn into a substance abuse problem."[1]

Today our Youth are confronted with many pressures as it relates to drugs and alcohol. There is peer pressure and social expectations that may cause minors to experiment with these substances without the ability to truly understand the consequences that are involved. Being open and real about the effects of drugs and alcohol with empathy and understanding, can help children and youth establish healthy habits and choices. Clear restrictions on their use are also important in setting boundaries.

---

1 (HealthLink BC, 2019)

B. Inclement Weather Conditions

Policy

1. In extremely hot or cold weather, Ministry Leads may use their discretion to determine if it is safe to take Children and Youth outside for programming.

2. Children and Youth are not to be forced to go outside if the temperature is below -10 degrees Celsius, or if there is a wind-chill advisory in effect, causing the temperature to feel below -10 degrees celsius. They are also to be kept indoors if the temperature is above 30 degrees Celsius or if a smog alert is in effect.

3. Ministry Personnel must use discretion when smog alerts are in effect, especially if there are Children and Youth with respiratory ailments in attendance.

4. In the event of a thunderstorm with lightning, Children and Youth are to remain inside.

5. In the event of a natural disaster, Children and Youth and Ministry Personnel are to remain indoors, away from windows. If required to go to the lowest part of the building, Ministry Personnel are to escort Children and Youth calmly.

6. In the event of inclement weather (heavy snow, tornado warning, etc.) the church may close due to travel warnings and high-risk of injury and danger. A recorded message is to be announced on the church voicemail, a notice placed on the website, and an email notice to be sent to all families.

Plan

- Children and Youth are kept indoors during dangerous weather conditions.
- Attendees and Ministry Personnel are notified in the case of a closure.
- Ministry Personnel are trained to recognize when weather conditions may be inappropriate for Children and Youth to spend time outdoors.

Protection

In Canada, with four different seasons, weather conditions are changeable, and therefore, churches must be prepared to handle all sorts of conditions and make sound decisions to protect everyone. This includes being able to recognize when temperatures are too extreme for children and youth to go outdoors as well as when the church itself should not open in the case of inclement weather. We do not want any families or ministry personnel coming to the church under high-risk situations.

C. Missing Person

Policy

The safety of Children and Youth will be given our highest priority. If a person goes missing, time is of the essence. As soon as an individual is found to be missing, all available Ministry Personnel must follow the steps below:

1. Conduct a preliminary search of their last known location.

2. Assemble all remaining Children and Youth together in a central safe location, enabling as many Screened Leaders as possible to search for the missing person. Split the Screened Leaders into two groups - one group to search, and one group to supervise the remaining Children and Youth. One person is designated as the primary point of contact.

3. The Primary Point of Contact must contact the Ministry Lead and Church Leadership immediately, and remain available to coordinate between the searchers, remaining Ministry Personnel, off-site leadership and outside groups.

4. The group supervising the Children and Youth must stay together and wait for further instructions from leadership. Do not send any minors to search for a missing person.

5. The searching group must appoint individuals to keep watch over points of entry or exit, and to reduce movement in the area by any other groups - under ideal circumstances, no one exits the area.

6. Remaining Leaders and Volunteers, (as many as possible without putting the remaining Children at risk) must begin by conducting a search of the "hot spots" - nearby, likely and dangerous areas - then move to less immediate areas.

7. Search both inside the building and outside the building. Search inside locations: cupboards, washrooms, closets, stairwells, classrooms, auditorium/sanctuary, baptismal tanks and offices. Search outside locations: parking lot, beach, river, swimming pool, nearby streets, parks, play grounds, railroad tracks, and ravines, etc.

8. At the 10 minute point of searching, the Primary Point of Contact must call 9-1-1 to notify the police and emergency officials of the missing person. Provide them with the individual's age, physical description (including a description of their clothing), last known location, and possible whereabouts in the building or community where the Child went missing. If possible, provide a photograph.

9. The Primary Point of Contact is to designate someone (themselves or a Church Leader) to notify the family members (in the case of a Child, their Parents) immediately after notifying the police.

10. Continue to search, cooperating with the police and local authorities.

11. Once the missing person is found, administer first aid as needed.

12. If a Child is found with another Adult, attempt to calmly and gently detain the Adult until the police arrive. If the Adult leaves, record a description of the individual as soon as possible if they are unknown, and provide it to the police.

13. Complete an Incident Report, and keep the report on file permanently.

14. If the media arrives on the scene, only the Church Leader should speak to the media.

Plan

- ○ One person is designated to coordinate the search and communication efforts.
- ○ Church Leadership are notified immediately.
- ○ Remaining children and youth are gathered together and a few screened personnel are tasked to supervise the minors as others search.
- ○ Police are notified after 10-15 minutes of searching.
- ○ Parents/Guardians are notified immediately after the police.
- ○ First aid is available to be administered as needed as soon as the individual is found. This includes all necessary equipment as well as trained personnel.
- ○ An Incident Report is completed after the individual is found and is kept on file permanently.
- ○ The Church Leader has been trained on how to approach the media and how to share information regarding the incident appropriately.
- ○ All Ministry Personnel have been trained on what to do in case of a missing child.

Protection

As we follow Plan to Protect®, we should be doing our utmost to prevent a missing child or vulnerable adult incident from occurring. This policy is designed to be put into place to swiftly and effectively take action to locate any missing person, and to notify and involve parents and the authorities at every point. A missing person should be an extremely rare occurrence. However, accidents and the unexpected do occur, and we must not take this issue lightly.

In 2019, Canada reported that 55% of missing persons reports involved children. In other words, more than half of the missing persons reports involved children!

Although missing child cases may involve abduction and accidents, most reported cases involve children who have run away. In Canada, 74% of missing children and youth reports (including male and female) were runaways. Children and youth may run away for many different reasons. For children, that may mean running away to avoid a certain problem they are faced with, or emotions they don't want to deal with. For youth, they may run away due to substance abuse. They may believe running away is the best solution to hiding their abuse from their parents. Other reasons children and youth may run away include:

o   Abuse (violence in the family)
o   Parents separating or divorcing or the arrival of a new stepparent
o   Death in the family
o   Birth of a new baby in the family
o   Family financial worries
o   Parents drinking alcohol or taking drugs
o   Problems at school
o   Peer pressure
o   Failing or dropping out of school

Oftentimes, members of the child's family may be part of the reason why they ran away. Hence, the child may have chosen to not disclose their problems to family members. As such, it is especially important that the community, including the church, is attentive to these varying possibilities. There may be possible signs of stress or discomfort a child exhibits prior to running away. If we pay extra attention to our children and youth, in addition to setting up preventative measures for all types of abuse, we can help minimize the chances of missing children incidents.

Protection continued...

The severity of missing child cases can vary greatly. Some cases may be a quick lost and found situation, whereas some may involve much more dangerous factors. However, a number of different things can happen when a child is lost, including choking, water danger, becoming stuck in tight places, seizures, abduction and more. Although it may not be necessary for everyone to panic immediately when a child has gone missing, having a system, and knowing when and how to act in those cases will minimize the chances of greater danger. We can never know what is happening to the child before they are found so, no matter the severity, every minute we spend waiting before reacting or calling emergency services is a minute wasted not bringing them back to safety.

In other cases, the missing person could be someone who suffers from dementia or Alzheimer's. If someone walks away from programming that is known to suffer from cognitive capacity, immediately call 9-1-1 and the primary caregivers. Many of the same principles for responding to a lost child would apply to adults suffering from dementia or Alzheimer's, if they walk away from a program.

For more information, check out **https://www.missingkids.org/codeadam**.

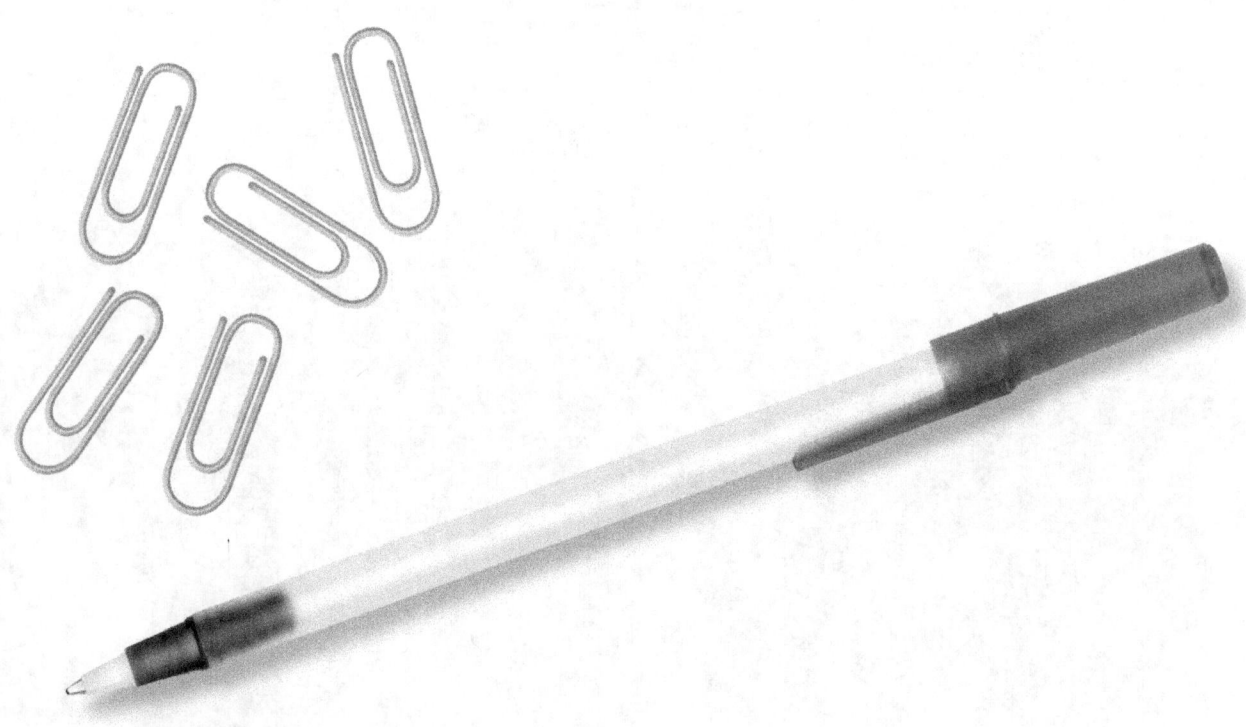

D. Lockdown Guidelines

Policy

These guidelines are to be put into action in the event of a lockdown or during a lockdown drill. Although each church is to draft their own lockdown policy with details pertaining to their specific needs and facilities, this policy will help give Church Leadership a place to start.

1. Identify green zones and red zones within the facility. Green Zones: More secure – rooms that have doors that lock. Red Zones: open areas, including gymnasiums and auditoriums.

2. As soon as the facility is put on "Lockdown Alert", the designated person in charge will announce "Code Red" to all classrooms and Ministry Personnel: "Announcement: Emergency Code Red, the facility is going into lockdown, repeat, Emergency Code Red, the facility is going into lockdown."

3. Immediately call 9-1-1, unless it is a situation where the police first alerted the church. Instruct all individuals present to shut off cell phones.

4. All present must clear away from red zones as quickly as possible. They are to go to the nearest green zone, or if an outside door is closer, they are to evacuate the building.

5. Prior to locking doors, those in charge of classrooms are to ensure that any individuals walking the halls within their classroom's proximity are ushered quickly into the room. The door must then be closed and locked. If the classroom door has a window, Ministry Personnel are to cover it and turn off the lights.

6. Those in charge of classrooms are to assist students in turning tables on their sides and position them away from the door and windows. The students are to then take refuge behind them.

7. Attendance is to be taken, including a list of all missing and extra students in the room. This list must be emailed to the office, and the teacher must take the list with them if directed to leave the classroom.

8. Custodians or ushers are to check all washrooms in the facility, remove any individuals who may be within, and lock the washrooms from the outside.

9. Everyone is prohibited from leaving green zones until they are instructed to do so by the designated person in charge or a police officer. Those in charge of classrooms are to remain in the rooms, maintain silence and keep the students calm. Do not contact the church office, the office will contact you when it is safe to do so.

10. When instructed to evacuate the building, do so quickly and silently.

11. Once the police arrive on the scene, they have the ultimate command of the incident and their instructions will be followed without protest.

12. At least twice during a calendar year, the church is to perform a lockdown drill. Church Leadership are to notify the church community of a lockdown drill the week or day prior to the drill.

13. Circumstances and details of the drill are to be recorded and kept on file. It is strongly recommended to have a debriefing with participants, and keep notes of these debriefings on file.

plan

These procedures should be implemented prior to the event of a facility lockdown or a lockdown drill.

- ○ Green and red zones have been identified in the facility.
- ○ The church community has been informed of the meaning of a Code Red.
- ○ The church community has been instructed on lockdown procedures.
- ○ Plans have been made to schedule at least two lockdown drills during a calendar year.
- ○ The church community has been given prior notification of a lockdown drill.
- ○ An individual has been designated responsible for the recording of the details and debriefing of each drill.

Protection

It is becoming more common for churches to be implementing security measures for the protection of parishioners, due to the number of high-profile attacks on places of worship. As an organization, we should no longer stand by the statement, "It won't happen here." Although we have seen historically that schools in Canada have been targeted by lockdowns more often than churches, the risk still exists.

Churches should be working to educate and empower ministry personnel to follow and maintain strict lockdown procedures to best protect the vulnerable persons in their care. Parents dropping off their children and youth into programs should be confident that the workers, and the organization as a whole, is armed with the tools and strategies to protect them under any circumstance.

These practices should be well communicated with parents, guardians and the church community in general to ensure a universal understanding of lockdown procedures. Consider "sending a newsletter to each home at the beginning of the [program] year, to inform parents of lockdown procedures and to encourage parents to reinforce with their children the importance of understanding the procedures and following ministry personnel direction. Parents [and other members of the church] need to be informed of where they should proceed in the event of an actual incident involving a lockdown. Communication with parents around the importance of lockdowns is vital. "Parents should be informed of what is expected should they arrive at [the church] during a drill, or if they are present within the [church] when a lockdown is called."[1] "Some parents say lockdown drills have the potential to scare the … [children], particularly younger ones, and real lockdowns create a culture of fear. … Police and school boards, however, say that while lockdown drills and real lockdowns might be controversial, they are here to stay because drills prepare students for the real thing and lockdowns imposed in the face of a threat have the potential to save lives."[2]

Organizations should take advantage of the help that police departments will provide throughout the planning process of lockdown procedures. "Given the dynamic, complex, and fluid nature of violent incidents, it is essential that continuous communication, assessment, and coordination by first responders and [church] administrators occur."[3]

---

1 (Government of Ontario, 2009)
2 (Draaisma 2007, 2)
3 (York Regional Police, 2018)

E. Fire and Emergency Evacuation

Policy

1. Whenever the fire alarm sounds, everyone is to leave the building and wait in the designated waiting area, even if it is a false alarm or a drill.
2. Ministry Personnel, Church Leadership, and selected members of the congregation are to be trained in Emergency Evacuation Policies and Procedures and must be prepared to assist in the event of an Emergency Evacuation. These Ministry Personnel and members of the congregation are to be referred to as Fire Marshals.
3. Ministry Personnel must not wait for Parents to pick up their Children when there is an alarm. Rather, they must immediately vacate the building with the Children and Youth and go to the designated location.
4. Congregation members are to immediately vacate the building. Parents are to be notified to meet their Children at the designated locations outside of the building. A fire alarm does not negate the need for appropriate sign-out and pickup of Children.
5. The congregation shall periodically conduct a "Fire Drill" in order to practice safe evacuation of the building, according to the procedures.
6. The Board, in coordination with Ministry Personnel, must be responsible to:
   a. Assure the periodic training of Ministry Personnel, Church Leadership, and additional selected members of the congregation in Emergency Evacuation Policies and Procedures;
   b. Schedule and carry out periodic "Fire Drills;"
   c. Periodically review and update the Emergency Evacuation Policies and Procedures.
7. Exits are to be maintained free of snow, ice and obstructions.
8. In the event that the Fire Department is called to the scene, the Fire Department (and other Emergency Responders) have authority to determine a course of action. Ministry Personnel, church members, and building occupants are to follow their directives.

Plan

- ○ Emergency Evacuation policies and procedures have been drafted and are updated periodically.
- ○ A designated area outside of the building has been identified for parents to pick up or meet their children.
- ○ Exits are regularly maintained and free of any obstructions.
- ○ Ministry Personnel, Church Leadership, and other selected members of the congregation have been trained in the Emergency Evacuation policies and procedures.
- ○ "Fire Drills" are conducted periodically.

Protection

In 2014, Canada saw 19,062 structural fires, occurring in residences, places of business, institutions, and other buildings.[1]

These fires can be caused by anything from faulty wiring to arson and is a risk that presents itself regardless of where you are located. Many buildings have a legal responsibility to have a fire safety plan. These plans are often required to be approved by the Chief Fire Official before it is implemented by the owner of the building. A part of these plans include scheduling regular Fire Drills to educate all occupants of the building on a safe exit plan in the event of an emergency. "Conducting effective fire drills helps building owners, property management and others responsible for fire safety within a building to:

- Provide scheduled opportunities for comprehensive fire emergency response training for supervisory staff and others;
- Determine whether supervisory staff competently respond in a timely manner to carry out their duties in accordance with the emergency fire and evacuation procedures;
- Determine whether sufficient supervisory staff are provided to carry out their duties;
- Assess the ongoing effectiveness of the emergency procedures under different fire scenario conditions, and
- Comply with [your local] Fire Code's mandatory requirement for conducting fire drills."[2]

"Examples for content for the plan may include instructions such as:

If you discover a fire:

- Leave the fire area immediately.
- Activate the fire alarm and/or alert other staff.
- If safe to do so, assist anyone in immediate danger.
- Close all doors behind you to confine the fire.
- Use exit stairwells to leave the building."[3]

You may want to conduct an audit of your organization to determine what resources you have available, what combustible or flammable materials may be in the building, what precautions are currently being taken to avoid fire risks, what fire alarms are in place and if they are in proper working order, have fire extinguishers been inspected, etc. There are many things that organizations may overlook – a practice that may not be in accordance with your local Fire Code. The risk of a fire is real and present, and to do your due diligence as the owner of the building, or a regular occupant of the building, you must ensure that you are compliant with the requirements of your local Fire Code and that you are practicing the best measures to protect those within your congregation.

---

1 (Statistics Canada, 2017)
2 (Office of the Fire Marshal and Emergency Management, 2016)
3 (Canadian Centre for Occupational Health and Safety, 2021)

Technology Concerns

A. Online Forums and Gatherings
B. Social Media
C. Internet and Computer Use
D. Photography and Video Recording

A. Online Forums and Gatherings

Policy

1. Online Forums and Gatherings must be hosted by the church's licensed and operated accounts only, no personal accounts may be used.

2. The church's licensed and operated accounts must be accessible to more than one Ministry Lead (passwords, usernames and email credentials).

3. To host an Online Forum/Gathering, Ministry Personnel must first secure permission in writing from the Ministry Lead overseeing the department or their Supervisor. Hosts must be screened and trained according to the Recruitment process for Ministry Personnel.

4. An Letter of Informed Consent must be prepared and submitted to the Parent prior to the event. Parents must sign and submit the Letter of Informed Consent to allow a student to participate utilizing an electronic signature platform (i.e., SmartWaiver or Docusign).

    a. Parents will be provided with an opt-in option on the Letter of Informed Consent to allow their Child(ren) to use a webcam while a session is being recorded.

    b. Parents will be notified of the documentation management and retention policies outlined in the church's Plan to Protect® policies and procedures.

    c. Any Children or Youth that do not have expressed, written permission from a Parent to use the webcam will not be permitted to do so.

5. For the duration of the meeting, Ministry Personnel will have the video platform in 'Moderator' mode to restrict the video and webcam sharing of other attendees.

    a. If the 'Moderator' mode is unavailable on the video platform, or the church deems it beneficial for attendees to use a webcam, only Children and Youth that have expressed written consent from a Parent to be recorded will be permitted to use a webcam. Those that do not have consent to be recorded will not be permitted to use their webcams.

6. Ministry Personnel will either:

    a. Remain on the video platform until all attendees have left before closing the session; OR,

    b. Close the session to end the meeting for all attendees.

7. Ministry Personnel are encouraged to use videos, fun games and songs to share with families, to limit direct attendee communication.

8. All persons (Children, Youth, Parents, Ministry Personnel) will be educated on the expectations for the use of the online platforms, both video and social media, to encourage safe and productive use.

9. If Ministry Personnel is found to be contacting Children or Youth through personal accounts, they will be subject to disciplinary action by the church.

10. In the event that conversation with a Child or Youth moves beyond regular program activities, Ministry Personnel must inform Church Leadership and provide a copy of the conversation immediately. Church Leadership will follow the procedure outlined in the Plan to Protect® manual for Suicide, Substance Abuse and Self-Injury. Procedures may include:

    a. Reporting to the proper authorities; or,

    b. Informing the Parents of the Child or Youth.

Policy continued...

For Children Grades 1-6:

In order to create a safe experience, the church must:

1. Maintain at least TWO screened, unrelated Adults (in accordance with the Recruitment and Screening section in the Plan to Protect® manual) in the church's Gatherings. This is a practice under the church's Plan to Protect® policy in all Children's ministry programs.
2. The church's host will be recording the program. The recordings are not to be posted online and will only be used for security and resource purposes.
3. Attendance is to be taken at each Forum/Gathering.
4. A Parent must be in the room at the beginning and at the end of a call. This is our check in and out process.
5. Parents must remain in the same room as their Children when they are on the call. Children must not be left in front of the computer alone in an isolated room.
6. Parents are requested to ensure that the call is played on a computer/device with speakers instead of earphones/headphones.
7. The church's Gatherings are not permanent to facilitate chat rooms. Parents are to be required to check in their Children in each Zoom Gathering. Hence, Children are not to be able to join the church's [Name of Platform, i.e., Zoom] Gatherings outside our pre-set program time.
8. Upon completion of the call, the attendance record and the recording must be sent to the Ministry Lead of the department.

For Youth Grades 7-12:

In order to create a safe experience, the church must:

1. Maintain at least TWO screened, unrelated Adults (in accordance with the Recruitment and Screening section in the Plan to Protect® manual) in the church's Gatherings. This is a practice under the church's Plan to Protect® policy in all our Youth ministry programs.
2. The church's host will be recording the program. The recordings are not to be posted online and will only be used for security and resource purposes.
3. Attendance is to be taken at each Forum/Gathering.
4. The church's Gatherings are not permanent chat rooms. Hence, Youth are not to be able to join the church's [Name of Platform, i.e., Zoom] Gatherings outside our pre-set program time.
5. Upon completion of the call, the attendance record and the recording must be sent to the Ministry Lead of the department and retained permanently.

Plan

- A licensed account has been created for the use of the church and login information has been provided to more than one Ministry Lead.

- Written permission has been secured from Church Leadership before hosting an Online Gathering.

- Parents have been notified of the documentation management and retention policies outlined in the church's Plan to Protect® policies and procedures via Letters of Informed Consent.

- Parents have granted written permission for their children to participate in programs online, including the guidelines for monitoring activity online.

- The video and security settings of the Gathering have been switched to 'Moderator' mode.

- Attendance records and recordings have been sent to the Ministry Lead of the department.

Protection

Online Forums and Gatherings provided a way for us to connect with students during times of self-isolation and quarantines. However, this form of connection is high-risk. For example, online platforms could provide the opportunity for communication outside of program activities, or unsupervised and private chats, or a child could be exposed to inappropriate imagery though screen sharing. We have heard of too many incidences of uninvited guests crashing (Zoom bombing) an online event exposing participants to harassment, discrimination and inappropriate material. Furthermore, since video conferencing takes place in a digital space, it may be easy to forget that isolation is a risk factor online as well as in person, and adequate supervision is just as necessary.

While a general policy for online interaction is useful, each platform comes with its unique features and unique risks. Understanding the platform that is being used in your programs, knowing how to activate all the safety features, and identifying the associated vulnerabilities is an important part of preparation and abuse prevention.

B. Social Media

Policy

1. Church members, adherents and Ministry Personnel are encouraged to demonstrate and model purity, integrity, transparency and accountability with all communications including those noted above.
2. Email or text communication with Children 12 years of age and under is prohibited.
3. Youth Ministry Personnel will agree to allow the Ministry Lead or designate access to their Social Media networks in order to facilitate regular supervision.
4. Communication with Youth 13 years of age and older via Social Media, telephone and texting is permitted under the following conditions:
   a. Communication with a Youth via email, text, Instagram, Snapchat, Facebook Messenger, or other Social Media networks will be monitored closely and only used with written Parental permission (Appendix 15).
   b. To avoid isolation on social media, one of the following must take place:
      i. Ministry Personnel may communicate with Youth via email with written Parental permission (Appendix 15). The Parents will be copied on all communications; or
      ii. In cases where Ministry Personnel contact Youth via email, text or Social Media without copying Parents, they must include another Ministry Personnel in the communications; or
      iii. Use a public Social Media option (wall-to-wall, church-owned pages and accounts). In either case, Parental permission to contact Youth directly is required.
   c. Ministry Personnel will limit their online communications with Youth via Social Media to daytime hours (8:00am-11:00pm).
   d. Online communication will not involve video messaging (FaceTime, Skype, etc.) in any form, unless it is a training post or group conference call approved by the Ministry Lead.
   e. In the rare occasion that a conversation with a Youth moves beyond communication of information, Ministry Personnel will notify their Ministry Lead immediately and submit a copy of the conversation to the Ministry Lead. Ministry Personnel will request the Youth to continue the conversation in person with the Ministry Lead.

Plan

- ◯ Approval for communication with youth outside of programs has been obtained and parameters for these interactions have been discussed with parents.

- ◯ The Board has established a philosophy and parameters for social media and communication.

- ◯ Parental permission has been secured from parents to communicate via computers, text, internet and social media.

- ◯ Ministry Personnel are using church-owned accounts to communicate with Children and Youth.

- ◯ At least two members of Church Leadership have access to the church-owned platform (username, password, etc.) and monitor use regularly.

Protection

The world has become witness to a technological era, in which new platforms for social media are continuously being developed. Social media provides us with numerous methods of communication, which can strengthen the relationships we have with one another. According to the 2019 Emarsys Report, approximately 3.2 billion people worldwide use a form of social media. With the increase of advancements in the way we communicate with each other, we also see increased risk among those using these platforms, often unsupervised. We have become witness to a new channel of bullying, online predators, and promotional material for recreational drug and alcohol use.

We cannot control what our children and youth see all the time—social media has provided many private avenues for children and youth to access outside of the public eye. Instead, churches should lead by example for those in our care and promote healthy digital footprints and lifestyles. Insurance companies also require that parameters be put in place for ministry personnel serving with the vulnerable sector.

"The internet is a fundamental part of daily life which means adults and children must be smart digital citizens."[1] Organizations should educate their leaders on the dangers of social media use, as children and youth are being exposed to growing risks communicated through their private accounts.

"With each new advancement in computer and telecommunications technology, access to new sources of information and cultural experience expands. However, as this access increases, so does the opportunity for predators to gain access to you and your child's private information. The fact makes it vital for you (especially parents) to understand the various dangers of online access and how to monitor information changes that may result from issues online."[1]

The technological era has brought the introduction of apps, social networking, online gaming, and video sharing, which present a number of growing risks including:

- "When creating a profile, some services require certain fields be completed but allow users to choose the information entered into others. In most cases, there are no restrictions on what can be added to a profile, including personal information and photos/videos.
- Teens may accept friend requests from individuals they have not met in person. Adults looking to victimize teens can quickly turn conversations sexual.
- Teens may be bullied or stalked by peers or other users on social networking sites.
- Once a message is sent or a post is made, control over that message or post is lost. Personal information, pictures and videos can be easily saved and/or shared with others.
- A teen may engage in private conversations, share private information or private photos, unaware of the lasting consequences. Once private information or material is sent, control over what happens with the information or material is lost.
- Some anonymous messaging apps allow teens to engage in conversations with strangers easily.
- The history of the communication through some apps may not be saved. Some chat and messaging apps may log the conversations but allow them to be easily deleted with the swipe of a finger.
- Teens can be easily influenced and coerced into situations where they quickly find themselves in over their head."[2]

---

1 (Rembert, 2020)
2 (ProtectKidsOnline.ca, 2020)

C. Internet and Computer Use

Policy

1. Church Leadership are to determine who will have access to the church Wi-Fi. Passwords are not to be distributed without permission from Church Leadership

2. Public computers are to be placed in open areas where the screen is easily visible. Users are to be held accountable through the use of sign-in and sign-out sheets, and/or a user password.

3. Internet filters are to be installed on each computer to limit access to certain types of content.

4. The Church Leadership are to appoint an authorized computer system's individual who is to periodically review the browser history as well as the documents downloaded onto church-owned computers.

5. An 'Acceptable Computer Use Policy' are to be developed and posted in the computer centre. (Appendix 27)

6. Ministry Personnel should closely monitor the use of their church owned devices and not allow minors to use these devices.

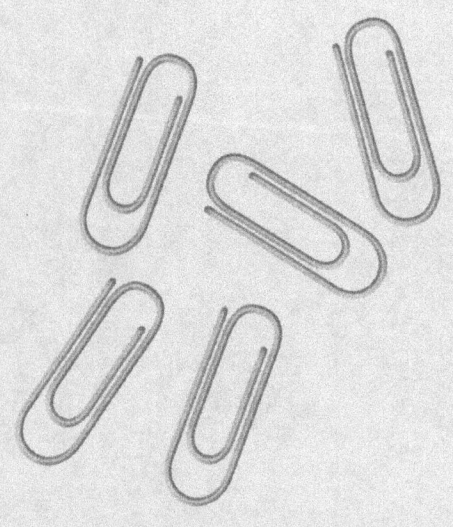

Plan

- ○ Computer areas have been set up to promote visibility and accountability, with clear lines of vision to all screens.

- ○ All computers require a sign-in system and Internet filters have been installed.

- ○ An authorized computer system's individual has been appointed to monitor the Internet filters and review browser history and downloaded documents.

- ○ Ministry Personnel have been appointed the responsibility of monitoring and supervising the computer centre.

- ○ An 'Acceptable Computer Use Policy' has been posted.

- ○ Approval for communication with children outside of programs have been obtained and parameters for these interactions have been discussed with parents.

Protection

We cannot control what our children and youth see all the time, but by setting up guidelines for our church, and through leading by example, we can help our church community develop healthy lifestyles.

"Child safety on the internet is everyone's business. Children must understand, in an age appropriate way, the risks they run on the Internet. And parents, teachers and caregivers must know the dangers as well."[1]

"In 1998, there were over 3,000 reports of child sexual abuse imagery online. Just over a decade later, yearly reports soared past 100,000. In 2014, that number surpassed 1 million for the first time. In 2018, there were 18.4 million, more than one-third of the total ever reported. Those reports included over 45 million images and videos flagged as child sexual abuse. Images were shared over Facebook Messenger, Google and Bing search engines, and cloud storage services."[2]

The prevalence of pornography is on the rise. One way that we demonstrate our love and care for each other is to protect each other from the dangers of pornography.

"There are a few risks for children who use the internet or other online services. Teenagers are particularly at risk because they often go online unsupervised and are more likely than younger children to participate in online discussions regarding companionship, relationships, or sexual activity. Some risks are:

- **Exposure to Inappropriate Material**
A child may be exposed to inappropriate material that is sexual, hateful, or violent in nature, or encourages activities that are dangerous or illegal. Children could seek out such material but may also come across it on the web via chat areas, social networking sites, email, or even instant messaging if they're not looking for it.

- **Physical Molestation**
A child might provide information or arrange an encounter that could risk his or her safety or the safety of other family members. In some cases child molesters have used chat areas, email, and instant messages to gain a child's confidence and then arrange a face-to-face meeting.

- **Harassment and Bullying**
A child might encounter messages via chat, email, on their social networking site or their cellular telephones that are belligerent, demeaning, or harassing. 'Bullies,' typically other young people, often use the Internet to bother their victims.

- **Viruses and Hackers**
A child could download a file containing a virus that could damage the computer or increase the risk of a 'hacker' gaining remote access to the computer; jeopardizing the family's privacy; and, perhaps, jeopardizing the family's safety.

- **Legal and Financial**
A child could do something that has negative legal or financial consequences such as giving out a parent's credit card number or doing something that could get them in trouble with the law or school officials. Legal issues aside, children should be taught good 'netiquette' which means to avoid being inconsiderate, mean, or rude."[3]

---

1 (Paul Gillespie, https://www.paulgillespiecounsulting.com/services_ParentsChildren.php)
2 (The US National Center for Missing and Exploited Children, reported in NY Times, 2019)
3 (Magid, 2003)

D. Photography and Video Recording

Policy

With a desire to capture memorable moments at the church, photography and video recording are to be closely monitored by Church Leadership. The AV Department and Ministry Departments must abide by the following guidelines:

1. Photography and video recording are to be done by designated Ministry Personnel who have been screened and trained in safeguarding policies and procedures.
2. For public church activities including services where video recording is to be done in the sanctuary, and with the church family together, it is required that signage be posted notifying those in attendance that the event will be captured on film. Individuals can either stay out of the line of the camera or, if necessary, opt out of the event.
3. For all Children and Youth ministry activities and programs, Parental permission must be secured prior to taking photographs of Children and Youth. Parental permission must be secured on an annual basis on the Registration Forms (Appendix 15);
   a. No photographs of Children or Youth are to be taken without prior written approval.
   b. No photographs are to be posted on the church's website, Facebook, Instagram, or other online social networks without Parental permission and only on sites monitored closely by Church Leadership.
4. To easily identify Children and Youth that are not to have their picture taken, they are to be clearly identified with either a sticker on their nametag or with an arm band. All effort must be made to adhere to the Parent's request.
5. No photographs of Children or Youth are to be tagged or labeled with the name of the individual at any time, including but not limited to bulletin boards, newsletters, websites, social media sites, or church bulletins.
6. When archiving and filing photographs and videos of Children and Youth, only those with written Parental permission can be kept for future use. Written permission forms must be kept permanently on file in the church office. Archived photos must be labeled and cross-referenced with Parental permission forms.

Plan

- ○ Only designated Ministry Personnel are responsible for photographing and video recording.
- ○ Parental permission has been secured for the current year on the Registration Forms.
- ○ Children and Youth who do not have Parental permission to be photographed or videotaped have been easily identified on their nametag.
- ○ Photos and videos of Children and Youth have not been tagged or labelled with any identifying information.
- ○ Archived photos and videos of Children and Youth have been labeled, cross-referenced with the Parental permission form, and secured on file in the church office.

Protection

As we live in a rapidly developing technological era, the sharing of media has become much more of a norm. With the ease of having phones capable of taking and storing hundreds of photos in minutes, organizations are tasked with determining their rights to take, use and publish photos of persons attending programming, and what is needed to be able to do so.

Rights to take and publish photos differ if they are for personal use, or for organizational or commercial use such as being posted on bulletins or websites. Canada's provinces follow different privacy legislation, which determine the rights and responsibilities that organizations have when taking photos and videos for commercial purposes. "For commercial activities, PIPEDA [Personal Information Protection and Electronic Documents Act] requires consent to distribute photographs depicting identifiable individuals, similar to its requirement for collecting personal information … If you are photographing people in the course of commercial activities, you should obtain permission from all subjects that will be identifiable within your photographs. For any type of use, you should obtain permission if you intend to publish or exhibit your photographs. This includes online distribution."[1]

The protection of a child's right to privacy is not only protected by provincial legislation such as PIPEDA, Freedom of Information and Protection of Privacy Act, and Personal Information Protection Act, but also through the international UN Convention on the Rights of the Child, which specifically protects children's privacy. Through this legislation, the Office of the Privacy Commissioner of Canada has "also taken the position that in all but exceptional cases, consent for the collection, use and disclosure of personal information of children under the age of 13 must be obtained from their parents or guardians."[2]

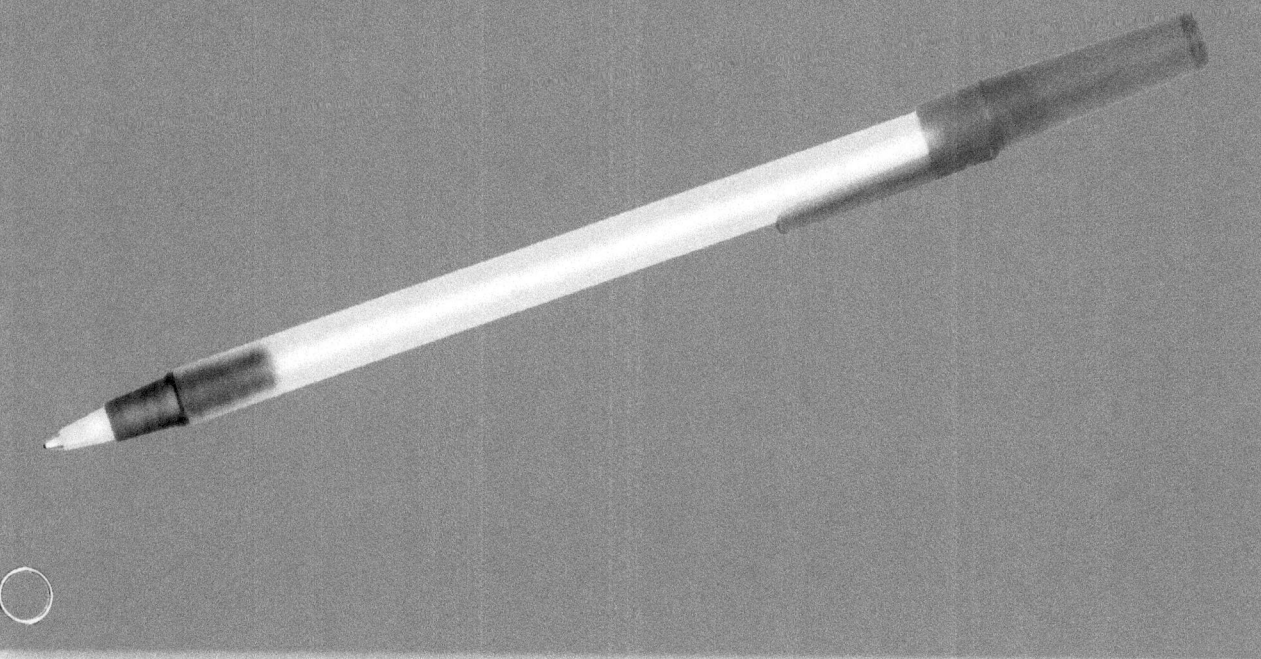

---

1 (Samuelson-Glushko Canadian Internet Policy and Public Interest Clinic (CIPPIC), n.d.)
2 (Zeeshan, 2019)

Facility Precautions

A. Modifying Your Facility
B. Security Systems and Cameras

A. Modifying Your Facility

Policy

1. Recognizing that there are many storage areas within the church, elevated precautions must be taken to monitor these areas. Storage closets and doors must be locked at all times except when in use. When doors are unlocked, additional Hall Monitors will be on duty to monitor these areas.

2. All windows in doors in Children's program areas are never to be covered in any way so as to keep clear sight lines into rooms.

3. Washroom facilities in the preschool area are for the sole use of Children.

4. Nursery doors are to be secured from the inside.

5. All electrical outlets are to be kept covered when not in use in the nursery and toddler classrooms.

6. Doors of rooms and closets must be locked when not in use during Children's programs.

For Accessibility:

1. Install ramps and automatic doors.

2. Consider elevators or stair lifts.

3. Provide handicap seating and space for wheelchairs.

4. Make washrooms accessible with wide doors, space for assistive devices, low sinks, and handrails.

5. Place signage and program materials accessible to those with limited vision.

6. Accommodate those with hearing loss.

Plan

- ○ All windows and doors are uncovered, to maintain a direct line of sight into classrooms.
- ○ There is a designated washroom for Children's use.
- ○ Classroom doors have locks on the inside of the rooms.
- ○ Electrical outlets are covered in the nursery and toddler classrooms.
- ○ Doors of closets and rooms that are not in use are locked.

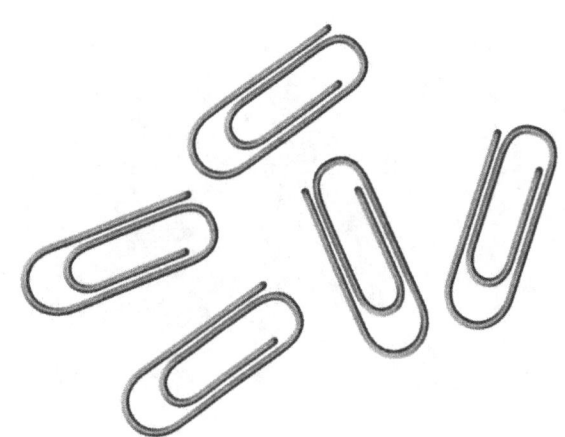

Protection

Children are naturally curious with an inherent desire to explore new spaces and try new things. While curiosity has its benefits, children are more vulnerable to engaging in dangerous activities without awareness. Even though we might think of this as applying only to babies and toddlers, accidental injury is the leading cause of death for children and youth up to the age of 14, with more than a third of these injuries happening at home, somewhere that we would naturally want to consider safe for our loved ones.[1]

While it is impossible to avoid all threats to injury, churches should take it upon themselves to practice safe premise modifications to best avoid these threats. Childproofing is not only a safety measure for the home, but also for your building.

Churches should identify high-risk zones within the building and be prepared with the tools to safeguard them. Something as simple as covering electrical outlets is both easy and inexpensive and can go a long way.

Having washroom facilities that are accessible and designed for protection is another way to ensure safety. Windows on washroom doors enable adults to assist young children while in view of other adults, and child-size toilets allow children to use the washroom with greater independence.

Inserting locks on the inside of classrooms is also a great way to protect our children by making sure that no one enters the room unnoticed. In the case of younger children, a radio transmitter can also be used to monitor activity in another room. Additional supervision by hall monitors and security within isolated areas of the building is also recommended to provide children with greater protection.

Furthermore, if facilities are being rented, we would recommend arriving early and doing a safety walk-through to remove hazardous and unsafe materials and objects. For example, if closets and storage areas do not have locks, prop the doors open.

Keep in mind that this list of suggestions is not exhaustive. Churches should always pay attention to the safety and security issues of their facilities and routinely monitor any risks.

1 (Nemours KidsHealth, n.d.)

B. Security Systems and Cameras

Policy

1. Security cameras are provided for the purpose of elevated safeguarding precautions, and to aid in investigations.

2. As the purpose of Plan to Protect® is to prevent injury, harm and abuse from happening, security cameras that are installed for recording purposes are not to be considered a replacement for Hall Monitors or elevated supervision.

3. Security cameras that are installed for the purpose of monitoring in real time, must be staffed during all activities and programs where Children, Youth and Vulnerable Adults are present.

Plan

- ○ Security cameras are installed and operating at all times.

- ○ Cameras are positioned at entrances and within any classrooms.

- ○ Ministry personnel have been scheduled with the task of monitoring security cameras.

- ○ Ministry personnel have been notified that they are not to depend on security cameras for safeguarding purposes.

Protection

Even if the church hires enough ministry personnel, supervision of children and youth always comes with certain risks. It is difficult for church leaders to always have their eyes on each and every child or youth. That is why installing security cameras within the church, especially in busy areas, is a good way to ensure safety for everyone.

When deciding on the type of security camera to install, answer the following question: Is the purpose for monitoring in real time for prevention purposes, or to be able to access recordings for investigative purposes? Cameras can help to monitor who is entering or leaving the facilities, and can be extremely useful in the case of a missing or lost child, allowing us to quickly locate individuals we are looking for. Other cameras allow us to look back on any situations in the case of a liability issue. There are many options available, as some cameras only provide the option of seven-day recordings, some others provide a 30-day recording.

Security cameras should not be the ultimate security measure in place. Supervision from staff, an appropriate ratio of volunteers, as well as other architectural precautions mentioned in this manual should be carefully implemented. However, security cameras provide an advantage of being able to view the facilities from a different perspective, and also record activities to review at a later date. They are an additional preventative measure that will benefit the church in many ways and should be properly installed regardless.

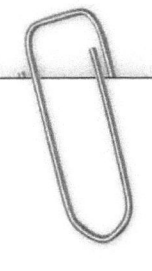

High Risk Activities

A. High Risk Activities
B. Transportation
C. Off-Site Event Planning
   a. Shared Activities
   b. Home Groups
D. Special Events and Overnight Policies
E. Shower and Locker Room Guidelines
F. Overnight Trips and Housing (Including Conferences, Camps, Hotels and Motels)
G. Billeting and Hosting

A. High Risk Activities

Policy

1. High risk activities include each of the following:

    a. Activities identified as having a higher risk, such as off-site events, water activities, extreme sports, online events, overnight events, billeting, transportation, mission trips, and small groups, and;

    b. Irregular activities that take place, including one-off events, yearly events, and new activities.

2. High risk activities that fall into the categories above may only take place under the following criteria:

    a. A risk assessment must be completed prior to the event;

    b. Permission must be granted from the Church Board or designate;

    c. Parents must be provided a Letter of Informed Consent one week in advance of the event;

    d. A qualified instructor or lifeguard has been appointed; and

    e. Ratios have been modified to provide elevated supervision.

3. In our church, we are committed to protecting Children, Youth and Vulnerable Adults. The following activities are prohibited:

    a. Uncontrolled free falls or jumps that exceed 8 feet;

    b. Driving at high speeds; and

    c. Minors driving all-terrain vehicles or motorized vehicles.

Plan

○ A list of any forbidden activities has been determined by the Board.

○ All high-risk activities have clear procedures or require signed approval from the Church Board or designate.

○ Anyone leading a high-risk activity has access to the appropriate procedures to ensure safety.

Protection

Some activities naturally come with a higher risk than others. In order to mitigate the increased risk, additional procedures should be put into place. Some activities are so high risk that your leadership may decide to simply abstain from those activities. This can be communicated in this policy to ensure that decisions on risk are properly documented and shared to all ministry personnel.

In some cases, you might find you engage in a high risk activity often enough that you build a policy or procedures for that activity. You can include that activity in this section. The following pages contain some of the higher-risk activities that we regularly see churches engage in.

B. Transportation

1. When planning off-site activities, Parents are to be encouraged to drop off and pick up their Children and Youth at the event location. For out of town events, commercial school carriers are to be used whenever possible.
2. Our first concern in transportation is the safety of the passengers. Drivers must obey all the rules of the road including the speed limits. Reckless or unsafe driving will not be tolerated.
3. When not using commercial carriers, all Ministry Personnel drivers transporting on behalf of the church during church activities must complete the following prior to an event:
    a. Be pre-approved by the Ministry Lead;
    b. Provide a copy of their valid driver's license;
    c. Provide a copy of their current automobile insurance policy;
    d. Have a minimum of five (5) years driving experience in good standing.
4. The number of occupants in vehicles transporting Children, Youth and Vulnerable Adults during church sponsored activities must not exceed the number of seat belts and each passenger must be in age-appropriate safety restraints. Seatbelts must be worn by everyone and remain fastened at all times the vehicle is in operation.
5. Children, Youth and Vulnerable Adults must never be left alone in a vehicle. At least two (2) Ministry Personnel must be in each vehicle transporting Children during church sponsored activities. Exceptions to this policy should only happen when Ministry Leads and Parents are informed, and there is more than one Child or Youth in the vehicle, avoiding isolation.
6. A copy of the 'Trips and Off-site Travel Form' (Appendix 22) will accompany each driver with the original left in the church office and filed permanently. The form contains information consisting of:
    a. Names and phone numbers of all participants
    b. Location of event and phone number(s)
    c. Drivers and vehicles involved
7. When transportation is being provided by your church, an Letter of Informed Consent for Transportation must be signed by Parents of minors (Appendix 23). The travel forms must be maintained and filed in the church office. Forms are to be kept on file permanently.

Plan

- ○ A copy of a valid driver's license and insurance coverage has been provided by all drivers.

- ○ Ministry Personnel have been informed of the need for drivers to have a minimum of five years driving history in good standing.

- ○ The Ministry Lead has ensured that supervision in cars complies with Ministry Personnel staffing guidelines.

- ○ Ministry Personnel have been advised to travel in as few vehicles as possible, and have been advised the risk is greatly reduced by using commercial buses with professional drivers.

- ○ Photocopied Authorization Forms have been sent with the driver and originals filed in the church office. Plans have been made to keep originals on file permanently.

- ○ Photocopied Travel Forms have been sent with the Ministry Lead for the duration of the event and originals have been kept on file permanently in the church office.

Protection

Transportation and safety considerations go hand-in-hand with liability considerations. By ensuring the safety of those travelling on the road, we are also protecting ourselves and the church from liability issues. For example, taking into account something as simple as the number of vehicles used to transport a group of students can change the probability of having an accident or liability issue. In addition, leaving transportation in the hands of an experienced driver, rather than an inexperienced driver, is also another easy step to taking the right precautions.

It is also important to note that if church leadership waives the recommended five year driving history policy and decides to utilize any youth drivers with less experience, parents must be notified of the increased risk and provided the opportunity to have their children not be driven by those individuals. Please check with the church's insurance company and church leadership prior to making this decision.

In addition, if you are considering taking on the role of a driver yourself rather than hiring another individual, it is often the case that: "...the church's insurance covers only the church for its legal liability, but does not cover you as the owner or driver of a personal vehicle. Your own insurance may not cover you if you are driving individuals for an event like this and/or you may not have sufficient third party liability coverage amount for carrying a carload or vanload of passengers."[1] If the driver does not own the vehicle they are driving, and the insurance is in the name of another person, we recommend the owner of the vehicle also grant written permission to use the vehicle for this purpose, as their insurance is primary. Please remember to check with the insurance agent or broker to make sure you are covered properly.

---

1 (Robertson Hall Insurance, 2007)

C. Off-Site Event Planning

Policy

1. Prior to any off-site trip the Ministry Lead must complete a risk assessment. The results of the risk assessment must be provided when securing approval to host the off-site event.

2. All off-site trips must be pre-approved by a Pastor.

3. A Letter of Informed Consent for the off-site trip will be given to the Parents no less than one week prior to the event. Information must include the exact location of the event, emergency phone numbers, a list of Adult Ministry Personnel attending the event, and any inherent risks of the event.

4. If there is travel involved or there are additional elements of risk to the activity, Parents will be informed of risks and required to provide clear permission for each element of risk.

5. Sufficient supervision by at least two screened Adults is required to ensure protection and safety for all involved.

6. Copies of Letters of Informed Consent, medical authorizations, and any additional Registration Forms for each Student must be kept on hand at each event. (Appendix 19)

7. Attendance of all Ministry Personnel, Children, Youth, and Occasional Observers must be recorded on the Trip and Off-Site Travel Forms. (Appendix 22) The Travel Form must be maintained and filed in the church office. Forms will be kept on file permanently.

Plan

- ○ A risk assessment has been completed.

- ○ All off-site trips have been pre-approved by a Pastor.

- ○ Written communication has been distributed to parents a minimum of one week in advance to off-site events with location, phone number(s) and attending Ministry Personnel.

- ○ Letters of Informed Consent have been distributed.

- ○ Supervision requirements have been met for off-site trips.

- ○ Ministry Personnel have been informed to take photocopies of authorization and consent forms along on each outing.

- ○ Travel and Attendance forms have been completed on all attending Youth and Ministry Personnel and filed permanently in the church office.

Protection

Similar to your responsibilities to children and youth attending programs at your premises, the church is responsible for what happens, whether it be on-site or off. From the time the child or youth is dropped off into your care, to the time that they are picked up, you are responsible and liable. As risk increases for off-site activities, reducing that risk becomes even more important. To take the additional precautions for safety and risk management will mean protecting yourself and protecting those in your care. Ensure that you follow proper steps in assessing, organizing and conducting off-site programs by knowing where you are going, the inherent risks presented by the activity or location, the transportation that is being arranged, what will happen when you are there, and ensure that everything is communicated in advance to both the parents and the ministry leads.

We recommend that all documentation, including Letters of Informed Consent (Appendix 19) and attendance forms be taken and maintained permanently. Maintaining documentation may seem cumbersome; we encourage you to refer to Documentation Management to help customize your information management system with fields that will help you track the information needed for Plan to Protect®.

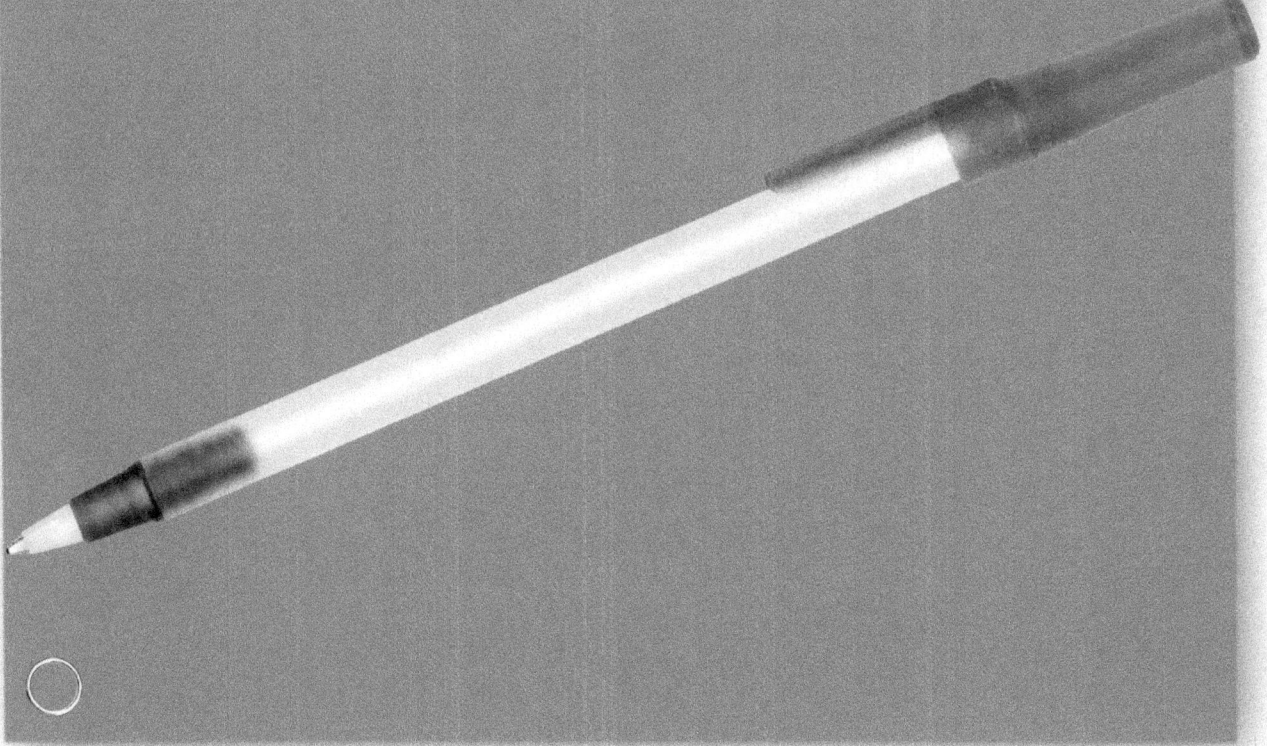

a. Off-Site Event Planning: Shared Activities

Policy

1. In the case that outside users, members, adherents or renters are granted permission to use the facility for activities involving Children, Youth and Vulnerable Adults, that are not direct ministries and activities of the Church, it is required that they provide a certificate of insurance, with no less than $2,000,000 Commercial General Liability coverage with abuse coverage and the Church be named as additional insured. The user or renter is also required to demonstrate that they have a full Child/Youth protection policy and protocol in place. If they lack an Abuse Prevention Policy, the Church will refer them to Plan to Protect® to secure their own copy of the *Plan to Protect®* manual.

2. In the case that the Church partners with other churches, agencies or community groups for the delivery of a joint activity or event with Children and/or Youth, the leadership of the Church requires that their insurance agent be consulted during the planning stage, to determine the risks, insurance coverage and shared liability. The Program Leader is required to obtain written opinion from the insurance agent acknowledging the status of insurance coverage for these joint activities.

Plan

- A certificate of insurance is requested from any outside user, member, adherent or renter using the facilities of the church.

- A Child/Youth protection policy and protocol is in place for any outside user or renter.

- If not, outside users are referred to Plan to Protect®.

- Leaders of the church are included in the planning stage of all joint activities and events with other churches, agencies or community groups.

- Known risks, insurance coverage and shared liability concerns are consulted with the church's insurance agent.

- Written opinion about insurance coverage from the church's insurance agent is obtained prior to any joint activities or events.

Protection

The facility of any church is meant to be a safe space for its members and especially the children and youth who attend the church's programs. Therefore, to ensure the safety of the space, those who use the space should be trusted people.

Benefits to renting out church property may include additional revenue for the church, especially if the property is underutilized during the week, or expansion of the church's vision and purpose, allowing the church to reach out to more people in the community. However, even though allowing outside users to use or rent facilities has its advantages, it is a process that requires extreme care and foresight.

Outside users must have sufficient financial resources and insurance protection to address damage or injuries resulting from negligent actions or lack of proper supervision on the church's premises. Users must take responsibility for the issues that arise during their use of the property if they wish to utilize the space. Improper usage by under-resourced groups could become a financial burden for the church and lead to liability concerns.

Renters should be able to provide a certificate of insurance of at least $2,000,000 (recommend $5,000,000) Commercial General Liability coverage and the church must be named as an additional insured. They should have a protection protocol and policy in place and if they do not, the church will should refer them to Plan to Protect® in order for them to obtain a manual. This also helps the church maintain arm's length from those activities.

Finally, aside from outside user groups, the church may also host shared activities or events with other churches and community groups. Although it may seem simpler and easier to trust these groups, it is still important that insurance agents are consulted regarding liability concerns. Otherwise, it is possible to run into a situation where liability is involved and find yourself unsure of who should be held accountable or the insurance companies debating over who is primary. Take the appropriate steps ahead of time and make sure that whatever happens at the church is done under proper counsel from your insurance company, guidelines, and awareness.

b. Off-Site Event Planning: Home Groups

Policy

The following protocols is to be adhered to for all group meetings hosted in homes:

1. Host homes and families must be approved by a Pastor.

2. At no time should Children be left unsupervised. One of the following two criteria for supervision must be in place:

   a. The Child must stay with the Parent at all times; or

   b. If Children are separated from their Parents, two Screened Adults must be assigned to supervise the Children; or one Screened Adult with the second Screened Adult acting in the role of a Hall Monitor to check on the group frequently throughout the event.

3. Children are never to be left unattended or left in the care of only Youth child care worker(s). There must always be a minimum of one Screened Adult and a Hall Monitor supervising the Children.

4. Programming for Children is to be planned in advance in conjunction with Church Leadership. Prior to each event, Parents should be notified of the activities that the Children will participate in. This includes but is not limited to verifying appropriate games, computer activity, and screen activity (i.e., TV, video, Netflix).

5. Children are **not** to be left alone with Unscreened Adults or Youth.

6. Home Group Leaders will be responsible to:

   a. Take attendance each time a group meets as part of a Cell/Home Group;

   b. The Attendance Form must include the date, location and the names of all Adults and Children in attendance;

   c. The attendance must include the age or grade of Children, participant's first and last name, full names of all Ministry Personnel and Occasional Observers attending on that date.

7. Each Home Group Leader must remit this Attendance Form within one week to the Pastor or Ministry Lead or to the church office.

8. These Attendance Forms are to be kept on file permanently.

plan

- ○ Host home has been pre-approved by a pastor.
- ○ Screened Adults are present to supervise Children or Youth when separated from their parents.
- ○ Parents have been informed in advance of the activities the Children or Youth will participate in.
- ○ Attendance has been taken.
- ○ Attendance Forms have been provided to the pastor or Ministry Lead.
- ○ Attendance Forms are filed permanently.

Protection

"Small groups can help us develop a greater sense of Christian community in a disconnected age. They can facilitate the formation of deeper Christian friendships, encourage greater spiritual accountability among church members, and become a natural opportunity for inviting unbelieving and unchurched (or underchurched) neighbors to interact with a covenant community."[1]

Home groups build community within your church and are great ways to create relationships with each other and your families. They provide deeper opportunities to discuss and share concerns, issues, stories, and Scripture. However, home groups also come with responsibility over those attending, particularly if vulnerable persons are present without a parent or guardian.

As home groups are a ministry of the church, the church may be held liable for injury, harm or abuse that occurs within the home. Unfortunately, we have heard too many stories of abuse occurring within home groups, when parents are upstairs in a Bible study. Therefore, the responsibility of the church to provide supervision for these persons remains unchanged.

When a church organizes or promotes home groups, these groups become an activity of the church and small group attendees may have an expectation of safety. Closeness comes with vulnerability, and that is good, but it can increase risks. Recognizing that small groups need guidance and resources allows us to provide a safer experience for attendees and appropriate tools for leaders.

---

1 (Boekestein, 2018)

D. Special Events and Overnight Policies

Policy

Field Trips and Special Events:

1. All off-campus activities are to be pre-approved by the Ministry Lead with Parents being notified at least one week prior to the outing.
2. Proper written Letters of Informed Consent and Registration and Medical Consent Forms are required for each individual participating in field trips and special events. Photocopies of the forms must be kept in the Ministry Lead's possession during trips and events with the originals filed in the church office. (Appendix 19 and 15)
3. All trips and outings are to be supervised by a minimum of two approved, unrelated Adult Ministry Personnel.
4. When planning local special events, it is preferred that Parents drop off and pick up their Children at the event location. For out of town events, it is preferred that a commercial carrier be employed.
5. Children and Youth may not be transported one-on-one. Mentoring relationships should be conducted in teams and in public places. Parents are encouraged to drop their Children or Youth off and pick them up.
6. All Ministry Personnel drivers transporting individuals during church activities must be pre-approved by the Ministry Lead, provide a copy of their valid driver's license and current automobile insurance in accordance with the church insurance policy, and have had a minimum of five years of driving experience.
7. Church vehicles are to be driven by Ministry Personnel that have been pre-approved by Church Leadership. These drivers are to be insured under the church automobile insurance policy.
8. The number of occupants in the vehicle are not to exceed the number of seat belts and each Child must be in age appropriate safety restraints. Seat belts must be worn by everyone and remain fastened at all times the vehicle is in motion.
9. Children are not to be left unattended in a vehicle.

Overnight Events:

1. All overnight activities are to be pre-approved by Church Leadership.
2. Proper written Letters of Informed Consent and Registration and Medical Consent Forms are required for each Child or Youth participating in overnight events. Forms must be kept in the Ministry Lead's possession during trips and events and a photocopy filed in the church office. The originals are to be kept on file permanently. (Appendix 19 and 15)
3. All overnight activities must have a minimum ratio of two Ministry Personnel for every 10 Children or Youth. Ministry Personnel are to be assigned a specific group of Children or Youth for who they are responsible. If both genders are in attendance, there must also be both male and female Ministry Leaders providing supervision.
4. All trips and outings must be supervised by a minimum of two approved, unrelated Adult Ministry Personnel.
5. When transportation is being provided by your church, a Letter of Informed Consent for Transportation must be signed. (Appendix 23) The travel forms must be maintained and filed in the church office. Forms are to be kept on file permanently.

Plan

- ☐ Ministry Lead approval has been given prior to execution of off-site trips.
- ☐ Church Leadership has given approval prior to execution of overnight trips.
- ☐ Consent forms and medical release forms have been obtained for every child or youth participating in off-site or overnight trips.
- ☐ Copies of valid driver's licences and insurance coverage have been provided by all drivers.
- ☐ It has been confirmed that all drivers have a minimum driving history of five years.
- ☐ All forms remain with Ministry Lead and copies filed with the church office.
- ☐ Plans have been made to keep all event forms permanently.

Protection

Off-site activities, overnight trips and retreats are often spiritual turning points for individuals. When it involves children, parents are trusting you to make wise choices. Again, thought and planning work together to ensure the success of these ministries. Scheduling, accommodations, meals, supervision, consent and transportation are just a few of the details needed to make these events happen.

We discovered that "Legal Guide for Day-to-Day Church Matters states that car, bus and van accidents are one of the top three types of injuries for which churches are repeatedly sued."[1] Let us help you think through some of the logistics of getting participants there and back safe and sound.

E. Shower and Locker Room Guidelines

Policy

1. Locker Rooms must be supervised at all times. Two Screened Adults must be present together in the dressing or locker room with Children or Youth while they are showering or changing; Ministry Personnel must not be alone with minors in this setting.

2. Out of respect for the Children and Youth, and to maintain a high standard of professionalism, Ministry Personnel will announce their arrival prior to entering a dressing or locker room.

3. Ministry Personnel are not permitted to change or shower at the same time as Children and Youth.

4. Separate facilities should be designated for both genders or, if these are not available, separate showering/changing times will be arranged.

5. The use of photographic or video recording devices, including cell phones, is prohibited in dressing or locker rooms at all times.

Plan

○ Procedures have been put into place so that an Adult is never alone in locker rooms with a minor.

○ In the case of a shortage of facilities, showers and changing schedules have been posted with the times for showering and changing.

Protection

We have learned from historical situations of abuse that change rooms and showers pose a high risk of abuse by coaches, and child-to-child abuse.

Don't let your guard down, but always stay alert. You can reduce situations of abuse and protect your ministry personnel from wrongful allegations of abuse by promoting good practices. It is very important to realize that while you have a duty to children with whom you work, so you also have a duty to yourself to prevent any accusations of abuse or improper behaviour with players.

Be aware of situations in which actions can be misconstrued or manipulated by others. Prevent any opportunity for an accusation to arise where a ministry personnel would not have someone that can testify on their behalf.

F. Overnight Trips and Housing

Policy

For the protection of our Children and Youth, the following guidelines will be followed prior to all off-site trips where overnight accommodations must be secured:

1. A notice with a Letter of Informed Consent (Appendix 19) will be sent home to Parents at least one week in advance, advising them that an overnight trip is being planned, which requires the team to stay in a conference centre/camp/hotel/motel. The notice will note:

   a. The inherent risks associated with the event;

   b. The precautions being taken to minimize the risk and to raise the level of safety provided for their Children and Youth; and,

   c. Specific sleeping and travel arrangements that have been planned.

2. The Parent must return the signed and witnessed Letter of Informed Consent which includes the required liability shields.

3. Ministry Personnel travelling with Children and Youth must complete the screening and training process outlined in this policy prior to departure. Screened and trained Ministry Personnel who are placed in a Position of Trust with Children and Youth must be known by the church for six months.

4. Any individuals travelling with the team who do not qualify as screened Ministry Personnel must have separate sleeping arrangements.

5. When travel plans require overnight housing, housing must be arranged in the homes of screened and approved billets, or in a conference centre, camp, or church where Children or Youth can stay together, and where more than one screened Adult can be assigned to each common sleeping area. (Refer to the policy on "Billeting and Hosting" on page 201). When this is not possible, and it is necessary that the group stay in hotels or motels, the following plans must be made so that Children and Youth have distinctly separate sleeping arrangements from Ministry Personnel. In these plans, safety will be prioritized using the following guidelines when possible:

   a. Hotel rooms will be all together in one wing of the hotel or motel; and

   b. Parents are encouraged to accompany the team, assigning the family to hotel rooms; or,

   c. Ministry Leads request the availability of suites with two or three bedrooms per suite and assign two Children or Youth of the same age to a separate room, set apart from the two Adult screened Ministry Personnel; or,

   d. Ministry Leads must assign two unrelated Adult Ministry Personnel to a hotel room with two or more Children or Youth; or,

   e. In hotel or motel rooms with adjoining doors, Ministry Leads must assign one Adult Ministry Personnel with two Children or Youth in each room. For accountability purposes, the door separating adjoining rooms must be kept ajar or open at all times. Children and Youth must have distinctly separate sleeping arrangements from other Adults.

   f. Ministry Personnel are never to be alone in a room with a Child or Youth.

Plan

- ○ Letters of Informed Consent outlining overnight housing arrangements have been sent, signed and returned.
- ○ Overnight housing arrangements for each night have been managed to ensure that room assignments, Ministry Personnel assignments and Children and Youth numbers meet specified requirements.
- ○ Curfews have been established.

Protection

Overnight trips can be especially exciting for young people. The chance to spend time with their friends in an off-site location makes for a fun adventure. This could be a mission trip or a retreat. The excitement students hold for these trips is wonderful, but it is also our job to ensure that the enthusiasm for the trip does not overshadow necessary safety precautions.

Off-site trips can help young people grow in many ways. They can help them build responsibility, teamwork and take in novel experiences. By putting in place plans to protect our students from vulnerable situations, we can provide them with a safe environment to engage with the purpose of the trip fully.

G. Billeting and Hosting

Policy

1. For the protection of our minors, it is required that all Adults residing in the home where billets are provided must complete the following screening process prior to hosting. Screening includes:

    a. A recommendation from a Pastor or member of Church Leadership

    b. A Criminal Record Check

2. Information guidelines are to be distributed to host homes no less than one week in advance of minors arriving at their home.

3. Any allergies and medications for minors will be communicated to the host home prior to arrival, with clear directions on how to manage allergies and medications.

4. Minors must always be billeted in teams or small groups of the same gender, must have distinctly separate sleeping arrangements from the household members, and are not to be left alone in the home without adequate adult supervision.

5. Curfews shall be established and enforced when minors are being billeted. All minors staying in host homes are to be informed of proper etiquette, rules and curfew guidelines.

Plan

- ◯ A recommendation has been secured by the Pastor or member of Church Leadership.

- ◯ Screening has been completed on all Adults living in host homes.

- ◯ Information guidelines for billeting have been distributed.

- ◯ Allergies have been reported prior to arriving at host homes.

- ◯ Curfews have been established.

- ◯ Minors have been informed of proper etiquette and curfew while staying in host homes.

Protection

This policy is to be applied as an addition to the Overnight Trips and Housing Policy found on page 199.

When we arrange for individuals to reside in host homes, it is likely that we are allowing them to enter the homes of individuals they are unfamiliar with. With that being said, it is extremely important that the hosts are not strangers to members of the church and have undergone Criminal Record Checks and a recommendation by the pastor or member of church leadership if youth will be assigned to the home.

Hosting someone with a billet means entering the personal space of a host family. They are staying in a new environment and therefore have less control and awareness within that home. As they reside in the house it is natural for them to grow more at ease and relaxed. Both of these can cause an increased vulnerability to dangers and abuse.

In addition to curfews and assigning a group of youth to each home, helping our youth understand the potential dangers of residing in a billet ahead of time is an essential measure to consider. By doing so, we can provide them with greater protection and awareness for their own safety as they enter host homes. Putting in place protective measures provides reassurance to all those who are involved with billets.

For future events, survey both the billet family and the youth after the stay to discover what went well and what did not go well.

> So, my dear brothers and sisters, be strong and immovable. Always work enthusiastically for the Lord, for you know that nothing you do for the Lord is ever useless. - 1 Corinthians 15:58, NLT

Child Protection Procedures

- Introduction
- Checklist of General Protection Procedures
- Case Study
- A. Staff to Student Ratios
- B. Proper Display of Affection
- C. Child-to-Child Sexual Play or Abuse
- D. Washroom Guidelines
- E. Receiving and Releasing Children

Introduction

We love kids!

Many people think we love policies. That is only partly true for we do believe policies can be your friend not your foe.

However, we value kids above policies and believe they deserve the HIGHEST STANDARD of protection.

Plan to Protect® is truly about creating that great place where kids will want to spend their time. It is that great place where they feel really safe. It is that place where they can be everything they are intended to be! It is that great place where they can learn what it means to be a follower of God. The policies and procedures in this chapter are also designed to keep Children safe in order that no one would hinder them from coming to faith or cause them to lose their faith.

In this chapter we focus on activities that are often unique to Children's ministry. Please also refer to the chapter titled, General Protection Procedures, as those procedures relate also to your ministry of protection.

"Parents, pastors, and children's ministry workers all have a responsibility to steward the children entrusted to us. What is a steward? It is one who is responsible for watching over someone else's stuff. ... Churches have a responsibility to steward the gift of children. Several hours a week, parents entrust this very precious gift of children to churches --- to watch over, instruct, and protect the kids under their care. Church workers should consider the time spent with other people's children not as a burden, but as a great privilege and important responsibility."
- Deepak Reju

Checklist of General Protection Procedures

- [ ] Ministry Personnel have been screened and trained.

- [ ] Ratios have been observed in Children's programming.

- [ ] The congregation and Ministry Personnel have been educated and informed on 'Appropriate Touch' and 'Inappropriate Touch' policies.

- [ ] Policies on 'Appropriate Touch' and 'Inappropriate Touch' have been posted in Children and Youth departments.

- [ ] Resources and training are provided for those who work in areas where there is a higher risk of abuse.

- [ ] Parents have been informed and encouraged to deal with their baby's toileting needs and to take their Children to the washroom prior to each class or service.

- [ ] Diaper changing policies have been posted and followed in the nursery.

- [ ] Hall Monitors have been trained and assigned to monitor washrooms.

- [ ] Sign-in and sign-out forms have been developed and their usage monitored weekly for babies to kindergarten Children. (Appendix 27)

- [ ] The policy for receiving and releasing of Children has been clearly communicated to all Ministry Personnel.

- [ ] A system for receiving and releasing Children has been established and monitored by the Ministry Lead.

- [ ] Ministry Personnel are educated in the discipline steps that are appropriate to use with Children and Youth.

- [ ] Classroom expectations have been clearly communicated to the Children and Youth.

- [ ] Group rules have been established.

- [ ] Incident Reports are being used.

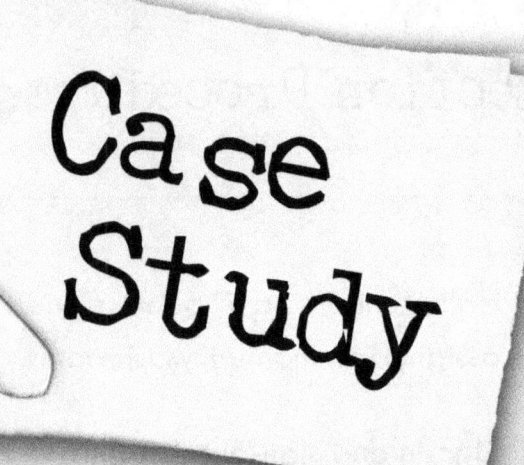

Case Study: Child Protection Procedures

One of the ministries your church has done this year is small cell groups. Each week, small groups meet in a congregation member's home for a meal and some time of fellowship. Together they pray, read the Bible or watch a video lesson. The small cell groups have been a great way for congregation members to get to know each other better and build stronger friendships.

During the small cell groups, Children of the families attending typically play together in the basement or bedrooms where they watch movies and hang out together.

The kids have a blast together. If an argument breaks out, one of the Parents comes to break it up. If there is a problem, one of the Children typically comes to get a Parent. However, most weeks, as long as they're not too loud, the Adults are able to focus on their prayer, Bible study and fellowship.

One evening, Bonnie and Jon had to leave early because Jon had an early morning appointment the next day. Bonnie went down the stairs to grab their five-year-old daughter, Sarah. When Bonnie descended the stairs, she noticed that all the kids were sitting on the couches focused on the TV, but Sarah wasn't there. Looking around, she noticed that 15-year-old Levi was also not there. Weird!

Looking around, Bonnie opened one of the guest bedroom doors and found Levi and Sarah alone. Sarah was sitting on Levi's lap, and he was tickling her. It made Bonnie feel really uncomfortable. What should she do?

Case Study continued ...

> ## Questions to Answer:
>
> - What responsibility does the church have to protect the Children during cell groups when the parents are upstairs?
>
> - What safeguarding steps should be in place to mitigate risk in church-run programs and activities?

Hindsight is 20/20:

We have a responsibility to protect Children in our care. Churches that sponsor small groups (often called cell groups or life groups), can be held liable for the activities that happen. If a ministry is sponsored and promoted within the church, Ministry Personnel should be screened and trained. Children should never be left unattended without Adult supervision and oversight. The church has an elevated duty to provide care for Children during church-run activities. Sarah's parents, the host family, and the church have shared responsibility to prevent abuse from occurring during cell groups in order to protect the Children in their care.

In this case study, we would recommend that Sarah be asked non-leading questions to determine if she was harmed. Based on what is discovered, if Child abuse did occur, the child protection agency must be notified (where there is more than a three year age difference). If there is evidence that abuse did occur, both Sarah and Levi will need to receive professional counselling. Abuse of a minor by a minor cannot be ignored as both Sarah and Levi may be victims of child abuse.

A. Staff to Student Ratios

Policy

1. Classroom settings must comply with established ratios for Adults and Children at all times. This includes off-site activities and trips. Established ratios are:

   - Two Ministry Personnel for every six infants (birth – 18 months)

   - Two Ministry Personnel for every 10 toddlers or preschoolers

   - Two Ministry Personnel for every 20 elementary-age Children

Plan

- Ratios have been observed in children's programming.

Protection

Safety and security are primary concerns for the children and families who attend our churches. At the same time, we are also concerned for the adults and youth who minister to children. We want to work towards providing a safe environment where effective ministry to children can take place. Adequate staffing of ministry personnel 16 years of age and older is one step in making that goal a reality. All minors serving in children's ministry should be supervised by adults, and they too need protection.

Teacher to student ratios promote positive learning and offer protection to the ministry personnel who serve our children. Please be aware that these ratios do not preclude the need to have two leaders present in a classroom.

Provincial standards for ratios differ across Canada; be sure to check with your province's standards to ensure your organization complies with local laws and regulations regarding teacher to student ratios.

B. Proper Display of Affection

Policy

Appropriate Touch:

1. Recognizing that Children need appropriate displays of affection that reflect pure, genuine and positive displays of God's love, appropriate touch with Children will be age and developmentally appropriate. We encourage Ministry Personnel to:
   - Hold a preschool Child who is crying,
   - Speak to a Child at eye level and listen with your eyes as well as your ears,
   - Hold a Child's hands when speaking, listening or walking him or her to an activity,
   - Gently hold the Child's shoulder or hand to keep his or her attention while you redirect the Child's behaviour,
   - Put your arm around the shoulder of a Child when comforting or quieting is needed,
   - Pat a Child on the head, hand, shoulder or back to affirm him or her.

2. All touch must be done in view of others.

Inappropriate Touch:

1. Recognizing that the innocence of Children must be protected, Ministry Leaders will be made aware that the following actions are deemed inappropriate and will not be permitted:
   - Do not kiss a Child or coax a Child to kiss you,
   - Do not engage in extended hugging and tickling,
   - Do not hold a Child's face when talking to or disciplining the Child,
   - Do not touch a Child in any area that would be covered by a bathing suit (strictly prohibited except in cases of diapering and assisting preschoolers as outlined in washroom policies),
   - Do not carry older Children and do not allow them to sit on your lap,
   - Avoid prolonged physical contact with any Child or Youth.

2. Ministry Personnel are not to be left alone with a Child or Youth.

Plan

- The congregation and ministry personnel have been educated and informed on 'Appropriate Touch' and 'Inappropriate Touch' policies.

- Policies on 'Appropriate Touch' and 'Inappropriate Touch' have been posted in Children's and Youth departments.

Protection

God created our senses to experience and celebrate the world He created. God created the sense of touch. Picture this: "It will be a gospel of cuddles and softly spoken words. These are the seeds out of which, by the grace of God, fuller faith may develop."[1] Physical touch is an important element in the communication of love and care.

We do not want our ministries to children and youth to be 'hands-off' ministries. There are simple do's and do not's to help guide us in our behaviour as we attempt to be reflections of God's love and character. Start by being aware of, and sensitive to, differences in sexual development, cultural differences, family backgrounds, individual personalities and the special needs of children.

---

1 (Sidebotham, 2003)

C. Child-to-Child Sexual Play or Abuse

Policy

1. If caregivers discover age-appropriate consensual Child-to-Child sexual play, use it as a teachable moment. Calmly figure out what happened by asking open-ended questions. Provide appropriate consequences and provide education in the area that appears most relevant to the situation. For example: learning names and functions of body parts, clarifying social rules and privacy, understanding how to respect their own bodies and others, identifying friendship vs. intimate relationships, and age-appropriate sexual education.

2. Reassure the Child that you care about them.

3. Fill out a Suspected Abuse Report Form, notify Parents and leadership, and respond appropriately.

4. If it is inappropriate sexual play, if there is an imbalance of power or authority, if there is a difference in age, ability or strength, if the actions are aggressive in nature or do not follow age of consent laws, fill out a Suspected Abuse Report Form and make a report to the proper authorities immediately.

5. Notify Parents as instructed by authorities.

6. Keep all documentation of Child-to-Child sexual play and abuse permanently.

Plan

- Resources and training are provided for those who work in areas where there is a higher risk of abuse.

Protection

Does child-to-child abuse or sexual play happen? Yes. According to the U.S. Department of Justice[1], 23% of all sexual offenders are under the age of 18. 40% of victims under the age of 6 are abused by juveniles; 39% of victims 7-11 years of age are abused by juveniles; and 27% of victims 12-17 years of age are abused by juveniles.

Inappropriate sexual behaviours are activities of a sexual nature between children which do not meet the definition of sexual abuse but are deemed undesirable due to their impact on each child's health and welfare. Problematic sexual behaviour is that which occurs frequently; occurs between children of widely different ages (3+ years) or different abilities; is initiated with strong, upset feelings, such as anger or anxiety; causes harm or potential harm; does not respond to typical discipline strategies; and involves coercion, force, or aggression.[2]

Protection continued...

Does child-to-child abuse or sexual play need to be reported? If it is inappropriate sexual play, if there is an imbalance of power or authority, if there is a difference in age, abilities or strength, if the actions are aggressive in nature or do not follow age of consent laws, fill out an incident report and report it to the proper authorities.

Inappropriate or abusive child-to-child sexual actions need to be reported to Child and Family Services because they exist to protect the community and to keep children safe. In the case of illegal sexual activity, juvenile court or family court will be required to establish a plan so that children will receive treatment and will not re-offend. It is also very important to note that some, not all, but some children who abuse other children were abused themselves and they may need help and protection.

Some things to remember: children under 12 are never charged with crimes. Child and Family Services can provide support and resources so that children can receive treatment. According to the National Center on Sexual Behaviour in Youth, research shows that among adolescents who receive treatment, rates of committing another sexual offense are low, from 3 to 14%.[3]

Other advantages of reporting appropriately include that the victim knows that they will be believed and supported, the offender can get the help they need, the professionals can make plans for treatment, and we make a statement about how serious we view child abuse. "Kids who have sexual behavior problems are needed to be seen really in the same way as any other child that has broken the law or who have behaviour problems. They are children. Their brains are still developing. They are still developing morally, socially, and interpersonally."[4]

> "Kids who have sexual behavior problems are needed to be seen really in the same way as any other child that has broken the law or who have behavior problems. They are children. Their brains are still developing. They are still developing morally and interpersonally."

---

1 (Snyder, H. N., PhD. (2000). Sexual Assault of Young Children as Reported to Law Enforcement: Victim, Incident, and Offender Characteristics. National Centre for Juvenile Justice, U.S. Department of Justice, Office of Justice Programs)
2 (NCSBY. Childhood Sexual Development. http://www.ncsby.org/node/59)
3 (Ibid.)
4 (Matthew Roberts, Jackson Co. Family Court)

D. Washroom Guidelines

Policy

1. Upon registering Children for programs, Parents will be notified to take their Children to the washroom prior to programs.

For Nursery:

1. Ministry Personnel are not required to change the diapers of young Children. It is the responsibility of a Child's Parents to change diapers.
2. Diaper changing procedures are clearly posted in the nursery diaper changing area. (Appendix 11)
3. In the rare case Ministry Personnel do change diapers, it is to be done only by a designated Adult Ministry Personnel and must be conducted within view of other Ministry Personnel.

For Preschool Children:

1. Preschool Children are not to go to the washroom alone.
2. One of the following are to be adhered to when accompanying preschool Children to the washroom:
   - Two Ministry Personnel are to escort a group of Children to the washroom, or,
   - One Ministry Personnel is to escort a group of Children to the washroom with one Hall Monitor appointed to assist with washroom and security duties.
3. No Ministry Personnel must ever be alone with a Child in an unsupervised washroom and they are never to go into the cubicle with a Child and shut the door.
4. When a preschool Child needs assistance in the washroom, Ministry Personnel may enter the washroom cubicle to assist utilizing the following guidelines:
   - The outside washroom door must be propped open and the Adult must stand in an open cubicle doorway,
   - Ministry Personnel will take into consideration the privacy of the Child.

For Elementary Children:

1. Elementary boys and girls are not to be sent to the washroom alone but should be accompanied by a buddy in the same age group.
2. Ministry Personnel are to escort the Children to the washroom and prop the door open to make sure that everything is in order. Ministry Personnel must then remain outside the washroom door and wait for the Children before escorting them back to the classroom.
3. Ministry Personnel are not to be alone with Children in an unsupervised washroom and are never to enter into the cubicle with a Child and shut the door.

plan

- ○ Parents have been informed and encouraged to deal with their baby's toileting needs and to take their children to the washroom prior to each class or service.

- ○ Diaper changing policies have been posted and followed in the nursery.

- ○ Hall monitors have been trained and assigned to monitor washrooms.

Protection

First things, first ... know where the washrooms are, and encourage parents to visit the washroom with the children before programs start.

Privacy and toileting needs are issues that face us every week in our work with children. We need to be practical. In the midst of the teaching process, think through how you will deal with children who have to go to the bathroom. The guidelines above are designed to protect the child as well as the ministry personnel.

Some churches, in cooperation with their families, have adopted a 'no diaper changing policy' to put parents and ministry personnel at ease. Should a parent not be accessible, an approved adult ministry personnel will change a baby's or toddler's diaper utilizing universal precautions posted in the diaper changing area. Use gloves, hand sanitizers and follow the steps listed in your nursery to sanitize the diaper changing area. In the nursery, for their protection, youth ministry personnel will not change diapers.

E. Receiving and Releasing Children

Policy

1. Receiving and releasing Children under the age of 6 is strongly monitored. A mandatory sign-in and sign-out form is to be used in all Children's programming. (Appendix 29)

2. Children are not to be dropped off in a classroom without Ministry Personnel present.

3. Babies and preschool Children are to only be released into the care of the Child's Parent or designate utilizing a signature, security number or identification card.

4. Parents and visitors are not to enter the nursery or preschool classroom when picking up their Child unless requested to do so.

For Elementary Students:

1. Younger elementary students and newcomers are to remain in the classroom until the Parent or designate comes to pick them up and the student demonstrates recognition.

2. Consideration must be given to security, church facilities and location when determining the age release of older elementary Children. Ministry Personnel are to ask on an informal basis whether the Child knows where to find his or her Parent. If the Child demonstrates uncertainty, the Ministry Personnel will keep the Child with them in the classroom until the Parent or designate picks up the Child.

Plan

- ○ Sign-in and sign-out forms have been developed and their usage monitored weekly for babies to kindergarten Children. (Appendix 29)

- ○ The policy for receiving and releasing of Children has been clearly communicated to all Ministry Personnel.

- ○ A system for receiving and releasing Children has been established and monitored by the Ministry Lead.

Protection

The church is responsible for the care of children when they are placed in our care. We have been advised by insurance companies that it is babies to kindergarten children who must be signed in by parents when being left in our programs. The signing in and releasing of elementary students needs to be closely monitored by the ministry lead to ensure that guidelines are followed. If a child is released to someone other than a parent, that designate should be introduced to the ministry lead and included on the registration form as someone that can pick up the child.

One small church told us that to make this policy work in their setting, they have the teacher take the student to the parents. A church plant has written in their parent information brochure that, "Parents are responsible for their children prior to being dismissed from the worship service. Parents are also responsible for their children after being dismissed from the children's program."[1] Again, communication is the key.

> "There is . . . no higher calling than to be called to minister to children. Nothing touches more closely to the very heart of God than discipling children."
> - Daryl Bursch

---

1 (Allison, 2006)

Youth Protection Procedures

- Introduction
- Checklist of General Protection Procedures
- Case Study

A. Physical Contact

B. Staff to Student Ratio

C. Mentoring

D. Youth-to-Youth Sexual Activity

- Youth Ministry Issues
    Counselling Youth
    Substance Abuse
    Suicide and Crisis Intervention

Introduction

Many people think we love policies. That is only partly true for we do believe policies can be your friend not your foe. When your organization puts policies and procedures in place, they are to help everyone get on the same page and moving in the same direction. However, Plan to Protect® is so much more than the draft policies and procedures you find in this manual.

Plan to Protect® is about your protection and the protection and longevity of your ministry and church. Don't be fooled though – Plan to Protect® is also truly creating that great place where kids will want to spend their time. It is that great place where they feel really safe. It is that place where they can be everything they are intended to be! It is that great place they can learn what it means to be a follower of God.

Many of the students in your ministries may not have great role models in their lives, whether that is parenting, a strong marriage, as a protective sibling, or even as a mentor. As you do life with the students in your ministries, you are role-modeling to them what followers and disciples of Jesus Christ should look and act like. There may not even be Adults in their life that are protecting them or holding others accountable for their actions. As you invest in the lives of your students today you are influencing the type of Parent, Spouse, Sibling, Friend, Adult they will become in the future.

We are so grateful for the many Youth pastors that have shared with us the best practices found in this module. They are amazing mentors that their students and the Parents of their students, and their Supervisors love and respect. Our prayer is that God will use these contributions to influence your Youth ministries.

Note: The Youth Protection Procedures in this module are not stand-alone policies and procedures. This section of the manual is supplementary material to be used with other (as important) sections of this manual, including Recruitment and Screening, General Protection Procedures, Documentation, and Reporting and Response.

"And Jesus grew in wisdom and stature, and in favor with God and man."
- Luke 2:52, NIV

Checklist of General Protection Procedures

☐ Ministry Personnel have been screened and trained.

☐ Physical contact guidelines have been clearly communicated and posted in the Youth department as well as in volunteer manuals and training.

☐ Adequate staffing has been maintained at all Youth events.

☐ Two unrelated Ministry Personnel have been assigned.

☐ Age difference requirement has been observed.

☐ A proposal and risk assessment for mentoring have been submitted to the Board for approval.

☐ The qualifications for mentors have been determined.

☐ All mentors for this ministry have been trained (including Plan to Protect® Orientation and Refresher training).

☐ The locations that are approved sites for mentoring to take place have been identified.

☐ Mentors have been carefully assigned with mentees.

☐ Letters of Informed Consent have been prepared for Parent permission.

☐ Resources and training are provided for those who work in areas where there is a higher risk of abuse.

Case Study

Youth Protection Procedures

Aaron stared down at the job description. He was thrilled that God had granted his heart's desire and called him to be a Youth Pastor. This was his first week on the job and the first thing he wanted to do was to connect with all the young people individually, meet them on their turf and get to know them. Once he got to know the kids, he would then begin to build up other Ministry Leaders in the church to work on his Youth ministry team.

He couldn't wait for opportunities to help kids work through their problems, and to challenge them to grow in their faith with Christ. He had been dreaming for years of taking kids out to do good deeds in the community. Already he had a busy week planned and had a counselling appointment scheduled.

Here was the challenge – how was he going to meet with the kids individually and still abide by protection procedures of not being alone with kids one-on-one? Didn't that defeat the idea of pastoring young people? Even if he met with two or three of them together, how could he arrange to pick just one of them up in the car, and drop the last one off?

Looking at his schedule, Aaron knew he needed to begin on the right foot with Youth protection … but the big question was how?

Monday:
- 12:00 p.m. Meet Sandy at the front door of Creston High School and take her to the McDonald's down the street for lunch.
- 3:00 p.m. Pick up John.
- 3:05 p.m. Pick up Trevor. Take John and Trevor to Jim's basketball game.

Tuesday:
- 7:30 a.m. Pick up Leanne for breakfast and drop her off at school for 9:00 a.m.

Wednesday:
- 12:00 p.m. Meet Todd and Josh at McDonalds, next to Creston High School.
- 3:00 p.m. Meet Victoria at St. George's High School for inner-city sandwich run.

Thursday:
- 7:00 p.m. Worship practice
- 9:00 p.m. Meet Jane for counselling at church.

Friday:
- 7:00 p.m. Youth group

Case Study continued ...

> This 'Youth Protection Procedures' section is a supplementary section and does not replace the 'Recruitment and Screening' and 'Reporting and Response' sections of Plan to Protect®. Unless noted differently in this section, those policies apply.

Hindsight is 20/20:

Aaron has the right heart for ministry. He is also very eager to begin his ministry and get to know the young people. Review and discuss Aaron's priorities and consider how Aaron can overcome the challenge of implementing Plan to Protect® in Youth ministry. Also review and discuss Aaron's schedule this week and come up with solutions as to how to overcome the challenges of his schedule. The answers are all found in 'Youth Protection Procedures'. We can often view the policies as a hindrance to ministry rather than as a friend to protect both the Youth and ourselves. Don't let the challenges in ministry defeat your passion and desire to spend time with your Youth. Be creative and come up with solutions — they are there for the finding.

A. Physical Contact

Policy

1. 'Physical Contact Guidelines' are to be posted in the Youth department.

2. Ministry Personnel are aware of what constitutes appropriate touch:
    a. one-arm hugs
    b. shoulder-to-shoulder hugs
    c. touch on the back or shoulder

3. Ministry Personnel must refrain from inappropriate touch at all times:
    a. chest-to-chest hugging
    b. extended hugging
    c. overexuberant affection
    d. lap-sitting
    e. kissing
    f. touching of thighs, knees or inappropriate spots of the body

4. Ministry Personnel must be cognizant of conduct that could be misinterpreted:
    a. horseplay
    b. tickling
    c. extended backrubs

5. All touch should be done in view of other people.

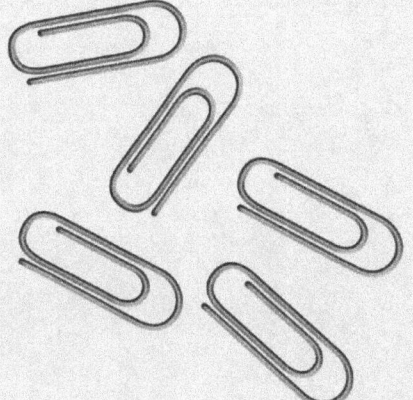

Plan

○ 'Physical Contact Guidelines' have been clearly communicated and posted in the youth department as well as in volunteer manuals and training.

Protection

Conduct that may seem innocent to one party but may be deemed inappropriate by another party or those watching on should be closely monitored and ministry personnel should be encouraged to refrain from this conduct.

It is important that leaders be 'adults that love and care about teens' – not adults who are trying to be kids or lengthen their youthfulness by being with kids. Students will more likely respond and love you appropriately if you act appropriately. Students will be more likely to respond inappropriately when you give signals that can be misinterpreted (or if you are intentionally sending inappropriate signals).

B. Staff to Student Ratio

Policy

1. Programs for Youth must comply with established staffing ratios as follows:
   - **Junior High events** – Two Ministry Personnel for every 16 students
   - **Senior High events** – Two Ministry Personnel for every 20 students
   - **Overnight/Off-Site events** – Two Ministry Personnel for every 10 students

2. There must be at least two unrelated Ministry Personnel at all events.

3. Overnight events with mixed genders must be accompanied by both male and female Ministry Personnel.

4. It is recommended that there be a five year gap between Ministry Personnel and the Youth they serve.

Plan

- ○ Adequate staffing has been maintained at all youth events.
- ○ Two unrelated ministry personnel have been assigned.
- ○ Age difference requirement has been observed.

Protection

Understanding that every situation is different, we always need to do everything we can to reduce the risk. It is never appropriate to take the easy road and look past important issues. Contact your church's lawyer and insurance company to see how they respond to the above ratios. Dialoguing and listening to their perspective will help you understand YOUR OWN personal risk as a leader if anything does happen.

As many youth ministries are served by married couples, it is critical to remember that another volunteer be assigned to the team. There is a compelling reason as a married individual will have less credibility when testifying on a matter involving her or his spouse. A spouse almost always would have a vested interest in not having the other spouse charged with something and so is far less likely to be believed. If it is not possible for someone to be assigned to work with the couple, the open door or window policy is again required along with the scheduling of a hall monitor.

C. Mentoring

Policy

1. Church Leadership must grant approval for a mentoring ministry to take place. Once approved, for the protection of those we mentor and for Ministry Personnel engaged in mentoring, the following policies are to be followed:
   a. The Ministry Lead is responsible for assigning mentees with mentors.
   b. Ministry Personnel granted to be mentors must be screened and trained according to recruitment and screening policies and procedures.
   c. Ministry Personnel are encouraged to meet with Youth in small group settings and in teams.
   d. Parental permission must be granted in writing using a Letter of Informed Consent.

2. If off-site mentoring, the following must take place:
   a. A risk assessment must be submitted to Church Leadership.
   b. The Ministry Lead must be informed of the time and place of the meeting prior to the meeting.
   c. Mentoring must be done in small groups, or in conjunction with another team of two.
   d. Mentoring can then take place at the church or an approved stationary public location, such as a coffee shop, library, restaurant, or campus cafeteria; and
   e. Separate transportation must be arranged (avoiding isolation in a vehicle).

3. If mentoring is not done in small groups, it may only take place at the church or in a public setting, in view of other people. Furthermore, these additional policies must be followed:
   a. The Ministry Lead must pre-approve the conducting of any one-on-one mentoring with the information being documented and filed.
   b. The public setting where mentoring takes place must be a static location, not subsequently moving to another location.
   c. One-on-one mentoring is permissible only for mentoring minors thirteen (13) years of age and older.
   d. The difference in the age between the mentor and the mentee must be five (5) years or more, subject to the mentor being a minimum of twenty-one (21) years of age, or older.

4. Mentors must avoid meeting in a home setting unless it is the home of the mentee, and the Parents are at home during the meeting and the mentoring happens in a common shared room (i.e., living room, family room, or dining room).

Plan

- ○ A proposal and risk assessment for mentoring have been submitted to the Board for approval.
- ○ The qualifications for mentors have been determined.
- ○ All mentors for this ministry have been trained (including Plan to Protect® Orientation and Refresher training).
- ○ The locations that are approved sites for mentoring to take place have been identified.
- ○ Mentors have been carefully assigned with mentees.
- ○ Letters of Informed Consent have been prepared for parent permission.

Protection

Mentoring, at its core, guarantees young people that there is someone who cares about them, assures them they are not alone in dealing with day-to-day challenges, and makes them feel like they matter. Research confirms that quality mentoring relationships have powerful positive effects on young people in a variety of personal, spiritual, academic, and professional situations.

A good mentor will always:
- Respect the person's dignity and worth;
- Work towards the best interest of the mentee, not their own;
- Avoid the temptation to force their help on anyone;
- Avoid manipulation and guilt techniques;
- Establish early on with the mentee the skills and lessons to be learned;
- Avoid exploiting trust or dependency;
- Share the bounds of confidentiality at the outset;
- Keep information confidential unless the person's welfare is at stake;
- Terminate the relationship if feelings of attraction begin in either party.

Protection continued...

If you are a mentor, or you oversee a mentoring program, we would encourage you to regularly assess how much one-on-one time is spent with each student under your care, the risks associated with the mentoring and all means of reducing the risk of harm and abuse.

Take all precautions for safety and protection for yourself and for the young people in your care. We would encourage any church that is offering or considering offering a mentoring program to discuss the risks with your insurance company to ensure that appropriate coverage will be in place.

All mentors should be screened and trained under Plan to Protect®. We would also encourage you to identify mentoring as a high-risk activity and establish specific policies for this activity with additional checks and balances for ensuring accountability and determining safe parameters for mentoring.

Most often mentors will be matched based on their gender. However, the same protection precautions need to be taken whether you are mentoring a male or female. Avoid isolation, including driving alone with a mentee in a vehicle and spending time together in locations where you are alone. Locations that we discourage mentors to take students alone include their homes, shopping malls, amusement centers, and parks. Ideal locations for mentoring include coffee shops, burger restaurants, the student's home when parents are present, or school and church events.

When mentoring, additional efforts need to be made for safety and ensuring accountability.
- Avoid isolation by teaming up with another mentor and two students.
- Contact the parents and discuss your plans.
- Secure written approval from parents and your ministry lead.
- Travel with your co-worker to pick up the young people and select a public place to meet. By choosing nearby tables or similar activities you can buddy together, complying with the requirements of your organization.
- It is crucial to celebrate the parent and child relationship, honoring their relationship above your own.
- Even if the parent wishes to provide blanket approval and seems disinterested, we recommend you role model accountability and strong leadership by notifying parents and your ministry lead in writing where, when and how the mentoring will take place.

Most parents are honoured and pleased to have you invest in the lives of their children. However, it is essential that mentors be accountable to parents and leadership and keep them informed of the dates, times and locations they are meeting with the student.

D. Youth-to-Youth Sexual Activity

Policy

1. If Ministry Personnel discover the occurrence age-appropriate consensual sexual activity, use it as a teachable and mentoring moment. Calmly discuss your concerns with open-ended questions. Provide education in the area that appears most relevant to the situation. For example: discussing the church's theological position, safety concerns, clarifying social rules and privacy, understanding how to respect and honour each other, identifying friendship vs. intimate relationships, and age-appropriate sexual education.

2. Reassure the young people that you care about them.

3. Fill out a Suspected Abuse Report Form, and respond appropriately by encouraging the Youth to discuss their relationship and activity with their Parents. If they are not willing to tell their Parents, it may be appropriate for Ministry Personnel to notify their Parents if you deem the Youth to be in an unsafe sexual relationship or if they are below the age of consent.

4. If it is inappropriate or not consensual sexual activity, if there is an imbalance of power or authority, if there is a difference in age, ability or strength, if the actions are aggressive in nature or do not follow age of consent laws, fill out a Suspected Abuse Report Form and make a report to the proper authorities immediately.

5. Notify Parents as instructed by authorities.

6. Keep all Suspected Abuse Report Forms and documentation permanently.

Plan

- Resources and training are provided for those who work in areas where there is a higher risk of abuse.

Protection

Does child-to-child abuse or sexual play happen? Yes. According to the U.S. Department of Justice[1], 23% of all sexual offenders are under the age of 18. 40% of victims under the age of 6 are abused by juveniles; 39% of victims 7-11 years of age are abused by juveniles; and 27% of victims 12-17 years of age are abused by juveniles.

Inappropriate sexual behaviours are activities of a sexual nature between children which do not meet the definition of sexual abuse but are deemed undesirable due to their impact on each child's health and welfare. Problematic sexual behaviour is that which occurs frequently; occurs between children of widely different ages (3+ years) or different abilities; is initiated with strong, upset feelings, such as anger or anxiety; causes harm or potential harm; does not respond to typical discipline strategies; and involves coercion, force, or aggression.[2]

Protection continued...

Does child-to-child abuse or sexual play need to be reported? If it is inappropriate sexual play, if there is an imbalance of power or authority, if there is a difference in age, abilities or strength, if the actions are aggressive in nature or do not follow age of consent laws, fill out an incident report and report it to the proper authorities.

Inappropriate or abusive child-to-child sexual actions need to be reported to Child and Family Services because they exist to protect the community and to keep children safe. In the case of illegal sexual activity, juvenile court or family court will be required to establish a plan so that children will receive treatment and will not re-offend. It is also very important to note that some, not all, but some children who abuse other children were abused themselves and they may need help and protection.

Some things to remember: children under 12 are never charged with crimes. Child and Family Services can provide support and resources so that children can receive treatment. According to the National Center on Sexual Behaviour in Youth, research shows that among adolescents who receive treatment, rates of committing another sexual offense are low, from 3 to 14%.[3]

Other advantages of reporting appropriately include that the victim knows that they will be believed and supported, the offender can get the help they need, the professionals can make plans for treatment, and we make a statement about how serious we view child abuse. "Kids who have sexual behavior problems are needed to be seen really in the same way as any other child that has broken the law or who have behaviour problems. They are children. Their brains are still developing. They are still developing morally, socially, and interpersonally."[4]

> "Kids who have sexual behavior problems are needed to be seen really in the same way as any other child that has broken the law or who have behavior problems. They are children. Their brains are still developing. They are still developing morally and interpersonally."

---

1 (Snyder, H. N., PhD. (2000). Sexual Assault of Young Children as Reported to Law Enforcement: Victim, Incident, and Offender Characteristics. National Centre for Juvenile Justice, U.S. Department of Justice, Office of Justice Programs)

2 (NCSBY. Childhood Sexual Development. http://www.ncsby.org/node/59)

3 (Ibid.)

4 (Matthew Roberts, Jackson Co. Family Court)

Youth Ministry Issues

Note: Churches and Ministry Personnel ministering to Youth may wish to consider these particular issues and how they relate to your Youth context, and determine if documented policies and plans are required for additional protection.

A. Counselling Youth

1. **Awareness of and adherence to the following ethics in counselling:**
   - Respect the person's dignity and worth as they are created in the image of God with huge potential!
   - Live, act and counsel in accordance with godly values.
   - Work towards their best interest, not yours.
   - Don't force your help on anyone. Be sure not to manipulate or use guilt in your counselling.
   - Fully inform them of where you are leading them.
   - Never exploit trust or dependency.
   - Share the bounds of confidentiality at the outset.
   - If feelings of attraction begin in either party, terminate counselling immediately.
   - If the relationship is destructive to you, terminate counselling immediately.
   - Never counsel if the person is under the influence of alcohol, drugs or illness.
   - Never create false expectations of favourable results.
   - Keep information confidential unless the person's welfare is at stake. As a general rule, only share information if the person consents.
   - All counsellors are legally bound to report physical abuse or neglect of a minor to the Department of Social Services or the police. Anyone who does not comply with this law is subject to a fine and/or a jail sentence.
   - Refer individuals requiring specialized physical, mental or emotional diagnosis, therapy or treatment to qualified health-care professionals.

   > All counsellors are legally bound to report physical abuse or neglect of a minor to the Department of Social Services or the police. Anyone who does not comply with this law is subject to a fine and/or jail sentence.

2. **Awareness of counselling issues that relate specifically to Youth:**
   - They need to form their own identity and self-esteem; you can help by building into their character.
   - They are adapting to rapid physical changes; this can add to the confusion in many situations.
   - They are adapting to sexual changes; weird feelings, fantasies and confusion, making decision-making more difficult.
   - They are struggling with dependence vs. independence; teens are beginning to move away from their Parents and yet know that they love and need them. This struggle can make them irritable, argumentative, irrational and difficult. Usually the conflicts arise from difference in opinion on how much freedom they can have. Don't take sides … ever!
   - There is an increasing importance of peer and intimate relationships; they need approval and often overreact to rejection.
   - They are forming all of their life-directing values and beliefs; most of these lessons (careers, lifestyles, behaviours and even problem solving) need to be learned experimentally.

- They need to develop a wider variety of social/interpersonal skills; dealing with conflict, coping, stress, temptation, study, productivity, interaction, authority or handling money all need to be understood an developed.

3. **Recognition of how Youth respond to problems:**
   - Repression is exhibited through denial, pushing aside and trying to forget. This often results in more serious behaviours such as eating disorders, anger, apathy, poor achievement, withdrawal or substance abuse.
   - Suppression is not an activity of denial but an attempt to hide it from others. Behaviours may be similar to repression but could be expressed through running away, substance abuse or suicide.
   - The antithesis of repression and suppression is expression. It is an obvious negative outward response that may be exhibited through anger, quitting school, lying, stealing, substance abuse, defiant behaviour or rebellion. These responses are a way of 'crying out for help' and may lead to serious depression.

> "It is important for churches and Christian charities to obtain appropriate coverage for the type, or types, of counselling conducted by employees and volunteers."

4. **Recognition of coverage issues that relate to counselling.**

"Unless designated as a professional counsellor, most types of counselling that occurs within Youth ministry is termed 'non-professional' counselling, which can roughly be defined as general instruction, advice or guidance of a religious nature provided by individuals who have certain recognized responsibilities, but who have no specialized training or qualifications. The only legal liability posed by this counselling is based on general legal principles that infer the existence of a standard duty of care required of any person in a position of responsibility, to act as any reasonable and prudent person would act in order to avoid harm or injury to another. Examples of non-professional religious counselling include elders, lay persons, Youth leaders, teachers, volunteer counsellors, peer counsellors, cell group leaders and certain employees."[1] We need to remember that there are different understandings of 'standard duty of care.' Government law will take precedent over church law.

"For non-professional counselling activities, there may exist a degree of coverage in general liability wording. In order to address the potential gap in coverage created by this exclusion, it is important for churches and Christian charities to obtain appropriate coverage for the type, or types, of counselling conducted by employees and volunteers. Organizations which provide any type of professional or non-professional counselling as part of their ministries or activities should arrange appropriate coverage under their general liability policy or under a separate professional liability policy. If coverage is arranged under a general liability policy, make sure that the policy wording is broad enough to include the type or types of counselling conducted by employees and volunteers, and the definition of bodily injury contained in the policy includes 'mental anguish.' If coverage is arranged under a separate policy, try to obtain a policy with an 'occurrence' rather than a 'claims made' basis in order to prevent future gaps in your coverage."[2]

---

1 (Robertson Hall Insurance)
2 (Ibid.)

B. Substance Abuse

1. **Prohibition of substance abuse at church-related events and services.**

2. **Observation of substance abuse indicators:**

   Social Indicators:
   - Family history of substance abuse
   - Changes in peer group
   - Uncharacteristic irritability or moodiness
   - Suspicion of and aggression towards friends, teachers, parents
   - Lying, theft, promiscuity, rebelliousness, antisocial behaviour
   - Withdrawal
   - Consistent failure to meet obligations

   Phyiscal Indicators:
   - Hangovers
   - Hand tremors
   - Appetite/weight gain or loss
   - Sleeping difficulties
   - Drawn appearance
   - Fatigue
   - Changes in hygiene, dress, grooming
   - Red eyes, dilated pupils
   - Vague, dull, confused

   Behavioural Indicators:
   - Low or deteriorating self-esteem
   - Loss of interest in usual activities
   - Grandiose feelings
   - Can't cope, easily frustrated
   - Impulsive behaviour
   - Depression, suicide attempts
   - Confusion, poor memory
   - Paranoid statements and feelings
   - Uncharacteristic irritability, moodiness
   - Withdrawal
   - Failure to meet obligations

C. Suicide and Crisis Intervention

1. **Awareness and detection of depression and suicidal tendencies among Youth:**

   Direct or indirect preoccupation with death:
   - Verbal or written suicidal statements/references
   - Giving away personal belongings
   - Writing of a will
   - Previous attempts

   Significant lifestyle changes:
   - Loss of significant person through death, divorce, separation
   - Loss of an object of affection (friend, boyfriend, girlfriend)
   - Loss of health
   - Financial difficulties
   - Loss of status

   Observable changes in behaviour or motivation:
   - Decreased academic performance
   - More attendance problems or lateness
   - Poor interpersonal relationships
   - Decrease in social activity
   - Substance abuse

   Observable changes in personality and emotions:
   - Feelings of helplessness, hopelessness, discouragement
   - Feelings that life is too painful or too difficult
   - Frequent crying, tantrums
   - Irritability, moodiness

   Physical or somatic changes:
   - Loss or increase in appetite
   - Headaches, stomach aches
   - Change in sleep patterns
   - Symptoms of substance abuse
   - Deterioration of hygiene or tidiness

2. **All threats of suicide must be responded to in the following way:**
   - Always take suicide threats seriously and respond accordingly:
     i. Don't minimize their pain.
     ii. Don't ask leading questions, rather reflect their feelings back to them.
     iii. Don't make promises that you can't keep.
     iv. Hear them out, listen and encourage.
   - Determine the seriousness of the individual's suicidal thoughts, noting the detail of the plan, including specific dates, times, methods and any advanced preparation already completed.
   - Remind them that God hasn't turned His back on them (Romans 8:38-39).
   - Assure them that you are concerned and you would like to put them in touch with someone who can help.
   - Don't take on the role of a therapist
   - Keep them safe. Inform Ministry Lead, Parents, and seek professional help.

Suicide and Crisis Intervention *continued...*

3. **Awareness of necessity for crisis intervention:**
   - Determine the need for professional assistance. If the situation is dangerous or you sense that it is beyond your ability, refer it to a professional sooner rather than later. Counselling takes time, energy and resources to deal effectively with certain situations.
   - Establish rapport
     i. Show warmth and interest.
     ii. Listen carefully.
     iii. Take them seriously.
   - Reduce anxiety
     i. You must remain calm and reassuring.
     ii. Don't offer pat answers like ... 'God will take care of you.'
     iii. Offer valid reassuring statements such as: 'Let's see what we can do about this. I think I can help. I know somebody that can help.'
   - Identify and prioritize the issues. Focus on the present and determine what needs to be done immediately.
   - Evaluate resources
     i. Personal: They have strengths, abilities, experiences and attitudes to draw on.
     ii. Interpersonal: Decide who you can depend on. Use other people to help.
     iii. Community: Draw on the expertise of the legal, medical, pastoral, welfare and tutoring resources available.
     iv. Spiritual: This is not necessarily a time to evangelize, but a time to remind them that God is with them.
   - Plan a course of action
     i. Outline a specific plan of action specific to their needs.
     ii. Encourage hope. Without hope, we are immobilized. Don't allow self-defeating statements such as: I'll never do it. Things will never change.
   - Follow-up
     i. Stay in contact as the steps you have laid out take place.
     ii. If they have been referred to other support networks, be sure to maintain contact with them.

Adult Protection Procedures

- Introduction
- Checklist of General Protection Procedures
- Case Study

A. Physical Contact
B. New Immigrant and Refugee Settlement
C. Personal Care
D. Mentoring Adults and Pastoral Care
E. Shelters, Recovery and Rehabilitation Ministries
F. Violence and Harassment
G. Financial Aid

Introduction

"Speak up for those who cannot speak for themselves, for the rights of all who are destitute. Speak up and judge fairly; defend the rights of the poor and needy." - Proverbs 31:8-9 (NIV)

When Plan to Protect® was first written in 1996 it was a manual for the protection of Children. Since then we have committed to not only speak on behalf of Children and young people but also to speak on behalf of those that are elderly and vulnerable due to the physical and mental disabilities that cause them to be dependent on others.

In this chapter we focus on activities that are often unique to Vulnerable Adults. Please also refer to the chapter titled General Protection Procedures, as those procedures relate also to your ministry of protection.

We are so grateful for the individuals that are advocates for Vulnerable Adults. Thank you for your relentless care and passion for the elderly and marginalized. This module in the Plan to Protect® manual could not have been written without the involvement of Cynthia Tam, Assistant Professor at the University of Toronto in the Department of Occupational Science and Occupational Therapy and Sarah Chaudhery, O.T. Reg. (Ont.).

"My grandmother had dementia, and in the last few years of her life, she encountered many fears. We would talk through the terror she felt and experienced in the institution where she lived. She would beg me to protect her from people that were hurting her. At the time, I was naive to the predators that would prey on and harm the elderly. I wish I knew 40 years ago what I know today. On the other hand, my mother-in-law (she was abused as a young girl) is an extremely happy and thankful Alzheimer's patient. Due to her lack of short-term memory, others could easily harm her. She is well into her 80's and is receiving such wonderful care and protection. Today my mother-in-law cheers us on and prays for the success of Plan to Protect® even though she cannot remember what transpired during the last 24 hours, she has not forgotten the abuse that she encountered as a young girl." ~ Melodie Bissell

Thank you for investing in the lives of Vulnerable Adults. As you minister to Vulnerable Adults through pastoral care and visitation, as a friend, or a caregiver, may you find joy in your service. Caregiving isn't for the weak, and caregivers need all the help they can get to keep them healthy physically, mentally, spiritually, and financially strong.

May your plan to protect include care for yourself as you care for others.

> "To care for those who once cared for us is one of the highest honors."
> - Tia Walker

Checklist of General Protection Procedures

- [ ] Ministry Personnel have been screened and trained.

- [ ] A strategy has been developed for Refugee Sponsorship and Settlement at the beginning of each program year in compliance with protection policies.

- [ ] Transitions are reviewed and planned one month in prior to the end of the Refugee Sponsorship and Settlement program. Paperwork is reviewed and summarized.

- [ ] Caregivers or family members remain present with Ministry Personnel and Vulnerable Adults when visitation occurs.

- [ ] Ministry Personnel seek permission from caregivers and leadership before providing any personal care and caregivers respect Ministry Personnel's choice on whether or not they would like to provide personal care.

- [ ] Ministry Leads are aware of the dangers inherent in the care relationship and have established clear boundaries.

- [ ] Mentors have been provided communication and appointment logs to track time with mentees.

- [ ] Individuals providing pastoral care have been reminded of the importance of maintaining a log of appointments with individuals requesting pastoral care.

- [ ] Separate transportation has been arranged.

- [ ] Ministry Personnel have signed confidentiality agreements.

- [ ] Visitation is conducted in teams of two screened and trained Ministry Personnel.

- [ ] Ministry Personnel serving with Vulnerable Adults have been screened and trained.

- [ ] A security plan has been put in place.

- [ ] Individuals have been trained to address aggressive or violent behaviour.

Case Study: Adult Protection Procedures

After a dearly loved woman named Abigail Cotes, a founding member of a church, passed away, family members lodged a civil lawsuit against the church, naming both the Board and the Pastor on the case. Criminal charges were also filed against the Pastor.

It was well known that Mrs. Cotes would leave a substantial legacy in her will to the church. However, months before Mrs. Cotes had passed away; she had changed her will without telling anyone. Instead of leaving the money to the church, Abigail named the Pastor and his wife as the beneficiaries of the funds.

Upon investigation, law enforcement discovered that the young Pastor and his wife had befriended Abigail Cotes for two years. This timing was soon after they had moved into the parish. Neighbours and friends reported that the Pastor would often visit offering to do errands for Abigail.

As the friendship developed, the Pastor and his wife confidentially shared with the older woman that instead of leaving the church in her will, she should revise her will and name them as the beneficiary. They had confided with her that they did not have money for a down payment on a home and were unsure if they could afford to have children. Family, friends and neighbours shared that Mrs. Cotes had been giving the couple large sums of cash and that the Pastor and his wife took advantage of her financially, at times asking her directly for money. Church leaders discovered that they were shopping for her and cashing her cheques.

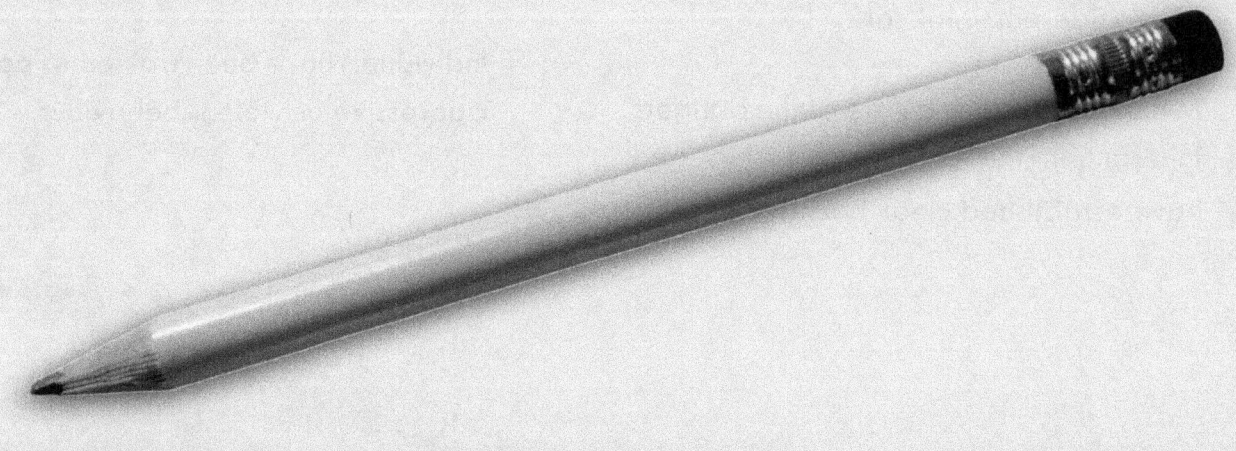

Case Study continued ...

> ### Questions to Answer:
>
> - What ways did the Pastor and his wife harm Mrs. Abigail Cotes?
>
> - What ways did the Pastor and his wife harm the church?
>
> - What requests should Church Leaders (the Board) make of Ministry Personnel when visiting Vulnerable Adults in their home?
>
> - How could this case study have been avoided?

Hindsight is 20/20:

This case study is one that we read about in newspapers and hear about in the news. The elderly are so often victims of financial and emotional abuse. Often the harm is not discovered until after someone passes away. Employees and Church Leaders have a responsibility to demonstrate their care not only for the congregation members but also on behalf of the church. The concept of duty of care identifies the relationship that exists between two people or a person and an organization. It establishes the responsibility that one owes the other, particularly the duty to exercise care concerning the interests of the other, including the protection from harm. The Pastor and his wife have not demonstrated their duty to care for the church. We encourage you, through position descriptions and staff policies, to communicate specific ways that Ministry Personnel will demonstrate their duty of care.

A. Physical Contact

Policy

1. Ministry Personnel must refrain from inappropriate touching at all times:
   a. Chest-to-chest hugging
   b. Extended side hugs
   c. Overexuberant affection
   d. Sexual activity
   e. Kissing on the mouth
   f. Touching of the thighs, knees, lower back, buttocks, or other inappropriate spots of the body
   g. Any form of touch that makes someone feel uncomfortable, i.e., attempting to forcefully hold their hand or any part of the body, or even trying to hug someone without their consent

2. Ministry Personnel are aware of what constitutes appropriate touch of Adults:
   a. One-arm hugs
   b. Shoulder-to-shoulder hugs
   c. Brief touch on the shoulder or hand

3. Ministry Personnel must be cognizant of conduct that could be misinterpreted and avoid these actions:
   a. Compliments regarding someone's body or clothing
   b. Whistling
   c. Tickling
   d. Offers of backrubs

Plan

○ Ministry Personnel have received training on appropriate touch and inappropriate touch during Orientation and Refresher Training.

Protection

Inappropriate physical touch and comments begin the dangerous slide to misconduct that can ruin a ministry, family, and lives.

Conduct that may seem innocent to one party may be deemed inappropriate by another party or those observing. Ministry personnel must hold themselves to a high standard of integrity of what is good.

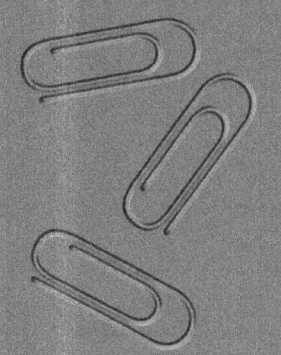

B. New Immigrant and Refugee Settlement

Policy

Newly arrived immigrants and refugees to Canada are vulnerable due to their dependency on others to assist with acclimation to a new country, culture, and in some cases a new language.

1. A plan and strategy for Refugee sponsorship and engagement has been approved by the Board and is reflective of both the Refugee Sponsorship Agreement Holder handbook and the Plan to Protect® policy. The plan:
   a. Requires all Refugee Sponsorship team members be screened and trained per the Plan to Protect® policy;
   b. Ensures Refugee family members are solely responsible for their own Children;
   c. Includes both oral and written translation;
   d. Remains in place until the Refugees are independent or no longer the legal responsibility of the church.
2. For the initial year of sponsorship and dependence, Ministry Personnel are not to assign the care of Refugee Children to minors under the age of 18 years old. Following this time, all Child protection procedures will be adhered to in accordance with the procedures outlined under the "Child Protection Procedures."
3. All care procedures will be followed as outlined in "General Protection Procedures," "Child Protection Procedures," and "Youth Protection Procedures." This includes Occasional Observers, personal care and washroom guidelines, dating, discipline, contacting opportunities, and transportation.

Temporary Housing
1. If temporary housing is provided with a church family, the following guidelines must be followed:
   a. All Adult members of the home must be appropriately screened and trained.
   b. Refugee family members will have distinctly separate sleeping arrangements from the other household members. Separate sleeping arrangements must be made available for each family member, or as preferred by the Refugees.
   c. The Refugee family members will be housed together, and Children are not to share a bedroom or bed with the host family Children.
   d. Children will accompany Parents to meetings and appointments whenever possible.
   e. If young Children are part of the family, all electrical outlets will be kept covered when not in use.
   f. Children will not be left alone in the care of any minors.
   g. For the protection of all parties, the host family will maintain a daily log of activities. This log is to be submitted to the church office on a monthly basis.

Plan

- ○ A strategy is developed for Refugee Sponsorship and Settlement at the beginning of each program year in compliance with protection policies:
    - It is ensured that training, the updating of files, and all aspects of Refugee Settlement are compliant with the policy and requirements outlined by the Sponsorship Agreement Holder.
    - All Refugee Settlement Volunteers follow all protocols of the Screening process.
    - All Child, Youth and Vulnerable Adult Protection Procedures as outlined in this manual are reviewed and included.
    - Expectations are communicated in writing to Refugees, in their language.
    - A strategy for compliance, including documentation retention, has been set.
- ○ Transitions are reviewed and planned one month prior to the end of the Refugee Sponsorship and Settlement program.
- ○ Paperwork is reviewed and summarized.
- ○ Required reports are provided.

Protection

Refugee settlement volunteers will be providing care and funding for refugees, so there will likely be an imbalance of authority, influence and control. Our goal is to help the refugee family become more confident and independent of the church. As this begins to happen, the imbalance will lessen, and the refugees will feel more at home in their community, and more in control of their environment. As such, refugee family members will be respected to make informed decisions regarding the care and supervision of their own children. This will require both oral and written translation. Until such time as the refugees are independent or no longer the legal responsibility of the church as A Constituent Group, these protection procedures will be in place.

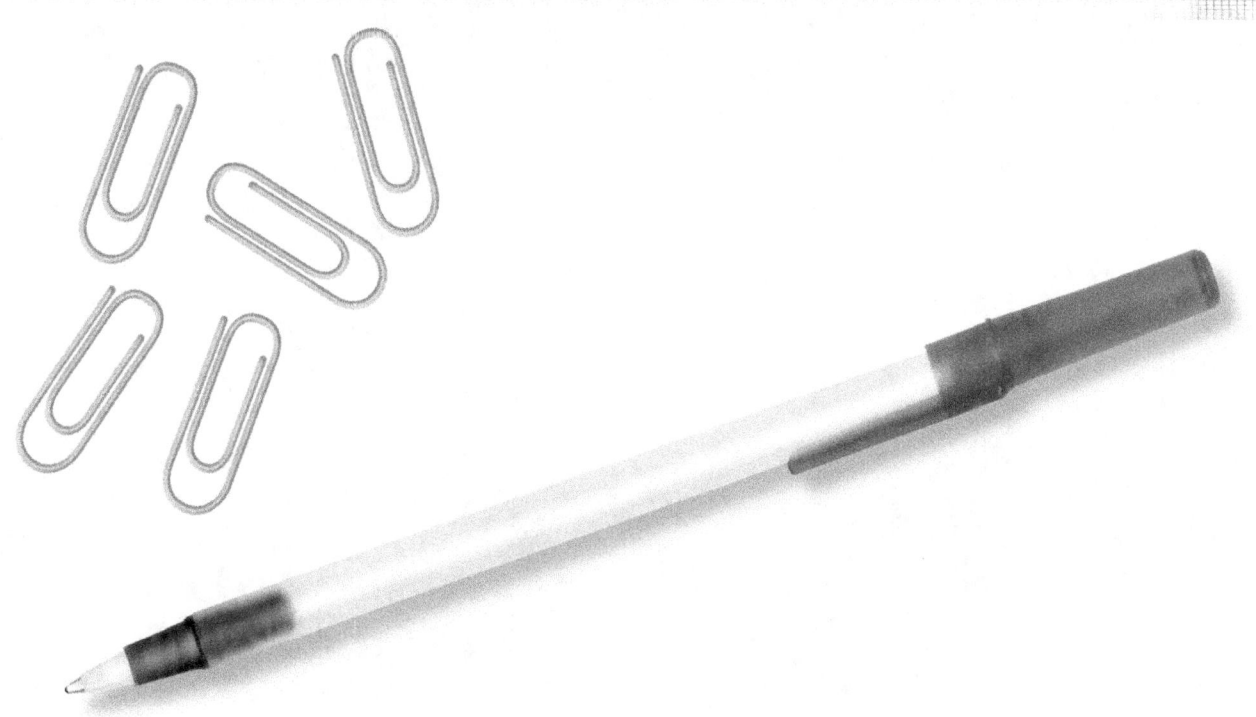

C. Personal Care

Policy

1. Personal Care is the responsibility of caregivers and family members, not Ministry Personnel.

2. Caregivers and family members may look forward to the respite of Ministry Personnel coming to visit the Vulnerable. It is at the Ministry Personnel's discretion if they wish to provide this extra level of care; however, at no time will Ministry Personnel be left alone in a home or behind closed doors with Vulnerable Persons.

Plan

- ○ Caregivers or family members will remain present with ministry personnel and Vulnerable Adults when visitation occurs.

- ○ Ministry personnel will seek permission from caregivers before providing any personal care and caregivers respect ministry personnel's choice on whether or not they would like to provide personal care.

- ○ Ministry personnel are aware of the dangers inherent in the care relationship and have established clear boundaries.

Protection

American painter, Walter Anderson, once said, "We're never so vulnerable than when we trust someone - but paradoxically, if we cannot trust, neither can we find love or joy." In the case of vulnerable adults, this quote stands especially true.

When ministry personnel and vulnerable adults form a connection, a relationship of trust is also built. Already vulnerable as they are, it is important that ministry personnel do not abuse the confidence entrusted in them. It may be the case that vulnerable adults seek greater care from ministry personnel during visitation. At the same time, it is also natural for ministry personnel to want to provide greater care for the adults they work with. However, it is important for both parties to understand that forming a bond during visitation should focus on developing a friendship and sharing an emotional connection.

In order to maintain a safe environment for both parties, appropriate boundaries should be set in place. This includes responsibilities of personal care. We do not want ministry personnel to be inappropriately crossing any boundaries, or assuming the role of a caregiver.

D. Mentoring Adults and Pastoral Care

Policy

1. Only Ministry Personnel approved by the Lead Pastor may mentor Adults or provide pastoral care under the umbrella of the church.

2. Mentoring and pastoral care must take place in a church office or a stationary public location, such as a coffee shop, library, restaurant or another public location, or a room with the door fully open.

3. Mentors are to maintain and submit monthly communication and appointment logs.

4. Individuals providing pastoral care must maintain a journal or calendar of appointments and a summary of pastoral care that has been provided.

5. When meeting off-site, separate transportation is to be arranged (avoiding opportunities for isolation).

Plan

- ○ Mentors have been provided communication and appointment logs to track time spent with mentees.

- ○ Individuals providing pastoral care have been reminded of the importance of maintaining a log of appointments with individuals requesting pastoral care.

- ○ Separate transportation has been arranged.

Protection

When mentoring or providing pastoral care it is recommended that there be two screened ministry personnel present. Exceptions to this guideline requires that meetings between two people should take place in public OR a second ministry personnel be in attendance nearby:

- This is to avoid being alone with someone who may be unstable, particularly on the first visit;
- This sets the tone that our presence is friendly but professional;
- This is to ensure that there are potential witnesses to inappropriate behaviour either on the part of the ministry personnel or the individual receiving care or mentorship;
- This allows ministry personnel to control the length of the visit.

We recognize the value of mentoring and discipleship programs. However, there is an inherent risk with these ministries as a relationship where an imbalance of power, authority, influence, and control is formed. Mentoring relationships can become an opportunity for unhealthy dependency, co-dependency and broken boundaries on either side of the relationship.

Being needed feels good. Being able to give and receive help is part of a healthy interdependent relationship (where we are mutually responsible to each other) safely and confidently.
Co-dependency is an adaptive coping mechanism used compulsively by those trying to find personal worth and value by meeting perceived needs of others.

Co-dependency is a mixed-up motivation to help. Helping becomes a "have to" out of a sense of guilt and survival instead of a "want to" out of a spirit of voluntary service.

Focus on the Family identifies indicators of unhealthy and co-dependent relationships:
You or a friend might be co-dependent if you:
- Are in a relationship marked by addiction or abuse.
- Take responsibility for helping others at the expense of your own needs.
- Seek love and worth through helping but live in fear of abandonment.
- Endure mistreatment and live in survival mode.
- Excuse and enable others' ongoing dysfunctional behaviours.
- Fail to set or keep personal boundaries.
- Become emotionally dependent on fixing, rescuing, and controlling others.
- Live with a lack of love, attention, security, fulfillment, and identity.
- Experience hurt, fear, anger, guilt, loneliness, and shame.
- Deny the reality and personal costs of staying in unhealthy relationships.

As a professional, good practices include maintaining a summary of appointments and care provided.

E. Shelters, Recovery and Rehabilitation Ministries

Policy

This policy is for ministries of the church where overnight housing and shelter is provided to individuals in recovery or seeking a safe residence.

Visitors

1. Visitors and non-housing Ministry Personnel are discouraged from coming to the residence, this includes Board members and Directors. In the rare occasion that this may occur, the visit must be scheduled well in advance when there is a minimum of two unrelated Ministry Personnel present.

2. No individuals of the opposite gender are allowed in the sleeping quarters of residences.

Guest Log

1. In the rare occasion where visitors do come to the shelter or residence, a guest log is to be maintained.

2. Guests' first and last names, along with the names of Ministry Personnel present must be acquired for every visit. The date and time of all guest comings and goings are to be captured on the guest log. The log will be retained permanently.

Confidentiality

1. Unless granted permission, the location of the residence must be kept confidential. It is a vital matter of the safety of residents and Ministry Personnel working and living in the house.

2. This specifically refers to any mention of:

    a. The ACTUAL STREET ADDRESS of the house;

    b. ANY IDENTIFYING CHARACTERISTICS of the house or programs, (i.e., description of buildings, neighbourhood, etc.)

3. No information shall be divulged without written, informed consent of Leadership.

4. In addition, Ministry Personnel taking participants on outings may not disclose to associates, friends, relatives or anyone that you encounter, that is not involved in shelter ministry, that the participant is part of the Shelter or Residence programs. Participants should only be referred to as 'friends'.

plan

- Ministry personnel and residents have been trained on the importance of confidentiality.
- Ministry personnel and residents have signed confidentiality agreements.
- Ministry personnel have been trained on how to introduce residents when off-site.
- A guest log is available for tracking visitor attendance.

protection

The protection of adult residents living in shelters, recovery centres and residential homes is of utmost importance. In some cases, adults have chosen to live in a shelter because their physical health and well-being has been threatened by a partner. In other settings, individuals have chosen to live in recovery or rehabilitation centres to break the bondage of alcohol and drug addictions. Organizations have a duty to care for the residents and the ministry personnel working in these shelters and homes.

F. Violence and Harassment

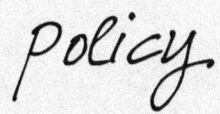

The church is committed to the prevention of violence and is ultimately responsible for the health and safety of individuals that come to our services and who work at the church. We will take reasonable steps to protect our Ministry Personnel and attendees from violence.

1. A security plan has been put in place. It is the responsibility of the Board and Church Leadership to ensure this policy and the supporting security plan are implemented and maintained, and that all Ministry Personnel have the appropriate information and instruction to protect them from violence within the church.
2. Ministry Leads are to adhere to this policy and the supporting security plan. Ministry Leads are responsible for ensuring that measures and procedures are followed by Ministry Personnel, and that they have the information they need to protect themselves.
3. Violent behaviour in any form is unacceptable from anyone. All concerns regarding violence or not feeling safe within the church must be reported to the Pastor or Chair of the Board.
4. Ministry Personnel must work in compliance with this policy. Everyone is encouraged to raise any concerns about violence and to report any violent incidents or threats. If it is an emergency, immediately call 9-1-1. Please complete an Incident Report Form and submit all concerns and complaints to the Pastor or Chair of the Board. The Board must be made aware of these incidents.
5. The Board and Church Leadership pledge to investigate and deal with all incidents and complaints of violence in a fair and timely manner, respecting the privacy of all concerned as much as possible.

Incidents of Aggressive and Violent Behaviour

1. To ensure the safety of participants, aggressive behaviour by an attendee will result in the request for them to leave the premises.
2. In an effort to discourage aggressive behaviour, Ministry Leads are to follow the disciplinary action policy guidelines.
3. If aggressive behaviour has occurred, the aggressive individual is to be required to stay home from the program for at least one event. Additional incidents are to result in a progressive number of days out of the program. In some cases, it may be necessary to impose permanent removal. This would be addressed on a case-by-case basis, and only after other reasonable alternatives have been exhausted. The Ministry Lead is to work with the individual, caregiver or guardian to identify behaviour triggers and look for solutions.
4. Complete an Incident Report Form for any act of violence.

plan

- ◯ A security plan has been put in place.
- ◯ Individuals have been trained to address aggressive or violent behaviour.

Protection

The church is never where we expect violence or harassment to occur. However, for centuries violence against the church and in the church has been prevalent. We live in a fallen world where violence can erupt at a moment's notice. We are not immune to such threats even when we gather to worship our Creator. Churches have become easy targets for violence and attacks.

Sometimes our fear of social pressures can cause churches to avoid addressing issues of human rights, harassment, and discrimination. However, these issues can escalate to violence or provoke aggressive behaviour and responses that themselves instigate violence.

Violence is the exercise of physical force or the attempt to cause physical force by a person against an individual that causes or could cause injury. It also includes statements or behaviours that are reasonable for a person to interpret as a threat to exercise physical force.

Because of this reality, churches must be prepared. A security plan should be put into place outlining:

- Who is on the security team?
- Who is responsible for security?
- At what point will law enforcement be called?
- When to execute the plan?
- How will the team communicate with each other?
- What will be communicated to ministry personnel?
- What will be communicated to the congregation?

Protection continued...

With or without a plan, the following seven recommendations have been adapted from an article that Joe Carter wrote with the Gospel Coalition to help churches prepare for and address violence[1]:

1. **Communicate to your congregation what your security plan is.** Church members should be aware of safety precautions, policies, and recommendations if someone poses a threat to the church.

2. **Be realistic about your security context as threats vary in kind, degree, and probability.** Hiring an off-duty police officer to patrol the lobby during morning services may be a prudent measure for the city church, but the rural church shouldn't overreact by implementing expensive security measures unless they deem it necessary.

3. **Think outside the church door.** Often our thoughts are providing security for those within the building, but Joe Carter also reminds us to protect those in the parking lot and those being dropped off for the service. Parking lot attendants can provide elevated security and patrol.

4. **Understand the singular threat of domestic violence.** The one threat every church should expect and prepare for is spillover of domestic violence into the church. Church leaders should be aware of which members of the congregation are vulnerable to violence in the home.

5. **Identify and prepare the guardians.** Identify key Ministry Personnel who are willing and able to lay down their lives to protect their brothers and sisters in Christ (John 15:13). Their regular duties may be as simple as having them regularly sit in pews close to the doors during church services or to be the one to dial 9-1-1 in an emergency. These "guardians" don't need to be police officers or former SEAL team veterans. They don't need to be the biggest and bravest in the congregation. All they need is the conviction that they will do whatever is in their power to protect the church from violence.

6. **Protect the Children.** Though you may have "guardians" sitting in the sanctuary, the whole congregation should be aware that their primary security responsibility should be to protect the children from violence.

7. **Prepare against anxiety and hardheartedness.** We must be cautious, but not fearful. We can't shut our doors to those who need to hear the gospel because of our anxiety about violence. As Paul tells us, "Do not be anxious about anything, but in every situation, by prayer and petition, with thanksgiving, present your requests to God. And the peace of God, which transcends all understanding, will guard your hearts and your minds in Christ Jesus." (Philippians 4:6-7, NIV)

---

1 (https://www.thegospelcoalition.org/article/7-ways-prepare-church-violence)

G. Financial Aid

Policy

1. Ministry Personnel may not distribute money or loans from their own resources.
2. Ministry Personnel are not to give money, or loans to individuals in their programs as a bribe or in exchange for any services or favours.
3. If an individual asks for aid, requests must be submitted in writing, with supporting documentation demonstrating the need to the Ministry Lead of the benevolent fund. Leadership must approve these funds, whether the aid is being provided personally or from the benevolent fund. Groceries and gift cards can be given in the case of need, but must be approved by the Board or benevolent committee.
4. All financial aid distributed by the church is to be accounted for by the finance department.

Plan

- ○ A benevolent fund policy has been established.
- ○ Ministry personnel have been trained when and how financial aid may be distributed.
- ○ Financial aid is being tracked for accountability purposes.

Protection

Churches have always been active in benevolence, doing acts of kindness or compassion for those in need. Individuals experiencing a personal crisis where they are in need of finances are vulnerable.

Distributing or exchanging money could lead to misunderstandings. Friends and family members of the individual may be suspicious of the motives of the ministry personnel if the individual tells them that ministry personnel are handling their money or giving them gifts or aid.

Whenever monies are being handled, there should be a minimum of two ministry personnel present to count and distribute the funds. This will protect ministry personnel from accusations of theft and it will protect the charitable status of the church.

Churches should consider writing a clear benevolence fund policy to help with this ministry of the church. This policy would include information on the following:
- How will your church assess the need?
- Who is eligible to receive such funding?
- What kind of support will you offer?
- What kind of support will you not offer?
- What will the priorities be?
- How will you document the need and the action?
- Who will administer benevolent funds?

Reporting and Response

- Introduction
- Reporting Abuse
- Case Study
- Response to Abuse
- Case Study
- Conclusion

Introduction

"My Youth Pastor raped me!"

Is it even possible to hear someone voice these words? One would think that a Youth Pastor, called by God, licensed by a denomination, appointed by Church leaders, voted in by a congregation to pastor and shepherd young people would be the last person to harm a student.

However, this Youth Pastor raped a teenage girl for years. As a result, this young woman spent years afraid to walk in the doors of a church, to look a male in the eyes, or even whisper a prayer. She self-injured, was hospitalized with an eating disorder, and experienced night terrors.

She shares with us that she was afraid to tell anyone. She is certain though that there were individuals in the church that suspected that there was something wrong. She recalls at one point hearing a Parent raise concerns to the Youth Pastor that he was showing favouritism to some of the girls in the youth programs. The Youth Pastor told the teen that the Lead Pastor challenged him on numerous occasions not to be alone with a minor. However, the abuse continued for years and no one reported it!

This story is not unique; we have heard different versions of it many times over. No segment of our society is immune to abuse, nor is any denomination or faith community.

Creating a ministry of protection includes praying that God would open our eyes to what is happening around us. To be alert, to be vigilant on behalf of the vulnerable sector. A Child may come to you and trust you with a secret they have been carrying. It may mean you observe indicators of abuse or hear an allegation of abuse by a family member or friend.

God may call us to stand in the gap and become a first responder in the life of a Child. If so, it is a privilege.

The duty to report abuse is the most important of all Child protection laws. In Canada, everyone is a mandatory reporter of Child abuse. In this module in the manual, we lay out recommended policies and procedures for reporting and responding to Child abuse and Vulnerable Adult abuse.

We report Child abuse, and we respond to Vulnerable Adult abuse.

Together let's plan to protect by reporting and responding to abuse.

Reporting Abuse

A. Hearing an Allegation or Suspicion of Child Abuse

B. Reporting Child Abuse

C. Hearing an Allegation or Suspicion of Abuse or Harassment Against an Adult

D. Reporting and Responding to an Allegation of Abuse or Harassment Against an Adult

E. Assessing and Investigating an Allegation or Suspicion of Abuse

F. Protecting Confidentiality and Dignity of the Victim and the Accused

G. Spiritual Abuse

H. Whistleblower Policy

Reporting Abuse

The phone call interrupted the Lead Pastor's study, but upon answering it, he recognized the voice of a faithful member of the congregation. Initially there was silence on the other end of the phone, followed by "Pastor, we are coming over to see you!"

Less than 30 minutes later, the couple had arrived at the church. They lacked the same warmth and greeting they normally would have given him, and it was apparent they had both been crying.

Over the course of the next hour, the story spilled forth – the couple took turns telling what they had heard first-hand from their 8 year old daughter. The details told were any pastor's worst nightmare.

The Parents informed the Lead Pastor that their daughter had reported to them the night before that the Assistant Pastor of the church had touched her where they had said no one ought to. It happened during Bible story time during Sunday School. Pastor Ben's hand went up her skirt and his fingers touched her private parts. He had whispered in her ear, and made her promise not to tell a soul, or God would be angry with her.

The pain was etched on their faces. They were completely broken.

Finally, the father went on to say that they had stayed up all night, praying and discussing what steps to take. Who would they tell? What would happen to their daughter and the church that they loved so dearly? The Parents had invested their lives and service in this church. They didn't want media attention drawn to their family, their daughter, nor did they want to bring any disgrace to the church. Finally, they told the Lead Pastor, that if he dealt with it and dismissed Pastor Ben, they would not report it to the officials.

As the sun went down, the three individuals in the Pastor's study agreed that the Assistant Pastor would be asked to leave the church. Graciously, Ben submitted his resignation after having admitted that "yes" he

Case Study continued ...

had fallen to temptation with the 8 year old.

Not prepared to deal with the fall-out in the church community, the Board members and the Lead Pastor arranged for a farewell party for the Assistant Pastor. Today, he serves as a lay person in his new church, teaching Sunday School on a rotation basis. He recently attended an anniversary celebration at the church and was warmly greeted and told how much he was missed.

Questions to Answer:

- What should the response of the Lead Pastor have been?
- Who should have been informed?
- Knowing there is no statute of limitations on child abuse, what could happen in the future?

Hindsight is 20/20:

As Christians, we do not know how to handle bad news. We never think abuse will happen in our churches and ministries. What about you? In our attempt to protect our churches and our community, we do the expedient thing, thinking we are above the laws of reporting to Social Services and protecting the Children that God has entrusted into our care. We encourage you to carefully, and prayerfully, read through 'Reporting Procedures'. Our prayer is that this will never happen during your watch as a leader in ministry, but, please be prepared if it does.

A. Hearing of an Allegation or Suspicion of Child Abuse

Policy

The following policies outline the recommended procedure and sequence for reporting suspected abuse cases.

1. For the protection of our Children, Youth and Adults, all allegations and/or suspicions of abuse against Children, Youth and Vulnerable Adults are to be taken seriously.

2. Immediately upon hearing of potential abuse or allegations of abuse of a Child or Youth, the Ministry Personnel must complete a Suspected Abuse Report Form documenting all pertinent information (Appendix 33). The victim must not be asked leading questions nor should the accused or any other parties be contacted at the point of completing the Suspected Abuse Report Form.

3. Make an immediate report to Child and Family Services. Reporting may be done in conjunction with the Lead Pastor or a Ministry Lead.

4. All forms must be kept permanently unless otherwise directed by legal counsel.

5. Reporters are requested to submit a copy of the Suspected Abuse Report Form to the Lead Pastor.

Plan

This plan is written for a situation where an allegation has been voiced or where suspected abuse has been identified.

- ○ Suspected Abuse Report Forms have been prepared and made accessible to Ministry Personnel.

- ○ Suspected Abuse Report Form has been completed with all pertinent information.

- ○ Lead Pastor has been notified.

Protection

All allegations, disclosures and suspicions of abuse must be taken seriously. An accusation of child sexual abuse may occur in any church, because realistically, no prevention strategy is 100 percent effective. Therefore, before hearing of an accusation or suspicion of abuse, churches need to develop policies and procedures for reporting and responding to sexual abuse allegations. Be aware that wrong actions can multiply the pain and liability inherent in an abuse case.[1]

"Reducing the Risk" highlights important issues to remember when dealing with an allegation of abuse. "First, be prepared mentally to receive an allegation. Do not express disbelief or respond in any way that minimizes the complaint or places blame upon the complainant. Comments like, "Did it only happen once?" and, "It doesn't sound that serious," need to be replaced with "I know how hard this must be for you," and, "We want to do everything within our power to help and support you."[2]

Second, be prepared for intense emotions from the complainant. Avoid asking any leading questions and doing your own investigation. Don't try to form conclusions concerning the truth of the complaint at this time. Rather, focus on three simple points:
- that the complaint is being taken seriously,
- that procedures exist for such complaints and that they will be followed to ensure proper follow-through, and,
- that the church desires to extend care and support in whatever ways possible to the victim and the victim's family."[3]

When completing the Suspected Abuse Report Form, be careful to simply gather the required information. Remember that it is not your responsibility to investigate or to draw conclusions, but rather to provide information about the victim, the alleged perpetrator, the nature of the suspected abuse and indicators of the suspected abuse. If the child is disclosing the abuse, write out what the child said along with your response to the child.

---

1 (Cobble, Hammer and Klipowicz 2003, 55)
2 (Cobble, Hammer and Klipowicz 2003, 55-6)
3 (Ibid.)

B. Reporting Child Abuse

Policy

1. Any person including, but not limited to, Ministry Personnel, who has reasonable grounds to believe that a Child is in need of protection, is legally required to immediately report the matter to Child and Family Services (Children's Aid) or the police. Reporting must be done orally by telephone or in-person.

2. A person who knowingly fails to report in these circumstances is in violation of the law and may be found to have committed an offence and may be subject to disciplinary action in the church.

3. If the abuse occurred within the context of the church, the Lead Pastor or his designate must notify the church's insurance provider and seek legal counsel upon hearing of a suspected child abuse case.

4. The church will notify and work in conjunction with denominational leadership in any and all allegations or suspicions of abuse that may have happened in the context of church ministry.

5. If the suspected abuse happened in the context of church ministries or was committed by a church member or attendee, the Parents of the victim must be notified by the Lead Pastor or by Church Leadership in conjunction with Child and Family Services and legal counsel.

Plan

This plan is written for a situation where an allegation has been voiced or where suspected abuse of a Child has been identified.

- ◯ Child and Family Services or the police have been notified of the allegation or suspicion of abuse.

- ◯ Legal counsel has been sought.

- ◯ Insurance provider has been contacted to satisfy the conditions of the policy and to ascertain potential liability and legal defence coverage.

- ◯ Parents of the victim have been notified if the allegation or suspicion involves ministry personnel.

- ◯ Denominational leadership have been notified if the allegation or suspicion happened in the context of church ministry.

Protection

"In Canada, the Child and Family Services Act states that anyone with a reasonable suspicion of child abuse has a legal responsibility to report the suspicion. ... An oral report to police officials or child protection authorities should take place within twenty-four hours of observable signs of abuse or receiving a report of abuse. A written report to the same officials or authorities should take place within seventy-two hours."[1] According to the 2006 Annual Church and Charity Law Seminar, the duty to report suspected child abuse cannot be delegated. Section 72 of the Act requires that any person obligated to report a child in need of protection should make the report directly to the Children's Aid Society and not rely on another person to make the report on their behalf.[2]

However, we have been advised that should a ministry lead, a teacher and a children's pastor become aware of an incident, one person may make a report to Child and Family Services on behalf of all three.

There are three means of learning that a child may be a victim of child abuse. The first means is that one has a suspicion of abuse. You may begin to recognize common indicators of abuse. In training, ministry personnel will learn the types of abuse and common indicators of that form of abuse. What constitutes reasonable grounds to report a suspicion of abuse? Reasonable grounds are what an average person, given his or her training, background and experience, exercising normal and honest judgment, would assume to be an action that needs attention. Do you see a pattern of indicators of abuse? Is the child in need of protection? If you observe a pattern of indicators, you must report the suspicion. No action would be taken against a person making a report unless it is made maliciously or without reasonable grounds for the belief. You do not need proof to call Child and Family Services, rather you can ask, "Is this something that I should report?"

The second means is through a disclosure of abuse. This is when a child discloses that someone has done something that constitutes abuse. During Plan to Protect® training, ministry personnel will learn the categories and definitions of abuse.

The third means is an allegation of abuse. An allegation of abuse may be communicated by someone other than a child.

The provincial and territorial child protection acts in Canada vary in terminology and the age of the child that falls under the act for protection. However, the acts have commonality as the report must be an immediate report, a direct report, and an on-going duty to report. Do not delay, in some cases the requirements states "forthwith." The report must be a direct report. Every person in Canada is a mandatory reporter of child abuse. This report should not be delegated to someone else. The person with the knowledge or suspicion of abuse has a direct duty to report and should be present when the report is made. Finally, there is an on-going duty to report. Even if you know Child and Family Services is already involved or a report has been made in the past, you have an on-going duty to report when new information or suspicions come to your knowledge.

---

1 (Swagman 2003, 44-5)
2 (Annual Church and Charity Law Seminar, 2006)

Protection continued...

The following characteristics may be indicators of abuse, although they are not necessarily proof. One sign alone does not constitute abuse and may simply be indicative of other issues. You need to ask God for discernment and wisdom as you watch for patterns or a combination of these warning signs. For additional indicators of abuse, see Appendix 31.

Physical signs may include:
- lacerations and bruises
- recurring nightmares
- irritation, pain, regular discomfort, or injury to the genital area
- difficulty sitting
- torn or bloody underclothing
- venereal or sexually transmitted disease

Behavioural signs may include:
- anxiety when approaching a child care area
- nervous, hostile, or rejecting behaviour toward one or more adults
- sexual self-consciousness
- acting out of sexual behaviours or other expressions of sexual knowledge beyond that appropriate for the child's age
- withdrawal from church, school, or sports activities
- withdrawal from friends and family[3]

Child abuse can happen at home. Child abuse can happen at school. Child abuse can happen at church. Having been placed in positions of trust, it is our responsibility, before God and before the governing authorities, to be aware and prepared to create safe places for our children and youth.

3 (Zarra 1997, 120)

C. Hearing an Allegation or Suspicion of Abuse Against an Adult

Policy

1. All allegations and disclosure of abuse or harassment against Adults are to be taken seriously.

2. Upon hearing an allegation or disclosure of abuse or harassment against an Adult, Ministry Personnel must complete a Suspected Abuse Report Form (Appendix 32) documenting all pertinent information. Do not ask the individual leading questions, and neither the accused nor any other parties should be contacted at the point of completing the Suspected Abuse Report Form.

3. All forms must be kept permanently unless otherwise directed by legal counsel.

4. Ministry Personnel are requested to notify the Lead Pastor that they have heard an allegation or disclosure of abuse.

5. If the abuse occurred within the context of the church, the Lead Pastor or his designate must notify the church's insurance provider and seek legal counsel upon hearing of a suspected abuse case.

6. If the abuse happened within the context of the church, leadership will notify and work in conjunction with denominational leadership in any and all allegations or suspicions of abuse that may have happened in the context of church ministry.

Plan

- ○ "Suspected Abuse Report Forms (for Adults)" have been prepared and made accessible to Ministry Personnel.

- ○ "Suspected Abuse Report Form (for Adults)" has been completed with all pertinent information.

- ○ Lead Pastor has been informed.

Protection

We are never prepared to hear an accusation of abuse or harassment. As pre-emptive as we may strive to be, no plan can be 100% preventative. Ministry personnel often gain a relationship of trust with the individual they have befriended, visited and worked with. This will provide an opportunity for them to express concerns.

'Reducing the Risk' highlights important issues to remember when dealing with an allegation of abuse or harassment. First, be prepared mentally to receive an allegation or to hear a disclosure. Do not express disbelief or respond in any way that minimizes the complaint or places blame upon the complainant. Comments like 'Did it only happen once?' and, 'It doesn't sound that serious,' need to be replaced with 'I know how hard this must be for you,' and, 'We want to do everything within our power to help and support you.'

"Second, be prepared for intense emotions from the complainant. Discerning and sensitive questions will be necessary to uncover some details. Don't try to form conclusions concerning the truth of the complaint at this time. Rather, focus on three simple points:
- that the complaint is being taken seriously,
- that procedures exist for such complaints and that they will be followed to ensure proper follow-through, and,
- that the church desires to extend care and support in whatever ways possible to the victim and the victim's family."[1]

When completing the Suspected Abuse Report Form (for Adults), be careful to simply gather the required information. Remember that it is not your responsibility to investigate or draw conclusions, but rather to gather information about the complainant, the alleged perpetrator, the nature of the suspected abuse or harassment and any indicators of the suspected abuse. Ask open questions and record direct words where possible.

---

1 (https://www.usccb.org/topics/marriage-and-family-life-ministries/when-i-call-help-pastoral-response-domestic-violence)

D. Reporting and Responding to an Allegation of Abuse or Harassment Against an Adult

Policy

1. All allegations, disclosures and suspicions of abuse and harassment against an Adult will be taken seriously and responded to with empathy.

2. If an allegation or suspicion of abuse represents a situation that is an emergency and a crime is about to be committed, immediately call 9-1-1 and report it to police.

3. If it is not an emergency or no imminent threat exists, and an accusation of abuse, harassment, misconduct or exploitation towards an Adult is made or suspected, the following guidelines are to be followed:

    a. If the Adult has the cognitive ability to make a report to police, then Ministry Personnel are to encourage the person to make that report, and support them in their decision, whatever they decide. At no time should the individual be discouraged or instructed not to call the police.

    b. If the Adult does not have the cognitive ability to make a report, then Ministry Personnel are to complete a Suspected Abuse Report Form (Appendix 32) and make a report to police, where the accusation involves a crime.

    c. In some cases, such as Long Term Care homes, additional laws define anyone who works with certain Adults as a Mandatory Reporter. In these cases, whether the Adult has the cognitive ability to make a report on their own or not, Ministry Personnel are to complete a Suspected Abuse Report Form (for Adults) and make a report to the mandated reporting agency.

4. If the Adult has the cognitive capacity to make a report, but is unwilling to do so, and no law requires mandatory reporting, Ministry Personnel should:

    a. Express concerns for the individual's well-being;

    b. Provide them the phone number to make the report in the future;

    c. Offer to be with them when they report it;

    d. Inform them about the laws in place regarding abuse and harassment and that they are not alone, that there are supports available to them;

    e. Encourage them to consider what to do next time;

    f. Arrange for a follow-up;

    g. Develop a safety plan.

5. Ministry Personnel and leadership are not to confront the accused as this may put the victim in more danger. They may offer pastoral care and professional counselling to the individual that disclosed the abuse but they are not to confront the accused about the abuse.

6. The church requests that when a report is made to police on behalf of an Adult who does not have the cognitive capacity to report on their own, in the case where a Ministry Personnel provides support to an Adult who makes their own report to police, or in a case where the Ministry Personnel is a Mandatory Reporter, that Ministry Personnel must notify the Lead Pastor that such a report has been made.

plan

This plan is written for a situation where an allegation or disclosure has been voiced or where suspected abuse or harassment against an Adult has been identified.

- ○ In the case of an emergency, the police have been notified.

- ○ Provincial Legislation on mandatory reporting for Elders and Vulnerable Adults has been consulted and shared to Ministry Personnel.

- ○ The Complainant with the cognitive ability to make a report has been encouraged to do so.

- ○ 'Suspected Abuse Report Form (for Adults)' has been completed and the allegation has been reported to police by Ministry Personnel where the Adult does not have the cognitive capacity to report on their own.

- ○ The Lead Pastor has been notified after a police report has been made, or after a Ministry Personnel completes a Suspected Abuse Report Form or Incident Report Form regarding Adult abuse.

Protection

This policy applies to, but is not limited to, abuse or harassment against an elderly person, an adult with physical or cognitive disabilities, and new immigrants. It may also apply to incidents of domestic abuse, harassment (sexual or psychological), or abuse where there is a power differential.

If an adult is not in immediate danger and they are cognitively capable of making a report on their own, it is their responsibility to make that report. Some complainants may know they are in danger but will resist all efforts of intervention. What we can do is support them and encourage them to seek help from law enforcement, professional therapists, and community services. Sadly, many times abuse and harassment come at the hands of very trusted individuals, and those being abused may fear the loss of a key relationship. Though we may care for them, ultimately whether or not to report a concern is their decision to make.

In Canada, reporting of abuse against an adult is not mandatory in most circumstances. An adult has the right to decide for themselves how they want to deal with an abusive situation. Unfortunately, this potentially leaves seniors and adults with disabilities in a very vulnerable situation. The only instance where reporting of suspected abuse of an adult is mandatory in Canada is when a person resides in a long-term care home (e.g., nursing home, senior home). When abuse is suspected to have happened in a long-term care facility, everyone, with the exception of residents themselves, is required to report allegations or suspicions of abuse to the Ministry of Long-Term Care.

Regardless of whether or not an individual is ready to report abuse or act in an abusive situation, we recommend you document your concerns. Documentation can help to show patterns of abuse, and can help to provide more appropriate care. Always share your concerns with a Lead Pastor or Board Member who can provide additional resources or guidance.

Church leaders should respond with empathy and care when they hear of domestic violence. If there are children in the home, exposure to domestic violence is a form of child abuse and must be reported to Child and Family Services.

According to the Conference of Catholic Bishops, "many church ministers want to help abused women but worry that they are not experts on domestic violence. Clergy may hesitate to preach about domestic violence because they are unsure what to do if an abused woman approaches them for help. We ask them to keep in mind that intervention by church ministers has three goals, in the following order:
- Safety for the victim and children;
- Accountability for the abuser; and
- Restoration of the relationship (if possible), or mourning over the loss of the relationship.
- We also encourage church ministers to see themselves as "first responders" who
- Listen to and believe the victim's story,
- Help her to assess the danger to herself and her children, and
- Refer her to counseling and other specialized services."[1]

---

1 (https://www.usccb.org/topics/marriage-and-family-life-ministries/when-i-call-help-pastoral-response-domestic-violence)

E. Assessing and Investigating an Allegation or Suspicion of Abuse

Policy

1. No persons, including Church Leadership, are to assume the function of assessing, substantiating or investigating the need for intervention or interpretation of suspected Child abuse or abuse against an Adult.

2. The church is to engage an external investigator to investigate allegations and disclosures of sexual misconduct and abuse of Adults.

3. The church and its individuals must avoid any undue interference when a report of Child abuse has been filed with Child and Family Services or the police. The church must ask how it can assist in helping and supporting the investigation and the victim. The church must maintain frequent communication and supportive relationships with those suspected or guilty of child abuse as long as these persons exhibit a willingness to listen, change and look to Christ for help. This does not exclude the need for hurting individuals to receive professional counselling.

4. The church must maintain frequent communication and supportive relationships with those suspected of abuse as long as the individual exhibits a willingness to listen. This does not exclude, or should it be at the expense of those that are victims and in need of professional counselling. A victim advocate must be appointed to walk alongside the victim.

5. The church is to support Ministry Personnel when they fulfill their duty to report abuse as outlined in the Plan to Protect® training and church policies.

Plan

This plan is written for a situation where an allegation has been voiced or where suspected abuse has been identified.

○ Church Leadership and Ministry Personnel have supported the Department of Social Services or the police in the course of an investigation and have offered to provide any necessary assistance.

○ Church Leadership and Ministry Personnel have adhered to the child protection acts, have supported those that made the report.

Protection

Ministry personnel and church leadership need to clearly understand that it is not our responsibility to investigate or to draw conclusions regarding allegations or suspicions of abuse. Our responsibility is to report the reasonable grounds of our belief that a child or youth is in need of intervention. Our responsibility is to support victims of abuse and seek truth and transparency.

"The devastation that follows an allegation of abuse is multi-layered, regardless of whether or not the allegation proves to be true. Clearly, prevention is the best defence. However, in the event that an abusive situation occurs – despite every effort to prevent it – the existence of, and adherence to clear policies and procedures will be an important factor in determining whether or not due diligence was exercised."[1]

It is not easy to make a report to Child and Family Services or the police. When ministry personnel make the report, it is imperative that church leadership provide support and care to the reporter. The reporter may experience compassion fatigue or come under great opposition after the report. It is always best to do what is in the best interest of the victim.

The greatest support we can lend to the process after a report of suspected abuse has been made is to provide thorough reports and records of child registration, attendance, workers' applications, references and screening forms.

As the church comes alongside the victim after an allegation has been made, church leaders need to be careful not to revictimize the victim. The church should also be aware that communication with the perpetrator should be done carefully and not before the police or Child and Family Services has given permission to do so.[2] The church needs to offer support and care and provide necessary services as we begin to work together in the journey to restore hope.

> "One of the greatest tests of our belief in the sovereignty of God is when we make a report of child abuse! If we believe in the sovereignty of God, we will rest knowing that God is ultimately in control."

---

1 (McCormick and Mitchell, 1999)
2 (Cobble, Hammer and Klipowicz 2003, 57)

Reporting and Response

F. Protecting Confidentiality and Dignity of the Victim and the Accused

Policy

1. During the process of reporting and response, all Ministry Personnel will be committed to prayer and strive to remain calm and hopeful.

2. Discretion must be observed and details of the suspected abuse must not be shared among the church community. Information should be shared on a need-to-know basis, expanding only as individuals are drawn into the response and investigation. Confidentiality for the suspected victim and the accused must be protected.

Plan

This plan is written for a situation where an allegation has been voiced or where suspected abuse has been identified.

○ Confidentiality will be maintained at all times.

Protection

"We must do all we can to make our ministries as safe as possible, and be alert and ready to help those who've been wounded – they are in our midst."[1] We have all read stories or met people who have been wounded by abuse, either as victims or as the accused. The church should offer to both a commitment to pray, a commitment to protect confidentiality and a commitment to uphold dignity as God begins the binding of their wounds.

"Sexual abuse is a problem in every community and every church. The statistics are horrifying – one in every three girls and at least one in every seven boys is victimized by sexual abuse."[2] "Statistics, however, only give us an idea of how widespread a problem is. They represent the tip of the iceberg and do not paint the whole picture. Neither do they capture the impact of the problem on the victim or the family struggling through the devastation of abuse. Child abuse and neglect is a broad topic that addresses a complex experience which is debilitating for children."[3]

To protect the confidentiality and the dignity of all involved, our desire would be that the suspected abuse not be shared with the church community at large. However, it would be naïve to think that all situations can be controlled at that level. "To say nothing creates suspicion and backlash that jeopardize the ministry of a church. To say everything can put the church and the leaders at legal risk."[4] Church leadership, in consultation with legal counsel, need to determine, throughout the process, who and what constitutes a need-to-know basis as they attempt to bring healing and wholeness to the church community.

---

1 (Hayes and Wagner 2004, 78)
2 (Leader, 2002)
3 (Hayes and Wagner 2004, 78, 83)
4 (Cobble, Hammer and Klipowicz 2003, 60)

G. Spiritual Abuse

Policy

1. The church is opposed to any form of spiritual abuse. Ministry Personnel are not to misuse their positions of authority or influence to manipulate or coerce others to act or believe in a certain way for the apparent benefit of the church or those in a position of authority.

2. Ministry Personnel are not to use scripture out of context or to use the Bible as a weapon to unduly manipulate an individual.

3. Ministry Personnel and Board members must attend additional professional development training on spiritual abuse awareness and prevention. Volunteers must receive training on the definition of spiritual abuse as part of their safeguarding training.

4. A whistleblower policy must be put in place to provide a safe contact to receive concerns about any form of injury, harm, and abuse. All complaints of spiritual abuse are to be brought to the attention of the Board and are to be fully investigated as outlined under the Whistleblower Policy.

5. Ministry Personnel are to be held accountable if they have been found to have misused their positions to unduly cause spiritual harm to another individual and are to be subject to progressive steps of discipline.

6. If an individual raises a concern about spiritual abuse, they are to be encouraged to seek out professional help and healing. Church Leadership are to assign a knowledgeable person to provide care to the individual, and where able, are to extend the offer of professional care and therapy to help with the recovery of the spiritual harm that has occurred.

Plan

- ○ Policies, procedures and training include the definition of spiritual abuse.

- ○ Community and ministry resources have been identified to help individuals that have been spiritually abused.

- ○ A whistleblower policy has also been put into place to provide a safe contact to raise issues of spiritual abuse.

Protection

According to bEmboldened Ministries, "Unhealthy religious experiences are prevalent and the wreckage from them is all around you. …. Harm is harm. Trauma is trauma. Pain, confusion, loss. We all know these emotions from some aspect of our own lives." bEmboldened Ministry[1] exists for those whose lives have been, presently are, and have the potential to be impacted by an unhealthy religious experience.

In human relationships there are areas of legitimate authority. When power or control is exercised beyond the appropriate boundaries of such authority, whether in the context of a religious organization or in individual relationships where spiritual authority is claimed, this constitutes spiritual abuse. This can happen when spiritual authority is misused to manipulate peoples' emotional responses (such as fear, guilt or shame) or loyalty, for the benefit of the church, institution or of another individual. Spiritual abuse may also include or underlie other forms of abuse such as sexual, physical, verbal, psychological or emotional abuse when these take place within the context of a religious organization.

Mary DeMuth provides 10 traits of spiritually abusive ministries[2]:

1. **Have a distorted view of respect.** They forget the simple adage that respect is earned, not granted. Abusive leaders demand respect without having earned it by good, honest living.
2. **Demand allegiance as proof of the follower's allegiance to Christ.** It's either his/her way or no way. And if a follower deviates, he is guilty of deviating from Jesus.
3. **Use exclusive language.** "We're the only ministry really following Jesus." "We have all the right theology." Believe their way of doing things, thinking theologically, or handling ministry and church is the only correct way. Everyone else is wrong, misguided, or stupidly naive.
4. **Create a culture of fear and shame.** Often there is no grace for someone who fails to live up to the church's or ministry's expectation. And if someone steps outside of the often-unspoken rules, leaders shame them into compliance.
5. **Often have a charismatic leader at the helm who starts off well, but slips into arrogance, protectionism and pride.** Where a leader might start off being personable and interested in others' issues, he/she eventually withdraws to a small group of "yes people" and isolates from the needs of others. These ministries and churches harbor a cult of personality, meaning if the central figure of the ministry or church left, the entity would collapse, as it was entirely dependent on one person to hold the place together.
6. **Cultivate a dependence on one leader or leaders for spiritual information.** Personal discipleship isn't encouraged. Often the Bible gets pushed away to the fringes unless the main leader is teaching it.
7. **Demand blind servitude of their followers, but live prestigious, privileged lives.** They live aloof from their followers and justify their material extravagance as God's favor and approval on their ministry. Unlike Jesus' instructions to take the last seat, they often take the first seat at events and court others to grant them privileges.
8. **Buffer him/herself from criticism by placing people around themselves whose only allegiance is to the leader.** These leaders and churches view those who bring up legitimate issues as enemies. Those who were once friends/allies swiftly become enemies once a concern is raised.
9. **Hold to outward performance but rejects authentic spirituality.** Places burdens on followers to act a certain way, dress an acceptable way, and have an acceptable lifestyle, but they often demonstrate licentiousness, greed, and uncontrolled addictions behind closed doors.

---

1 (https://www.beemboldened.com)
2 (https://www.marydemuth.com/spiritual-abuse-10-ways-to-spot-it)

Protection continued...

10. **Use exclusivity for allegiance.** Followers close to the leader or leaders feel like lucky insiders. Everyone else is on the outside, though they often long to be in that inner circle. If someone on the inner circle speaks up about abuses, lapses in character, illegal acts, or strong-arming, that insider immediately moves to an outsider. Fear of losing their special status often impedes insiders from speaking up.

Alternatively, Scot McKnight and Laura Barringer in their book *A Church Called Tov: Forming a Goodness Culture That Resists Abuses of Power and Promotes Healing* speaks to the seven elements that make up the "circle of tov."

A tov church will proactively:
- Nurture empathy, and resist a narcissist's culture
- Nurture grace, and resist a fear culture
- Put people first, and resist institution creep culture
- Tell the truth, resist false narratives, and form a truth-telling culture
- Nurture justice, and resist the loyalty culture
- Nurture service, and resist the celebrity culture
- Nurture Christlikeness, and resist the leader culture

The last of these essentially summarizes the whole circle. A tov church will be a Christlike church.

May we all embrace a culture that reflects the goodness of God while nurturing Christlikeness in each other.

> "The bad news and the good news about culture can be summed up in the same statement: A rooted culture is almost irresistible. If the reinforcing culture is toxic, it becomes systematically corrupted and corrupts the people within it. Like racism, sexism, political ideologies, and success-at-all-costs business, a corrupted culture drags everyone down with it. On the other hand, if the reinforcing culture is redemptive and healing and good (tov), it becomes systematically good. A tov church culture will instinctively heal, redeem, and restore."
>
> *A Church Called Tov*, Scot McKnight and Laura Barringer, p. 17

> "Trust does not negate questioning, love does not negate accountability, and leadership does not negate humanity." - Naomi Wright

H. Whistleblower Policy

Policy

1. The church is to act with due diligence in its investigation and follow through on all allegations of misconduct. They are to do their utmost to protect any whistleblower from reprisal, dismissal or any other retaliation.
2. The church is not to tolerate any harassment or victimization (including informal pressures) and is to take appropriate action to protect the whistleblower when they raise a concern in good faith, even if they are mistaken. Any harassment or victimization of a whistleblower may result in disciplinary action against the person responsible.
3. In situations where we have a legal duty to report child abuse, no internal investigation is to take place until such time as an investigation has been conducted by law enforcement or the child protection agency.
4. Any investigations into allegations arising from whistleblowing are not to influence or be influenced by any other Ministry Personnel procedures to which the whistleblower may be subject.
5. All concerns are to be treated in confidence and every effort is to be made not to reveal the identity of the whistleblower if that is their wish. If a concern cannot be resolved without revealing the identity of the whistleblower, steps forward are to be determined in collaboration with the whistleblower. This policy encourages the whistleblower to put their name to their allegation whenever possible.
6. Church Leadership has overall responsibility for the maintenance and operation of this policy. The church is to maintain a record of concerns raised and outcomes (in a form which does not endanger confidentiality) and is to report as necessary to the governmental, or other legal authority as required by law.
7. The church is to respond to every complaint or allegation. Within 10 working days of a concern being raised, a member of Church Leadership is to write to the whistleblower to:
   a. Acknowledge that the complaint or allegation has been received;
   b. Indicate how the matter will be dealt with;
   c. Give an estimate of how long it will take to provide a final response;
   d. Indicate whether any initial inquiries have been made;
   e. Supply the whistleblower with information on support mechanisms;
   f. Tell the whistleblower whether further investigations will take place and if not, why not.
8. Where appropriate, the matters raised may:
   a. Be referred to the next level of leadership;
   b. Be referred to the Board of Directors;
   c. Be referred to the disciplinary process;
   d. Be referred to the police;
   e. Be referred to an external investigator; or
   f. Form the subject of an independent inquiry.
9. The church is to take steps to minimize any difficulties which the whistleblower may experience as a result of raising a complaint or allegation.
10. If a complaint or allegation is not confirmed by an investigation, no action is to be taken against a whistleblower. If, however, a complaint or allegation is made frivolously, maliciously or for personal gain, disciplinary action may be taken against the complainant.
11. Subject to legal constraints, the church is to inform the whistleblower of the outcome of any investigation.

plan

- Church Leadership has developed a plan and processes for responding to whistleblower complaints and determining how to take steps forward.

- Ministry personnel have been made aware of their right to protection if they raise a concern.

- Ministry personnel have been made aware of the disciplinary action to be taken if a concern is raised for frivolous or malicious reasons.

Protection

When there is something seriously wrong within the activity of an organization, ministry personnel will often be the first to realize it. However, they may feel that speaking up would be disloyal to their colleagues, family members, clients or constituents. They may also fear harassment or victimization from others within their organization. In these circumstances, they may find it easier to ignore the concern rather than report what may just be a suspicion of malpractice or abuse.

Churches should make it clear that anyone can raise concerns in confidence without fear of victimization, subsequent discrimination or disadvantage. Examples of whistleblower reports include but are not limited to, sexual harassment comments, spiritual abuse, misuse of donations, grooming behaviour, slander, etc. All concerns should be taken seriously. These concerns, may fall outside the scope of other procedures, including the reporting of child abuse or suspicion of child abuse, places of risk, illegal activity, personal injury or injury to a colleague, and breaches of the policy or code of conduct. In those situations, please also refer to specific policy statements that address those issues.

Response to Abuse

A. Spiritual Response and Counsel for the Victim
B. Biblical Response and Discipline for the Accused or Convicted
C. Media Relations
D. Ongoing Investigation
E. Offender's Policy

Case Study

Response to Abuse

I serve as a staff pastor at my church. One Sunday after church, Mike, a consistent attendee for the last few months tells me that he has a big problem. We meet the following Tuesday to talk about it and in the midst of our conversation, he tells me that he was convicted of sexually abusing a Child while overseas. He tells me that he is still struggling with attraction to Children and that he was recently kicked out of his apartment for telling the landlord that he was attracted to the Children of a family that lived there. In a lot of distress, he asks me, "not to kick him out of the church."

I immediately contact the Lead Pastor and after consultation with him, we tell the rest of the Elders Board as well as the District Superintendent. The elder responsible for Plan to Protect® in our church reviews our procedures to make sure we are following protocol. On advice from our District Superintendent, I called the editor of Plan to Protect® as well as our lawyer.

In the short term, we informed those in charge of the Children's Ministry of the specific threat prior to the next Sunday. In addition, I told Mike that the Children's area on the third floor was off-limits and that there would be no tolerance of him being there under any circumstance.

The following week, we met as a Board to deal with the situation and then as a Board, we met with Mike who was gracious enough to meet with our request. Mike shared his struggle with us, the abuse, his time in prison, his current temptations, and how he is trying to put his life back together. We prayed with him. We talked about what type of structures we could put into place to protect him and the church. One of the major problems to overcome was who to tell. Mike wanted as few people to know as possible, fearing that if everyone knew that it would be impossible for him in the church. We considered telling everyone who had Children, but instead decided to tell the Children's Ministry Personnel and the deacons in the church in addition to the pastors and Elders Board who already knew. An Offender's Covenant was then drafted to send to Mike outlining the following stipulations and we consulted with our lawyer once again. Mike was required to submit to the following:

"1. Upon entry into the church on Sunday morning, you will check in with one of two designated elders. In addition, you will "buddy up" with a designated peer who knows of your situation. This buddy up system will be in place for all meetings in church including prayer meetings, fellowship meetings or any other events.
2. The whole third floor of the Children's area is off-limits.
3. There will be no interaction with families with Children under 12 who do not know of your situation.
4. The church will be off-limits during our Children's day camp and any other events that are deemed to be high risk.

Any failure to meet the above policy will result in the church being off-limits to you."

Case Study continued ...

Mike agreed to sign the Offender's Covenant as he recognized that this was for his protection also. In addition, my Lead Pastor or myself met with Mike often weekly over several months. There were no reported incidents and Mike complied with the stipulations. We thank God for the opportunity to function as the body of Christ, upholding our brother in his need. We learned to love as Christ loved. It was also a reminder that we are all vulnerable to hidden sin and need to be watchful for ourselves and each other. We have grown with Mike through our time together. Mike has since left the city and we pray the same precautions will be taken at his next church.

Questions to Consider:

- Did the church follow the protocol for this situation?
- What did the church do right?
- Where do you feel the church may have been remiss?
- Do you believe the appropriate people were notified? Too many, or not enough?
- What precautions do you feel the church could assume to protect the children and youth in this situation?
- What other requirements could be included in the Offender's Covenant?
- Discuss with your leadership team how you would deal with a similar scenario in your church.

Hindsight is 20/20:

Unfortunately, this case study is also true and very alarming. We applaud the church for responding with love and grace during a difficult time. Often we think that this could not happen in our church. Please read carefully through the section, 'Response to Allegations,' and consider how you can respond with love and grace to the accused, assist with extending and facilitating compassion and healing to the victim while ensuring confidentiality.

A. Spiritual Response and Counsel for the Victim

Policy

1. The church is committed to providing a trauma-informed response, prioritizing the needs of the victim.

2. For the protection of everyone, all allegations and/or suspicions of abuse are to be taken seriously and handled with the utmost care. The suspected victims are to be treated with dignity and respect.

3. During the process of reporting and response, all Ministry Personnel are to be committed to prayer and strive to remain calm and hopeful.

4. Situations of abuse must be handled forthrightly with due respect for people's privacy and confidentiality. Discretion must be observed and details of the suspected abuse must not be shared among the church community. Information must be shared on a need-to-know basis, expanding only as individuals are drawn into the response and investigation. Confidentiality for the victim must be protected.

5. Church Leadership are to seek opportunity to provide individual care and counsel both for the abuse victim and their family. In consultation with the individual, a victim advocate will be assigned to support the victim. Church Leadership are to determine the need for professional assistance and evaluate and designate resources as needed and able.

6. The victim will be empowered to make decisions and granted opportunity for their voice to be heard. At no time will the victim be asked to sign a non-disclosure agreement in relation to the incident of abuse.

Plan

This plan is written for a situation where an allegation has been voiced or where suspected abuse has been identified and a report has been submitted.

- ○ Discretion has been observed and offered at all times along with confidentiality and dignity extended to the suspected victim and their family.

- ○ Individuals have been designated to provide care and counsel to both the suspected victim and their family.

- ○ Professional counsel has been recommended as required.

- ○ Resources have been allocated as deemed needed and available.

Protection

One mom shared the pain of discovering her five-year-old daughter had been abused by a 16-year-old volunteer in a worship room filled with kids and leaders. Where are our children safe? Her questions are profound, " … since God is a God of truth, aren't we to honor the truth regardless of how it'll impact our church's future? And since our children belong first and foremost to God, aren't we to do everything in our power to keep them safe? Especially in our churches? Especially since our children can't defend themselves?"[1]

"Shepherds are protectors of lambs as well as grown up sheep."[2] It takes great courage to choose to right a wrong. Victims who take this first step deserve support and protection throughout the many difficult steps to come.

God's healing can begin as the church initiates steps of care and support. We recommend that someone be appointed to ensure that the church fulfills its responsibility. The church must reach out to the victim and the victim's family as they attempt to rebuild trust.

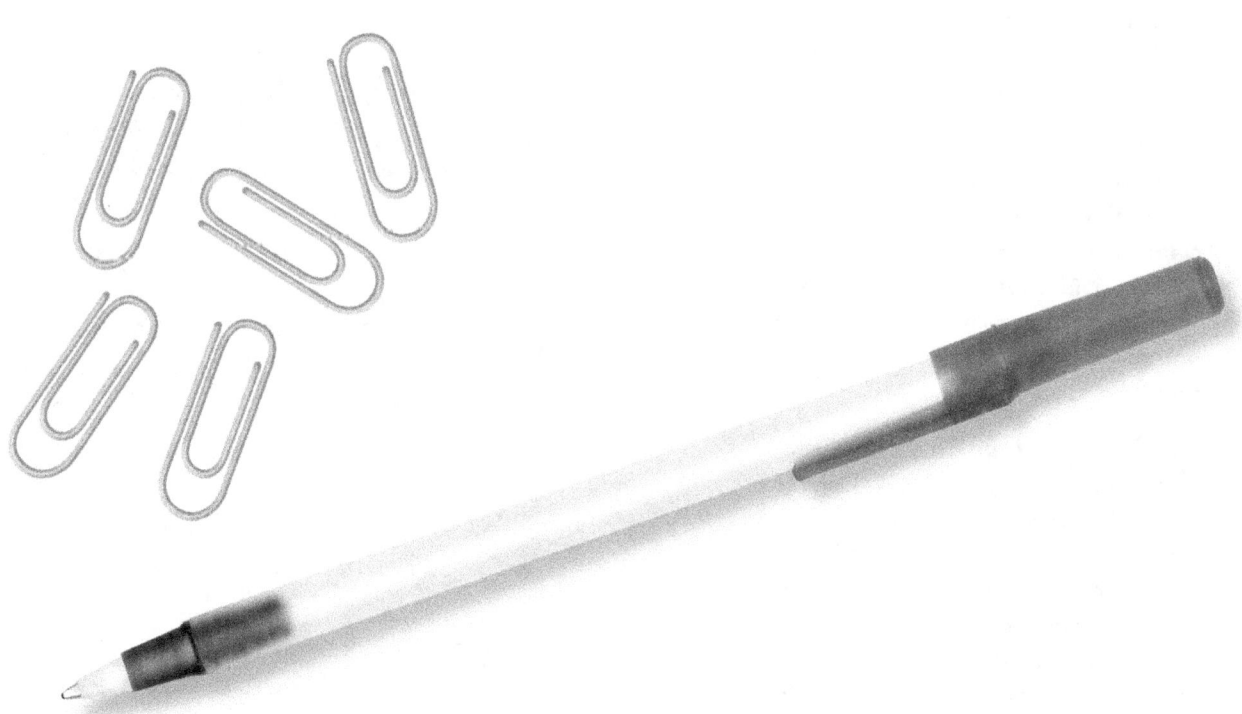

1 (Davis 2006, 58)
2 (Zarra 1997, 9)

Reporting and Response

B. Biblical Response and Discipline for the Accused or Convicted

Policy

1. The accused is to be treated with dignity and respect. Ministry Personnel, accused of abuse, must be relieved temporarily of all of their duties until an investigation is completed. Arrangements will be made to either maintain or suspend income until the allegations are cleared or substantiated if applicable.

2. It is the responsibility and right of Church Leadership to exercise and practice church discipline as outlined in Matthew 18 and as stipulated in denominational guidelines.

3. Church Leadership are to seek opportunity to provide individual care and counsel both for the accused and their family. Church Leadership are to determine the need for professional assistance and evaluate and designate resources as needed and able.

4. Anyone accused of abuse to Children or Youth is to be prohibited from having access to Children or Youth until they are cleared of any and all charges. Clear written guidelines are to be provided to the individual with restricted activities and areas of the church that they are not permitted to use.

5. Anyone convicted of Child abuse will be prohibited from having access to Children or Youth. Church Leadership may designate an individual to be responsible to be informed whenever the convicted person attends church activities and to accompany the convicted person while on church property. Clear written guidelines are to be provided to the individual listing restricted areas and access points on the church property.

Plan

This plan is written for a situation where an allegation has been voiced or where suspected abuse has been identified and a report has been submitted.

- ○ The accused has been removed from ministry involvement until his or her name is cleared by officials.

- ○ Guidelines for those with convictions have been identified to restrict access to vulnerable persons.

- ○ Discretion has been observed and offered at all times along with confidentiality and dignity extended to the accused and their family.

- ○ An individual has been designated to provide care and counsel to both the accused and their family.

- ○ Professional counsel has been recommended as required.

- ○ Resources have been allocated as deemed needed and available.

Plan continued...

○ Individuals have been notified of suspected abuse on a need-to-know basis.

○ On a need-to-know basis, individuals have been notified of convicted abusers attending the church.

○ Restrictions for contact with minors and restrictions regarding church premises have been clearly communicated to individuals accused of or convicted of abuse to children and/or youth.

Protection

In the Canadian legal system, the accused is innocent until proven guilty. False accusations can be made. Legal counsel strongly cautions the broadcasting of untruths. Confidentiality is critical. For example, ministry personnel and board members should not discuss information about an accusation with their spouses.

The church's response to the accused is critical in restoring the person to health. "Faithful response to the accused abuser will include acknowledgment not only that he or she is a person of sacred worth; but also that he or she must stop the abusive behaviour, prayerfully repent and turn in a new direction. Faithful response will include removing the accused from his or her position as a worker with children and youth until the allegations are fully investigated and resolved. It does not necessarily mean that the accused will at some future time be placed again in a position of trust involving children and youth."[1]

Churches must speak out against abuse and take the necessary precautions to prevent further incidents from happening.

---

1 (Thornburg Melton 2003, 54)

C. Media Relations

Policy

1. It is the responsibility of the Church Leadership and Lead Pastor to designate a spokesperson to speak on behalf of the church to media and to the public in relation to any crisis or allegation of abuse. All inquiries must be directed to this person and comment must not be made by other individuals unless given permission to do so.

2. Public statements must be well prepared and presented under the guidance of legal counsel.

3. The media spokesperson is to cooperate with the media to communicate our deep concern about the incident and reaffirm our commitment to cooperate with the investigation.

Plan

- A media spokesperson has been designated by church leadership.
- A public statement has been prepared for media spokesperson under the guidance of legal counsel.

Protection

Cases of abuse in a church often result in extensive media coverage. One individual needs to be designated as the spokesperson for the church, however, "A team of members need to be ready to deal with media, legal matters, counselling issues and financial aspects of the church if an accusation is made. Responding to the media takes education and understanding that there could be grave legal ramifications."[1]

Church leadership must prepare a statement for public use should an allegation of abuse occur. "Having a carefully prepared statement is far superior to making no comment. This is an opportunity to influence public opinion positively by emphasizing an awareness of the problem of abuse and harassment, a concern for victims and the extensive steps the church has taken to reduce the risk and provide a safe church. Let the media know that the church takes the risk of abuse seriously and that the church has acted responsibly. Describe all the precautions the church has taken and the policies the church has implemented. This is no time for silence or 'no comment'. Take the initiative in maintaining a positive public image of your church."[2]

1 (Woodruff and Kasper 2001, 96)
2 (Cobble, Hammer and Klipowicz 2003, 6)

Protection continued...

Church leadership should have a well crafted Crisis Response Plan in place which can be put into action as soon as a crisis comes to light. Plan to Protect® offers a Crisis Management certification course for church leaders.

In an allegation of abuse against a child, the statement below is suggested wording for a public response:

> We believe that our children and our youth are gifts from God and that they are the future of His church. So, we at _____ Church are committed to protecting the children and youth entrusted to our care. All ministry personnel are screened and trained and policies have been set to provide for the safety and security of our students. It is always tragic when children are abused or exploited and we are distressed and shocked by any accusation of child abuse. We are committed to do everything in our power to address any needs in this situation and to cooperate with the investigation. For the welfare of those involved, all information has been directed to the police and the Department of Social Services.

In an allegation of harassment or abuse against an adult, the statement below is suggested wording for a public statement. (This does not constitute legal advice):

> At _____ Church, we are committed to safeguarding and are gravely concerned about any allegation or disclosure of sexual harassment or abuse. All ministry personnel including staff are screened and trained and policies have been set to provide for the safety and security of our congregation. We are committed to do everything in our power to address any needs in this situation and will immediately launch an investigation and if charges are laid against the individual, we will cooperate with law enforcement.

"Courage faces fear
and thereby masters it."
- Dr. Martin Luther King Jr.

D. Ongoing Investigation

Policy

1. Full cooperation must be given by all parties to civil authorities under the guidelines of legal counsel.

2. At no time should Church Leadership or its individuals either engage in denial, minimization or blame, or admit responsibility which could prejudice the case or cause increased liability to the church.

3. A confidential follow-up report with conclusions and action taken must be documented by the Lead Pastor following a report of abuse. This report should be placed in a confidential Ministry Personnel file and kept permanently.

4. Church Leadership are to inform others of any ongoing investigation strictly on a need-to-know basis. In consultation with legal counsel, a trauma-informed summary report will be shared with the complainant, accused and the congregation.

Plan

This plan is written for a situation where an allegation has been voiced or where suspected abuse has been identified and a report has been submitted.

○ Cooperation has been offered to civil authorities with the guidance of legal counsel.

○ All actions have been documented and filed with the church office and kept permanently.

Protection

"Rebuilding the lives shattered by abuse begins by focusing on three primary concerns:
- healing of the lives of the victims,
- repentance, reparation, and eventual restoration of the perpetrator, and,
- rebuilding of trust and oneness in the church community."[1]

1 (Zarra 1997, 91)

E. Offender's Policy

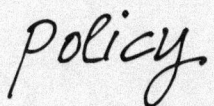

This policy relates to Offenders, meaning individuals who have been convicted of sexual crimes against Children or Youth who wish to attend the church on a consistent basis.

1. Offenders of Child sexual abuse may attend the church on a regular basis if they enter into an Offender's Covenant Agreement with the leadership of the church.

2. Two delegates from the Board and the Lead Pastor are to meet with the individual and inform the individual that the church requires Offenders to enter into an Offender's Covenant Agreement (Appendix 41) in order for them to attend the church on a regular basis.

3. The Covenant Agreement is to be written and signed by the Lead Pastor, two representatives of the Board, and the individual, making up the accountability team.

4. The Offender's Covenant must include the following:

   a. Who is to be informed when the Offender will be at the church.

   b. What part of the building the Offender may come to.

   c. Locations in the building the Offender is not allowed to go to (Children and Youth wings of the church).

   d. Where in the sanctuary the Offender may sit (recommend the front of the sanctuary with one of the accountability team members).

   e. Restriction to take pictures at the church.

   f. Restrictions for befriending and spending time with families with Children.

   g. When the Offender uses the washroom, one of the chaperones are to first check the washroom to make sure there are no Children in the washroom. If there is a Child in the washroom they are to wait until the Child is done before entering.

   h. Restrictions from participating in programs with Children and Youth, i.e., church property during special Children's events (such as VBS, mid-week Children's/Youth programs, etc.).

   i. The requirement for annual review and signature of the Offender's Covenant Agreement by the accountability team.

   j. The consequences if the covenant is broken.

5. Information regarding an individual's convictions are to only be disclosed to the members of the Board, the Pastor, key Ministry Leaders and individuals involved in supporting the Covenant Agreement or on a limited need-to-know basis.

Plan

- ☐ The Board is notified if someone discloses a history of committing abuse or a conviction so that there is a process and parameters put in place.

- ☐ An Offender's Covenant has been put in place for any individual who has been convicted of crimes against Children, Youth or Vulnerable Adults.

- ☐ When the individual is involved in programs, they do so with members of their covenant team present and they abide by the agreement.

- ☐ There is an ongoing process in place to identify who needs to know and to disclose in an appropriate manner.

Protection

Churches can be messy spaces. We love our kids and want to keep them safe, but we also believe in forgiveness and redemption and want to create spaces for individuals who seek reconciliation with God to continue their journey. A covenant agreement provides a framework for such an individual to do so in a safe and transparent manner.

Churches are now wanting to embrace a ministry of reconciliation and restorative justice. Restorative justice refers to a way of responding to crime, or to other types of wrongdoing, injustice or conflict, that focuses primarily on repairing the damage caused by the wrongful action and restoring, insofar as possible, the well-being of all those involved.

For the protection of children, youth and those that were harmed in the past, as well as for those who are known to have a history of crimes against children and youth, clear parameters should be put into place restricting such an individual from having access to the vulnerable.

Information regarding an individual's convictions should only be disclosed on a need-to-know basis to the board, the pastor and some ministry personnel. If the individual is a parent with children attending church, which may afford opportunity for the individual to have more access to other children (i.e., pickup and drop-off, and social events), then the need-to-know circle should be expanded to those families.

The Offender's Covenant (Appendix 41) has been adapted from *Smart Justice* written by Diane Roblin-Lee.

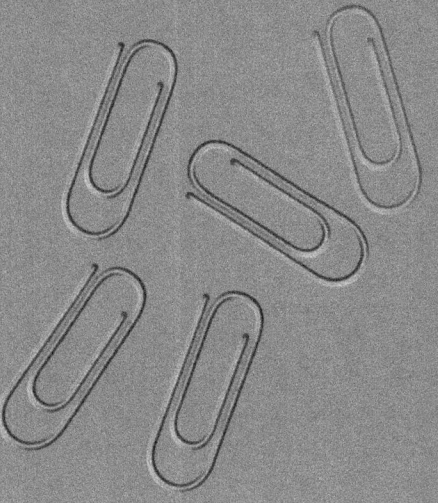

Conclusion

This brings to a close this version of Plan to Protect® A Safeguarding Guide for Children, Youth and Adults Church Edition. This resource has not been written by just one author, rather, it represents the efforts of many, many individuals who have stepped up to the plate with a passion and commitment to protect the vulnerable, to guard the church, and to raise the voices of victim-survivors of abuse. It is a collection of best practices gleaned from experts in the field, and many, many church partners that have been putting into practice the recommendations of Plan to Protect® during this time.

While working tirelessly on this resource, I (Melodie) have also been pursuing my doctoral studies at the Toronto School of Theology, University of Toronto. Just recently I successfully defended my thesis The Experience of Spiritual Healing Among Adult Victim-Survivors of Child Sexual Abuse: A Phenomenological Study.

The question I raised in my thesis was: Do the experiences of victim-survivors of child sexual abuse offer a rich resource for churches to learn better ways to support individuals on their journey to spiritual healing?

The answer was yes! A resounding yes! In the study I sat down with six brave victim-survivors of abuse and asked them their stories of spiritual healing from abuse. The abusers were individuals that represented Christian faith and leadership within the church. Their abusers wore many hats, including church elders, deacons, fathers, a grandparent, Sunday School teachers, a pastor, a youth leader, a missionary, and a boarding parent.

My goal in undertaking my research study was to hold the posture of being a lifelong learner as I have a deep interest in the issues, having dedicated my life to the prevention of abuse.

Sixteen common themes emerged from the interviews with the six individuals who were part of the doctoral research study. The learnings are so important that we could not go to print with the manual without sharing them as the conclusion.

Plan to Protect® has always been about prevention. We want to help you prevent abuse against Children, Youth and Adults. However, we sadly know from experience that abuse happens. The church's response when abuse happens will either contribute to the damage and trauma that the victim will experience, or will be instrumental in their healing—be that physical, emotional, or spiritual.

We are confident that the themes identified in the research may reflect the experiences of other victim-survivors seeking spiritual healing as they live within a faith community. This belief is based on courses, readings, and personal discussions outside of the scope of this study. We share these 16 discovered themes with you as food for thought and further discussion:

1. Child sexual abuse happened within churches and homes representing Christian faith, and because of fear, shame, blame, and guilt, a high percentage of the participants did not disclose their abuse to those closest to them.
2. Victim-survivors testify to discovering spiritual healing of child sexual abuse, but they speak of it as a lifelong journey as there were helpful and not harmful events that occurred as part of the healing process.
3. Victim-survivors of abuse experience triggers that bring back painful memories of abuse. Some of these triggers are tied to the church or symbols of the faith and included, but are not limited to, a smell, a well-known Bible passage, a worship song or hymn, a phrase, and a big black Bible.
4. The care of victim-survivors of abuse means knowing and recognizing coping mechanisms and being able to have caring and intentional conversations to shepherd the victim-survivors.

5. There is a need for Christian leaders to receive professional development on the importance of referring individuals to professional counsellors when dealing with child sexual abuse and following up with the individual after referral.
6. Pastors, church leaders, counsellors, and professors need to receive more training on power differentials, the impact of child sexual abuse, and unhealthy conversations concerning exploring an individual's sexual history and experience.
7. Pastors and Christian leaders must overcome their fears and concerns (including but not limited to the impact on their churches and ministries, congregation responses, lawsuits and motivations), in order to transform their churches into safe places conducive to support the healing process.
8. Individuals who advocate for a safe church may be boldly and courageously advocating on their own behalf as a victim-survivor of abuse, or on behalf of Children in their midst so that the Children will not have to experience the suffering they personally experienced.
9. God has called individuals to journey with the victim-survivors of abuse to share in their redemptive stories.
10. God uses people (within and outside the church) to nurture the healing process, more so than a church's programs, sermons, teachings, or events.
11. Care of victim-survivors of abuse involves being present and available while these individuals experience and overcome the pain in their lives.
12. The practice of spiritual disciplines can provide a means by which God reveals his presence and speaks to those who are suffering within the context of role-modelling and discipleship.
13. To rebuild the walls of protection and nurture spiritual healing of victim-survivors of child sexual abuse, the church is encouraged to work collaboratively with other community stakeholders, such as physicians, family members, friends, and therapists.
14. There may come a time in a victim-survivor's life when they no longer desire to be defined by their past.
15. Hurt people may hurt people. However, hurt people may also be the ones God uses to care for those in need.
16. Victims of child sexual abuse suffer intensely, physically, emotionally, mentally, and spiritually, but can and do experience healing. With personal encounters with God, the people who have made them feel safe and the spiritual practices they engaged in, spiritual healing can be realized.

This research has been deeply transformative in my life and practice through the courses attended, the writing of the comprehensive paper and thesis, and the research and analysis among the participants.

When we first set out to write Plan to Protect®, our intention and goal was never just to write a policy and procedure handbook. Rather, it was always with a deep desire to protect the vulnerable and to encourage the church to pursue excellence in safeguarding. During the past 25 years we have written hundreds of policies and procedures, and trained tens of thousands of people. We have coached people on mitigating risk and qualifying for abuse coverage all with an aim to prevent abuse from happening.

However, we truly believe that by sharing these themes as the conclusion of this resource, we are coming full circle and reminding ourselves and our readers that this is always about protecting the vulnerable. Protecting their innocence and protecting their spiritual well-being so that they truly can live the "abundant life"[1] intended for them. My research has been deeply transformative for me as I find that now I incorporate daily the voice of the victim – both in prevention and response. I believe that this will also be transformative for you, the church.

If you wish to receive a copy of the doctoral research, please contact me directly at **melodie.bissell@sympatico.ca**.

For more information regarding our services at Plan to Protect®, contact **info@plantoprotect.com**.

Living for an audience of One,

Melodie Bissell, D.Min.
President
Plan to Protect®

---
1 (John 10:10, NASB)

Appendices and Bibliography

Introduction to Appendices

If you need it, we have created it! If you are a member of Plan to Protect® and for some reason you believe something is missing, please contact us at **info@plantoprotect.com**.

Within the pages of the Appendices section of the Plan to Protect® manual, we have compiled every draft policy in the manual. We have included the Implementation Strategy, the extensive plan section which is a TO DO list to implement every policy and procedure statement. With the assistance of our Advisory Council we have drafted a template for every form that you will need.

With the purchase of the manual, you have access to the full Appendices section in Word format. Please refer to page 2 for your key to the download page of the Plan to Protect® website.

The forms are customizable.

Disclaimer: All rights reserved with the exception that permission is granted to the purchaser of this manual the right to reproduce for the sole use of your local church for training purposes and customized policy development. No portion of this book may be posted on the internet or shared with other organizations and churches without written permission from Plan to Protect®. Permission is granted to the purchaser and/or bearer of this published work a single license of the registered trademark Plan to Protect®. This use of the license is restricted to organizations that credit the majority of their abuse prevention policy to the Plan to Protect® manual. The registered trademark symbol must accompany the phrase Plan to Protect®.

When modifying the policy, procedures and appendices, organizations are strongly encouraged to seek legal counsel as well as counsel from their insurance company who can give written opinion concerning the specifics of their particular situation.

Note: The best practices found in the Appendices of the manual are not stand-alone. The Appendices are supplementary material to be used with other (as important) sections of this manual, including Recruitment and Screening, Training, Documentation, General Protection Procedures, Child, Youth and Vulnerable Adult Protection Procedures, and Reporting and Response.

We are grateful for the network of advisory council members that have contributed to the 100+ pages of the Appendices.

Did you know we have a service desk available for Plan to Protect® Members? One of the benefits of membership with Plan to Protect® is ongoing email and phone support. Visit our website at **www.plantoprotect.com** to select the membership level best suited for your needs.

If you are not a member of Plan to Protect® and questions arise as you begin to implement the manual, please visit the FAQ section of our website at **https://www.plantoprotect.com/faq/** or consider joining our network of members.

Frequently Asked Questions

Where do I even begin to deal with Plan to Protect®?
We recognize that implementing an abuse prevention plan is an overwhelming task. Don't be tempted to take any shortcuts - it will be manageable if you break it up in bite-sized pieces. Follow the Implementation Strategy section and let the manual guide you step by step.

What's new in this manual that's different from the previous three versions of Plan to Protect®?
This version of the manual includes:
- **Updated information** on new safety issues facing the church.
- **Recent quotes and case studies** related to the need for an effective plan for safety in every church.
- **An overhaul of the training section**, helping you to orient and determine your needs.
- **Policies related to new issues** arising since the previous manuals, including:
    - Mentoring
    - New Immigrants and Refugees
    - Online Forums and Gatherings
    - Sexual Harassment and Misconduct
- **New layout** making safety in the church easier to assess and implement, including new sections dedicated to Documentation Management and Adult safety concerns.
- **Updated forms** provided in the appendices covering most of the activities carried out by church ministries to Children, Youth, and Adults.

We've spent a lot of time working with Plan to Protect®. How do updates affect all of the work we have done to date?
Your hard efforts to date will not be affected by newer versions of Plan to Protect®. You can continue to build on the work you have already done and become very familiar with the new manual. Assess your progress and see where there may be opportunities for your organization to improve how you provide safe programs.

As a smaller organization, we know everyone who attends our church. Is all of Plan to Protect® really necessary?
This issue of abuse is not limited in its scope. It affects organizations regardless of size, function or geography. And regrettably, it is also present in our churches. Over the past 25 years we have heard hundreds of stories of abuse that have occurred and yes, many of those acts of abuse and misconduct have occurred in smaller churches and rural, or ethnic communities.

We implemented Plan to Protect® years ago but have not kept it up to date – how do we get back on track?
Plan to Protect® involves both an extensive implementation stage and a commitment to maintain the program through process management. Many of the organizations we surveyed acknowledged that they do a few of the steps in Plan to Protect®, but not 100%. It is not necessary to start over, but rather pick up where you left off. Take time to become acquainted with this new version of Plan to Protect® and assess where you are and what needs to be done. We have recently developed our Five Steps to Safeguarding. We encourage you to review them and go back to Step #1 and pick up the pieces that have fallen through the cracks:
1. Take our complimentary assessment,
2. Maintain certification for your Administrator and Trainer (this includes accessing our policy updates and training materials),
3. Screen and train your staff and volunteers,
4. Maintain your plan and stay abreast of best practices,
5. Network with others committed to safeguarding and nurture the healing of those that have been abused within and without the church.

So take the Assessment! Our Administrator/Leader Certification course is a great way to learn how to administer, implement and maintain Plan to Protect® - it is a great resource to help you get back on track.

We are concerned about putting policies in place. If we do, then we have to make sure we comply with them and we don't know how we can do this; it's a lot of work. We are thinking it is better to not put the policies in place, than to have them and not comply with them. Isn't that right?

From a general business perspective, it is true that creating company policies means that businesses and organizations must comply with the policies. However, there is a significant difference between creating an administrative risk or burden by adopting an employee fringe benefit program that is not required by law and creating a risk by not implementing policies and procedures that help ensure compliance to existing labour laws and other government regulations. Vulnerable sector protection is a matter that the federal and provincial governments take very seriously and one that no organization can afford to ignore. The costs of non-compliance can far exceed the nuisance and cost of compliance.

Negligence in employment covers several actions in tort law, mainly when an employer is responsible for the accident (or other tortuous act) caused by the employee. The employer in this case is negligent in providing the employee with the ability to create this situation. A person who is claiming negligence must prove that the defendant owed them a duty of care, that this duty was breached and that the claimant was injured as a result of the duty breach. This duty exists only if the injury is labeled as "reasonably foreseeable" (can cause the harm of the type which occurred at the current accident). The claimant must also be the person for whom the harm would be a "reasonably foreseeable consequence." Generally, the law divides Negligence in Employment into four scenarios: negligent hiring, negligent retention, negligent supervision and negligent training.

- **Negligent Hiring:** Negligent hiring refers to a situation where the employer hires the employee, while ignoring the evidence in some of his or her work records that pointed to the fact that the accident could occur. This is one of the cornerstones of negligence in employment, because at this point everything depends on the actions of the employer and their professional skills in hiring employees. All the other scenarios can include some factors that appear later during the working process, but hiring is the moment when only the employer is guilty for possible future incidents. Negligent hiring could be an underlying factor in a scenario that could be prevented by the hirer alone. Additional investigation may uncover some facts about a potential employee. It is best for the hirer to conduct interviews, verify work and educational histories, check references and conduct a background check on any potential employee.

- **Negligent Retention:** This type of negligence occurs when the people in charge failed to remove an employee from a position of authority or responsibility after it became clear that the employee wasn't capable of handling the responsibility. The consequences of this type of negligence are probably the most serious; a non-professional person with authority can cause huge losses for an organization.

- **Negligent Supervision:** Negligent supervision occurs when a party fails to monitor or control the actions of an employee. As with the other types of negligence, it may result in injuries or losses if the work of an employee was not observed correctly.

- **Negligent Training:** Negligent training occurs when a party fails to provide adequate training of an employee or fails to make the employee aware of certain aspects of the working process which results in injuries or losses.

We wrote policies many years ago, we are now wondering what updates should we be considering for our policies?

If you haven't updated your policies within the last five years, your policies are likely out of date and may not reflect the changes within our society. The following are some areas for discussion:
- **Screening** – Discuss the inclusion of the following checks in your screening of new candidates: reference checks, interviews, and criminal record checks, local police indices, and pardoned crimes of a sexual nature. Also discuss the value of renewing these checks every three-to-five years.
- **Documentation** – Documentation that is kept permanently is encouraged, as there is no statute of limitations on child abuse. Discuss how you are maintaining documentation; organizations are encouraged to maintain documentation (under lock and key) in order to demonstrate their duty of care to Ministry Personnel, Children, and Youth.

- **Social media and photography policies** – Discuss ways that these policies can establish parameters and address staff members' access to children and youth via social media beyond the parameters of program and photography permissions.
- **Gender** – Discuss plans for accommodating individuals who do not identify with their gender of birth and requests to access programs, washrooms, shower rooms, and housing. Consider ways to incorporate a welcoming environment, reasonable accommodation, and protect their privacy. Previously, it had been recommended that Children be assigned to Ministry Personnel of the same gender in situations such as the assistance of young Children in the washroom, transportation to and from events, and mentoring relationships. Discuss replacing the wording about gender with wording about Children being assigned to two screened, unmarried Adults who will provide supervision and oversight.
- **Child registration** – Consider challenges that guardians might encounter when registering a Child. For example, with the number of single-parent families and the rising divorce rate, you may need to revise their policies and procedures for the registration, sign-in, and sign-out of minors.
- **Small groups** – Life groups and home groups pose one of the greatest risks, as Children are often left unsupervised or alone with other Children of varying ages without Adult supervision, which could create an opportunity for Child-to-Child abuse. Discuss whether the same level of screening and Adult supervision on a weekend service or church event is being applied to childcare in these settings.
- **Trips and activities** – Most activities and trips also pose an elevated risk of injury and harm. While many organizations have been using waivers for years, there is a growing body of cases that suggest that Parents cannot waive the rights of their Child to initiate a claim. Such documents may not be enforceable in court; however, charities are encouraged to use waivers drafted by legal counsel to ensure that the waivers employed are enforceable.
- **Prohibited activities** – Don't wait for a serious accident or fatal injury to discuss prohibited activities. Some examples of prohibited activities are bungee jumping, white-water rafting, driving all-terrain or motorized vehicles, rock climbing, and using weapons (i.e., archery bows).
- **Review your reporting policies** – One of the biggest changes and gaps we've noticed in policies is in relation to reporting and responding to abuse. Each state, province or territory has its own legislation; however, all of the provinces and territories in Canada mandate reporting that no longer applies only to people in administration, professional, and leadership roles within an organization. For example, every person living in Canada, including volunteers, has a duty to report child abuse. Ontario has recently increased the age of Children protected by the law from 16 to 18 years of age.
- **Alcohol and drug use** – Considering that drug and alcohol use policies can intersect with issues around employees, volunteers, testing, and human rights among other things, these policies should be created in consultation with legal counsel.

At Plan to Protect® we provide policy templates and customized policies for our clients and members. Don't hesitate to reach out to us to ask for a quote on these services.

There are so many variations on Criminal Background Checks in Canada - can you help us understand the difference?
In Canada, there are primarily three components of a Criminal Record Check. When working with the vulnerable sector we recommend you complete all the steps of screening including an interview, 2-3 reference checks, a Vulnerable Sector Check or Enhanced Criminal Record Check, Training and a Covenant of Care.
There are many acronyms when it comes to Criminal Record Checks or Criminal Background Checks in Canada. Here is a quick summary of the checks that are the most common:

- **CPIC**   Canadian Police Information Check
  Includes:
  1. Search of the Canadian Police Information Centre
  2. Locally held police information searches the Canadian Police Information Centre (CPIC) within the National Repository of Criminal Records, including Investigative, identification and Ancillary banks plus Local Police Records which includes Police Information Portal (PIP) based on the candidate's name and date of birth. The results provided are returned as Negative or Additional Check recommended.

- **E-PIC** Enhanced CRC
The Enhanced search will discover any Canadian Criminal Convictions that have not been pardoned or discharged as well as identifiers that additional information may be present related to the candidate. Search result details are not released to third parties, however, candidates identified by the Enhanced search are recommended to attend their Local Police Detachment for a detailed report or submit fingerprints. Candidates who obtain results independently from their Local Police may share results with the organization requesting a search.
- **VSC/VSS** Vulnerable Sector Search
Includes:
1. Canadian Police Information Check;
2. Locally held police information, including pending charges and 'persons of interest'
3. Check of the national pardoned sex offender database

Third party providers of Criminal Record Checks, including our Enhanced Criminal Record Checks cannot access the pardoned offender database. Plan to Protect® is recommending that you send new candidates directly to the police station to secure a Vulnerable Sector Check. Plan to Protect® ScreeningCanada is able to provide Enhanced Criminal Record Checks, however, they do not include the pardoned component of the VSC/VSS. A fingerprint comparison would verify whether or not the individual is the individual that was convicted of a crime.

Can we send a video/DVD home for training instead of holding a training program?
The best training option is to hold on-site, face-to-face training in a group setting where there is opportunity for interaction and discussion and a walk-through of your facilities. We would encourage you to pursue the highest level of training for your personnel, and avoid shortcuts. However, in the rare occasion when individuals cannot attend the scheduled group training seminar, we would encourage the individual to take our on-line training or live webinar. Plan to Protect® trainers cannot distribute our copyright materials including PowerPoints and training.

Why does Plan to Protect® recommend a 6-month waiting period?
Yes, we do recommend a 6-month waiting period for newcomers to the church. If someone is new, they should take time to get to know the church or school and for the church or school to get to know them. The prospective volunteer can begin the screening near the tail end of the six months.

This recommendation mirrors many insurance company requirements. However, some exceptions may apply, for example if the individual is a new staff member, or an intern coming from a local college, or if they have transferred from another church within your denomination. Though it is important to note that in all of these situations, if a 6-month waiting period is not possible because of your type of organization (camp, community group, nursing home) an additional reference should be added from another organization where they volunteered or worked in the past. Ideally the person would have also been serving in a similar capacity.

What is considered a "clean" driving record? Is there any leeway in this definition?
While clean is a relative term, along with our advisory council, we would consider a clean driver's history of someone who has been licensed for five (5) years or more and has less than two (2) minor infractions.

A minor infraction would include backing up (unsafe, illegal, improper), brakes (none, inadequate, improper), and other offenses (speeding with less than 2 points deducted), failure to stop at a stop sign, driving imprudently. If they had less than two of these, you could consider it a clean driver's history.

A major infraction would include distracted driving, a learning driver driving unaccompanied, failure to obey a school crossing stop sign, failure to report an accident, improper passing of a school bus, improper passing/speeding in a school or playground zone, careless driving. If a driver has a major infraction, be wary of using them, especially if the infraction was recent. We recommend you contact your insurance company if you have concerns.

A Serious or Criminal infraction would include DUI, speeding 50kms above posted limit, driving uninsured, refusing a breathalyzer, failure to remain at an accident, or racing. If they have a serious or criminal conviction, we do not recommend they drive on behalf of your organization.

What you are really looking for is a pattern of unsafe driving behaviour. Typically, one to two (1-2) minor infractions in a three to five (3-5) year period can happen. But again, check with your insurance company.

How much freedom do we have to make changes to the volunteer application in the Plan to Protect® manual?
The Plan to Protect® manual is not a policy but a recommended plan to establish policy and procedures for your organization. We have provided you 100+ pages of templates and forms in Word document format for your use. Don't hesitate to adapt them for your organization. The templates that we have provided to you - including the application - were carefully reviewed by legal counsel and insurance companies. The Volunteer Application was crafted by a lawyer specializing in employment and human rights law. We recommend you avoid questions that would conflict with human rights issues, i.e., age, gender, ethnicity, and marital status. We do though however recommend you ask pertinent questions that will help gather critical information for you to make an informed decision regarding the candidate, including area of interests, experience, and past criminal convictions. As always, we strongly recommend that you have your own legal counsel review your policy and procedures when you establish a customized Plan to Protect®. Once legal counsel has reviewed your policy and forms, they will be ready for board approval. Don't miss these critical steps!

We find it difficult to collect all the forms back from our people – any suggestions?
This is a common challenge that many organizations face. Encourage prospective personnel to complete their forms prior to the time they attend training. If that doesn't work, set aside time during the training session for the forms to be filled out and submitted. Police jurisdictions vary in their requirements for submitting forms and collecting results. If your police jurisdiction permits you to submit all the police records checks at one time, and have the results sent directly to the organization, this will minimize the turn-around time and avoid having you wait for individuals to bring them into you. Another option to consider is Plan to Protect® ScreeningCanada; for a reasonable fee we will provide police records checks compliant with PIPEDA and Canadian privacy and human rights legislation and available within 24 hours. For additional help in recruiting and screening volunteers, see our Admin/Leader course.

If an organized activity runs short on screened helpers, is it OK for Parents/Caregivers to help out or can we also include other people connected to our organization to assist? What do we do if we cannot meet our staff to vulnerable person ratio?
We recommend that you have a screened Hall Monitor observing the activity rooms and available if Children/Youth/Adults need supervision when going to the washroom. We would strongly recommend that you manage your ratios according to Plan to Protect® with screened workers. We do not recommend using unscreened workers, even if they are Parents or Caregivers, because the participants may then identify them as individuals who they can trust. Your participants do not know the difference between screened workers or non-screened workers.

All individuals placed in a Position of Trust should be screened. Adhere to ratios for supervision, and any exception to two unrelated screened, Adult workers in the activity room should be cause to have the door open with a Hall Monitor acting as a second overseer.

Thinking ahead and screening additional staff will be helpful for these occasions. It may be advantageous to have some plans in your back pocket for those occasions where you are thrown a curve ball. The courts will hold you to the same level of protection and care even during the challenge of staff shortages.

Is it even possible to keep all the Attendance Forms and personnel files permanently?
One of the keys to demonstrating due diligence is to keep documentation on file. There is a lot of misunderstanding about the length of time documentation should be kept. Unlike financial records which should be kept for seven years, in Canada there is no time limit (called a statute of limitations) on bringing criminal charges for sexual assault – meaning you can swear a criminal complaint and file charges at any point in your lifetime.

Therefore, for the protection of the organization, and to be able to demonstrate that you fulfilled your duty of care and due diligence in protecting those under your care, documentation should be kept permanently.

An important filing system is critical to maintain attendance records and personnel forms. Attendance records can be retained electronically, which will minimize maintaining a paper trail. Ensure a procedure is in place for backups of electronic files and recording dates and revisions. Originals should be maintained of police records checks and signed application forms. Scanning and electronically filing documentation of interviews, reference checks and attendance at training seminars can also minimize paper files. Our Admin/Leader course can provide additional resources in documentation management.

How do I determine reasonable grounds for reporting suspected abuse to the authorities?
Reasonable grounds are what an average person, given his or her training, background and experience, exercising normal and honest judgment, would assume to be an action that needs attention. No action should be taken against a person making a report unless it is made maliciously or without reasonable grounds for the belief. See appendix 31 for a list of characteristics to watch for in helping you determine reasonable grounds and for definitions of abuse. These characteristics may be indicators of abuse, although they are not necessarily proof. One sign alone does not constitute abuse and may simply be indicative of other issues.
For specific guidelines for what constitutes reasonable suspicion and duty to report please visit your province's Children's Aid website.

What would you do if another Child was threatening the safety of the environment? For example, sexual comments to other Children and leaders, as well as profanities. What is the policy here? What are the steps to take?
We would recommend that you follow discipline/anti-bullying steps here: Give a verbal warning, a written warning (including a notice to the Parent/Caregiver), and if it happens again a suspension from the program for a week. If the Child does not stop then you can elevate this with a longer suspension from the program. You could also require the Parent to sit in the program with their Child for a few weeks.

Also, recognize that the behaviour the Child is exhibiting may be an indicator of abuse. If you see a pattern, you should notify Child and Family Services. If there is a 3-5 year age difference between two Children involved in such conduct we would suggest you also contact Child and Family Services and ask what your legal duty is in this situation. Child and Family Services will assess the situation and determine if you have a duty to report.

Our Hall Monitors have asked us what exactly they should do if they walk in on an abusive situation - especially sexual abuse - where the perpetrator could run. Can you make suggestions on how they should respond?
As with any volunteer or staff member, we would recommend that if they walk in on, observe, or have a suspicion of any form of abuse (including sexual misconduct), that they should immediately record and report it. If the individuals involved are of the age of majority, the Hall Monitor should notify the Senior Leader and document their observation and conversation, submitting this to leadership. Many organizations have a whistleblowing policy in place for this purpose.

If one or both of the individuals involved are minors, the Hall Monitor should immediately call for the abuse or misconduct to cease, remove the individual from the situation, and at the earliest opportunity document their observation, conversations and actions on the Suspected Abuse Report Form. The Hall Monitor should also notify organization leadership and immediately contact Child and Family Services or Children's Aid Society. Nothing should delay the report to the appropriate protection authorities. If the individuals are a Child and Adult (not a family member), the caregivers of the individual should be notified by the Senior Leader or designate. Caregivers should also be notified if Children or Youth are engaged in abusive behaviour (including sexual misconduct) with each other.

Appendices & Bibliography

If the sexual engagement is between minors of the same age and it appears to be consensual, Parents should be notified but child protection authorities would not need to be notified. If the sexual engagement involves minors but there is an age difference of three years or if it is not consensual, child protection authorities should be notified along with the Parents. No Parent or other individual, regardless of position or leadership duties has the right to tell you not to fulfill your legal duty to report to child protection authorities.

Should we avoid all high-risk activities and play in our programs?
We believe that risk should be managed not eliminated or completely avoided. There are benefits to risk. Many educators and child development professionals encourage Risky Play. Risky play can be defined as a thrilling and exciting activity that involves a risk of physical injury, and play that provides opportunities for challenge, testing limits, exploring boundaries and learning about injury risk. For example, "risky play" for Children and young people provide many benefits, including:
- Confidence that they can accomplish difficult tasks
- Pushing them beyond their comfort zone
- Emotional well-being
- Thrill of the adventure
- Links between movement and thought

If Children and young people are not allowed to explore and learn through playing and taking part in positive activities, they will not learn how to judge risks and manage them for themselves. The skills a Child or young person learns through play and other activities can act as a powerful form of prevention in other situations where Children and young people are placed in positions of risk.

At Plan to Protect® we do not believe that all risk should be avoided in Child and Youth programming. We do believe that organizations should be planning on how to protect Children and young people as part of the programming.

Determining whether to retain the risks that are associated with an activity should be a leadership decision. Program personnel should present a well thought out and researched plan on the benefits that will be gained by doing the high-risk activity versus consequences that could result from doing the activity.

Do your homework, present your written plan to your leadership, contact your insurance company to determine if the risk can be transferred to your insurance policy, and share the risks with Parents so they can make an informed decision whether or not to allow their Child to participate. We also encourage you to communicate in brochures, signs, newsletters, etc.: "Risky play is encouraged here." We want Children to feel safe to take risks - to be daring. We cannot guarantee that accidents will not happen.

TABLE OF CONTENTS
Appendices & Bibliography

Appendix 1	Implementing Plan to Protect - Risk Assessment
Appendix 2	Plan to Protect® Policies - A Compiled Guide
Appendix 3	Ministry Application Form
3a	Release of Information and Declaration of Intent
3b	Declaration of Faith
3c	Ministry Personnel Application Form Approval Checklist
3d	Code of Conduct and Covenant of Care
Appendix 4	Ministry Personnel Application Form for Youth Working with Children
Appendix 5	Suggested Script for Telephone Follow-Up When Screening Applications
Appendix 6	Confidential Record of Reference Checks
Appendix 7	Ministry Personnel Reference Form
Appendix 8	Ministry Personnel Interview Form
Appendix 9	Sample Interview Questions
Appendix 10	Ministry Personnel Renewal Application Form
Appendix 11	Diaper Changing Procedure / Handwashing Hints
Appendix 12	Infection Control Procedures
Appendix 13	Bloodborne Pathogens and Infectious Diseases
Appendix 14	Guidelines for the Development of AIDS/HIV Church Policies
Appendix 15	Registration and Medical Consent Form
Appendix 16	Medication Form
Appendix 17	Liability Shields
Appendix 18	Incident Report
Appendix 19	Letter of Informed Consent

TABLE OF CONTENTS
Appendices & Bibliography

Appendix 20	Off-Site Tips Sheet
Appendix 21	Off-Site Activity Report Form
Appendix 22	Trips and Off-Site Travel Form
Appendix 23	Letter of Informed Consent for Transportation
Appendix 24	Emergency Info Card
Appendix 25	Volunteer Driver Agreement
Appendix 26	Driving Contract
Appendix 27	Acceptable Computer Use Policy
Appendix 28	Computer Policy Agreement for Ministry Personnel
Appendix 29	Sign-In / Sign-Out Sheet
Appendix 30	Talking to a Potentially Abused Child
Appendix 31	Symptoms of Molestation and Abuse
Appendix 32	Suspected Abuse Report Form (Adult)
Appendix 33	Suspected Abuse Report Form (Child) **33a** Suspected Abuse Follow-Up Report Form
Appendix 34	Suspected Abuse Follow-Up Guidelines
Appendix 35	Fire Prevention Procedure Checklist
Appendix 36	Insurance / Lawyer Checklist
Appendix 37	Abuse Prevention Declaration - Churches/Charitable Organizations
Appendix 38	Billeting Checklist
Appendix 39	Provincial Acts on Child Abuse
Appendix 40	Confidentiality Agreement
Appendix 41	Offender's Covenant

TABLE OF CONTENTS — Appendices & Bibliography

Appendix 42	Terms of Reference for Plan to Protect® Committee
Appendix 43	Sample Job Description - Plan to Protect® Administrator
Appendix 44	Sample Job Description - Plan to Protect® Trainer
Page 418	Plan to Protect® Services
Page 419	Bibliography

IMPLEMENTING PLAN TO PROTECT®
RISK ASSESSMENT

Appendix 1

Risk Category	Risk Factor	Yes/ True	No / Not True
Degree of Isolation	The Ministry Personnel may have an opportunity to be alone with Children/Youth or Vulnerable Persons.		
Degree of Supervision/ Leadership	The Ministry Personnel has limited or no supervision or is considered a person in a leadership role with authority. Children/Youth and Vulnerable Persons would have contact with this person and consider them to be an authority figure.		
	The activities of the Ministry Personnel are in a place where activities are not observed or monitored regularly.		
Access of Property	The Ministry Personnel may have access to personal property or money of persons served.		
	The Ministry Personnel has access to confidential information related to Children/Youth and Vulnerable Persons.		
Degree of Physical Contact	This role requires the Ministry Personnel to have physical contact with Children/Youth or Vulnerable Persons.		
Vulnerability of Persons Served	Persons served have language or literacy barriers.		
	Persons served are immobile.		
	Persons served have challenges that contribute to their vulnerability (e.g., physical, psychological, and situational).		

Appendix 1

Risk Category	Risk Factor	Yes/ True	No / Not True
Degree of Physical Demands	The activity involves potential danger to persons served (e.g., rock climbing, using a stove).		
	The activity involves potential stress (e.g., Children upset by visit to elderly in palliative care).		
Degree of Trust	The Ministry Personnel develops close, personal relationships with the Children/Youth or Vulnerable Persons they serve.		
	Parents and caregivers entrust Children/Youth or Vulnerable Persons into this individual's care (e.g., teaching, visiting, mentoring, tutoring, nursery care).		
	The position involves transportation of Children/Youth or Vulnerable Persons.		
	The Ministry Personnel contributes to making career decisions or other important decisions of persons served.		
Degree of Inherent Risk	The activity heightens potential for the Ministry Personnel to be in contact with bodily fluids or disease of persons served.		
	The activity exposes persons served to operation or handling of potentially dangerous equipment (e.g., playground equipment, lawnmower).		
	The activity exposes the persons served to handling toxic substances or results in exposure to poor air quality, noise, etc. (e.g., demolition in an inner-city mission).		

PLAN TO PROTECT® POLICIES - A COMPILED GUIDE

Appendix 2

PROTECT THROUGH IMPLEMENTATION

A. The Plan to Protect Committee
1. A Plan to Protect® committee will oversee the implementation of Plan to Protect® including, but not limited to, the screening and training of all Ministry Personnel. On the committee, the following portfolios will be assigned:
    1. Chair
    2. Administration
    3. Screening
    4. Training
    5. Liaison with the Board
    6. Members at Large

2. The Plan to Protect® committee reports to the Board and will provide an annual report to the Board and congregation. The report must include the following:
    1. Members of the Plan to Protect® Committee
    2. Number of active Ministry Personnel screened and trained serving in a Position of Trust
    3. Status of abuse insurance coverage
    4. Number of Trainings held
    5. Date and findings of the annual audit
    6. Highlights of the past year
    7. Professional development completed
    8. Goals for the upcoming year
    9. Items of praise and prayer requests

PROTECT THROUGH RECRUITMENT AND SCREENING

Human Rights and Discrimination
1. The church is committed to treating people fairly, with respect and dignity, when hiring and recruiting, in accordance with applicable provincial human rights law.
2. Ministry Personnel will conduct their hiring and recruiting practices in line with applicable provincial human rights laws.
3. Ministry Personnel will avoid asking questions that violate applicable provincial human rights legislation in interviews and when checking references.
4. The church will be transparent about how applicable provincial human rights law permits religious organizations in certain circumstances to give preference in hiring persons or to hire only persons who are members of the same religious group or meet a creed-based qualification.

A. Recruitment and Screening Process
1. All ministry departments engaging the vulnerable sector must adhere to the recruitment and screening process.
2. Church Leadership and/or the Ministry Lead determine if an individual is a suitable or potential candidate for ministry.
3. Prospective Ministry Personnel are to submit to the recruitment and screening process managed by the Ministry Lead. Individuals will submit and complete the following:
    a. Ministry Application Form (Appendix 3),
    b. Adhere to six month waiting period,

c. Sign Statement of Faith,
   d. Face-to-face interview,
   e. Reference checks,
   f. Police records check,
   g. Training, and
   h. Final approval from Church Leadership.
4. Ministry Personnel must complete the recruitment and screening process prior to being placed in a Position of Trust.
5. Ministry Personnel who serve Children, Youth and Adults must have a personnel file kept with church records. These files are to be kept permanently.

B. Qualifications for Ministry

1. A minimum six-month waiting period prior to serving is required for individuals wanting to work in ministries serving the vulnerable sector. All prospective Ministry Personnel will have regularly attended the church for the previous six months.
   • Exceptions can be made in circumstances where the Ministry Personnel have transferred from another church of the same denomination in which they have been long-time members and are ministry workers in good standing or they are being employed by the church. In these circumstances, reference checks must be received from at least three individuals, including one from their previous minister or children's ministry director.

2. Ministry Personnel serving in a Position of Trust or leadership are members or adherents in good standing who support the doctrines, direction and by-laws or constitution of the church.

3. Individuals that have been accused, or convicted, or are under the suspicion of crimes against Children and/or Youth, or who have been convicted of violent crimes will not have any involvement in ministries or programs where Children or Youth participate until such time as they have been found innocent or the accusation has been found unsubstantiated.

C. Ministry Application Form

1. Prospective Ministry Personnel are to complete a Ministry Application Form. (Appendix 3) Student leaders are to complete the Ministry Application Form for Youth Working with Children. (Appendix 4)
   a. A verifiable witnessed signature is required for the protection of all parties.
   b. Individuals who transfer from another congregation unknown to the Church Leadership must include contact information or a reference from a pastoral staff member of their previous church.
   c. In accordance with PIPEDA[1] regulations, the Ministry Application Forms must include the reason for which the information is being collected.

2. Ministry Application Forms are to be kept confidential and available only to the Ministry Lead, Church Leadership and/or the Plan to Protect® team.
   a. Ministry Application Forms are to be kept in a secure location.
   b. Ministry Application Forms are to be kept on file permanently.

Appendix 2

D. Reference Checks

1. Designated Screening Personnel will conduct a minimum of two reference checks on all prospective Ministry Personnel. (Appendix 5)
    a. Prospective Ministry Personnel must sign a liability release before reference checks are conducted.
    b. Be sure that the references provided fit within the acceptable categories for Adults and for Youth who work with Children.
    c. Reference checks are conducted by telephone to confirm the suitability and appointment of prospective Ministry Personnel.

E. Interview

1. Face-to-face interviews will be conducted by the Ministry Lead or an individual approved by Church Leadership. (Appendix 8)

F. Criminal Record Checks

1. The Screening Committee must identify the criminal record checks available within their region.
2. Criminal record checks must be conducted on all Ministry Personnel serving the vulnerable sector.
    a. Criminal record checks are to be renewed every three years.
    b. Criminal record checks are to be conducted on all Ministry Personnel 18 years of age and older and are to be kept on file permanently.
3. If a prospective Ministry Personnel has had a history with the Child Welfare Agency, a request may be made by the Church Leadership for the individual to sign consent for a child welfare check.

G. Screening of Youth

1. Minors who apply to work and volunteer shall complete the same screening requirements as Adult Personnel with the following exceptions:
    a. No Criminal Record Check is required for applicants under the age of 18. When an active Youth volunteer turns 18, they will submit a Criminal Record Check within 3 months to continue volunteering.

H. Red Flags and Disqualifiers

1. Screening Personnel are to be trained on identifying red flags during the screening process.
2. During the screening process, Screening Personnel are to be alert to any red flags that may disqualify prospective Ministry Personnel from working with the vulnerable sector. When a red flag is identified, Screening Personnel are to bring the red flag to the attention of the Lead Pastor or their delegate.
3. Screening Personnel are to keep information confidential and information regarding red flags and disqualifiers will only be shared on a need to know basis.
4. The following red flags are to be automatic disqualifiers:
    a. Any convictions of crimes against Children, Youth or Vulnerable Adults or violent crimes, including but not limited to:
    - Child abuse, sexual or otherwise
    - Abduction, murder, or manslaughter
    - Incest
    - Rape
    - Sexual assault
    b. Violent crimes wherein a weapon was used

5. The Lead Pastor and the Board are to make a decision to disqualify or not to disqualify someone from a Position of Trust due to one or more red flags. Depending on the severity of the red flag, the decision may be made in conjunction with legal counsel and the insurance company. Their decision, reasoning, and steps taken to mitigate any potential risks are to be documented and kept permanently. No exceptions are to be made for convictions that fall under automatic disqualifiers.

6. Documentation is to be maintained permanently for all prospective Ministry Personnel applying to be Ministry Personnel. If someone does not qualify for a Position of Trust, the reason for disqualifying the candidate is to be kept confidential but is to be included on their personnel record which is to be kept under lock and key.

I. Plan to Protect Training

1. An initial Orientation training on abuse prevention education is required for all Ministry Personnel serving with Children, Youth and Adults. This applies to all employees, Board Members, Screening Personnel, Leaders and Volunteers, and anyone else in a Position of Trust.

2. Training must be conducted by a qualified trainer. The training must include a review of the Plan to Protect® Policy and all safeguarding procedures. Ministry Personnel are to be educated about their obligation to report suspected abuse and on how to recognize and identify the symptoms of abuse and molestation.

3. All Ministry Personnel are required to attend Orientation training prior to placement. All Ministry Personnel are required to attend annual Refresher training sessions thereafter.

4. Attendance is to be taken at all training events and noted in the Ministry Personnel file for each individual present. All Ministry Personnel must sign an agreement form (Appendix 3a) confirming they have read, understood and are willing to comply with the Plan to Protect® policies and procedures.

J. Code of Conduct and Covenant of Care

1. Upon completion of screening and training, Ministry Personnel must sign a Covenant of Care and Code of Conduct attesting that they will abide by the Plan to Protect® policies, procedures and training.

2. The Covenant of Care and Code of Conduct is to be signed on an annual basis.

K. Approval Process

1. The Board is to appoint an individual that is to approve candidates that have completed the screening process.

2. All Ministry Personnel are to be approved by Church Leadership upon completion of recruitment and screening process.

   a. Approval must be signed and dated.

3. The recruitment and screening process must be completed within a three month period of time

   a. Workers in process of completing the recruitment and screening process are not to be placed in a Position of Trust.

   b. Access to Children are to be limited until final approval is received.

Appendix 2

PROTECT THROUGH DOCUMENTATION MANAGEMENT

A. Plan to Protect® Program Maintenance

1. A strategy for program maintenance will be developed and reviewed at the beginning of each ministry year to ensure training, the updating of files and the physical environment are compliant with policy.

B. Documentation

1. Registration Forms, Attendance Records, and Letters of Informed Consent must be collected and kept on file.
2. Incident Reports must be written and submitted on all accidents and injuries.
3. Suspected Abuse Report Forms must be written for all suspicions, allegations and disclosures of abuse.
4. Documentation on screening and involvement of Ministry Personnel will be compiled in Ministry Personnel files.
5. All documents will be scanned, saved as a PDF or saved on the cloud in a secure format that cannot be easily manipulated. A secure backup of documentation will be retained, and files will not be overwritten.
6. Documentation mentioned within this policy must be retained permanently.

C. Documentation Storage and Retention

1. As there is no statute of limitations for child abuse in Canada, and extended statute of limitations for crimes and personal injury related to Vulnerable Adults in Canada, all documentation pertaining to program activities involving Children, Youth and Vulnerable Adults shall be kept and stored permanently following the church's document retention procedures, and in compliance with the areas below.
2. Wherever possible, forms must be legible, include the date, location and full names of everyone present or involved, and include any explanatory notes which provide context. The individual who completed a form must be identifiable.
3. This policy applies to all documentation created and gathered in relation to Children, Youth and Vulnerable Adults. The documentation to be retained includes, but is not limited to:
    a. All documentation gathered during Recruitment, Screening, Training of Ministry Personnel
    b. Ministry Personnel files
    c. Files created during the planning, supervision, and implementation of program activities
    d. Insurance policies
    e. Registration Forms
    f. Attendance Forms
    g. Disciplinary memos of Ministry Personnel
    h. Letters of Informed Consent (Releases and Waivers)
    i. Transportation records
    j. Rental agreements
    k. Incident Forms
    l. Suspected Abuse Forms
    m. Any follow-up or additional information attached to such forms as is necessary to provide a clear picture of the church's activities, participants, and supervision

Documentation storage and backup

1. All documents and files pertaining to the church's activities, participants and supervision will be stored in a locked cabinet accessible only to authorized Ministry Personnel. A backup will be maintained, containing copies of all documents.

2. Physical backup will take place off-site, in a fire and water resistant location.
3. Backups of all documents will be made weekly, and added to the physical back-up on a monthly basis.
4. An online backup of all files will be maintained, hosted on a server located off-site.
5. Online storage will be password protected and secure (preferably encrypted). All information stored on the server will be done in an unalterable format (i.e., PDF or password protected) where possible, and the ability to delete items be removed.
6. Scans of all documents will be made weekly, and added to the online storage on a monthly basis. Where possible, use software that tracks all changes to stored information.

Access to archived documentation
1. Archived documentation may be needed from time to time, to verify someone's past history, for audit purposes, or to ensure accuracy. In all cases where the archived, stored information must be accessed, care will be taken to adhere to a transparent process. Individuals accessing archived files must have a clear, articulated reason, and always do so under the supervision of at least one other authorized Ministry Personnel.

D. Personal Information and Privacy

1. The protection of personal information is all of our responsibility. Therefore, it is the responsibility of everyone serving to ensure that personal information provided is kept confidential according to this policy.

2. All Ministry Personnel that have access to personal information must sign a Confidentiality Agreement.

3. The collection of personal information is limited to what is necessary for the identified purposes and will be collected by fair and lawful means. Personal information must only be used and disclosed for the purposes for which it was collected, except with consent or as required by law. It will be retained only as long as it is necessary to fulfill those purposes. In most cases, information that relate to minors and Ministry Personnel serving with minors will be retained permanently as there is no statute of limitations on child abuse in Canada.

4. Personal information must be as accurate, complete and up-to-date as is necessary. Personal information must be protected by adequate safeguards. Information about a church's privacy policies and practices must be readily available to individuals upon request.

5. An individual has the right of access to personal information about themself and has the right to seek correction. Both these rights are subject to some exceptions as specified in each statute. The church must provide the means for an individual to challenge their compliance with the above principles. Please refer anyone requesting information to the Church Office Administrator.

PROTECT THROUGH PROGRAM DEVELOPMENT

General Protection Procedures

Administrative Policies

A. Planning for Safety

1. All Ministry Personnel must ensure a safe environment in their planning and evaluating of activities.

2. Safety precautions must be posted and highly visible for Children, Youth and Vulnerable Adults.

Appendix 2

B. Supervision of Ministry Personnel

1. For the protection of our Children, Youth and Vulnerable Adults, supervision of all Ministry Personnel will be intentional and will take place through formal and informal visits to classrooms and programs by a Ministry Lead or a Pastor.

C. Lifestyle

1. For the protection of everyone, Ministry Personnel are to be committed to maintaining a consistent spiritual life including prayer, Bible reading, attendance at relevant events, planning meetings and worship services.

2. Ministry Personnel are to be role models of integrity at all times. Ministry Personnel are to refrain from activities that are illegal or could be considered morally and biblically questionable.

D. Ministry Personnel Identification

1. Ministry Personnel are clearly identified with a nametag or approved clothing which identifies them to Parents, Children and Newcomers.

E. Registration and Compliance with PIPEDA

1. At the beginning of every ministry year, all program participants are to submit completed Registration and Medical Consent Forms, (Appendix 15) signed by their Parent. These forms are to be photocopied and originals maintained and filed permanently. The photocopies should be taken on all off-site trips and outings in case emergency medical assistance is required and the Parent cannot be notified.

2. The Registration and Medical Consent Form will not replace specific Letter of Informed Consent Forms for activities that involve an elevated risk or for overnight trips.

3. The inclusion of 'liability shields' on permission forms has been considered for activities that involve a level of risk. (Appendix 17)

4. A release and permission statement will be included on all Registration Forms releasing the church from unforeseen and accidental damages.

    I/We, the parents or guardians named above, authorize the Ministry Personnel of _____ Church to sign a consent for medical treatment and to authorize any physician or hospital to provide medical assessment, treatment or procedures for the participant named above.

    I/We, named above, undertake and agree to indemnify and hold blameless the Ministry Personnel, _____ Church, its pastors and Board from and against any loss, damage or injury suffered by the participant as a result of being part of the activities of the _____ Church as well as of any medical treatment authorized by the supervising individuals representing the church. This consent and authorization is effective only when participating in or traveling to events of the _____ Church.

5. A statement will be included on all Registration Forms which stipulates the purpose and extent for collecting personal information.

Purposes and Extent:

_____ Church is collecting and retaining this personal information for the purpose of enrolling your Child in our programs, to assign the Student to the appropriate classes, to develop and nurture ongoing relationships with you and your Child, and to inform you of program updates and upcoming opportunities at our church. This information

_____ Appendix 2

will be maintained permanently as it is a requirement of our insurance company and legal counsel. If you wish _____ Church to limit the information collected, or to view your Child's information, please contact us.

F. Attendance

1. Attendance must be taken each time a classroom or program is in session. These attendance records are kept on file permanently.

2. A record will be kept of Ministry Personnel on duty in each classroom or program. This record will be maintained with the record of attendance and kept on file permanently.

3. Attendance records must include the date, time, and classroom and everyone present (including visitors) during the program.

G. Outside User Groups (Renters and Service Providers)

For the church to be a safe space for all users, the following policies apply to all groups who use the space, whether they have a connection to the church or not:

1. All Service Providers, Visitors* and Renters must sign-in upon arrival at the front desk and sign-out when they leave. The individual's name, the date and the time is to be clearly noted. This information is to be kept on file in the Activity Log for that day and kept permanently.

*Note: This does not apply to individuals joining public events as attendees.

2. If Service Providers are onsite when programming is happening for Children, Youth or Vulnerable Adults, the Service Providers are to be clearly identified with a uniform or a nametag and are to always be accompanied and supervised by Ministry Personnel.

3. The criteria for Renters or outside user groups to use the church's facility include:

    a. Renters must complete a Rental Agreement which must be approved by the Board or by a Ministry Lead.

    b. Renters must provide a certificate of insurance, with no less than $2,000,000 Commercial General Liability coverage and the church be named as additional insured.

    c. Renters must provide evidence that they have a strong abuse prevention policy and protocol in place*, including but not limited to screening and training of staff and volunteers, and minors may not be left unsupervised.

    d. They must abide by the following for all activities where Children, Youth or Vulnerable Adults are present:

        i. Two Screened Workers providing oversight; or

        ii. One Screened Worker providing oversight where Parents accompany their Children, or Caregivers accompany Vulnerable Adults.

*Note 2: If these individuals and groups lack an Abuse Prevention Policy, we are not to provide them with one, rather, we will refer them to Plan to Protect® to secure their own copy of the *Plan to Protect*® manual.

4. In the case that the church partners with other churches, agencies or community groups for the delivery of a joint activity or event with Children, Youth or Vulnerable Adults in attendance, Church Leadership requires that their insurance agent be consulted during the planning stage, to determine risks, insurance coverage and shared liability. A Ministry Lead is required to obtain written opinion from the insurance agent acknowledging the status of insurance coverage for these joint activities.

Appendix 2

H. Misconduct and Accountability

1. Ministry Personnel are to refrain from all forms of misconduct.

2. It is the responsibility of the Board, Lead Pastor and Ministry Leads to hold each other and their direct reports accountable. Every member of a church must be accountable for their actions that could impact the reputation of the church, no one is exempt. This flows both up and down in in reporting concerns. For example: Ministry Personnel are to be supervised and held accountable by Ministry Leads, Ministry Leads are to be supervised and held accountable by Staff Members, Staff Members are to be supervised and held accountable by the Lead Pastor, and the Lead Pastor is to be supervised and held accountable by the Board as a collective body.

3. As a community of faith, we reserve the right and freedom to bring to the attention of individuals and Church Leadership anything we believe is compromising their integrity, walk with God, or could bring harm to the reputation of the church and cause of Christ. If a person does not feel safe to confront the individual (i.e., in the case of abusive behaviour), we urge them to follow the whistleblower policy (See Whistleblower Policy on page 273).

4. Individuals with concerns must follow Matthew 18 when confronting an individual unless they feel unsafe to do so. Matthew 18 calls for individuals to confront the individual alone first, and if they do not feel that the concern has been taken seriously, they are to bring in another. In the case of the church, they must then bring in the individual's Supervisor, followed by the Church Board.

5. When traveling, Ministry Personnel are to avoid meetings in hotel rooms of another individual other than an immediate family member.

6. With reasonable cause, Church Leadership reserves the right to look at staff computers, cell phones, and tablets that are primarily used for ministry purposes. This includes but is not limited to photographs and communication. Upon request, these devices must be turned over immediately. Staff Members must provide their passwords for their primary ministry electronic devices to the Office Administrator upon request.

7. All petty cash and expenses must be accounted for.

8. If a person is involved in a situation where a boundary is violated, or something occurs that is out of the ordinary or could be misinterpreted, or where such a violation or occurrence is alleged, he or she must immediately report it and discuss it with a Supervisor. If the Ministry Lead is unwilling, unable, or unavailable for discussion, he or she must seek out a Board Member or the Pastor to discuss the issue.

I. Disciplinary Action of Ministry Personnel

When a Policy or Procedure of the church has not been adhered to, the following progressive disciplinary actions are to be taken, depending on the given nature of the offence. Serious offences such as physical or sexual abuse, assault or theft will have zero tolerance (See steps 3 and 4).

Step 1 - Verbal Warning

1. Ministry Personnel are to be given a verbal warning regarding the unacceptable behaviour or action.

2. Ministry Personnel are to be given an explanation of when and how the undesirable behaviour or action took place. This will include the reason as to why the behaviour or action was unacceptable, such as a reminder of relevant policy or training.

3. Ministry Personnel are to be given an opportunity to explain the situation and their actions. This is an opportunity to give their side of the story.

4. Ministry Personnel are to be given a description of desirable or acceptable behaviour or actions.

5. Ministry Personnel are to be reminded that they signed a Covenant of Care affirming they would abide by the Policy and Procedures of the church. A copy of this may be given to them.

6. Ministry Personnel are to be informed of further disciplinary steps that will be taken if unacceptable behaviour continues.

7. Ministry Personnel are to be notified that a note will be added to their file with a record of the verbal warning.

Step 2 - Written Warning

1. Ministry Personnel are to be given a written warning regarding unacceptable behaviour or action in the event that the behaviour or action had either been discussed in a previous verbal warning or the behaviour or action was considerably severe in nature.

2. MInistry Personnel are to be given an explanation of when and how the undesirable behaviour or action took place. This will include the reason why the behaviour or action was unacceptable.

3. Ministry Personnel are to be given an opportunity to explain the situation and their actions. This is an opportunity to give their side of the story.

4. Ministry Personnel are to be given a description of the desirable or acceptable behaviour or actions.

5. Ministry Personnel are to be provided with a copy of the written warning and another will be placed in their Ministry Personnel file and shared with a Ministry Lead or Pastor.

6. Ministry Personnel are to be reminded that they signed a Covenant of Care affirming they would abide by the Policy and Procedures of the church. A copy of this should be given to them.

7. Ministry Personnel are to sign the document as proof of receipt.

8. Ministry Personnel are to be notified that future infractions will be addressed with further progressive disciplinary actions up to and including termination.

9. At this point it is recommended that the individual take additional professional development training in the area of the infraction or attend Plan to Protect® Orientation or Refresher Training again. See **www.plantoprotectschool.com**.

Step 3 - Suspension

1. Ministry Personnel are to be given written documentation regarding the suspension in relation to the unacceptable behaviour or action, in the event that the behaviour or action had either been discussed in a previous verbal or written warning, or the behaviour or action was considerably severe in nature.

2. Documentation must include information on the offence, the length and terms of the suspension and why the individual has been suspended.

3. Ministry Personnel are to be given an explanation of when and how the undesirable behaviour or action took place. This will include the reason why the behaviour or action was unacceptable.

4. Ministry Personnel are to be given a description of the desirable or acceptable behaviour or actions.

5. Ministry Personnel are to be provided a copy of the suspension documentation and another copy will be placed in their Ministry Personnel file.

6. Ministry Personnel are to sign the document as proof of receipt.

7. Ministry Personnel are to be notified that future infractions will be addressed with further progressive disciplinary actions up to and including termination.

——— Appendix 2

8. Church Leadership are to be notified that an individual has been suspended.

9. During the suspension, the individual may be required to take additional professional development training in the area of the infraction and re-attend Plan to Protect® Abuse Prevention Orientation or Refresher Training. See **www.plantoprotectschool.com**.

PLEASE NOTE: Ministry Personnel suspended due to suspicions or allegations of abuse may have no contact with vulnerable individuals and may not be placed in a Position of Trust during their suspension. The suspension will **NOT** be overturned unless they have been cleared of any and all allegations or suspicions of abuse.

Where applicable, legal counsel, an insurance company representative, and Child and Family Services must be consulted prior to termination and reinstatement.

Step 4 - Termination

1. Church Leadership must be consulted and notified prior to termination of any Ministry Personnel.

2. Ministry Personnel are to be given written documentation regarding the termination and the breach of policy or process, or inappropriate behaviour or action leading to and justifying the termination.

3. Documentation must include information on the offence and any previous disciplinary steps documented.

4. Ministry Personnel are to be given a description of when and how the unacceptable behaviour or action took place. This will include the reason why the behaviour or action was unacceptable.

5. Ministry Personnel are to be given a description of desirable or acceptable behaviour or actions.

6. Ministry Personnel are to be provided with a copy of the termination notice and another copy will be placed in the Ministry Personnel's file. Ministry Personnel file documentation is to be kept permanently, even after termination.

7. Ministry Personnel are to be escorted from the location while maintaining the dignity of the terminated Ministry Personnel.

8. Where possible, the reasons for dismissal are to be kept confidential.

9. At Church Leadership's discretion, the individual may be encouraged to attend services, bring their Children to programs, and participate in community events held at the church.

Personal Interactions

A. Occasional Observers

1. Occasional Observers who join a class will have their attendance recorded and kept on file with the classroom attendance for that day. Visitors do not need to be screened or trained. Visitors will be clearly identified as guests and should be coached on proper protocols for guests. Since they have not been screened and approved, they will not be placed in a Position of Trust with Children who are not their own. Occasional Observers should not be regular attenders in a classroom.

B. Bullying

1. Our Children, Youth, Vulnerable Adults, and Ministry Personnel have a right to a caring, respectful and safe church environment. An anti-bullying policy will therefore be in effect at all times and will be clearly communicated and enforced among participants and Ministry Personnel. All Ministry Personnel will take action to prevent bullying, teach against it, and assist and support Children, Youth and Vulnerable Adults who are being bullied. Bullying in any form will not be tolerated.

Appendix 2

2. Bullying is defined as unwanted, aggressive behaviour that involves a real or perceived power imbalance and is repeated or has the potential to be repeated.

   Types of Bullying:

   a. Verbal Bullying

   b. Social Bullying

   c. Physical Bullying

   d. Cyber Bullying

   e. Racial Bullying

   f. Homophobic Bullying

   g. Sexual Harassment

3. Any incidents, reports or suspicions of bullying will be acknowledged, reviewed and dealt with appropriately and immediately. All incidents, reports or suspicions of bullying must be reported immediately to the Ministry Lead.

4. Appropriate action will take place based on the situation. Possible action may include, but is not limited to:

   a. Completing an Incident Report (Appendix 18) after each incident;

   b. Notifying both sets of Parents after each individual incident;

   c. Providing a warning that bullying will not be tolerated;

   d. Suspension for one day/event if bullying persists;

   e. Suspension for three days/events after next incident;

   f. Prohibiting the bullies from participating in programs if the bullying does not stop;

   g. If necessary and appropriate, contacting and consulting with police.

5. All attempts will be made to work towards change of behaviour with the person who is bullying. Counseling and support will be recommended and if possible provided for the victim of bullying.

a. Harassment and Discrimination

1. Our church is committed to fostering an environment that is free of discrimination and harassment and one in which all individuals are treated with respect and dignity. Every attendee of our church community has a right to equal treatment with respect to the receipt of services and facilities without discrimination or harassment based on the following prohibited grounds: race, ancestry, place of origin, colour, ethnic origin, citizenship, creed, sex, sexual orientation, age, marital status, family status, or disability.

2. A right to freedom from discrimination and harassment is also applicable where someone is treated unequally because she/he is in a relationship, association or dealing with a person or persons identified by one of the prohibited grounds of discrimination.

3. Every attendee of our church community, especially screened Ministry Personnel, is responsible for creating an environment which is free of discrimination and harassment. Those found to have engaged in such conduct will be subject to discipline.

Appendix 2

4. Individuals who have committed an act of harassment will be subject to progressive steps of discipline. Acts of sexual harassment will result in immediate suspension and if an investigation finds that it was found to be substantiated, will result in immediate termination.

C. Discipline and Classroom Management

1. The following forms of punishment are not permitted:
    a. Corporal punishment of a Child or Youth by Ministry Personnel;
    b. Deliberate harsh or degrading measures that would humiliate a Child or Youth, or undermine their self-respect;
    c. Depriving a Child or Youth of their basic needs;
    d. Locking or confining a Child or Youth in a room separate from others.

2. All discipline and group management are to be conducted in a loving and caring environment. All attempts are to be made to prevent discipline problems from arising and to avoid the need for remedial discipline. All attempts to provide discipline are to adhere to the following:

    Preventative Discipline:
    a. Create a loving, caring atmosphere.
    b. To gain respect, you must grant respect.
    c. Model self-discipline and structure in your own life.
    d. Prepare exciting and interesting activities with short transitions in-between.
    e. Arrange your environment in an age-appropriate way and for learning.
    f. Establish and communicate realistic expectations for the Children and Youth.
    g. Be sure the activities that you provide are meaningful and age-appropriate.
    h. Be fair and consistent with all Children and Youth.
    i. Be sure your focus is on positive actions and reward positive behaviour.
    j. Be aware of Children and Youth with special needs and bring their needs to the attention of the Ministry Lead.

    Remedial Discipline:
    a. Deal with problems individually.
    b. Explain to the Child or Youth why the behaviour is unacceptable and instruct them how to do it correctly.
    c. Redirect the Child or Youth to positive action.
    d. Explain the consequences of unacceptable behaviour by defining the correct way to behave as well as the result of the wrong behaviour.
    e. Offer choices that are acceptable to both you and the Child or Youth.

3. Group rules are to be established to clearly communicate the expectations required of Children and Youth. Some suggested rules are:
    a. One voice talking at a time, and always use inside voices.
    b. Use good manners.
    c. Respect each other.
    d. Quiet hands get answered.
    e. Obey directions the first time.

Appendix 2

   f. Keep your hands and feet to yourself.
   g. Be friendly.

4. Ministry Personnel must complete an Incident Report form when an individual is removed from a program or activity or if a Child is returned to their Parents. The Incident Report Form must include the behaviour that resulted in the discipline step, the steps taken and the expected outcome prior to returning.

D. Contacting Opportunities

1. Ministry Personnel may meet with Children, Youth and Vulnerable Adults only during the parameters of ministry programming.

2. Ministry Personnel are to avoid any activity that would involve being isolated with a Child, Youth or Vulnerable Adult and are only to meet in group settings.

3. Any requests for exceptions to this policy must be submitted in writing to Church Leadership. Permission must be granted in writing by both Church Leadership and Parents for each event utilizing an Letter of Informed Consent.

a. Counselling and Pastoral Care

1. Ministry Personnel are prohibited to counsel the vulnerable sector unless the counselling is approved by the Board, and then only by professional counsellors with appropriate insurance in place.

2. Pastors and Board members may engage in pastoral care but must refer clients to a professional counsellor if they show signs of being affected by the following, or if they require or request specific counselling to deal with any of the following:
   a. suicidal ideation,
   b. signs of mental illness,
   c. gender dysphoria,
   d. self-injury
   e. working through a history of substance abuse, or
   f. past trauma.

3. Pastoral care and counselling must be done in a church office during church office hours, when another Ministry Personnel is also on-site.

E. Gift Giving

1. The church requires that all Ministry Personnel demonstrate our commitment to treating all individuals impartially. Ministry Personnel will demonstrate the highest standards of ethics and conduct in all matters when dealing with:

   a. Children, Youth and Vulnerable Adults

   b. All vendors and suppliers, both existing and potential

   c. Employees, Volunteers and prospective Ministry Personnel

   d. Any individual or organization with whom they come into contact

—— Appendix 2

To demonstrate our commitment to these standards and behaviour, all Ministry Personnel must abide by the following gift giving policy requirements:

2. Ministry Personnel are to refrain from giving gifts to Children, Youth or Vulnerable Adults unless the gift is given to everyone in a class or group setting and is in no means in exchange for services or favours.

3. No gifts of any kind, that are offered by vendors, suppliers, Parents, potential employees or volunteers, potential vendors and suppliers, or any other individual or organization — no matter the value — will be accepted by Ministry Personnel at any time, on or off the work premises if it is given as a means to receive benefit or a bribe including any business courtesy offered. This could include a product discount or any other benefit if the benefit is not extended to all Ministry Personnel, i.e., sale, special accommodation, registration spot, etc.

4. Exempted from this policy are gifts such as t-shirts, pens, trade show bags and all other tchotchkes that employees or volunteers obtain, as a member of the public, at events such as conferences, training events, seminars and trade shows, that are offered equally to all members of the public attending the event. This includes:

    a. Food, beverages, and tchotchkes provided at events, exhibitor trade show floor locations, press events, and parties funded by conference or event sponsors.

    b. Cards, thank you notes, certificates, or other written forms of thanks and recognition.

    c. Food, beverages, moderately priced meals and tickets to local events that are supplied by and also attended by current customers, partners, and vendors or suppliers in the interest of building positive business relationships.

5. When a gift is offered, and it does not fall under the exceptions policy, Ministry Personnel are required to professionally inform vendors, potential vendors and others of this policy and the reasons the church has adopted the policy.

6. Ministry Personnel will request that vendors respect our policy and not purchase and deliver any gift for our employees, a department, an office, or the church, at any time, for any reason.

7. Certain gifts given to or received by Ministry Personnel may be appropriate given a context or situation outside of the scope of this policy. Church Leadership may make a written exemption to this policy detailing the reasoning and scope of their decision for any gift.

F. Dating

1. Ministry Personnel may not pursue a dating, emotional, or physically intimate relationship with a minor, or someone in a ministry in which they serve.
2. Ministry Personnel are to immediately self-disclose to the Board any and all intimate (psychological or sexual) relationships that begin.

G. Home Visits

1. Ministry Personnel must secure permission in writing from the Ministry Lead to visit individuals that are deemed Vulnerable Adults in their home.

2. Ministry Personnel are never to visit a Child in a home without a Parent present at all times.

3. Ministry Personnel are to maintain and submit monthly communication/visitation logs.

4. Ministry Personnel are to abide by the church's visitation procedures in order to protect both parties in these situations - the visitor and the visited.

H. Hospital and Nursing Home Visits

1. There must be at least two (2) unrelated Ministry Personnel at all events and for all visitation to hospitals and nursing centres, or the door must remain open with family members, nursing staff, or caregivers nearby or present.

2. When visiting Children or Youth in a hospital, a Parent or family member should be present, or visitation must be done with Parental permission and in teams of two Screened Adults. The door must remain open.

3. When visiting Vulnerable Adults in hospitals and nursing centres, a Family Member or Personal Caregiver must also be present or visitation must be conducted in teams of two Screened Adults. In hospitals and nursing centers, visitation must be conducted in teams of two or the door must be left open.

4. Ministry Personnel must avoid scenarios where they are left alone in a hospital room or nursing home room.

I. Disabilities and Personal Support Workers

1. On Registration Forms, Parents and Caregivers are encouraged to list known disabilities. Upon registration, Ministry Leads are to determine how best to provide inclusive programming for individuals with disabilities. Ratios will be adjusted to provide additional support needed.

2. Ministry Personnel are to receive training on accessibility for individuals with disabilities.

3. If the church is unable to provide accommodations and support for individuals with disabilities, personal support workers may accompany the individual to the program.

4. All personal support workers shall comply with the church's screening and training process prior to taking responsibility over any individual.

5. If a personal support worker is personally hired and screened by a Child or Youth's Parents then the Parents will provide a signed form identifying the support worker as a private hire and provide copies of the criminal record check and references conducted.

6. A personal support worker who is not hired or screened by the church may only take responsibility over the individual they were hired to support, but may not supervise any other participants in a program, activity, or event.

7. All documentation regarding personal support workers and their screening procedures will be kept on file permanently.

J. Gender Identity

1. In the beginning, God created humans as relational beings, the inherent design of male and female reflecting God's image. Sexuality, our maleness and femaleness, is a dimension of our embodied existence. Sexual difference and complementarity are thus good features of our identity. While identity, fulfillment, and the path to human flourishing are founded on a relationship with the Creator, in Genesis we learn that God made sex an expression of intimacy, love, and self-giving, to be experienced between one man and one woman in a lifelong covenant.

2. Given the inherent dignity of all persons, the church will not tolerate the harassment, discrimination or any language of hate or loathing towards those who hold a differing view on human sexuality. Ministry Personnel and members of the church must treat all persons, regardless of gender, belief or sexuality, with respect and compassion. It is our desire to create a place of welcome and grace, and we are committed to creating a safe environment for all individuals. In light of this commitment, the church will take every reasonable step to ensure that its learning, working and living environments are maintained free from harassment and discrimination.

3. Every individual has a right to equitable treatment without discrimination with respect to accessing the activities or facilities of the church. No person shall be asked or required to 'prove' their gender (e.g., by providing a doctor's note, identity documents, etc.) in order to gain access to these opportunities.

4. Everyone who associates with the church community is encouraged to communicate using respectful, gender-inclusive language. Those who identify as a gender other than their biological sex should confirm with the church the name(s) and pronoun(s) by which they prefer to be referred. Everyone within the church community is encouraged to respect these preferences in their communication.

5. Intentionally addressing anyone within the church community by the incorrect name or gender pronoun is considered by the church to be a form of harassment and discrimination. Inadvertent slips or honest mistakes are not covered by this provision, but intentional and persistent refusal to acknowledge or use an individual's preferred or changed name or pronoun is unacceptable.

6. Disclosing the gender status of an individual associated with the church community without explicit and directly expressed consent or in the absence of a "need to know" circumstance is generally known as "outing". Outing in any form is not supported by the leadership of the church as it is recognized as a form of harassment that puts the individual's physical, emotional and psychological safety at risk.

7. The church will make reasonable efforts to ensure that all members of the church community can use washrooms with safety, privacy and dignity, regardless of their gender identity or gender expression.

8. Individuals within the church community have the right to express legitimate concerns about human rights violations they may experience in their interaction and engagement at the church without fear of reprisal. On the other hand, complaints made in bad faith are strongly discouraged since any accusation or complaint of harassment or discrimination is a matter that can cause considerable hardship to the person who is the subject of the complaint.

9. If individuals associated with the church community request counselling or guidance concerning Gender Dysphoria or Gender Identity Disorder, all Ministry Personnel and congregants are to notify a Pastor who will arrange for appropriate counselling.

Health and Safety

A. Health and Safety Guidelines

1. Ministry Leads and Ministry Personnel are encouraged to be certified and trained in first aid.

Appendix 2

2. The names and contact information of individuals who are certified in first aid are to be posted in the Children's and Youth program areas for easy access, with a Master List maintained by the Office Manager.

3. Ministry Leads must be informed of any individual(s) having severe allergies. The information is to be posted in the Children's and Youth departments for easy access and Ministry Personnel who have the individual(s) in their care must be informed.

4. The cleaning and sanitation of toys and table surfaces must be done after each use.

Illness:

1. An individual who is ill and could therefore expose others to illness are not to be received into the program room. Factors to consider are:

   a. Fever, unusual fatigue, irritability, coughing, sneezing, runny nose and eyes, vomiting, diarrhea, inflamed mouth and throat

   b. Individuals showing signs of a contagious illness such as viruses, pink eye, measles, chickenpox, or any other communicable disease that could be spread by touch or by coming in close proximity

Medications:

2. Ministry Personnel are not to give or apply any medications (i.e., Tylenol, Polysporin, vitamins, etc.) without written authorization from a physician and Church Leadership.

3. Any prescription medication must be brought in the original container with the doctor's prescription, dosage and date clearly printed on the label. Parents must fill out a medication form and sign dosage instructions. Medication must be presented to the Ministry Lead or designate on duty in the Child's room and handed over at sign-in. (Appendices 15 and 16)

4. When medication is brought for a Child, the medication is to be kept in a locked box in the cupboard or refrigerator. This also applies to non-prescription substances such as tobacco and cigarettes brought by Youth to events.

5. Dosage times must be recorded in the daily journal or Attendance Form for all staff to see.

6. At dosage time, the Ministry Lead or designated health worker must double check the medication form and instructions, dispense medication to the Child and sign the form noting the amount and time medication was given.

7. In the extreme case where EpiPens and puffers are needed for allergies or asthma, written instructions are to be provided by the Parent to the Ministry Lead. Requests should be written, signed, dated and filed permanently.

8. Topical medications for diaper changing purposes are to be used only when instructed and provided by the Parent.

Dealing with Cuts or Injuries Involving Blood:

1. Universal precautions must be used when administering any kind of first aid. (Appendix 12)

2. Blood pathogen policies are to be posted in classrooms.

3. When an individual is injured, they are to be separated from others. The area where the injury occurred or where any blood may have dropped on the floor or toys is also to be isolated.

4. Ministry Personnel need to ensure that no other individuals have had contact with any of the blood from the cut or injury.

—— Appendix 2

5. Non-latex gloves are to be used when bandaging the injury, avoiding contact with mouth, ears and eyes.

6. Extreme care must be taken in cleaning up all blood and bloody bandages and the safe and secure removal of waste and disposal of gloves to a secure waste removal container.

7. Hands are to be washed carefully with sterilizing soap available in the first aid kit.

8. When ministering to individuals with HIV or AIDS, specific guidelines for the education and care of these individuals are to be developed and followed (Appendix 14).

Emergencies:

1. Emergency and evacuation procedures are to be reviewed semi-annually by the Pastor and the Board. These procedures are to be posted in a visible place in each classroom stating the planned route of escape to the nearest exit.

2. Pastors, in communication with the Ministry Lead, are to arrange for annual fire and evacuation drills.

3. A first aid kit must be kept in each classroom with Ministry Personnel being educated on the kit's contents.

4. In addition to the first aid kits in each room, a master first aid kit must be available to the church's building and in any church-owned vehicle.

5. Each kit must contain a pair of disposable non-latex gloves, disinfectant towelettes, two or three 4" x 4" gauze pads for blood absorption, small scissors and bandages.

6. A Parent must be contacted when an injury, accident or medical emergency occurs that involve their Child. Incident reports are to be completed for any and all accidents (Appendix 18). Injuries are to be reported to the Ministry Lead.

a. Severe Allergies

1. Parents and Caregivers are responsible for notifying the church of any known allergies which their Children have. This information is to be noted on their Registration Form.

2. Upon permission of Parents, the notification of severe allergies are to be posted in the Child's classroom for high visibility, including a picture of the Child, a list of his or her allergies and typical signs of reaction. Ministry Personnel assigned to care for the Child must be made aware of the allergy and the treatment required if a reaction occurs.

3. In recognition of individuals with severe nut allergies, we are to promote a nut-free environment, where no nut products should be served.

b. Immunizations

1. It is the responsibility of the church and Ministry Personnel to demonstrate their care for the families they serve to ensure those providing care are vaccinated.
2. All Children, Youth and Ministry Personnel should stay current with their immunizations as recommended or mandated by Health Canada and the Public Health Agency of Canada and Province.
3. It is the responsibility of the Parent to ensure immunizations are current and to notify the church if there are immunization exemptions.
4. At such time that the church is alerted to the requirement of an immunization, a written notice will be sent home.

c. Drugs and Alcohol

1. The legalization of cannabis does not change the church's legal obligation to provide a safe workplace and programs. Ministry Personnel are not to be impaired while serving or working at the church.

2. During employment or volunteer service, the church has zero tolerance for the possession and/or consumption of illegal drugs and misuse of alcohol at any time.

3. Ministry Personnel will take action to prevent the abuse of drugs and alcohol, teach against it, and promote a safe environment for everyone.

4. The church will take steps to ensure individuals who are impaired or whose ability to work is affected by consuming substances such as alcohol and drugs, including cannabis, are removed from the premises, unless accommodation has been provided for medicinal use.

5. Individuals under the influence of drugs or alcohol will be escorted off the premises as they may pose a risk to other individuals. Children and Youth removed in this way will be separated from others until their Parents arrive to collect them. Any time an individual is removed from the premises due to drugs or alcohol, an Incident Form must be completed and a report made to the Ministry Lead.

6. Ministry Personnel cannot possess or consume alcohol or cannabis during program hours or at any time during hours of service, unless prescribed by a physician, as outlined in this policy.

7. Ministry Personnel may not possess or consume alcohol or drugs (legal or non-legal) where minors are present or where Ministry Personnel are responsible for the supervision and oversight of minors.

8. If minors are found to be in the possession of alcohol or non-medicinal drugs, it will be confiscated and reported to the police. The police should be asked if they would like the items turned over or destroyed. An Incident Report must be completed and Parents notified.

9. All Ministry Personnel working with Children, Youth and Vulnerable Adults are required to notify their Ministry Lead of their use of prescription and non-prescription medication which may produce side effects causing them to be under the influence of the medication or left impaired by the medication. If such medication is prescribed, Ministry Personnel may be required to provide relevant documentation by a physician. The church reserves the right to verify with a physician (either with such Ministry Personnel's own physician or an independent medical examination) that Ministry Personnel can safely continue to perform their duties. If the church determines from the examination or medical information that the Ministry Personnel is unable to safely perform his or her duties, the church will not grant continued service in ministry for the period of time that the Ministry Personnel remains impaired. The church is committed to respecting the privacy of Ministry Personnel, and Children, Youth and Vulnerable Adults.

10. Ministry Personnel that travel on behalf of the church are expected to conduct themselves in a professional and positive manner at all times. Irresponsible consumption of alcohol or cannabis at any time during employment, volunteer service or engagement with the church may result in immediate termination. Therefore, Ministry Personnel should exercise responsible alcohol and drug consumption when off-site, including after working hours. Any consumption should be conducted in a way that does not impede Ministry Personnel's capacity or ability to respond competently to situations that arise and in a way that does not negatively impact the reputation of the church. Ministry Personnel are prohibited from wearing church uniforms when purchasing or consuming alcoholic beverages, or while smoking or purchasing cigarettes or cannabis.

11. Ministry Personnel whose duties include driving must not be under the influence of any drugs or alcohol while operating a motor vehicle. It is important for church drivers and the passengers to be fully functional and alert when operating or driving in a motor vehicle. When church drivers are transporting other members of

the church or any Children, Youth or Vulnerable Adults on behalf of the church in commercial vehicles, such as a rented vehicle, or in their own vehicles, there is a zero alcohol and cannabis consumption policy for those drivers for a full 24 hours prior to the scheduled time of departure.

B. Inclement Weather Conditions

1. In extremely hot or cold weather, Ministry Leads may use their discretion to determine if it is safe to take Children and Youth outside for programming.

2. Children and Youth are not to be forced to go outside if the temperature is below -10 degrees Celsius, or if there is a wind-chill advisory in effect, causing the temperature to feel below -10 degrees celsius. They are also to be kept indoors if the temperature is above 30 degrees Celsius or if a smog alert is in effect.

3. Ministry Personnel must use discretion when smog alerts are in effect, especially if there are Children and Youth with respiratory ailments in attendance.

4. In the event of a thunderstorm with lightning, Children and Youth are to remain inside.

5. In the event of a natural disaster, Children and Youth and Ministry Personnel are to remain indoors, away from windows. If required to go to the lowest part of the building, Ministry Personnel are to escort Children and Youth calmly.

6. In the event of inclement weather (heavy snow, tornado warning, etc.) the church may close due to travel warnings and high-risk of injury and danger. A recorded message is to be announced on the church voicemail, a notice placed on the website, and an email notice to be sent to all families.

C. Missing Person

The safety of Children and Youth will be given our highest priority. If a person goes missing, time is of the essence. As soon as an individual is found to be missing, all available Ministry Personnel must follow the steps below:

1. Conduct a preliminary search of their last known location.

2. Assemble all remaining Children and Youth together in a central safe location, enabling as many Screened Leaders as possible to search for the missing person. Split the Screened Leaders into two groups - one group to search, and one group to supervise the remaining Children and Youth. One person is designated as the primary point of contact.

3. The Primary Point of Contact must contact the Ministry Lead and Church Leadership immediately, and remain available to coordinate between the searchers, remaining Ministry Personnel, off-site leadership and outside groups.

4. The group supervising the Children and Youth must stay together and wait for further instructions from leadership. Do not send any minors to search for a missing person.

5. The searching group must appoint individuals to keep watch over points of entry or exit, and to reduce movement in the area by any other groups - under ideal circumstances, no one exits the area.

6. Remaining Leaders and Volunteers, (as many as possible without putting the remaining Children at risk) must begin by conducting a search of the "hot spots" - nearby, likely and dangerous areas - then move to less immediate areas.

7. Search both inside the building and outside the building. Search inside locations: cupboards, washrooms, closets, stairwells, classrooms, auditorium/sanctuary, baptismal tanks and offices. Search outside locations: parking lot, beach, river, swimming pool, nearby streets, parks, play grounds, railroad tracks, and ravines, etc.

Appendix 2

8. At the 10 minute point of searching, the Primary Point of Contact must call 9-1-1 to notify the police and emergency officials of the missing person. Provide them with the individual's age, physical description (including a description of their clothing), last known location, and possible whereabouts in the building or community where the Child went missing. If possible, provide a photograph.

9. The Primary Point of Contact is to designate someone (themselves or a Church Leader) to notify the family members (in the case of a Child, their Parents) immediately after notifying the police.

10. Continue to search, cooperating with the police and local authorities.

11. Once the missing person is found, administer first aid as needed.

12. If a Child is found with another Adult, attempt to calmly and gently detain the Adult until the police arrive. If the Adult leaves, record a description of the individual as soon as possible if they are unknown, and provide it to the police.

13. Complete an Incident Report, and keep the report on file permanently.

14. If the media arrives on the scene, only the Church Leader should speak to the media.

D. Lockdown Guidelines

These guidelines are to be put into action in the event of a lockdown or during a lockdown drill. Although each church is to draft their own lockdown policy with details pertaining to their specific needs and facilities, this policy will help give Church Leadership a place to start.

1. Identify green zones and red zones within the facility. Green Zones: More secure – rooms that have doors that lock. Red Zones: open areas, including gymnasiums and auditoriums.

2. As soon as the facility is put on "Lockdown Alert", the designated person in charge will announce "Code Red" to all classrooms and Ministry Personnel: "Announcement: Emergency Code Red, the facility is going into lockdown, repeat, Emergency Code Red, the facility is going into lockdown."

3. Immediately call 9-1-1, unless it is a situation where the police first alerted the church. Instruct all individuals present to shut off cell phones.

4. All present must clear away from red zones as quickly as possible. They are to go to the nearest green zone, or if an outside door is closer, they are to evacuate the building.

5. Prior to locking doors, those in charge of classrooms are to ensure that any individuals walking the halls within their classroom's proximity are ushered quickly into the room. The door must then be closed and locked. If the classroom door has a window, Ministry Personnel are to cover it and turn off the lights.

6. Those in charge of classrooms are to assist students in turning tables on their sides and position them away from the door and windows. The students are to then take refuge behind them.

7. Attendance is to be taken, including a list of all missing and extra students in the room. This list must be emailed to the office, and the teacher must take the list with them if directed to leave the classroom.

8. Custodians or ushers are to check all washrooms in the facility, remove any individuals who may be within, and lock the washrooms from the outside.

9. Everyone is prohibited from leaving green zones until they are instructed to do so by the designated person in charge or a police officer. Those in charge of classrooms are to remain in the rooms, maintain silence and keep the students calm. Do not contact the church office, the office will contact you when it is safe to do so.

10. When instructed to evacuate the building, do so quickly and silently.

11. Once the police arrive on the scene, they have the ultimate command of the incident and their instructions will be followed without protest.

Appendix 2

12. At least twice during a calendar year, the church is to perform a lockdown drill. Church Leadership are to notify the church community of a lockdown drill the week or day prior to the drill.

13. Circumstances and details of the drill are to be recorded and kept on file. It is strongly recommended to have a debriefing with participants, and keep notes of these debriefings on file.

E. Fire and Emergency Evacuation

1. Whenever the fire alarm sounds, everyone is to leave the building and wait in the designated waiting area, even if it is a false alarm or a drill.

2. Ministry Personnel, Church Leadership, and selected members of the congregation are to be trained in Emergency Evacuation Policies and Procedures and must be prepared to assist in the event of an Emergency Evacuation. These Ministry Personnel and members of the congregation are to be referred to as Fire Marshals.

3. Ministry Personnel must not wait for Parents to pick up their Children when there is an alarm. Rather, they must immediately vacate the building with the Children and Youth and go to the designated location.

4. Congregation members are to immediately vacate the building. Parents are to be notified to meet their Children at the designated locations outside of the building. A fire alarm does not negate the need for appropriate sign-out and pickup of Children.

5. The congregation shall periodically conduct a "Fire Drill" in order to practice safe evacuation of the building, according to the procedures.

6. The Board, in coordination with Ministry Personnel, must be responsible to:

    a. Assure the periodic training of Ministry Personnel, Church Leadership, and additional selected members of the congregation in Emergency Evacuation Policies and Procedures;

    b. Schedule and carry out periodic "Fire Drills;"

    c. Periodically review and update the Emergency Evacuation Policies and Procedures.

7. Exits are to be maintained free of snow, ice and obstructions.

8. In the event that the Fire Department is called to the scene, the Fire Department (and other Emergency Responders) have authority to determine a course of action. Ministry Personnel, church members, and building occupants are to follow their directives.

Technology Concerns

A. Online Forums and Gatherings

1. Online Forums and Gatherings must be hosted by the church's licensed and operated accounts only, no personal accounts may be used.

2. The church's licensed and operated accounts must be accessible to more than one Ministry Lead (passwords, usernames and email credentials).

3. To host an Online Forum/Gathering, Ministry Personnel must first secure permission in writing from the Ministry Lead overseeing the department or their Supervisor. Hosts must be screened and trained according to the Recruitment process for Ministry Personnel.

4. An Letter of Informed Consent must be prepared and submitted to the Parent prior to the event. Parents must sign and submit the Letter of Informed Consent to allow a student to participate utilizing an electronic signature platform (i.e., SmartWaiver or Docusign).

    a. Parents will be provided with an opt-in option on the Letter of Informed Consent to allow their Child(ren) to use a webcam while a session is being recorded.

b. Parents will be notified of the documentation management and retention policies outlined in the church's Plan to Protect® policies and procedures.

   c. Any Children or Youth that do not have expressed, written permission from a Parent to use the webcam will not be permitted to do so.

5. For the duration of the meeting, Ministry Personnel will have the video platform in 'Moderator' mode to restrict the video and webcam sharing of other attendees.

   a. If the 'Moderator' mode is unavailable on the video platform, or the church deems it beneficial for attendees to use a webcam, only Children and Youth that have expressed written consent from a Parent to be recorded will be permitted to use a webcam. Those that do not have consent to be recorded will not be permitted to use their webcams.

6. Ministry Personnel will either:

   a. Remain on the video platform until all attendees have left before closing the session; OR,

   b. Close the session to end the meeting for all attendees.

7. Ministry Personnel are encouraged to use videos, fun games and songs to share with families, to limit direct attendee communication.

8. All persons (Children, Youth, Parents, Ministry Personnel) will be educated on the expectations for the use of the online platforms, both video and social media, to encourage safe and productive use.

9. If Ministry Personnel is found to be contacting Children or Youth through personal accounts, they will be subject to disciplinary action by the church.

10. In the event that conversation with a Child or Youth moves beyond regular program activities, Ministry Personnel must inform Church Leadership and provide a copy of the conversation immediately. Church Leadership will follow the procedure outlined in the Plan to Protect® manual for Suicide, Substance Abuse and Self-Injury. Procedures may include:

    a. Reporting to the proper authorities; or,

    b. Informing the Parents of the Child or Youth.

For Children Grades 1-6:

In order to create a safe experience, the church must:

1. Maintain at least TWO screened, unrelated Adults (in accordance with the Recruitment and Screening section in the Plan to Protect® manual) in the church's Gatherings. This is a practice under the church's Plan to Protect® policy in all Children's ministry programs.

2. The church's host will be recording the program. The recordings are not to be posted online and will only be used for security and resource purposes.

3. Attendance is to be taken at each Forum/Gathering.

4. A Parent must be in the room at the beginning and at the end of a call. This is our check in and out process.

5. Parents must remain in the same room as their Children when they are on the call. Children must not be left in front of the computer alone in an isolated room.

6. Parents are requested to ensure that the call is played on a computer/device with speakers instead of earphones/headphones.

7. The church's Gatherings are not permanent to facilitate chat rooms. Parents are to be required to check in their Children in each Zoom Gathering. Hence, Children are not to be able to join the church's [Name of Platform, i.e., Zoom] Gatherings outside our pre-set program time.

8. Upon completion of the call, the attendance record and the recording must be sent to the Ministry Lead of the department.

For Youth Grades 7-12:

In order to create a safe experience, the church must:

1. Maintain at least TWO screened, unrelated Adults (in accordance with the Recruitment and Screening section in the Plan to Protect® manual) in the church's Gatherings. This is a practice under the church's Plan to Protect® policy in all our Youth ministry programs.
2. The church's host will be recording the program. The recordings are not to be posted online and will only be used for security and resource purposes.
3. Attendance is to be taken at each Forum/Gathering.
4. The church's Gatherings are not permanent chat rooms. Hence, Youth are not to be able to join the church's [Name of Platform, i.e., Zoom] Gatherings outside our pre-set program time.
5. Upon completion of the call, the attendance record and the recording must be sent to the Ministry Lead of the department and retained permanently.

B. Social Media

1. Church members, adherents and Ministry Personnel are encouraged to demonstrate and model purity, integrity, transparency and accountability with all communications including those noted above.
2. Email or text communication with Children 12 years of age and under is prohibited.
3. Youth Ministry Personnel will agree to allow the Ministry Lead or designate access to their Social Media networks in order to facilitate regular supervision.
4. Communication with Youth 13 years of age and older via Social Media, telephone and texting is permitted under the following conditions:
   a. Communication with a Youth via email, text, Instagram, Snapchat, Facebook Messenger, or other Social Media networks will be monitored closely and only used with written Parental permission (Appendix 15).
   b. To avoid isolation on social media, one of the following must take place:
      i. Ministry Personnel may communicate with Youth via email with written Parental permission (Appendix 15). The Parents will be copied on all communications; or
      ii. In cases where Ministry Personnel contact Youth via email, text or Social Media without copying Parents, they must include another Ministry Personnel in the communications; or
      iii. Use a public Social Media option (wall-to-wall, church-owned pages and accounts). In either case, Parental permission to contact Youth directly is required.
   c. Ministry Personnel will limit their online communications with Youth via Social Media to daytime hours (8:00am-11:00pm).
   d. Online communication will not involve video messaging (FaceTime, Skype, etc.) in any form, unless it is a training post or group conference call approved by the Ministry Lead.
   e. In the rare occasion that a conversation with a Youth moves beyond communication of information, Ministry Personnel will notify their Ministry Lead immediately and submit a copy of the conversation to the Ministry Lead. Ministry Personnel will request the Youth to continue the conversation in person with the Ministry Lead.

C. Internet and Computer Use

1. Church Leadership are to determine who will have access to the church Wi-Fi. Passwords are not to be distrubuted without permission from Church Leadership

2. Public computers are to be placed in open areas where the screen is easily visible. Users are to be held accountable through the use of sign-in and sign-out sheets, and/or a user password.
3. Internet filters are to be installed on each computer to limit access to certain types of content.
4. The Church Leadership are to appoint an authorized computer system's individual who is to periodically review the browser history as well as the documents downloaded onto church-owned computers.
5. An 'Acceptable Computer Use Policy' are to be developed and posted in the computer centre. (Appendix 27)
6. Ministry Personnel should closely monitor the use of their church owned devices and not allow minors to use these devices.

D. Photography and Video Recording

With a desire to capture memorable moments at the church, photography and video recording are to be closely monitored by Church Leadership. The AV Department and Ministry Departments must abide by the following guidelines:

1. Photography and video recording are to be done by designated Ministry Personnel who have been screened and trained in safeguarding policies and procedures.
2. For public church activities including services where video recording is to be done in the sanctuary, and with the church family together, it is required that signage be posted notifying those in attendance that the event will be captured on film. Individuals can either stay out of the line of the camera or, if necessary, opt out of the event.
3. For all Children and Youth ministry activities and programs, Parental permission must be secured prior to taking photographs of Children and Youth. Parental permission must be secured on an annual basis on the Registration Forms (Appendix 15);
    a. No photographs of Children or Youth are to be taken without prior written approval.
    b. No photographs are to be posted on the church's website, Facebook, Instagram, or other online social networks without Parental permission and only on sites monitored closely by Church Leadership.
4. To easily identify Children and Youth that are not to have their picture taken, they are to be clearly identified with either a sticker on their nametag or with an arm band. All effort must be made to adhere to the Parent's request.
5. No photographs of Children or Youth are to be tagged or labeled with the name of the individual at any time, including but not limited to bulletin boards, newsletters, websites, social media sites, or church bulletins.
6. When archiving and filing photographs and videos of Children and Youth, only those with written Parental permission can be kept for future use. Written permission forms must be kept permanently on file in the church office. Archived photos must be labeled and cross-referenced with Parental permission forms.

Facility Precautions

A. Modifying Your Facility

1. Recognizing that there are many storage areas within the church, elevated precautions must be taken to monitor these areas. Storage closets and doors must be locked at all times except when in use. When doors are unlocked, additional Hall Monitors will be on duty to monitor these areas.
2. All windows in doors in Children's program areas are never to be covered in any way so as to keep clear sight lines into rooms.
3. Washroom facilities in the preschool area are for the sole use of Children.
4. Nursery doors are to be secured from the inside.
5. All electrical outlets are to be kept covered when not in use in the nursery and toddler classrooms.

6. Doors of rooms and closets must be locked when not in use during Children's programs.

For Accessibility:

1. Install ramps and automatic doors.

2. Consider elevators or stair lifts.

3. Provide handicap seating and space for wheelchairs.

4. Make washrooms accessible with wide doors, space for assistive devices, low sinks, and handrails.

5. Place signage and program materials accessible to those with limited vision.

6. Accommodate those with hearing loss.

B. Security Systems and Cameras

1. Security cameras are provided for the purpose of elevated safeguarding precautions, and to aid in investigations.

2. As the purpose of Plan to Protect® is to prevent injury, harm and abuse from happening, security cameras that are installed for recording purposes are not to be considered a replacement for Hall Monitors or elevated supervision.

3. Security cameras that are installed for the purpose of monitoring in real time, must be staffed during all activities and programs where Children, Youth and Vulnerable Adults are present.

High Risk Activities

A. High Risk Activities

1. High risk activities include each of the following:

    a. Activities identified as having a higher risk, such as off-site events, water activities, extreme sports, online events, overnight events, billeting, transportation, mission trips, and small groups, and;

    b. Irregular activities that take place, including one-off events, yearly events, and new activities.

2. High risk activities that fall into the categories above may only take place under the following criteria:

    a. A risk assessment must be completed prior to the event;

    b. Permission must be granted from the Church Board or designate;

    c. Parents must be provided a Letter of Informed Consent one week in advance of the event;

    d. A qualified instructor or lifeguard has been appointed; and

    e. Ratios have been modified to provide elevated supervision.

Appendix 2

3. In our church, we are committed to protecting Children, Youth and Vulnerable Adults. The following activities are prohibited:

   a. Uncontrolled free falls or jumps that exceed 8 feet;

   b. Driving at high speeds; and

   c. Minors driving all-terrain vehicles or motorized vehicles.

B. Transportation

1. When planning off-site activities, Parents are to be encouraged to drop off and pick up their Children and Youth at the event location. For out of town events, commercial school carriers are to be used whenever possible.

2. Our first concern in transportation is the safety of the passengers. Drivers must obey all the rules of the road including the speed limits. Reckless or unsafe driving will not be tolerated.

3. When not using commercial carriers, all Ministry Personnel drivers transporting on behalf of the church during church activities must complete the following prior to an event:
   a. Be pre-approved by the Ministry Lead;
   b. Provide a copy of their valid driver's license;
   c. Provide a copy of their current automobile insurance policy;
   d. Have a minimum of five (5) years driving experience in good standing.

4. The number of occupants in vehicles transporting Children, Youth and Vulnerable Adults during church sponsored activities must not exceed the number of seat belts and each passenger must be in age-appropriate safety restraints. Seatbelts must be worn by everyone and remain fastened at all times the vehicle is in operation.

5. Children, Youth and Vulnerable Adults must never be left alone in a vehicle. At least two (2) Ministry Personnel must be in each vehicle transporting Children during church sponsored activities. Exceptions to this policy should only happen when Ministry Leads and Parents are informed, and there is more than one Child or Youth in the vehicle, avoiding isolation.

6. A copy of the 'Trips and Off-site Travel Form' (Appendix 22) will accompany each driver with the original left in the church office and filed permanently. The form contains information consisting of:
   a. Names and phone numbers of all participants
   b. Location of event and phone number(s)
   c. Drivers and vehicles involved

7. When transportation is being provided by your church, an Letter of Informed Consent for Transportation must be signed by Parents of minors (Appendix 23). The travel forms must be maintained and filed in the church office. Forms are to be kept on file permanently.

C. Off-Site Event Planning

1. Prior to any off-site trip the Ministry Lead must complete a risk assessment. The results of the risk assessment must be provided when securing approval to host the off-site event.

Appendix 2

2. All off-site trips must be pre-approved by a Pastor.

3. A Letter of Informed Consent for the off-site trip will be given to the Parents no less than one week prior to the event. Information must include the exact location of the event, emergency phone numbers, a list of Adult Ministry Personnel attending the event, and any inherent risks of the event.

4. If there is travel involved or there are additional elements of risk to the activity, Parents will be informed of risks and required to provide clear permission for each element of risk.

5. Sufficient supervision by at least two screened Adults is required to ensure protection and safety for all involved.

6. Copies of Letters of Informed Consent, medical authorizations, and any additional Registration Forms for each Student must be kept on hand at each event. (Appendix 19)

7. Attendance of all Ministry Personnel, Children, Youth, and Occasional Observers must be recorded on the Trip and Off-Site Travel Forms. (Appendix 22) The Travel Form must be maintained and filed in the church office. Forms will be kept on file permanently.

a. Off-Site Event Planning: Shared Activities

1. In the case that outside users, members, adherents or renters are granted permission to use the facility for activities involving Children, Youth and Vulnerable Adults, that are not direct ministries and activities of the Church, it is required that they provide a certificate of insurance, with no less than $2,000,000 Commercial General Liability coverage with abuse coverage and the Church be named as additional insured. The user or renter is also required to demonstrate that they have a full Child/Youth protection policy and protocol in place. If they lack an Abuse Prevention Policy, the Church will refer them to Plan to Protect® to secure their own copy of the *Plan to Protect®* manual.

2. In the case that the Church partners with other churches, agencies or community groups for the delivery of a joint activity or event with Children and/or Youth, the leadership of the Church requires that their insurance agent be consulted during the planning stage, to determine the risks, insurance coverage and shared liability. The Program Leader is required to obtain written opinion from the insurance agent acknowledging the status of insurance coverage for these joint activities.

b. Off-Site Event Planning: Home Groups

The following protocols is to be adhered to for all group meetings hosted in homes:

1. Host homes and families must be approved by a Pastor.

2. At no time should Children be left unsupervised. One of the following two criteria for supervision must be in place:

    a. The Child must stay with the Parent at all times; or

    b. If Children are separated from their Parents, two Screened Adults must be assigned to supervise the Children; or one Screened Adult with the second Screened Adult acting in the role of a Hall Monitor to check on the group frequently throughout the event.

3. Children are never to be left unattended or left in the care of only Youth child care worker(s). There must always be a minimum of one Screened Adult and a Hall Monitor supervising the Children.

—— Appendix 2

4. Programming for Children is to be planned in advance in conjunction with Church Leadership. Prior to each event, Parents should be notified of the activities that the Children will participate in. This includes but is not limited to verifying appropriate games, computer activity, and screen activity (i.e., TV, video, Netflix).
5. Children are **not** to be left alone with Unscreened Adults or Youth.
6. Home Group Leaders will be responsible to:
    a. Take attendance each time a group meets as part of a Cell/Home Group;
    b. The Attendance Form must include the date, location and the names of all Adults and Children in attendance;
    c. The attendance must include the age or grade of Children, participant's first and last name, full names of all Ministry Personnel and Occasional Observers attending on that date.
7. Each Home Group Leader must remit this Attendance Form within one week to the Pastor or Ministry Lead or to the church office.
8. These Attendance Forms are to be kept on file permanently.

D. Special Events and Overnight Policies

Field Trips and Special Events:
1. All off-campus activities are to be pre-approved by the Ministry Lead with Parents being notified at least one week prior to the outing.
2. Proper written Letters of Informed Consent and Registration and Medical Consent Forms are required for each individual participating in field trips and special events. Photocopies of the forms must be kept in the Ministry Lead's possession during trips and events with the originals filed in the church office. (Appendix 19 and 15)
3. All trips and outings are to be supervised by a minimum of two approved, unrelated Adult Ministry Personnel.
4. When planning local special events, it is preferred that Parents drop off and pick up their Children at the event location. For out of town events, it is preferred that a commercial carrier be employed.
5. Children and Youth may not be transported one-on-one. Mentoring relationships should be conducted in teams and in public places. Parents are encouraged to drop their Children or Youth off and pick them up.
6. All Ministry Personnel drivers transporting individuals during church activities must be pre-approved by the Ministry Lead, provide a copy of their valid driver's license and current automobile insurance in accordance with the church insurance policy, and have had a minimum of five years of driving experience.
7. Church vehicles are to be driven by Ministry Personnel that have been pre-approved by Church Leadership. These drivers are to be insured under the church automobile insurance policy.
8. The number of occupants in the vehicle are not to exceed the number of seat belts and each Child must be in age appropriate safety restraints. Seat belts must be worn by everyone and remain fastened at all times the vehicle is in motion.
9. Children are not to be left unattended in a vehicle.

Overnight Events:
1. All overnight activities are to be pre-approved by Church Leadership.
2. Proper written Letters of Informed Consent and Registration and Medical Consent Forms are required for each Child or Youth participating in overnight events. Forms must be kept in the Ministry Lead's possession during trips and events and a photocopy filed in the church office. The originals are to be kept on file permanently. (Appendix 19 and 15)
3. All overnight activities must have a minimum ratio of two Ministry Personnel for every 10 Children or Youth. Ministry Personnel are to be assigned a specific group of Children or Youth for who they are responsible. If both genders are in attendance, there must also be both male and female Ministry Leaders providing supervision.

4. All trips and outings must be supervised by a minimum of two approved, unrelated Adult Ministry Personnel.
5. When transportation is being provided by your church, a Letter of Informed Consent for Transportation must be signed. (Appendix 23) The travel forms must be maintained and filed in the church office. Forms are to be kept on file permanently.

E. Shower and Locker Room Guidelines

1. Locker Rooms must be supervised at all times. Two Screened Adults must be present together in the dressing or locker room with Children or Youth while they are showering or changing; Ministry Personnel must not be alone with minors in this setting.

2. Out of respect for the Children and Youth, and to maintain a high standard of professionalism, Ministry Personnel will announce their arrival prior to entering a dressing or locker room.

3. Ministry Personnel are not permitted to change or shower at the same time as Children and Youth.

4. Separate facilities should be designated for both genders or, if these are not available, separate showering/changing times will be arranged.

5. The use of photographic or video recording devices, including cell phones, is prohibited in dressing or locker rooms at all times.

F. Overnight Trips and Housing

For the protection of our Children and Youth, the following guidelines will be followed prior to all off-site trips where overnight accommodations must be secured:

1. A notice with a Letter of Informed Consent (Appendix 19) will be sent home to Parents at least one week in advance, advising them that an overnight trip is being planned, which requires the team to stay in a conference centre/camp/hotel/motel. The notice will note:
   a. The inherent risks associated with the event;
   b. The precautions being taken to minimize the risk and to raise the level of safety provided for their Children and Youth; and,
   c. Specific sleeping and travel arrangements that have been planned.

2. The Parent must return the signed and witnessed Letter of Informed Consent which includes the required liability shields.

3. Ministry Personnel travelling with Children and Youth must complete the screening and training process outlined in this policy prior to departure. Screened and trained Ministry Personnel who are placed in a Position of Trust with Children and Youth must be known by the church for six months.

4. Any individuals travelling with the team who do not qualify as screened Ministry Personnel must have separate sleeping arrangements.

5. When travel plans require overnight housing, housing must be arranged in the homes of screened and approved billets, or in a conference centre, camp, or church where Children or Youth can stay together, and where more than one screened Adult can be assigned to each common sleeping area. (Refer to the policy on "Billeting and Hosting" on page 201). When this is not possible, and it is necessary that the group stay in hotels or motels, the following plans must be made so that Children and Youth have distinctly separate sleeping arrangements from Ministry Personnel. In these plans, safety will be prioritized using the following guidelines when possible:
   a. Hotel rooms will be all together in one wing of the hotel or motel; and

Appendix 2

b. Parents are encouraged to accompany the team, assigning the family to hotel rooms; or,

c. Ministry Leads request the availability of suites with two or three bedrooms per suite and assign two Children or Youth of the same age to a separate room, set apart from the two Adult screened Ministry Personnel; or,

d. Ministry Leads must assign two unrelated Adult Ministry Personnel to a hotel room with two or more Children or Youth; or,

e. In hotel or motel rooms with adjoining doors, Ministry Leads must assign one Adult Ministry Personnel with two Children or Youth in each room. For accountability purposes, the door separating adjoining rooms must be kept ajar or open at all times. Children and Youth must have distinctly separate sleeping arrangements from other Adults.

f. Ministry Personnel are never to be alone in a room with a Child or Youth.

G. Billeting and Hosting

1. For the protection of our minors, it is required that all Adults residing in the home where billets are provided must complete the following screening process prior to hosting. Screening includes:

    a. A recommendation from a Pastor or member of Church Leadership

    b. A Criminal Record Check

2. Information guidelines are to be distributed to host homes no less than one week in advance of minors arriving at their home.

3. Any allergies and medications for minors will be communicated to the host home prior to arrival, with clear directions on how to manage allergies and medications.

4. Minors must always be billeted in teams or small groups of the same gender, must have distinctly separate sleeping arrangements from the household members, and are not to be left alone in the home without adequate adult supervision.

5. Curfews shall be established and enforced when minors are being billeted. All minors staying in host homes are to be informed of proper etiquette, rules and curfew guidelines.

CHILD PROTECTION PROCEDURES

A. Staff to Student Ratios

1. Classroom settings must comply with established ratios for Adults and Children at all times. This includes off-site activities and trips. Established ratios are:
    - Two Ministry Personnel for every six infants (birth – 18 months)
    - Two Ministry Personnel for every 10 toddlers or preschoolers
    - Two Ministry Personnel for every 20 elementary-age Children

B. Proper Display of Affection
Appropriate Touch:

1. Recognizing that Children need appropriate displays of affection that reflect pure, genuine and positive displays of God's love, appropriate touch with Children will be age and developmentally appropriate. We encourage Ministry Personnel to:

Appendix 2

- Hold a preschool Child who is crying,
- Speak to a Child at eye level and listen with your eyes as well as your ears,
- Hold a Child's hands when speaking, listening or walking him or her to an activity,
- Gently hold the Child's shoulder or hand to keep his or her attention while you redirect the Child's behaviour,
- Put your arm around the shoulder of a Child when comforting or quieting is needed,
- Pat a Child on the head, hand, shoulder or back to affirm him or her.

2. All touch must be done in view of others.

Inappropriate Touch:
1. Recognizing that the innocence of Children must be protected, Ministry Leaders will be made aware that the following actions are deemed inappropriate and will not be permitted:
   - Do not kiss a Child or coax a Child to kiss you,
   - Do not engage in extended hugging and tickling,
   - Do not hold a Child's face when talking to or disciplining the Child,
   - Do not touch a Child in any area that would be covered by a bathing suit (strictly prohibited except in cases of diapering and assisting preschoolers as outlined in washroom policies),
   - Do not carry older Children and do not allow them to sit on your lap,
   - Avoid prolonged physical contact with any Child or Youth.

2. Ministry Personnel are not to be left alone with a Child or Youth.

C. Child-to-Child Sexual Play or Abuse

1. If caregivers discover age-appropriate consensual Child-to-Child sexual play, use it as a teachable moment. Calmly figure out what happened by asking open-ended questions. Provide appropriate consequences and provide education in the area that appears most relevant to the situation. For example: learning names and functions of body parts, clarifying social rules and privacy, understanding how to respect their own bodies and others, identifying friendship vs. intimate relationships, and age-appropriate sexual education.

2. Reassure the Child that you care about them.

3. Fill out a Suspected Abuse Report Form, notify Parents and leadership, and respond appropriately.

4. If it is inappropriate sexual play, if there is an imbalance of power or authority, if there is a difference in age, ability or strength, if the actions are aggressive in nature or do not follow age of consent laws, fill out a Suspected Abuse Report Form and make a report to the proper authorities immediately.

5. Notify Parents as instructed by authorities.

6. Keep all documentation of Child-to-Child sexual play and abuse permanently.

D. Washroom Guidelines

1. Upon registering Children for programs, Parents will be notified to take their Children to the washroom prior to programs.

Appendix 2

For Nursery:
1. Ministry Personnel are not required to change the diapers of young Children. It is the responsibility of a Child's Parents to change diapers.
2. Diaper changing procedures are clearly posted in the nursery diaper changing area. (Appendix 11)
3. In the rare case Ministry Personnel do change diapers, it is to be done only by a designated Adult Ministry Personnel and must be conducted within view of other Ministry Personnel.

For Preschool Children:
1. Preschool Children are not to go to the washroom alone.
2. One of the following are to be adhered to when accompanying preschool Children to the washroom:
    - Two Ministry Personnel are to escort a group of Children to the washroom, or,
    - One Ministry Personnel is to escort a group of Children to the washroom with one Hall Monitor appointed to assist with washroom and security duties.
3. No Ministry Personnel must ever be alone with a Child in an unsupervised washroom and they are never to go into the cubicle with a Child and shut the door.
4. When a preschool Child needs assistance in the washroom, Ministry Personnel may enter the washroom cubicle to assist utilizing the following guidelines:
    - The outside washroom door must be propped open and the Adult must stand in an open cubicle doorway,
    - Ministry Personnel will take into consideration the privacy of the Child.

For Elementary Children:
1. Elementary boys and girls are not to be sent to the washroom alone but should be accompanied by a buddy in the same age group.
2. Ministry Personnel are to escort the Children to the washroom and prop the door open to make sure that everything is in order. Ministry Personnel must then remain outside the washroom door and wait for the Children before escorting them back to the classroom.
3. Ministry Personnel are not to be alone with Children in an unsupervised washroom and are never to enter into the cubicle with a Child and shut the door.

E. Receiving and Releasing Children

1. Receiving and releasing Children under the age of 6 is strongly monitored. A mandatory sign-in and sign-out form is to be used in all Children's programming. (Appendix 29)

2. Children are not to be dropped off in a classroom without Ministry Personnel present.

3. Babies and preschool Children are to only be released into the care of the Child's Parent or designate utilizing a signature, security number or identification card.

4. Parents and visitors are not to enter the nursery or preschool classroom when picking up their Child unless requested to do so.

For Elementary Students:
1. Younger elementary students and newcomers are to remain in the classroom until the Parent or designate comes to pick them up and the student demonstrates recognition.

2. Consideration must be given to security, church facilities and location when determining the age release of older elementary Children. Ministry Personnel are to ask on an informal basis whether the Child knows where to find his or her Parent. If the Child demonstrates uncertainty, the Ministry Personnel will keep the Child with them in the classroom until the Parent or designate picks up the Child.

YOUTH PROTECTION PROCEDURES

A. Physical Contact

1. 'Physical Contact Guidelines' are to be posted in the Youth department.

2. Ministry Personnel are aware of what constitutes appropriate touch:
   a. one-arm hugs
   b. shoulder-to-shoulder hugs
   c. touch on the back or shoulder

3. Ministry Personnel must refrain from inappropriate touch at all times:
   a. chest-to-chest hugging
   b. extended hugging
   c. overexuberant affection
   d. lap-sitting
   e. kissing
   f. touching of thighs, knees or inappropriate spots of the body

4. Ministry Personnel must be cognizant of conduct that could be misinterpreted:
   a. horseplay
   b. tickling
   c. extended backrubs

5. All touch should be done in view of other people.

B. Staff to Student Ratio

1. Programs for Youth must comply with established staffing ratios as follows:
   - **Junior High events** – Two Ministry Personnel for every 16 students
   - **Senior High events** – Two Ministry Personnel for every 20 students
   - **Overnight/Off-Site events** – Two Ministry Personnel for every 10 students

2. There must be at least two unrelated Ministry Personnel at all events.

3. Overnight events with mixed genders must be accompanied by both male and female Ministry Personnel.

4. It is recommended that there be a five year gap between Ministry Personnel and the Youth they serve.

C. Mentoring

1. Church Leadership must grant approval for a mentoring ministry to take place. Once approved, for the protection of those we mentor and for Ministry Personnel engaged in mentoring, the following policies are to be followed:

a. The Ministry Lead is responsible for assigning mentees with mentors.
b. Ministry Personnel granted to be mentors must be screened and trained according to recruitment and screening policies and procedures.
c. Ministry Personnel are encouraged to meet with Youth in small group settings and in teams.
d. Parental permission must be granted in writing using a Letter of Informed Consent.

2. If off-site mentoring, the following must take place:
   a. A risk assessment must be submitted to Church Leadership.
   b. The Ministry Lead must be informed of the time and place of the meeting prior to the meeting.
   c. Mentoring must be done in small groups, or in conjunction with another team of two.
   d. Mentoring can then take place at the church or an approved stationary public location, such as a coffee shop, library, restaurant, or campus cafeteria; and
   e. Separate transportation must be arranged (avoiding isolation in a vehicle).

3. If mentoring is not done in small groups, it may only take place at the church or in a public setting, in view of other people. Furthermore, these additional policies must be followed:
   a. The Ministry Lead must pre-approve the conducting of any one-on-one mentoring with the information being documented and filed.
   b. The public setting where mentoring takes place must be a static location, not subsequently moving to another location.
   c. One-on-one mentoring is permissible only for mentoring minors thirteen (13) years of age and older.
   d. The difference in the age between the mentor and the mentee must be five (5) years or more, subject to the mentor being a minimum of twenty-one (21) years of age, or older.

4. Mentors must avoid meeting in a home setting unless it is the home of the mentee, and the Parents are at home during the meeting and the mentoring happens in a common shared room (i.e., living room, family room, or dining room).

D. Youth-to-Youth Sexual Activity

1. If Ministry Personnel discover the occurrence age-appropriate consensual sexual activity, use it as a teachable and mentoring moment. Calmly discuss your concerns with open-ended questions. Provide education in the area that appears most relevant to the situation. For example: discussing the church's theological position, safety concerns, clarifying social rules and privacy, understanding how to respect and honour each other, identifying friendship vs. intimate relationships, and age-appropriate sexual education.

2. Reassure the young people that you care about them.

3. Fill out a Suspected Abuse Report Form, and respond appropriately by encouraging the Youth to discuss their relationship and activity with their Parents. If they are not willing to tell their Parents, it may be appropriate for Ministry Personnel to notify their Parents if you deem the Youth to be in an unsafe sexual relationship or if they are below the age of consent.

4. If it is inappropriate or not consensual sexual activity, if there is an imbalance of power or authority, if there is a difference in age, ability or strength, if the actions are aggressive in nature or do not follow age of consent laws, fill out a Suspected Abuse Report Form and make a report to the proper authorities immediately.

5. Notify Parents as instructed by authorities.

6. Keep all Suspected Abuse Report Forms and documentation permanently.

Appendix 2

ADULT PROTECTION PROCEDURES

A. Physical Contact

1. Ministry Personnel must refrain from inappropriate touching at all times:
    a. Chest-to-chest hugging
    b. Extended side hugs
    c. Overexuberant affection
    d. Sexual activity
    e. Kissing on the mouth
    f. Touching of the thighs, knees, lower back, buttocks, or other inappropriate spots of the body
    g. Any form of touch that makes someone feel uncomfortable, i.e., attempting to forcefully hold their hand or any part of the body, or even trying to hug someone without their consent

2. Ministry Personnel are aware of what constitutes appropriate touch of Adults:
    a. One-arm hugs
    b. Shoulder-to-shoulder hugs
    c. Brief touch on the shoulder or hand

3. Ministry Personnel must be cognizant of conduct that could be misinterpreted and avoid these actions:
    a. Compliments regarding someone's body or clothing
    b. Whistling
    c. Tickling
    d. Offers of backrubs

B. New Immigrant and Refugee Settlement

Newly arrived immigrants and refugees to Canada are vulnerable due to their dependency on others to assist with acclimation to a new country, culture, and in some cases a new language.

1. A plan and strategy for Refugee sponsorship and engagement has been approved by the Board and is reflective of both the Refugee Sponsorship Agreement Holder handbook and the Plan to Protect® policy. The plan:
    a. Requires all Refugee Sponsorship team members be screened and trained per the Plan to Protect® policy;
    b. Ensures Refugee family members are solely responsible for their own Children;
    c. Includes both oral and written translation;
    d. Remains in place until the Refugees are independent or no longer the legal responsibility of the church.
2. For the initial year of sponsorship and dependence, Ministry Personnel are not to assign the care of Refugee Children to minors under the age of 18 years old. Following this time, all Child protection procedures will be adhered to in accordance with the procedures outlined under the "Child Protection Procedures."
3. All care procedures will be followed as outlined in "General Protection Procedures," "Child Protection Procedures," and "Youth Protection Procedures." This includes Occasional Observers, personal care and washroom guidelines, dating, discipline, contacting opportunities, and transportation.

Temporary Housing
1. If temporary housing is provided with a church family, the following guidelines must be followed:
    a. All Adult members of the home must be appropriately screened and trained.
    b. Refugee family members will have distinctly separate sleeping arrangements from the other household members. Separate sleeping arrangements must be made available for each family member, or as preferred by the Refugees.

  c. The Refugee family members will be housed together, and Children are not to share a bedroom or bed with the host family Children.
  d. Children will accompany Parents to meetings and appointments whenever possible.
  e. If young Children are part of the family, all electrical outlets will be kept covered when not in use.
  f. Children will not be left alone in the care of any minors.
  g. For the protection of all parties, the host family will maintain a daily log of activities. This log is to be submitted to the church office on a monthly basis.

C. Personal Care

1. Personal Care is the responsibility of caregivers and family members, not Ministry Personnel.

2. Caregivers and family members may look forward to the respite of Ministry Personnel coming to visit the Vulnerable. It is at the Ministry Personnel's discretion if they wish to provide this extra level of care; however, at no time will Ministry Personnel be left alone in a home or behind closed doors with Vulnerable Persons.

D. Mentoring Adults and Pastoral Care

1. Only Ministry Personnel approved by the Lead Pastor may mentor Adults or provide pastoral care under the umbrella of the church.

2. Mentoring and pastoral care must take place in a church office or a stationary public location, such as a coffee shop, library, restaurant or another public location, or a room with the door fully open.

3. Mentors are to maintain and submit monthly communication and appointment logs.

4. Individuals providing pastoral care must maintain a journal or calendar of appointments and a summary of pastoral care that has been provided.

5. When meeting off-site, separate transportation is to be arranged (avoiding opportunities for isolation).

E. Shelters, Recovery and Rehabilitation Ministries

This policy is for ministries of the church where overnight housing and shelter is provided to individuals in recovery or seeking a safe residence.

Visitors

1. Visitors and non-housing Ministry Personnel are discouraged from coming to the residence, this includes Board members and Directors. In the rare occasion that this may occur, the visit must be scheduled well in advance when there is a minimum of two unrelated Ministry Personnel present.

2. No individuals of the opposite gender are allowed in the sleeping quarters of residences.

Guest Log

1. In the rare occasion where visitors do come to the shelter or residence, a guest log is to be maintained.

2. Guests' first and last names, along with the names of Ministry Personnel present must be acquired for every visit. The date and time of all guest comings and goings are to be captured on the guest log. The log will be retained permanently.

Appendix 2

Confidentiality

1. Unless granted permission, the location of the residence must be kept confidential. It is a vital matter of the safety of residents and Ministry Personnel working and living in the house.

2. This specifically refers to any mention of:

    a. The ACTUAL STREET ADDRESS of the house;

    b. ANY IDENTIFYING CHARACTERISTICS of the house or programs, (i.e., description of buildings, neighbourhood, etc.)

3. No information shall be divulged without written, informed consent of Leadership.

4. In addition, Ministry Personnel taking participants on outings may not disclose to associates, friends, relatives or anyone that you encounter, that is not involved in shelter ministry, that the participant is part of the Shelter or Residence programs. Participants should only be referred to as 'friends'.

F. Violence and Harassment

The church is committed to the prevention of violence and is ultimately responsible for the health and safety of individuals that come to our services and who work at the church. We will take reasonable steps to protect our Ministry Personnel and attendees from violence.

1. A security plan has been put in place. It is the responsibility of the Board and Church Leadership to ensure this policy and the supporting security plan are implemented and maintained, and that all Ministry Personnel have the appropriate information and instruction to protect them from violence within the church.

2. Ministry Leads are to adhere to this policy and the supporting security plan. Ministry Leads are responsible for ensuring that measures and procedures are followed by Ministry Personnel, and that they have the information they need to protect themselves.

3. Violent behaviour in any form is unacceptable from anyone. All concerns regarding violence or not feeling safe within the church must be reported to the Pastor or Chair of the Board.

4. Ministry Personnel must work in compliance with this policy. Everyone is encouraged to raise any concerns about violence and to report any violent incidents or threats. If it is an emergency, immediately call 9-1-1. Please complete an Incident Report Form and submit all concerns and complaints to the Pastor or Chair of the Board. The Board must be made aware of these incidents.

5. The Board and Church Leadership pledge to investigate and deal with all incidents and complaints of violence in a fair and timely manner, respecting the privacy of all concerned as much as possible.

Incidents of Aggressive and Violent Behaviour

1. To ensure the safety of participants, aggressive behaviour by an attendee will result in the request for them to leave the premises.

2. In an effort to discourage aggressive behaviour, Ministry Leads are to follow the disciplinary action policy guidelines.

3. If aggressive behaviour has occurred, the aggressive individual is to be required to stay home from the program for at least one event. Additional incidents are to result in a progressive number of days out of the program. In some cases, it may be necessary to impose permanent removal. This would be addressed on a case-by-case basis, and only after other reasonable alternatives have been exhausted. The Ministry Lead is to work with the individual, caregiver or guardian to identify behaviour triggers and look for solutions.

4. Complete an Incident Report Form for any act of violence.

Appendix 2

G. Financial Aid

1. Ministry Personnel may not distribute money or loans from their own resources.

2. Ministry Personnel are not to give money, or loans to individuals in their programs as a bribe or in exchange for any services or favours.

3. If an individual asks for aid, requests must be submitted in writing, with supporting documentation demonstrating the need to the Ministry Lead of the benevolent fund. Leadership must approve these funds, whether the aid is being provided personally or from the benevolent fund. Groceries and gift cards can be given in the case of need, but must be approved by the Board or benevolent committee.

4. All financial aid distributed by the church is to be accounted for by the finance department.

REPORTING AND RESPONSE

Response to Abuse

A. Hearing of an Allegation or Suspicion of Child Abuse

The following policies outline the recommended procedure and sequence for reporting suspected abuse cases.

1. For the protection of our Children, Youth and Adults, all allegations and/or suspicions of abuse against Children, Youth and Vulnerable Adults are to be taken seriously.

2. Immediately upon hearing of potential abuse or allegations of abuse of a Child or Youth, the Ministry Personnel must complete a Suspected Abuse Report Form documenting all pertinent information (Appendix 33). The victim must not be asked leading questions nor should the accused or any other parties be contacted at the point of completing the Suspected Abuse Report Form.

3. Make an immediate report to Child and Family Services. Reporting may be done in conjunction with the Lead Pastor or a Ministry Lead.

4. All forms must be kept permanently unless otherwise directed by legal counsel.

5. Reporters are requested to submit a copy of the Suspected Abuse Report Form to the Lead Pastor.

B. Reporting Child Abuse

1. Any person including, but not limited to, Ministry Personnel, who has reasonable grounds to believe that a Child is in need of protection, is legally required to immediately report the matter to Child and Family Services (Children's Aid) or the police. Reporting must be done orally by telephone or in-person.

2. A person who knowingly fails to report in these circumstances is in violation of the law and may be found to have committed an offence and may be subject to disciplinary action in the church.

3. If the abuse occurred within the context of the church, the Lead Pastor or his designate must notify the church's insurance provider and seek legal counsel upon hearing of a suspected child abuse case.

4. The church will notify and work in conjunction with denominational leadership in any and all allegations or suspicions of abuse that may have happened in the context of church ministry.

Appendix 2

5. If the suspected abuse happened in the context of church ministries or was committed by a church member or attendee, the Parents of the victim must be notified by the Lead Pastor or by Church Leadership in conjunction with Child and Family Services and legal counsel.

C. Hearing an Allegation or Suspicion of Abuse Against an Adult

1. All allegations and disclosure of abuse or harassment against Adults are to be taken seriously.

2. Upon hearing an allegation or disclosure of abuse or harassment against an Adult, Ministry Personnel must complete a Suspected Abuse Report Form (Appendix 32) documenting all pertinent information. Do not ask the individual leading questions, and neither the accused nor any other parties should be contacted at the point of completing the Suspected Abuse Report Form.

3. All forms must be kept permanently unless otherwise directed by legal counsel.

4. Ministry Personnel are requested to notify the Lead Pastor that they have heard an allegation or disclosure of abuse.

5. If the abuse occurred within the context of the church, the Lead Pastor or his designate must notify the church's insurance provider and seek legal counsel upon hearing of a suspected abuse case.

6. If the abuse happened within the context of the church, leadership will notify and work in conjunction with denominational leadership in any and all allegations or suspicions of abuse that may have happened in the context of church ministry.

D. Reporting and Responding to an Allegation of Abuse or Harassment Against an Adult

1. All allegations, disclosures and suspicions of abuse and harassment against an Adult will be taken seriously and responded to with empathy.

2. If an allegation or suspicion of abuse represents a situation that is an emergency and a crime is about to be committed, immediately call 9-1-1 and report it to police.

3. If it is not an emergency or no imminent threat exists, and an accusation of abuse, harassment, misconduct or exploitation towards an Adult is made or suspected, the following guidelines are to be followed:

    a. If the Adult has the cognitive ability to make a report to police, then Ministry Personnel are to encourage the person to make that report, and support them in their decision, whatever they decide. At no time should the individual be discouraged or instructed not to call the police.

    b. If the Adult does not have the cognitive ability to make a report, then Ministry Personnel are to complete a Suspected Abuse Report Form (Appendix 32) and make a report to police, where the accusation involves a crime.

    c. In some cases, such as Long Term Care homes, additional laws define anyone who works with certain Adults as a Mandatory Reporter. In these cases, whether the Adult has the cognitive ability to make a report on their own or not, Ministry Personnel are to complete a Suspected Abuse Report Form (for Adults) and make a report to the mandated reporting agency.

4. If the Adult has the cognitive capacity to make a report, but is unwilling to do so, and no law requires mandatory reporting, Ministry Personnel should:

    a. Express concerns for the individual's well-being;

    b. Provide them the phone number to make the report in the future;

    c. Offer to be with them when they report it;

    d. Inform them about the laws in place regarding abuse and harassment and that they are not alone, that there are supports available to them;

    e. Encourage them to consider what to do next time;

    f. Arrange for a follow-up;

    g. Develop a safety plan.

5. Ministry Personnel and leadership are not to confront the accused as this may put the victim in more danger. They may offer pastoral care and professional counselling to the individual that disclosed the abuse but they are not to confront the accused about the abuse.

6. The church requests that when a report is made to police on behalf of an Adult who does not have the cognitive capacity to report on their own, in the case where a Ministry Personnel provides support to an Adult who makes their own report to police, or in a case where the Ministry Personnel is a Mandatory Reporter, that Ministry Personnel must notify the Lead Pastor that such a report has been made.

E. Assessing and Investigating an Allegation or Suspicion of Abuse

1. No persons, including Church Leadership, are to assume the function of assessing, substantiating or investigating the need for intervention or interpretation of suspected Child abuse or abuse against an Adult.

2. The church is to engage an external investigator to investigate allegations and disclosures of sexual misconduct and abuse of Adults.

3. The church and its individuals must avoid any undue interference when a report of Child abuse has been filed with Child and Family Services or the police. The church must ask how it can assist in helping and supporting the investigation and the victim. The church must maintain frequent communication and supportive relationships with those suspected or guilty of child abuse as long as these persons exhibit a willingness to listen, change and look to Christ for help. This does not exclude the need for hurting individuals to receive professional counselling.

4. The church must maintain frequent communication and supportive relationships with those suspected of abuse as long as the individual exhibits a willingness to listen. This does not exclude, or should it be at the expense of those that are victims and in need of professional counselling. A victim advocate must be appointed to walk alongside the victim.

5. The church is to support Ministry Personnel when they fulfill their duty to report abuse as outlined in the Plan to Protect® training and church policies.

Appendix 2

F. Protecting Confidentiality and Dignity of the Victim and the Accused

1. During the process of reporting and response, all Ministry Personnel will be committed to prayer and strive to remain calm and hopeful.

2. Discretion must be observed and details of the suspected abuse must not be shared among the church community. Information should be shared on a need-to-know basis, expanding only as individuals are drawn into the response and investigation. Confidentiality for the suspected victim and the accused must be protected.

G. Spiritual Abuse

1. The church is opposed to any form of spiritual abuse. Ministry Personnel are not to misuse their positions of authority or influence to manipulate or coerce others to act or believe in a certain way for the apparent benefit of the church or those in a position of authority.

2. Ministry Personnel are not to use scripture out of context or to use the Bible as a weapon to unduly manipulate an individual.

3. Ministry Personnel and Board members must attend additional professional development training on spiritual abuse awareness and prevention. Volunteers must receive training on the definition of spiritual abuse as part of their safeguarding training.

4. A whistleblower policy must be put in place to provide a safe contact to receive concerns about any form of injury, harm, and abuse. All complaints of spiritual abuse are to be brought to the attention of the Board and are to be fully investigated as outlined under the Whistleblower Policy.

5. Ministry Personnel are to be held accountable if they have been found to have misused their positions to unduly cause spiritual harm to another individual and are to be subject to progressive steps of discipline.

6. If an individual raises a concern about spiritual abuse, they are to be encouraged to seek out professional help and healing. Church Leadership are to assign a knowledgeable person to provide care to the individual, and where able, are to extend the offer of professional care and therapy to help with the recovery of the spiritual harm that has occurred.

H. Whistleblower Policy

1. The church is to act with due diligence in its investigation and follow through on all allegations of misconduct. They are to do their utmost to protect any whistleblower from reprisal, dismissal or any other retaliation.

2. The church is not to tolerate any harassment or victimization (including informal pressures) and is to take appropriate action to protect the whistleblower when they raise a concern in good faith, even if they are mistaken. Any harassment or victimization of a whistleblower may result in disciplinary action against the person responsible.

3. In situations where we have a legal duty to report child abuse, no internal investigation is to take place until such time as an investigation has been conducted by law enforcement or the child protection agency.

— Appendix 2

4. Any investigations into allegations arising from whistleblowing are not to influence or be influenced by any other Ministry Personnel procedures to which the whistleblower may be subject.
5. All concerns are to be treated in confidence and every effort is to be made not to reveal the identity of the whistleblower if that is their wish. If a concern cannot be resolved without revealing the identity of the whistleblower, steps forward are to be determined in collaboration with the whistleblower. This policy encourages the whistleblower to put their name to their allegation whenever possible.
6. Church Leadership has overall responsibility for the maintenance and operation of this policy. The church is to maintain a record of concerns raised and outcomes (in a form which does not endanger confidentiality) and is to report as necessary to the governmental, or other legal authority as required by law.
7. The church is to respond to every complaint or allegation. Within 10 working days of a concern being raised, a member of Church Leadership is to write to the whistleblower to:
    a. Acknowledge that the complaint or allegation has been received;
    b. Indicate how the matter will be dealt with;
    c. Give an estimate of how long it will take to provide a final response;
    d. Indicate whether any initial inquiries have been made;
    e. Supply the whistleblower with information on support mechanisms;
    f. Tell the whistleblower whether further investigations will take place and if not, why not.
8. Where appropriate, the matters raised may:
    a. Be referred to the next level of leadership;
    b. Be referred to the Board of Directors;
    c. Be referred to the disciplinary process;
    d. Be referred to the police;
    e. Be referred to an external investigator; or
    f. Form the subject of an independent inquiry.
9. The church is to take steps to minimize any difficulties which the whistleblower may experience as a result of raising a complaint or allegation.
10. If a complaint or allegation a not confirmed by an investigation, no action is to be taken against a whistleblower. If, however, a complaint or allegation is made frivolously, maliciously or for personal gain, disciplinary action may be taken against the complainant.
11. Subject to legal constraints, the church is to inform the whistleblower of the outcome of any investigation.

Response to Abuse

A. Spiritual Response and Counsel for the Victim

1. The church is committed to providing a trauma-informed response, prioritizing the needs of the victim.

2. For the protection of everyone, all allegations and/or suspicions of abuse are to be taken seriously and handled with the utmost care. The suspected victims are to be treated with dignity and respect.

Appendix 2

3. During the process of reporting and response, all Ministry Personnel are to be committed to prayer and strive to remain calm and hopeful.

4. Situations of abuse must be handled forthrightly with due respect for people's privacy and confidentiality. Discretion must be observed and details of the suspected abuse must not be shared among the church community. Information must be shared on a need-to-know basis, expanding only as individuals are drawn into the response and investigation. Confidentiality for the victim must be protected.

5. Church Leadership are to seek opportunity to provide individual care and counsel both for the abuse victim and their family. In consultation with the individual, a victim advocate will be assigned to support the victim. Church Leadership are to determine the need for professional assistance and evaluate and designate resources as needed and able.

6. The victim will be empowered to make decisions and granted opportunity for their voice to be heard. At no time will the victim be asked to sign a non-disclosure agreement in relation to the incident of abuse.

B. Biblical Response and Discipline for the Accused or Convicted

1. The accused is to be treated with dignity and respect. Ministry Personnel, accused of abuse, must be relieved temporarily of all of their duties until an investigation is completed. Arrangements will be made to either maintain or suspend income until the allegations are cleared or substantiated if applicable.

2. It is the responsibility and right of Church Leadership to exercise and practice church discipline as outlined in Matthew 18 and as stipulated in denominational guidelines.

3. Church Leadership are to seek opportunity to provide individual care and counsel both for the accused and their family. Church Leadership are to determine the need for professional assistance and evaluate and designate resources as needed and able.

4. Anyone accused of abuse to Children or Youth is to be prohibited from having access to Children or Youth until they are cleared of any and all charges. Clear written guidelines are to be provided to the individual with restricted activities and areas of the church that they are not permitted to use.

5. Anyone convicted of Child abuse will be prohibited from having access to Children or Youth. Church Leadership may designate an individual to be responsible to be informed whenever the convicted person attends church activities and to accompany the convicted person while on church property. Clear written guidelines are to be provided to the individual listing restricted areas and access points on the church property.

C. Media Relations

1. It is the responsibility of the Church Leadership and Lead Pastor to designate a spokesperson to speak on behalf of the church to media and to the public in relation to any crisis or allegation of abuse. All inquiries must be directed to this person and comment must not be made by other individuals unless given permission to do so.

Appendix 2

2. Public statements must be well prepared and presented under the guidance of legal counsel.

3. The media spokesperson is to cooperate with the media to communicate our deep concern about the incident and reaffirm our commitment to cooperate with the investigation.

D. Ongoing Investigation

1. Full cooperation must be given by all parties to civil authorities under the guidelines of legal counsel.

2. At no time should Church Leadership or its individuals either engage in denial, minimization or blame, or admit responsibility which could prejudice the case or cause increased liability to the church.

3. A confidential follow-up report with conclusions and action taken must be documented by the Lead Pastor following a report of abuse. This report should be placed in a confidential Ministry Personnel file and kept permanently.

4. Church Leadership are to inform others of any ongoing investigation strictly on a need-to-know basis. In consultation with legal counsel, a trauma-informed summary report will be shared with the complainant, accused and the congregation.

E. Offender's Policy

This policy relates to Offenders, meaning individuals who have been convicted of sexual crimes against Children or Youth who wish to attend the church on a consistent basis.

1. Offenders of Child sexual abuse may attend the church on a regular basis if they enter into an Offender's Covenant Agreement with the leadership of the church.

2. Two delegates from the Board and the Lead Pastor are to meet with the individual and inform the individual that the church requires Offenders to enter into an Offender's Covenant Agreement in order for them to attend the church on a regular basis.

3. The Covenant Agreement is to be written and signed by the Lead Pastor, two representatives of the Board, and the individual, making up the accountability team.

4. The Offender's Covenant must include the following:

    a. Who is to be informed when the Offender will be at the church.

    b. What part of the building the Offender may come to.

    c. Locations in the building the Offender is not allowed to go to (Children and Youth wings of the church).

    d. Where in the sanctuary the Offender may sit (recommend the front of the sanctuary with one of the accountability team members).

    e. Restriction to take pictures at the church.

    f. Restrictions for befriending and spending time with families with Children.

Appendix 2

    g. When the Offender uses the washroom, one of the chaperones are to first check the washroom to make sure there are no Children in the washroom. If there is a Child in the washroom they are to wait until the Child is done before entering.

    h. Restrictions from participating in programs with Children and Youth, i.e., church property during special Children's events (such as VBS, mid-week Children's/Youth programs, etc.).

    i. The requirement for annual review and signature of the Offender's Covenant Agreement by the accountability team.

    j. The consequences if the covenant is broken.

5. Information regarding an individual's convictions are to only be disclosed to the members of the Board, the Pastor, key Ministry Leaders and individuals involved in supporting the Covenant Agreement or on a limited need-to-know basis.

MINISTRY PERSONNEL APPLICATION FORM _____ Appendix 3

In our desire to reduce the risk of abuse within our church ministries, we believe this information is necessary to protect our children, our youth and our volunteers and to effectively place our volunteers in ministry positions. Thank you in advance for your partnership.

Personal Information

Full Name _____

Address _____

Postal Code _____ Email _____

Phone Number (H) _____ (C) _____

Personal History

Please provide a copy of your employment resume and/or list any employers with which you have worked in the past 20 years, including name and address of employer, dates of your employment, your position, and a contact person.

_____

_____

_____

_____

Hobbies, Interests or Skills

_____

_____

_____

Appendix 3

Spiritual History

How long have you attended _____ Church? _____

Do you regularly attend (2 or more services a month)? ❑ Yes ❑ No
Are you a member? ❑ Yes ❑ No
If not, are you willing to attend a membership seminar? ❑ Yes ❑ No
When did you accept Christ as your Savior? _____

Have you been baptized? ❑ Yes ❑ No
If not, are you willing to attend a baptismal seminar? ❑ Yes ❑ No

In a brief paragraph, please outline your spiritual journey.
_____
_____
_____
_____
_____
_____

List any gifts, training, education or other qualifications that you believe you have, that have prepared you to minister with children or youth.
_____
_____
_____
_____

Ministry Information and Experience

Churches I attended in the last five years are as follows:

1. Name of Church _____ Phone Number _____
   Address _____
   Dates Attended _____ Member or Adherent _____

_____ Appendix 3

2. Name of Church _____ Phone Number _____

   Address _____

   Dates Attended _____ Member or Adherent _____

My present and previous ministry experience is as follows:

1. Name of Church/Organization _____

   Dates and Description of Ministry _____

   Pastor or Ministry Supervisor _____ Phone Number _____

2. Name of Church/Organization _____

   Dates and Description of Ministry _____

   Pastor or Ministry Supervisor _____ Phone Number _____

Information About your Ability to Work with Children and Youth

In order to provide a safe and secure environment for our church's children and youth, we believe it is necessary to ask the following questions as part of our application process. All information will be kept in confidence by church leadership and the *Plan to Protect®* team and will not be disclosed by the church unless required by law. Answering 'yes' to any of the following questions may not necessarily prevent you from volunteering with the church. Thank you in advance for your understanding.

1. Are there any circumstances involving your lifestyle or history that ❏ Yes ❏ No
   could call into question your ability to work safely with children or youth
   in a Christian environment? (e.g. use of pornography, use of illegal substances, etc.)

2. Have you ever been convicted or found guilty of a criminal offence ❏ Yes ❏ No
   for which a pardon has not been granted? (Note: this does not include
   minor traffic violations). If yes, please list offence(s) and the date(s) of conviction:

   _____

3. Have you ever been expelled from or had your employment terminated by ❏ Yes ❏ No
   any organization or employer for assault or violence against any person,
   or for assault, violence or impropriety with children, youth or vulnerable persons?

4. Have you ever been investigated by the Child Welfare Agency or any other ❏ Yes ❏ No
   organization for suspected child abuse?

5. Have you ever been a defendant or respondent in a civil lawsuit or human ❏ Yes ❏ No
   rights complaint or other legal proceeding in which you were alleged to
   have abused or engaged in violence, harassment or other immoral or
   illegal behaviour or conduct involving children, youth or vulnerable persons?

_____ Appendix 3

6. Do you have any health concerns which could impact your ability to ❑ Yes ❑ No
   perform the functions of the volunteer position for which you are applying?
   (Please note that such health concerns may not prevent you from holding the
   position for which you have applied)

7. Do you have any contagious diseases or conditions of which we should be ❑ Yes ❑ No
   aware, and which we may need to take steps to protect against transmission
   should you volunteer at the church?

References

Please provide the names of three individuals, excluding relatives, who could provide a reference for you. Include at least one reference from outside the church.

1. Name of Reference _____ Day Phone _____
   How long you have known this person: _____ Evening Phone _____
   Address _____
   Nature of Relationship _____

2. Name of Reference _____ Day Phone _____
   How long you have known this person: _____ Evening Phone _____
   Address _____
   Nature of Relationship _____

3. Name of Reference _____ Day Phone _____
   How long you have known this person: _____ Evening Phone _____
   Address _____
   Nature of Relationship _____

RELEASE OF INFORMATION AND DECLARATION OF INTENT

Appendix 3a

I hereby give the church consent to verify the information provided by me in this Ministry Personnel Application Form and to contact the references and current and former employers listed above and to obtain and verify any information from them (and any other persons that the church determines might be able to provide relevant information) that may be relevant to my application.

I grant my permission for the church to perform a police records check on me, and I will sign and return the attached "Release of Information and Declaration of Intent" for such purpose.

I further grant the church permission to perform an internet search on me and to review and consider any information found by me on the internet.

I understand that if the church approves my volunteer application and later determines, in its discretion, at any time that I am not suitable for volunteer service in the church or for the volunteer position for which I am applying, the church may terminate my volunteer service or volunteer position for any reason without advance notice.

If the church approves my application for a volunteer position, I will sign any documents that the church requires and will at all times cooperate fully with the staff of the church in the fulfillment of my duties and will keep all confidential information I encounter in my role as a volunteer, confidential.

If at any time I determine that for any reason I am unable to support or adhere to or follow the policies, procedures or doctrine of the church, I will inform the church and will resign my volunteer position.

I hereby acknowledge that, to the best of my knowledge, the information contained in this Ministry Personnel Application Form is true and correct.

Signature of Applicant _____

Printed Name _____ Date _____

Signature of Witness _____

Printed Name _____ Date _____

Information received is confidential and is being gathered for the purposes of considering your application for volunteer ministry with the church and for determining what, if any church ministries, you may be suited for in future.

Application Form
© Plan to Protect® 2022

DECLARATION OF FAITH

Appendix 3b

NOTE: PLEASE INSERT YOUR STATEMENT OF FAITH HERE

MINISTRY PERSONNEL APPLICATION FORM
APPROVAL CHECKLIST
(For Office Use Only)

Appendix 3c

Name of Applicant _____

1. Ministry Interview Date _____

   Name of Interviewer _____

2. References Checked ❏ Date Completed _____

3. Criminal Record Check Received ❏ Date Completed _____

4. *Plan to Protect*® Training Completed ❏ Date Completed _____

5. Annual Training Date(s)
   ❏ Date _____
   ❏ Date _____
   ❏ Date _____
   ❏ Date _____

Application Form
© Plan to Protect® 2022

CODE OF CONDUCT AND COVENANT OF CARE ── Appendix 3d

Code of Conduct

As a (volunteer / staff member) at _____ Church, you have a duty to care for the people who make up our community, to steward our resources, and to treat our equipment with respect. Whatever your role will be, we expect all personnel to maintain a friendly and positive attitude. We ask every staff member and volunteer to read, understand and adhere to the guidelines of this Code of Conduct so we can overcome challenges and obstacles when working together in a team setting.

1. Respect and honor the mission and values of _____ Church.
2. Respect _____ Church property. Always ask for permission and follow instructions before using equipment or facilities.
3. Respect those who have different beliefs, lifestyles and cultures. We have zero tolerance for discrimination or harassment of others on the basis of religion, economic status, disability, age, gender, or social condition.
4. Direct questions, concerns or requests to Leadership and ask for help when needed.
5. Volunteers - sign in and out of all volunteer opportunities.
6. Volunteers and staff - arrive on time for service and notify your Ministry Lead as soon as possible if unable to fulfill your commitment.
7. Maintain a lifestyle that reflects positively on our church and on our values as a church.
8. Maintain the confidentiality of all proprietary or privileged information learned about the church, its programs, volunteers, staff, community members, partners or others to which they are exposed while serving. Do not reveal sensitive information to anyone outside of the church and only share information under the direction of the Board or Senior Leadership.
9. Do not contact organizations or individuals on behalf of _____ Church unless directed by the Board or Senior Leadership. Actions requiring prior approval of the Board include, but are not limited to, public statements to the press, use of our logo, coalition agreements, political initiatives, or lobbying efforts with other organizations.
10. Avoid engaging in any forms of harassment or abuse. Harassment refers to verbal or physical or sexual conduct that is unsolicited, offensive, and detrimental to an individual. Report any inappropriate behaviour (including harassment) immediately to Senior Leadership or the Board.
11. Refrain from the following behaviours while on church property (including the parking lot) or during service hours: smoking, gambling, or consuming alcoholic beverages and recreational drugs.
12. Comply with the screening and training policies, Plan to Protect® Policies, Privacy Policy, Information Release and this Code of Conduct.
13. Immediately inform the church in writing of any status change of your vulnerable sector check result and any recent arrests, or conviction in criminal offences and/or unresolved charges.
14. I recognize that a breach of the Code of Conduct and Covenant of Care could result in progressive steps of discipline, including the possibility of termination of activities with _____ Church. Volunteers - Understand that the volunteer/church relationship is not a contract of employment and can be terminated at any time by either the volunteer or _____ Church.

I agree to the Code of Conduct.

Signature _____

Printed Name _____ Date _____

CODE OF CONDUCT AND COVENANT OF CARE

Covenant of Care

I (Name) _____ have read, understand and agree to comply with all the Plan to Protect® policies and procedures of _____ Church to protect the health and safety of Children, Youth and Adults at all times.

I also acknowledge the paramount importance of safeguarding in all respects all of those to whom we minister, especially Children, Youth and Adults and commit to providing a caring environment by:

- Adhering to the Code of Conduct;
- Following all of the directives of the policies;
- Complying with the information given in my orientation and refresher trainings;
- Avoiding opportunities to be alone with a vulnerable person;
- Using appropriate language;
- Not changing diapers or taking children to the washroom alone;
- Showing no bias on account of gender, ethnic background, skin colour, intelligence, age, religion, or socio-economic status;
- Respecting confidentiality and privacy, except in cases where I am legally bound to report; and
- Striving to be bring glory to God in my speech, behaviour and actions.

Signature _____

Printed Name _____ Date _____

MINISTRY PERSONNEL APPLICATION FORM
FOR YOUTH WORKING WITH CHILDREN

Appendix 4

In our desire to reduce the risk of abuse within our church ministries, we believe this information is necessary to protect our children and our volunteers and to effectively place our volunteers in ministry positions. Thank you in advance for your partnership.

Personal Information

Full Name _____ Grade _____

Address _____

Postal Code _____ Email _____

Phone Number (H) _____ (C) _____

Name of Parents _____ Phone Number _____

Are your parents supportive of your ministry involvement? ❏ Yes ❏ No

If not, please explain
_____
_____

Hobbies, Interests or Skills
_____
_____
_____

Volunteer Experience and Part-time Jobs
_____
_____
_____

Spiritual History

How long have you attended _____ Church? _____

_____ Appendix 4

Do you regularly attend? (2 or more services a month) ❑ Yes ❑ No

When did you accept Christ as your Saviour? _____

In a brief paragraph, please describe what your faith means to you.

_____

_____

_____

_____

Ministry Questionnaire

Describe why you would like to be part of our children's ministry team.

_____

_____

What strengths or assets would you bring to our children's ministry program?

_____

What areas of concern do you have in working with children?

_____

_____

Do you see yourself as a team player? Please explain. ❑ Yes ❑ No

_____

Please list the area of ministry in which you would like to serve.

_____

Appendix 4

References

List three adults that you've known for at least one year and who have a definite knowledge of your character and ability to work with children. You may include one reference from a relative, but must also include references from your youth pastor, employer or teacher.

1. Name of Reference _____

Daytime Phone Number _____ Evening Number _____

Address _____

Nature of Relationship _____

How long have you known this person: _____

2. Name of Reference _____

Daytime Phone Number _____ Evening Number _____

Address _____

Nature of Relationship _____

How long have you known this person: _____

3. Name of Reference _____

Daytime Phone Number _____ Evening Number _____

Address _____

Nature of Relationship _____

How long have you known this person: _____

Signature of Applicant _____

Printed Name _____ Date _____

Signature of Parent/Guardian _____

Printed Name _____ Date _____

Information received is confidential and is being gathered for the purposes of screening ministry personnel and placing them into ministry with children. The information gathered here will be used for the purposes of supporting the ministries at _____ Church.

SUGGESTED SCRIPT FOR TELEPHONE FOLLOW-UP WHEN SCREENING APPLICATIONS

Appendix 5

"Hello, this is _____ , calling from _____ Church.

_____ (Name of Volunteer) has applied to be a volunteer in our children/youth ministries and has indicated on their application that you might be willing to act as a personal reference. We have a program in our church called Plan to Protect® which is designed to protect our children and youth as well as our volunteers. We do a reference check on all our volunteers working in our ministries.

May I ask you a few questions?

How long you have known _____ ? In what capacity? _____

1) What are _____ 's strengths? Weaknesses?

2) How would you describe the type of person _____ is and how he or she relates to others, especially children or youth?

3) Would you describe _____ as someone who follows through with commitments he or she makes?

4) How does _____ respond to supervision?

5) Is there any conduct you have observed that you would call into question?

6) Do you have any concerns with _____ working with children or youth in any of our ministries?

Thank you for your time. We really appreciate it.

Note: Record all information (using additional paper as necessary) on the Confidential Record of Reference Checks Form immediately following the call, keep notes in a confidential and secure location and return them promptly to _____ .

Reference: United Church of Canada, Camping Standards Manual, pgs. 23 - 25

CONFIDENTIAL RECORD OF REFERENCE CHECKS

Appendix 6

Name of Volunteer _____

REFERENCE #1

Name of Reference or Church Contacted _____

Date of Contact _____

Person Contacting the Reference or Church _____

Method of Contact ❑ telephone ❑ letter ❑ personal conversation

Summary of Contact

_____

_____

_____

REFERENCE #2

Name of Reference or Church Contacted _____

Date of Contact _____

Person Contacting the Reference or Church _____

Method of Contact ❑ telephone ❑ letter ❑ personal conversation

Summary of Contact

_____

_____

_____

REFERENCE #3

Name of Reference or Church Contacted _____

Date of Contact _____

Person Contacting the Reference or Church _____

Method of Contact ❑ telephone ❑ letter ❑ personal conversation

Summary of Contact

_____

_____

_____

Confidential Record of Reference Checks
© Plan to Protect® 2022

MINISTRY PERSONNEL REFERENCE FORM

Appendix 7

(Name of Volunteer) _____ has applied to be a volunteer in our children/youth ministries and has indicated on their application that you might be willing to act as a personal reference. We have a program in our church called *Plan to Protect*® which is designed to protect our children and youth as well as our volunteers. We do a reference check on all our volunteers working in our ministries. Your response will remain confidential. Thank you for your cooperation.

Please forward this information to:
_____
_____
_____

Your Name _____ Phone Number _____

Address _____

1. Describe your relationship with this person.
_____
_____
_____

2. How long have you known this person?
_____
_____
_____

Ministry Personnel Reference Form
© Plan to Protect® 2022

Appendix 7

3. Please use the following scale to respond to the following:

1 – low   2 – below average   3 – average   4 – very good   5 – excellent

How would you rate this individual in the following areas?

a. Ability to work with other volunteers	1 2 3 4 5
b. Ability to follow through on commitments	1 2 3 4 5
c. Ability to relate to children or youth	1 2 3 4 5
d. Level of spiritual maturity	1 2 3 4 5

4. What are the applicant's greatest strengths?

_____
_____
_____
_____

5. Would you entrust the care of your child or youth to the applicant without any concern, reservation or hesitation?

_____
_____
_____

6. Do you have concerns regarding this person working with children or youth? If so, please explain.

_____
_____
_____
_____

Signature _____

Printed Name _____ Date _____

Ministry Personnel Reference Form
© Plan to Protect® 2022

MINISTRY PERSONNEL INTERVIEW FORM _____ Appendix 8

Name of Applicant: _____

Have you completed the Ministry Personnel Application Form? ❏ Yes ❏ No

Has anyone explained the types of ministries that we provide as a church ❏ Yes ❏ No
and which might provide you with an opportunity for volunteer service?

What prompted you to be interested in the ministry that you identified on your Ministry Personnel Application Form? (Indicate the ministry that interests them)

_____

_____

_____

Would you be willing to attend the training session associated with that ministry? ❏ Yes ❏ No

Have the potential ministry personnel review their spiritual journey and compare responses with those indicated on the Spiritual History of the Ministry Personnel Application Form. Note any significant omissions or questions that arise.

_____

_____

_____

Review the items listed under Confidential Information on the Ministry Personnel Application Form and note any significant omissions or questions that arise.

_____

_____

On what date would you be available? _____

What is the minimum length of your commitment? _____

Thank you for your interest in serving.

Signature of Interviewer _____

Printed Name _____ Date _____

Ministry Personnel Interview Form

SAMPLE INTERVIEW QUESTIONS

Appendix 9

This list is provided as a sample of interview questions that can be asked in an interview. Don't forget to take notes during the interview and add the notes to the candidate's file.

Introduction Questions:
1. Tell us about yourself.
2. What do you know about the programs that are held at _____?
3. Why do you believe you are a strong candidate for this role?
4. What skills and qualifications are essential for success in the position of _____?
5. How does this position fit with your school and career goals?
6. What do you believe is the most difficult part of being a supervisor of people?
7. How would your team members describe you?
8. How would a past supervisor describe you?
9. List three things former coworkers would say about you.
10. Why do you want to work/volunteer at the church?
11. Why have you chosen to work with children/youth?
12. What are your top three strengths?
13. What is one area where you would like to grow?

Behavioural and Judgement Questions: (With young people, if the candidate does not have an incident or story, consider restating the question as a scenario question. This may call for you to restate the question in different words. Behavioural and Scenario questions demonstrate the ability to make judgement decisions on the spot).

14. Describe a time at any job, or volunteer position, where you were faced with problems which tested your coping skills. What did you do?
15. Give an example of a time when you had to be relatively quick in coming to a decision.
16. Tell us about a time when you had to use your spoken communication skills in order to get a point across that was important to you.
17. Give us an example of a time where you had to use your fact-finding skills to gain information for solving a problem, and then tell us how you analyzed the information to come to a decision.
18. Give an example of an important goal you have set and tell us about your success in reaching it.
19. In your previous experience working with children/youth, tell us about a time that you helped resolve a particularly difficult parent or customer complaint.
20. Tell us about a time when you cared for children/youth and had to handle a behavioural problem?
21. Give us an example of a time when you had to go above and beyond the call of duty in order to complete a task.
22. Describe a time when you felt the children/youth in your care were unsafe. What did you do?
23. Tell us about a time when you put the needs of another ahead of your own or a time you fostered a safe environment for others?

24. Give an example of a situation when you had to work on several tasks at a time. How did you prioritize your work? How did you plan your time between different activities?
25. Describe what teamwork means to you.
26. What did you do in your last job/volunteer position to contribute toward a teamwork environment?
27. Describe a situation in which you were able to positively influence the actions of others in a desired direction.
28. Tell us about a time you had to seek the involvement of a supervisor or leader to resolve a problem.
29. You and your team members are responsible for working together to ensure a fun, loving, and safe environment for the children/youth. How would you go about it?
30. Give an example of how you have provided leadership to a child/youth and encouraged them to make good decisions.
31. One of the values of this organization is respect of diversity and inclusion. How do you see yourself contributing to this happening?
32. Give us an example of a time you had to take a stand against the action of your peers.
33. Tell me about a time when you had a conflict with a friend or an employer or an authority figure of some kind (teacher, parent, coach).
34. Describe a time when you decided on your own that something needed to be done and you took on the task to get it completed.
35. Describe a situation in which you had to be creative. What did you find challenging and/or exciting about this?

Concluding Questions:

36. What aspect of this role do you believe will be the greatest challenge for you?
37. What is one area that will be difficult for you working with children/youth?
38. What do you consider the most important responsibility of this role?
39. If you were hired, what ideas/talents could you contribute to the programs and the team?
40. Do you have any questions for me?

Thank you so much for this interview!

MINISTRY PERSONNEL RENEWAL APPLICATION FORM

Appendix 10

In our desire to reduce the risk of abuse within our church ministries, we believe this information is necessary to protect our children and our volunteers and to effectively place our volunteers in ministry positions. Thank you in advance for your partnership. Information received is confidential and is being gathered for the purposes of screening ministry personnel and placing them into ministry with children or youth. The information gathered here will be used for the purposes of supporting the ministries at _____ Church.

Name _____

Phone Number _____

Has your address changed in the last year?   ❑ Yes ❑ No

New Address _____

In what ministry program(s) are you currently involved?
_____

In what other ministry program(s) do you plan to become involved?
_____

Have you at any time ever:
- Been arrested for any reason?   ❑ Yes ❑ No
- Been convicted of, or pleaded no contest to a crime?   ❑ Yes ❑ No
- Been arrested or convicted for any abuse related crimes?   ❑ Yes ❑ No

Are you aware of:
- Having any traits or tendencies that could pose any threat to children, youth or others?   ❑ Yes ❑ No
- Any reason why you should not work with children, youth or others?   ❑ Yes ❑ No

If the answer to any of these questions is 'yes', please explain in detail:
_____

Application Verification and Release

I recognize that the organization to which this application is being submitted is relying on the information contained herein. Accordingly, I attest and affirm that all of the information that I have provided is absolutely true and correct. I agree to abide by all the policies and procedures of _____ Church and to protect the health and safety of the children or youth at all times.

Signature _____

Printed Name _____ Date _____

_____

Reference: Guidelines for Ministry Workers, Brotherhood Mutual Insurance Company, July 2000

DIAPER CHANGING PROCEDURE / HANDWASHING HINTS

Appendix 11

1. Wash your hands.
2. Put on gloves.
3. Place baby on a clean, disposable surface.
4. Remove soiled diaper and place in plastic bag.
5. Clean diaper area with wipes and place in plastic bag.
6. Follow parent's instructions regarding application of powder or lotion.
7. Put clean diaper on baby.
8. Remove disposable cover from change table and spray area with bleach solution.
9. Remove gloves, place in plastic bag and dispose of plastic bag.
10. Wash your hands.

HAND WASHING HINTS

1. Wash hands with running water and soap.
2. Wash front and back of hands – don't forget between the fingers.
3. Wash hands for 15 – 30 seconds.
4. Dry hands with disposable towel.
5. Turn off faucet with disposable towel.

INFECTION CONTROL PROCEDURES

Appendix 12

1. Wear disposable gloves when:
   a. Accompanying a child to the toilet
   b. Changing diapers
   c. In potential contact with blood (i.e., nosebleed)

   If an emergency precludes use of gloves when in contact with blood, thoroughly wash with soap and water. Change gloves between each new child contact.

2. Change diapers on disposable wax paper sheets. Dispose of diaper, gloves and wax paper sheets in cover trash container.

3. Wash hands (antiseptic wipe is OK)
   a. After accompanying a child to the toilet
   b. After changing a diaper
   c. After assisting a child with wiping his/her nose
   d. Before food preparation

4. Have a child wash hands
   a. After toileting
   b. After contact with nasal secretions
   c. Before eating (antiseptic wipe is OK)

   Use only disposable towels.

5. Disinfect toy if child is seen to put it in his/her mouth.

6. Use disinfecting solution to
   a. Wipe spills
   b. Clean diaper changing tables
   c. Clean soiling from blood, urine or feces
   d. Clean all equipment after each session

7. Place the following in covered trash cans:
   a. Diapers
   b. Trash contaminated with blood, urine or feces
   c. Used rubber gloves

Reference: Christ Community Church - Omaha, Nebraska

Infection Control Procedure
© Plan to Protect® 2022

BLOODBORNE PATHOGENS AND INFECTIOUS DISEASES

Appendix 13

The following is a compilation of guidelines on dealing with bloodborne pathogens (any microorganism or virus that can cause disease that is carried through the blood) and infectious diseases. We have used three different resources that we felt had applications for use in church settings.

Studies of school and residential settings reflect a parallel between the inefficiency of transmission of bloodborne pathogens and the extent to which risk is adequately controlled by common hygienic measures. . . . Children who have bloodborne pathogen infections should not be excluded from daycare, group homes or foster care. There is no reason for excluding children who do not exhibit aggressive behaviour and who do not have medication conditions facilitating transmission.[1] The benefits of an unrestricted setting outweigh the risk of the child acquiring harmful infections. The risk of transmitting the virus to others is almost nonexistent.[2] "All educational and public health departments are strongly encouraged to inform parents, children and educators about AIDS and its transmission."[3]

1. Common infectious diseases may be contracted from dirt and waste encountered in ministry areas. Wash your hands with soap and running water at regular intervals throughout the day.[4]

2. All bodily fluids must be treated as though they are infectious, as bloodborne pathogens could be present in any child. Confidentiality laws may prevent you from knowing those infected with the HIV (virus that causes AIDS) or AIDS virus. By treating all bodily fluids as infectious, you protect not only yourself, but others.[5]

3. Latex gloves are required when handling any discharges from another person's body, particularly body fluids containing blood. Hands must be thoroughly washed with soap and running water when finished.[6]

Persons who are exposed to an infected child's body fluids and excrement should know that the child is infected and should know procedures to follow to prevent transmission. Disposable diapers should be used and soiled diapers should be placed in a plastic bag before discarding. Feces can be flushed down the toilet. Latex gloves should be worn if open sores are present on the caretaker's hands. Any open sore on the infected child should also be covered.[7] Hands should be washed after exposure to blood and body fluids and before caring for another child.

4. Contaminated disposable latex gloves and other contaminated materials should be disposed in plastic-lined waste containers.[8]

5. You need to develop an awareness of situations or dangers that may put you or others at risk. For instance, do not pick up broken glass with bare hands but use a brush and dustpan instead. You need to avoid punctures with objects that may contain blood from others. Carefully dispose trash that contains sharp objects. Use containers that cannot be broken or penetrated.[9]

1, 5	Preventing the Transmission of Bloodborne Pathogens in Healthcare and Public Service Setting, Canada Communicable Disease Report - Supplement V23S3, May 1997
2, 3, 4, 7	Guidelines Regarding Children and Infants with AIDS, Love in Action, Annapolis, MD
6	Universal Precautions, Alliance Academy, Quito Equador
8, 9	Universal Precautions, Alliance Academy, Quito Equador

Bloodborne Pathogens and Infectious Diseases

Appendix 13

6. Surfaces that have blood or other potentially infectious materials containing blood on them must be cleaned with an approved disinfectant or a 1:10 solution of liquid household bleach and water. This disinfectant must be mixed daily and must sit for ten minutes before use.[10]

7. An HBV (virus causing Hepatitis B) vaccination should be pursued within 24 hours if you have had an 'exposure incident'. An 'exposure incident' is when there is blood contact through an open sore, injury by a contaminated sharp object or by a blood splash into your eyes, nose or mouth.[11]

8. If you are responsible for administering first aid, it is strongly recommended that you receive current instruction. For instance, the rescuer needs to use a resuscitation mouthpiece when administering CPR so that there is no direct mouth-to-mouth contact.[12]

9. Individuals involved in the care and education of a preschool-aged child infected with HIV, HBV, or HCV should be informed of the child's infective status only if such knowledge is necessary to ensure proper care of the child and to detect situations in which there is potential for transmission. Parental consent is required for the disclosure of a child's infective status and should be made on a case-by-case basis respecting the child's and family's right to privacy. Decisions about education and care for children infected with the AIDS virus should be made by a team including the child's physician, public health personnel, parents or guardian and church staff.[13] The records of children with AIDS should be kept confidential. Parental consent must be given to the agency releasing pertinent medical information to those administering care to the child.

10. A more restricted environment is advised for infected preschool-age children, for children who cannot control their bowels or bladder, for children who display such behaviour as biting and scratching and for infected children who have uncovered oozing sores. These children should be cared for and educated in settings that minimize the exposure of other children to their blood and body fluids.[14]

Decisions regarding vaccination of children and workers who have contact with the child should be discussed with public health officials.[15]

The hygienic practices of an infected child may improve as the child matures, or they may deteriorate if the child's condition worsens. For these reasons, the need for a restricted environment should be re-evaluated regularly.[16]

10, 11, 12, 13 Universal Precautions, Alliance Academy, Quito Equador
14 Guidelines Regarding Children and Infants with AIDS, Love in Action, Annapolis, MD
15 Preventing the Transmission of Bloodborne Pathogens in Healthcare and Public Service Setting, Canada Communicable Disease Report - Supplement V23S3, May 1997
16 Guidelines Regarding Children and Infants with AIDS, Love in Action, Annapolis, MD

GUIDELINES FOR THE DEVELOPMENT OF AIDS/HIV CHURCH POLICIES

1. Any written policy should begin with a statement indicating that the intent of the congregation is to include HIV positive or symptomatic AIDS individuals in the church programs, not to exclude them.

2. Policy should be based on scientific and medical facts rather than in response to fears or lack of information.

3. Policy should be age-specific, providing guidelines for dealing with infants and toddlers as opposed to older youth and adults.

4. Any written policy the congregation decides to adopt should be the culmination of an education program that focuses on church leadership as well as the congregation as a whole. The education and awareness program will help prepare members of the church to deal with AIDS and HIV by updating them on medical facts and ministry opportunities while challenging them to become involved.

5. Written policy should include a component of prevention education that the church sees as its responsibility, including teaching its members that abstinence from sexual activity until marriage, faithfulness within marriage and abstinence from drug use of any kind are the only ways to totally prevent transmission of HIV.

For more information on how to develop policies relating to HIV/AIDS, contact those responsible for infection control at your local hospital or Public Health Agency.

Reference: Developing Church AIDS/HIV Policy Statements, Children's AIDS Funds, Washington DC

REGISTRATION AND MEDICAL CONSENT FORM

Appendix 15

Information received is confidential and is being gathered for the purposes of serving your child while in the care of _____ Church. Any medical information collected here serves to authorize _____ Church, and its staff and volunteers, to obtain medical assistance in emergencies. This form should be completed annually by the parent/caregiver.

Student's Name _____ Date of Birth _____

Address _____

Phone Number _____ Parents' Work Number _____

Health Card Number _____

Family Doctor _____ Phone Number _____

Allergies _____

In case of an emergency, contact _____

Does your child have any physical, emotional, mental, behavioural concerns or limitations that staff should be aware of? ❏ Yes ❏ No

If yes, please explain:
_____
_____

Will your child bring any medication with them? ❏ Yes ❏ No
If yes, please list.
_____
_____

Registration and Medical Consent Form
© Plan to Protect® 2022

_____ Appendix 15

The safety of your child is our primary concern. Precautions will be taken for their well-being and protection.

I/we, the parents or guardians named below, authorize Pastor _____ or one of _____ Program Personnel to sign a consent for medical treatment and to authorize any physician or hospital to provide medical assessment, treatment or procedures for the participant named above.

I/we, named below, undertake and agree to indemnify and hold harmless Program Personnel, _____ Church, and its leaders from and against any loss, damage or injury suffered by the participant as a result of being part of the activities of _____, as well as of any medical treatment authorized by the supervising individuals representing _____ . This consent and authorization is effective only when participating in or traveling to events sponsored by _____ _____ Church.

Communication

A policy is in effect that communication is to be used solely for the dissemination of information. Please sign below to grant permission for Youth Program Personnel (staff and volunteers) to communicate with your child via telephone, email, social media and text:

❑ Telephone (home / work / cell) ❑ Social Media Networks
❑ Email ❑ Text messages

Photos

Please sign below to grant permission for the reasonable use of pictures containing your child in any or all of the following ways:

❑ Brochures/Promotional material ❑ Organization
❑ Website ❑ Newsletters
❑ Videotaping

_____ Appendix 15

Purposes and Extent

_____ is collecting and retaining this personal information for the purpose of enrolling your child in our programs, to assign the student to the appropriate classes, to develop and nurture ongoing relationships with you and your child, and to inform you of program updates and upcoming opportunities at our organization. This information will be maintained indefinitely as it is a requirement of our insurance company and legal counsel.
If you wish _____ to limit the information collected, or to view your child's information, please contact us.

Parent / Guardian Options

I have read, understood and agree with above and sign it to cover all Youth Program activities for the program year effective as stated below. A separate Letter of Informed Consent will be sent home for off-site activities and activities of elevated risk.

Parents'/Guardian Signature _____

Printed Name _____ Date _____

This permission form is effective: (DATE) _____ to _____

MEDICATION FORM

Appendix 16

Child's Name: _____

Dr. : _____ Phone #: _____

Date	Name of Medication	Dosage	Time Required	Parent Signature	Dose Given	Time Given	Staff Signature

LIABILITY SHIELDS

Appendix 17

Liability shields are written contracts or agreements between a sponsoring organization and a participant, or if the participant is a minor, the participant's parents or legal guardian. These shields operate to identify the risks associated with a particular activity and to reduce or eliminate the potential legal liability of the sponsoring organization. They also provide better communication between the sponsors and participants.

Christian charitable organizations should strongly consider utilizing liability shields as an important tool in their risk management program.

Liability Shields include:

Waiver or Release of Liability - A contractual agreement between two parties whereby one party (the participant or "releasor") agrees to voluntarily release the other party (the sponsoring organization or "releasee") from legal liability in certain circumstances.

Indemnity Agreement - Usually forming part of a waiver agreement, it serves as a formal undertaking by the participant to indemnify, save and hold harmless the sponsor from any litigation expenses, legal fees and liability damage awards.

Informed Consent - Also forming part of a waiver agreement, it is a clearly worded description of the proposed activity or event that includes a thorough explanation of the inherent risks associated with participation in that activity. A consent form does not relieve an organization from responsibility for its own negligence. It seeks only to relieve the sponsor for the inherent risks of the activity itself and allows it to make a defence of liability claims on the basis of assumption of risk by the participant. To be effective, the form must fully disclose to the participant, or their parents/guardians, the specific risks associated with the proposed activity. By signing the consent a participant acknowledges that they have both read and understood the risks involved and agree not to initiate any legal action for harm resulting from the described risks.

Permission Forms - A well-drafted permission slip ensures parental knowledge and consent for their children's participation. When parents are informed about the nature and extent of the proposed activity and its risks, they will feel more involved in the decision-making process and will be less likely to claim that, "had I known, I would never have let my child participate". Also with a properly worded and signed permission form that includes consent for emergency medical treatment and disclosure of any existing medical conditions, a parent or guardian will be less likely to claim that the organization infringed on their authority, control or custody over the child.

Guidelines For An Effective Waiver Or Release Of Liability

i) Provide advance notice of the requirement to sign a waiver as a prerequisite for participation in the proposed activity, preferably forming part of the initial information and registration package.

ii) The waiver language should include a clear and objective description of the inherent risks associated with the proposed activity or event. It should also make specific reference to assumption of risk on the part of the participant.

iii) The design, format and content of a waiver document should be clear and in plain language. Emphasis should be placed on boldly printed headings such as "release of liability", "waiver of claims", "waiver of legal rights including the right to sue", "please read carefully", and so on, so that there is no uncertainty as to the intent of the document.

iv) The participant should be clearly identified on the waiver form, including information such as name, address, telephone number, date of birth, signature, witness and date, in order to defend allegations that the document was never signed.

v) Waivers should be limited to no more than a single page in order to avoid any legal challenge that the length of the document made it incomprehensible or that the releasor only looked at the signature page.

For the complete article, see www.robertsonhall.com Resource Articles, Facing the Risk: Liability Shields

Reference: Robertson Hall Insurance, London ON.

INCIDENT REPORT

Appendix 18

The incident report should be completed as soon as possible after the incident occurs and should include as detailed a description of the situation as possible.

Student Name/s _____

Phone Number _____

Address _____

Nature of Injury/Incident
_____
_____

Incident Date _____ Incident Time _____

Incident Location _____ Event Title _____

All Leaders Present _____

What happened?
_____
_____

Why did it happen?
_____
_____

What action was taken?
_____
_____

Contacted Parents ❑ Yes   ❑ No

Parents' Response
_____
_____
_____

Leader's Name _____ Signature _____

Witness Name _____ Signature _____

Incident Report
© Plan to Protect® 2022

LETTER OF INFORMED CONSENT

Appendix 19

Student Name/s _____

Activity: _____ Date of Activity: _____

Details of the Activity: (include location/time/sleeping arrangements/mode of transportation/driver/ activities upon arrival/ratios of student to staff/explanation of any and all risk which the students will be participating in i.e., rock climbing/bungee jumping/white water canoeing/water skiing) _____
_____

Dear Parent:
We are planning an activity as part of our programming that requires your permission prior to participation. We have provided you the details of the activity and request that you complete and sign the permission form. The safety of your child is our primary concern. Precautions will be taken for their well-being and protection.

Permission Form and Consent:

Student's Name _____ Date of Birth _____

Address _____

Phone Number _____

Parents' Work Number _____ Health Card Number _____

Family Doctor _____ Phone Number _____

In case of an emergency, contact _____

I hereby consent to the participation of my/our child(ren) in this supervised activity.

While every precaution is taken for the safety and good health, some sports and activities carry with them the inherent risk of personal injury beyond the risks associated with many of the recreational activities at (organization). I/we understand and accept these risks and agree that by allowing my child to participate in those activities, he/she may be taking part in a recreational activity that presents the potential for personal injury.

I/we, the parents or guardians named below, authorize the Director or one of the (organization's) Personnel to sign a consent for medical treatment and to authorize any physician or hospital to provide medical assessment, treatment or procedures for the participant named above.

I/we, named below, undertake and agree to indemnify and hold blameless (organization's), its Personnel, its Directors and Board from and against any loss, damage or injury suffered by the participant as a result of being part of the activities of the (organization), as well as of any medical treatment authorized by the supervising individuals representing the (organization). This consent and authorization is effective only when participating in or traveling to events of the (organization).

❑ I have read, understood and agree with above. Activity: _____

Parent / Guardian Signature _____

Printed Name _____ Date _____

Letter of Informed Consent
© Plan to Protect® 2022

OFF-SITE TIPS SHEET

Appendix 20

- ☐ Give the event details including date of event, departure and arrival time, location, supervising adults, and ministry leader approval to parents well in advance of the date and request consent from them.

- ☐ See that you have an 'Emergency Contact Card' for each student and bring them with you.

- ☐ Leave a list of students on the trip at church office.

- ☐ Leave a contact number for the person in charge of the event at the church office.

- ☐ Leave contact number for destination at church office.

- ☐ Communicate the nature of the trip to parents and ensure that consent has been given for each student.

- ☐ If drivers are used, make sure that the proper consent forms have been filled out.

- ☐ If location changes unexpectedly, ensure that this is communicated clearly to the parents/guardians.

- ☐ Leave a map to the off-site location at the church office.

Off-Site Tips Sheet
© Plan to Protect® 2022

OFF-SITE ACTIVITY REPORT FORM

Appendix 21

I would like to take _____ on the following activity:

_____

_____

This activity will take place on_____

from _____ to _____

The other adult(s) who will assist me is/are:

_____

_____

_____

I will ensure that each student has both a parental consent and medical release form for this activity. I will not transport more individuals in any vehicle than is legally allowed according to the passenger rating of the vehicle.

☐ Ministry Lead Approval   Signature of Ministry Lead _____

Signature _____ Date _____

Off-Site Activity Report Form
© Plan to Protect® 2022

TRIPS AND OFF-SITE TRAVEL FORM

Appendix 22

Group _____

Destination _____

Contact Number _____

Departure		Return	
Date		Date	
Time		Time	
ETA		ETA	

Driver's Name	Vehicle

Leader's Name	Phone Number

Student's Name	Phone Number

Trips and Off-Site Travel Form
© Plan to Protect® 2022

LETTER OF INFORMED CONSENT FOR TRANSPORTATION

Appendix 23

Student's name _____

Transporting from and to locations: From: _____ To: _____

Date(s) of transportation: _____

Dear Parent: (organization name) has arranged transportation to and from church activities on your behalf for your child(ren).

Details of the activity: (include location/time/mode of transportation/driver/ratios of student to staff)
_____

While every precaution is taken for the safety and good health, some activities including transportation carry with them the inherent risk of personal injury. Your permission is required to provide this transportation. Please carefully read the following information and consent form. If you are in agreement, please sign this and return it to the church.

PERMISSION

I give permission for my child/charge ("child") to be transported in a motor vehicle driven by the individual identified to an event at the specified location on the date indicated. I understand that my child is expected to follow all applicable laws regarding riding in a motor vehicle and is expected to follow the directions provided by the driver and/or other adult volunteers. I understand that participation in the identified event is not a requirement for participation in (name of organization's) activities.

I have read, understand, and discussed with my child that:

(1) They will be traveling in a motor vehicle driven by an adult and accompanied by a second adult and they are to wear their safety-belt while traveling;
(2) They are expected to respect each other, the vehicles they ride in, and the people they travel with during the trip;
(3) Riding in a motor vehicle may result in personal injuries or death from wrecks, collisions or acts by riders, other drivers, or objects; and
(4) They are to remain in their seats and not be disruptive to the driver of the vehicle.

I recognize that by participating in this activity, as with any activity involving motor vehicle transportation, my child may risk personal injury or permanent loss. I hereby attest and verify that I have been advised of the potential risks, that I have full knowledge of the risks involved in this activity, and that I assume any expenses that may be incurred in the event of an accident, illness, or other incapacity, regardless of whether I have authorized such expenses.

Student's Name _____ Date of Birth _____

Address _____

Phone Number _____ Parents' Work Number _____

Health Card Number _____ Family Doctor _____

Phone Number _____ In case of an emergency, contact _____

I hereby consent to the participation of my/our child(ren) in this supervised activity.

I/we, the parents or guardians named below, authorize the Director or one of the (organization's) Personnel to sign consent for medical treatment and to authorize any physician or hospital to provide medical assessment, treatment or procedures for the participant named above.

I/we, named below, undertake and agree to indemnify and hold blameless (organization's), its personnel, its Directors and Board from and against any loss, damage or injury suffered by the participant as a result of being part of the activities of the (organization), as well as of any medical treatment authorized by the supervising individuals representing the (organization). This consent and authorization is effective only when participating in or traveling to events of the (organization).

I have read, understood and agree with above. Activity: _____

Parent / Guardian Signature _____

Printed Name _____ Date _____

Letter of Informed Consent for Transportation
© Plan to Protect® 2022

EMERGENCY INFO CARD　　　　　　　　　　　　　　　　　　　　　　　　Appendix 24

EMERGENCY INFORMATION CARD

Student's Name _____

Parent's Name _____

Home Number _____

Emergency Contact Number _____

Known Allergies _____

Health Card Number _____

Family Physician _____

EMERGENCY INFORMATION CARD

Student's Name _____

Parent's Name _____

Home Number _____

Emergency Contact Number _____

Known Allergies _____

Health Card Number _____

Family Physician _____

Emergency Info Card
© Plan to Protect® 2022

VOLUNTEER DRIVER AGREEMENT   Appendix 25

"Trip Driver" is defined as any person authorized by the leadership of _____ [organization] who has agreed to be a driver for a certain trip while they are driving their own or another licensed automobile.

This will authorize _____ (Name of staff or volunteer)

1. To transport children and/or youth participating in the regular events of _____
   [organization]
OR
2. To transport children and/or youth participating in the following activity: _____
_____

Vehicle information: Make: _____ Year: _____ License #: _____

All "trip drivers" including volunteer drivers are advised that in order to ensure the automobile liability insurance coverage are not invalidated that the following are enforced:
   A) Use a licensed automobile which carries valid third-party liability insurance as required under legislation in our province.
   B) Provide the Board with prompt written notice, with all available particulars, of any accident arising out of the use of a licensed automobile during a trip on business of the Board.
   C) Be aware that the Board's Excess Liability Insurance comes into effect only after the "trip driver's" insurance has been exhausted.

I. Declaration to be signed by Driver:
- I declare that I am licensed in _____ [province] and my vehicle is insured by valid automobile insurance as required by provincial law.
- That the vehicle is mechanically fit and that there are seatbelts in working condition for all passengers. The vehicle has car seats for all passengers under 40 lbs., and booster seats for children between 40 lbs. and 59 lbs. Seat belts are required for anyone over 8 years and more than 60 lbs.
- I will follow the manufacturer's vehicle guidelines regarding air bags and acknowledge that children should not be seated in the front seat of any vehicle, especially under the age of 10.

Signature _____ Date _____

Insurance Company _____ Policy # _____

II. Declaration to be signed by the owner of the vehicle, if the volunteer does not own the vehicle.
- I declare that I have authorized _____ to drive my vehicle to transport children and/or youth participating in the events listed on this form.
- He/she is licensed to carry passengers and is fully insured under the vehicle liability insurance as required by provincial legislation.
- That the vehicle is mechanically fit and that there are seatbelts in working condition for all passengers. The vehicle has booster seats for all passengers under 40 lbs.

Signature _____ Date _____

Date _____ Organization _____

Program Lead's Signature _____

Reference: Volunteers in Your School: Practices and Screening Procedures, pg. 46

DRIVING CONTRACT

Appendix 26

I Agree:

1. To be a safe, responsible driver.
2. To follow all provincial and state licensing laws and to abide by any additional requirements placed on me by _____ Church.
3. To abide by any restrictions that are put in place by _____ Church (how many passengers, speed, etc).
4. Never to drive when I have been using alcohol or drugs.
5. To avoid distractions when I am behind the wheel, including loud music, eating, drinking, using a cell phone, or engaging in distracting conversations with other passengers.
6. To take responsibility for telling authorities and _____ Church supervisor when an accident or problem with the vehicle has taken place.
7. To take responsibility for any accidents that occur because of poor judgment on my part.
8. To follow all provincial and state driving laws (speed limits, construction zones, etc).
9. To always notify an _____ Church supervisor if I am tired and do not feel that I can continue to drive.

Driving Restrictions:

1. All drivers must be 25 years of age or older.
2. All drivers must hold a valid driver's license.
3. Under no circumstances will a sanctioned _____ Church driver allow a student to drive a vehicle.

I understand that if I do not follow any of these guidelines my ability to drive will be jeopardized. A _____ Church supervisor has the right and authority to take away my driving privileges for the church at any time.

Your signature below means that you have read the preceding statements and guidelines, that you agree to them, that you will abide by them, and that if at any time you cannot agree to the preceding you will notify _____ Church supervisor and will discontinue driving for the church.

Signature _____

Printed Name _____ Date _____

ACCEPTABLE COMPUTER USE POLICY

By using these public computers, you agree to abide by these guidelines:

1. All users must sign-in and sign-out when using public computers, including name, date and time.
2. Public computers are only open for public access during posted hours. Staff and volunteers reserve the right to ask anyone to leave the Center at any time for any reason.
3. Be polite. Do not use abusive or threatening messages to or about others.
4. Use appropriate language in conversation and online.
5. Obscene or sexually explicit material may not be accessed on these computers.
6. Illegal online activity or websites may not be accessed on these computers.
7. Sharing of copyrighted material, including piracy of books, movies or computer software is not allowed on these computers.
8. Only staff members are permitted to load software on these computers.
9. Damaging or attempting to harm our or others' data, computer equipment, or network performance is prohibited.

Any violation of the regulations above may cause access privileges to be revoked and may result in additional disciplinary actions.

User's Full Name: _____

User Signature: _____ Date: _____

COMPUTER POLICY AGREEMENT
FOR MINISTRY PERSONNEL

Preamble

Everything must be done in order to protect the children in our care against harmful materials and predators on the Internet. All Ministry Personnel have a responsibility for the ethical and appropriate use of the computers and the Internet in our centers. The following details this more fully.

Contexts for Use

Computer equipment, access to the organization's network and an Internet connection will be used in the performance of your job for legitimate business. All users have a responsibility to use these computer resources and the Internet in a professional, lawful and ethical manner. Occasional limited appropriate personal use of the computer is permitted if such use does not interfere with the user's or any other employee's job performance; have an undue effect on the computer or organization network's performance; or violate any other policies, provisions, guidelines or standards of this or any other agreement of the organization.

Inappropriate Activities

The following list is not exhaustive but gives examples of inappropriate computer-based activities:
- Using tech resources to create, view or share offensive, pornographic, discriminatory or demeaning media
- Using technology resources without appropriate permission or access
- Using technology resources to harass, insult or attack others
- Sharing or copying another's work without his/her consent
- Violating copyright laws or other legal contracts
- Installing unauthorized software on organization's equipment

Consequences

Failure to comply with these policies will be taken seriously. Any inappropriate use of the computer or the Internet technologies, particularly that which puts our children's and youth's protection in jeopardy, is grounds for disciplinary action and/or termination.

Disclaimer

The organization recognizes that it is difficult to avoid at least some contact with objectionable material while using the Internet. Even innocuous search requests may lead to sites with highly offensive content. Additionally, having an e-mail address on the Internet may lead to receipt of unsolicited e-mails containing offensive content. Users accessing the Internet do so at their own risk; the organization is not responsible for material viewed or downloaded by users from the Internet. Employees will not be held accountable for inappropriate material sent to them or inadvertently viewed. All inappropriate material received should be deleted immediately.

Lack of Privacy/Organization's Rights

The user expressly waives any right of privacy in anything they create, store, send or receive using the organization's computer equipment or Internet access. User consents to allow the organization's personnel access to and review of all materials created, stored, sent or received by user through any organization network or Internet connection. The organization has the right to monitor and log any and all aspects of its computer system including, but not limited to, monitoring Internet sites visited by users, monitoring chat and newsgroups, monitoring file downloads, and all communications sent and received by users. Employees should have no expectation of privacy in anything they create, store, send or receive using the organization's computer equipment.

The organization has the right to utilize software that makes it possible to identify and block access to Internet sites containing sexually explicit or other material deemed inappropriate in the workplace.

Personal Accountability

It is recommended that all users consider installing an accountability program like Covenant Eyes or X3Watch. The organization grants permission to install such software on all equipment with Internet access. For an employee who has been cited for inappropriate Internet use, the organization may require that such software be installed.

SIGN-IN / SIGN-OUT SHEET

Appendix 29

Date _____ Time _____

Department _____

Ministry Personnel	

ID Number	Child's Name	Sign In	Sign Out	Special Instructions

Sign-in / Sign-out Sheet
© Plan to Protect® 2022

TALKING TO A POTENTIALLY ABUSED CHILD

When a Child Discloses Abuse or Neglect
Children who may have been abused or neglected are particularly vulnerable. It is critical that, in responding to their needs, we take every caution to avoid upsetting or traumatizing them any further.

If the child is in immediate danger, call police first.

When talking to the child, be sensitive to his or her needs and follow the general guidelines below. Your primary role is to support the child, gather basic information and report it to a child welfare worker as quickly as possible.

Stay calm and listen. An abused or neglected child needs to know that you are calm and available to help. If you react with shock, outrage or fear, you might inhibit the child and make him or her feel more anxious or ashamed. A calm response supports the child to tell you what has happened. It also provides some reassurance that what the child is experiencing can be talked about and worked through together.

Go slowly. It is normal to feel inadequate or unsure about what to do or say when a child tells you about abuse or neglect. Do not let this discomfort rush you into asking questions. Remember to proceed slowly. Gentle questions, such as "Can you tell me more about what happened?" are helpful.

Be supportive. Reassure the child that he or she has not done anything wrong. Children need support and reassurance when discussing abuse or neglect. It is helpful to let children know that:
- they are not in trouble with you, the child welfare worker or the police (if they are involved)
- they are safe with you
- you are glad that they have chosen to tell you about this
- they have done the right thing in telling you about this
- you are sorry that they have been hurt or that this has happened to them
- you will do everything you can to make sure they get the help they need
- you know others who can be trusted to help solve this problem.

Get only the essential facts. Once you have enough information and reason to believe that abuse or neglect has occurred, stop gathering facts and be supportive. The child may be interviewed in depth by a child welfare worker and, if there is a criminal investigation, by the police; to avoid the stress of multiple interviews, limit your discussion to finding out generally what took place. If you need more information, be sure to ask how, when, who and what questions. Avoid using why questions. They can suggest indirectly that the child may have done something wrong and increase the child's reluctance to discuss the matter.

Tell the child what will happen next. Children who disclose their abuse feel anxious and vulnerable about what people think of them and what will happen next. Tell them only what you know (e.g., that they are not in trouble, and that you will help) and avoid making promises. For example, do not promise that the alleged perpetrator won't get into trouble. Provide only reassurance that is realistic and achievable. Discuss with the child what you think will happen next and who will be involved.

Appendix 30

Make notes. As soon as possible after the child's disclosure, write down as much as you can of what the child told you. This will help ensure accuracy when reporting to the appropriate authority. (Direct disclosures may be admissible in court, so accuracy is important.)

When there are Indicators of Child Abuse or Neglect

Children do not always tell us about their abuse or neglect, and sometimes the indicators are not obvious. When you see indicators and are talking to children about possible abuse or neglect, the following points may be helpful:

- **Choose your approach carefully.** The child may be fearful or reluctant to talk about what happened.

- **Be relaxed and casual.** If you appear anxious or exhibit strong feelings, the child may withdraw.

- **Keep it private.** Make sure you have enough time and a private setting with little chance for interruptions. The child is more likely to confide in you in a place where he or she feels safe.

- **Be neutral.** Express your concerns to the child in a neutral and objective manner and seek or ask for their explanation for the indicators you have observed.

- **Be a good listener.** Pay attention and express your confidence in the child. This shows your genuine concern for his or her safety and well-being.

Questioning techniques:
Ask general, open-ended questions
- Do ask – "Do you want to tell me more about that?"
- Do not ask – "Why did this happen?"

State observations
- Observe – "I see you have welts on your legs."
- Do not ask – "Have you been beaten?"

Validate feelings
- Validate – "I see that you are upset."
- Don't analyse – "You must hate your father for doing that!"

Express concern
- Say – "I need to know that you are safe; let's try to get you some help."
- Don't make promises – "Everything will be alright if you report this."

SYMPTOMS OF MOLESTATION AND ABUSE

Appendix 31

Ministry Personnel should be aware of the physical signs of abuse and molestation, as well as behavioural and verbal signs that a victim may exhibit. The following characteristics may be indicators of abuse, although they are not necessarily proof. One sign alone does not constitute abuse and may simply be indicative of other issues. Here is where you need to ask God for discernment and wisdom as you watch for patterns or a combination of these warning signs.

Possible Signs of Physical Abuse

- Hostile and aggressive behaviour toward others
- Fearfulness of parents and/or other adults
- Destructive behaviour toward self, others and/or property
- Inexplicable fractures or bruises inappropriate for child's developmental stage
- Burns, facial injuries, pattern of repetitious bruises

Possible Signs of Sexual Abuse

- Unusually advanced sexual knowledge and/or behaviour for child's age and developmental stage
- Depression – cries for no apparent reason
- Promiscuous behaviour
- Runs away from home and refuses to return
- Difficulty walking or sitting
- Bruised or bleeding in vaginal or anal areas
- Exhibits frequent headaches, stomach aches, extreme fatigue
- Sexually transmitted diseases

Possible Signs of Emotional Abuse

- Exhibits severe depression and/or withdrawal
- Exhibits severe lack of self-esteem
- Failure to thrive
- Threatens or attempts suicide
- Speech and/or eating disorders
- Goes to extremes to seek adult approval
- Extreme passive/aggressive behaviour patterns

Possible Signs of Neglect

- Failure to thrive
- Pattern of inappropriate dress for climate
- Begs or steals food; chronic hunger
- Depression
- Untreated medical conditions
- Poor hygiene

Possible Signs of Abuse in Church Settings

- Unusual nervousness or anxiety about being left in a church class
- Reluctance to participate in church activities that were previously enthusiastically approached
- Comments such as, "I don't want to be alone with … " in reference to a child care worker or teacher
- Nightmares including a child care worker or teacher as a frightening character
- Unexplained hostility toward a child care worker or teacher
- Preferential treatment to one individual
- Secretiveness
- Lack of accountability

SUSPECTED ABUSE REPORT FORM (ADULT)　　　　　　　　　　　　　　　　Appendix 32

Date _____　　Name of Adult _____

Address _____

Postal Code _____

Phone _____

Parents'/Caregivers' Names (if applicable) _____

Name of Person Filing Report _____

Name of Pastor Receiving Report _____

Name of alleged perpetrator _____ ❏ M ❏ F

Relationship between suspected victim and alleged perpetrator _____

Nature of suspected abuse　❏ physical　❏ sexual　❏ emotional/psychological
　　　　　　　　　　　　　　❏ neglect　❏ financial　❏ other

Indications of suspected abuse (including facts, physical signs and course of events)

_____

_____

If the Adult is reporting, what did they say? (Give quotes where possible)

_____

_____

What was your response?

_____

_____

Action taken (i.e., Was an emergency call made to 9-1-1? Did the Adult make the report for themselves? Did they express that they weren't ready to make a report?)

_____

_____

Signature _____

Printed Name _____ Date _____

The above information will serve as a guide and will be necessary if a formal report is filed with the police or appropriate government agency. All information received is to be kept STRICTLY CONFIDENTIAL and not shared with anyone or influenced by anyone.

This document should be sealed and labelled and stored under lock and key.

Suspected Abuse Report Form (Adult)
© Plan to Protect® 2022

SUSPECTED ABUSE REPORT FORM (CHILD)   Appendix 33

Date _____ Name of Student _____

Age of Student _____ Grade _____ Birthdate _____

Address _____

Postal Code _____ Phone Number _____

Parents' Names _____

Siblings' Names _____

Name of Person Filing Report _____

Name of Pastor Receiving Report _____

Name of Social Worker _____ Phone Number _____

Name of alleged perpetrator _____ ❑ M ❑ F

Relationship between suspected victim and alleged perpetrator _____

Nature of suspected abuse: ❑ physical ❑ sexual ❑ emotional ❑ neglect

Indications of suspected abuse (including facts, physical signs and course of events)

_____
_____
_____

Action taken (including date and time)

_____

If a child is reporting: What did the child say? (Give quotes where possible.)

_____
_____
_____

What was your response?

_____
_____

Signature _____

Printed Name _____ Date _____

The above information will serve as a guide and will be necessary if a formal report is filed with the police or appropriate government agency. All information received is to be kept STRICTLY CONFIDENTIAL and not shared with anyone or influenced by anyone.

This document should be sealed and labelled and stored under lock and key.

Suspected Abuse Report Form (Child)
© Plan to Protect® 2022

SUSPECTED ABUSE FOLLOW-UP REPORT FORM   Appendix 33a

To Be Completed by Program Leader/Lead Pastor (separately from Appendix 33)

Date _____

Date of Suspected Abuse Form (Appendix 33) being addressed _____

Name of Student _____

Age of Student _____ Grade _____ Birthdate _____

Address _____

Postal Code _____ Phone Number _____

Details as reported to you:

_____
_____
_____
_____

Conclusions:

_____
_____
_____
_____

Action taken (including dates and times):

_____
_____
_____
_____

Lead Pastor's Signature _____

Printed Name _____ Date _____

The above information will serve as a guide and will be necessary if a formal report is filed with police or appropriate government agency. All information received is to be kept STRICTLY CONFIDENTIAL and not shared with anyone or influenced by anyone.

Suspected Abuse Follow-Up Report Form
© Plan to Protect® 2022

SUSPECTED ABUSE FOLLOW-UP GUIDELINES

Appendix 34

Filing a suspected abuse report with the Child Welfare Agency (CWA) can be an overwhelming experience. In order to assist you with this process, here are some suggested steps to take, or points to consider regarding reporting to CWA, dealing with staff, informing leadership, and following up with the family. It is important to note, however, that these are considerations only, and that each report should be assessed on a case by case basis. Always keep in mind that the safety of the child is paramount, even if it may jeopardize your relationship with the family.

Dealing with the Child Welfare Agency

- Once a suspected abuse report is filed, the person who made the report should make the call to CWA
    - If more than one ministry leader is involved, you may all be in the room to make the call together
- The person making the report can request to be advised as to the outcome of their report to CWA
- When making a report, you will be asked to provide a full report of the incident or condition that causes you to be concerned for the child
    - You can begin your call anonymously to explore the appropriateness of the referral
- Communicate to CWA that the church wants to be a support to the family and to inform you when it would be appropriate to speak directly with the family
- Upon receiving the report, CWA will
    - Assess the seriousness of the report
    - If deemed necessary, an investigation will begin immediately where a child is deemed to be at an "immediate risk"
    - Investigations will begin within 7 days
    - All serious allegations of child abuse are referred to the police by the child protection worker. You will also be asked other relevant identifying information about the family (names of family members, address, etc.)
    - Custodial parents will be interviewed as well as any parent or caretaker alleged to have harmed the child. Other persons, such as siblings, relatives, neighbors, community professionals, who are considered to possibly have information relevant to the reported situation, may also be interviewed.
    - Parents (and the child where appropriate) can expect to be informed by the child protection worker of the outcome of the CWA investigation, and their ongoing role if any.

Appendix 34

Dealing with the Family

When a report of suspected abuse is made regarding a child in your church, responding to the family appropriately is very important. Again, the safety of the child is of primary concern here, and it may not always be wise to inform them that the report is being made. If they ask you if you have filed a report, it is always best to be honest, open, supportive and transparent when you respond while you keep the child's safety in mind.

Following up with the family is very important, but it can be tricky to know when to become involved. It is important to note that the Child Welfare Agency, as part of their program, asks parents if they have support groups that they desire to partner with should they need assistance and ongoing help. If the church is identified by the parents in this way, CWA will involve the church in this process. At this point, the church leaders involved can speak openly with the parents regarding the report in question and offer support. This being the case, when a report is made to CWA , it would be helpful to offer the support of the church with any needs that may arise as a result.

Dealing with the Board

The person reporting the incident and the ministry lead should be informed about the report and contact the Lead Pastor. Board members need only be involved in situations when the church has liability; i.e., The abuse happened on-site, or a church-run camp or event, however, you may believe it prudent to inform the Board members in cases of potential liability. In the case of an allegation against Ministry Personnel, more parties will need to be involved such as insurance agents, lawyers, and pastoral staff. Confidentiality is very important here out of respect for the family.

FIRE PREVENTION PROCEDURE CHECKLIST

The responsibility for fire safety lies with the church leadership.

- Contact your local fire department to ensure that your building is up to code.

- Partner with a fire department representative to develop a Fire Safety Plan for your church.

- Post fire routes in each room where children are served.

- Develop an emergency escape plan.

- Train ministry personnel and other associated ministry leaders regarding the plan (For example, you may need to utilize ushers or other staff to assist with carrying babies from the nursery in case of fire. Consider including them in your training nights.)

- Inform parents of the fire safety procedures that will be followed in the case of a fire in the building. Assure parents that their children will be removed from the building by ministry personnel and will be reunited with them once outside the building.

- Propose performing a fire drill during a peak ministry time.

- Contact the fire department and set up a time for them to perform a fire drill during your ministry time.

INSURANCE / LAWYER CHECKLIST

Appendix 36

- Review Plan to Protect® policies, including policies specific to your church, with your insurance company for approval to qualify for abuse coverage.

- Review regular insurance checklist sent to church (See example checklist provided by Insurance Company).

- Review the coverage required for drivers used for church functions.

- Review the coverage necessary when providing services off of church property (camps, administering of medication by a nurse hired by the camp, playgrounds, etc.)

- Seek legal counsel for the protection plan adopted by the church.

- Inquire with your insurance broker, agent or company to determine whether your liability insurance policy contains any exclusions or limitations for abuse claims. Unfortunately, most insurance policies exclude abuse coverage for churches and children's and youth organizations. In fact, the new Insurance Bureau of Canada's (IBC) recommended liability policy forms contains a standard of abuse exclusion. Without proper abuse coverage, church assets and personal assets are potentially at risk. Most legal professionals recommend occurrence form general liability protection for bodily injury from abuse claims and caution church leaders to be aware of insurance conditions, limitations, sub-limits and claims-made coverage that might restrict coverage for abuse claims that are made now and in the future.

- Inquire about how corporated or unincorporated status may affect the church in relation to liability issues and potential personal liability for Board members and congregational members.

ABUSE PREVENTION DECLARATION
CHURCHES/CHARITABLE ORGANIZATIONS

Appendix 37

Name of organization/policyholder: _____

Address: _____

Please have an authorized representative of your organization review the following declarations, mark the appropriate box for your response and return the original signed copy for underwriting review by your insurance company. Retain a copy for your records.

Declarations

A. Our organization has implemented a formal written abuse prevention *Plan to Protect®* for the children, youth and/or vulnerable adults in our care. ❏ Yes ❏ No

B. Our formal prevention plan contains the following measures:

1. A written statement of policy confirming our organization's commitment to: ❏ Yes ❏ No
   a. a safe environment by preventing harm to those in our care,
   b. protecting our childrens' and youth ministry workers from false allegations, and
   c. declaring zero tolerance for abuse, harassment or neglect.

2. Our prevention plan assists workers by defining physical, sexual and emotional abuse, child neglect, harassment, inappropriate touching and improper discipline. ❏ Yes ❏ No

3. We have mandatory Screening measures for all workers (including all employees, ministers, staff, board members and volunteers) serving in any position involving work with children, youth or vulnerable adults, including the following:

PLEASE CHECK IF YES:	EMPLOYEES/ MINISTERS	VOLUNTEERS
Signed Employee/Volunteer Application (including ministry agreement and release for references and criminal record checks)	❏	❏

Criminal Record Checks: (i.e. C.P.I.C. and V.S.V.)
• New Applicants – checked prior to eligibility
• Existing Workers – re-checked as follows:
  • Camping and Short-Term Missions Organizations – Annually
  • Schools, Day Cares and Nurseries – Every Three (3) years, or less
  • Churches and All Other Organizations – Every Five (5) years, or less
Note: For Existing Workers being re-checked or for New Applicants under 25 years of age, a C.P.I.C. and F.I.P can be done in lieu of a C.P.I.C. and V.S.V.
☐ C.P.I.C. means named-based Police Check through Canadian Police Information Centre
☐ V.S.V. means Vulnerable Sector Verification (Screening)
☐ F.I.P. means Firearms Interest Police query (available through Third Party Providers)
	❏	❏

Background Reference Checks (minimum 2) for new Employees/Volunteers	❏	❏
Personal Interviews for new Employees/Volunteers	❏	❏
Minimum 6-month waiting period for volunteers who are new to your organization prior to eligibility	N/A	❏

Appendix 37

4. We have implemented written procedures to prevent abuse and harassment through the following Operational Procedures:
(Please check if yes)
- ❏ Prohibiting corporal punishment and inappropriate touching, affection or discipline
- ❏ 'Two adult rule' (unrelated) for off-premises contact with children and youth (refer to "Good/Better/Best" Guidelines)
- ❏ Addressing health, safety and sanitation issues to prevent child neglect
- ❏ Age appropriate supervision of washroom breaks (refer to 2011 Abuse Prevention Newsletter – FAQ Question 3)
- ❏ Avoiding activities that could easily lead to allegations of abuse or harassment, such as unsupervised Internet access, individual photography of children and vehicle transportation by a worker alone with unrelated minors
- ❏ Obtaining written parental consent for sponsored off-premises or overnight activities and field trips
- ❏ Implemented a social networking policy for youth programs addressing appropriate content and confidentiality issues
- ❏ Keeping confidential screening documentation on file indefinitely for all workers, including original Criminal Record Checks
- ❏ Annual or bi-annual internal audit, including report to board

5. We have modified or altered our premises (owned or rented) to prevent or discourage abuse incidents by ensuring the following:
(Please check if yes)
- ❏ 'Two-adult rule', and/or 'open door policy' and/or windows in all classrooms and/or designated monitors circulating periodically from room to room, for surveillance and to protect workers against false allegations
- ❏ Controlled access and parental sign-in/sign-out for nursery facilities
- ❏ Parental sign-in/sign-out for children's programs under Grade 1 age
- ❏ Adequate lighting inside and outside of building(s) where children's/youth activities take place

6. We conduct training for all children's and youth ministry workers and other workers in positions of trust with minors or vulnerable adults to assist them in understanding the issue of abuse, abuse prevention and the legal responsibility to report actual or alleged incidents, including the following: (Please check if yes)
- ❏ Initial training for all new workers
- ❏ Annual refresher training for Operational Procedures, Premises and Responding protocol (refer to items 4., 5. and 7. of the Declaration Form)

7. In cases of suspected or alleged abuse, our written protocol for responding includes the following:
(Please check if yes)
- ❏ We will immediately complete an incident report form
- ❏ We will fulfill statutory reporting obligations to child protective agencies or police authorities
- ❏ Without admitting legal liability or making public statements prior to obtaining legal counsel, we will assure a compassionate response to the alleged victim and their family
- ❏ We will maintain confidentiality for the alleged victim and alleged perpetrator
- ❏ We will immediately suspend the alleged perpetrator pending outcome of investigation

Note: For any boxes left unchecked, please attach a written explanation signed by the authorized representative of the organization. Approval is subject to underwriting review. Please keep a photocopy of this Declaration Form for your records and for your internal auditing purposes.

We, the undersigned, duly authorized to make representations on behalf of the organization/corporation applying for coverage eligibility under a contract of liability insurance (new policy or renewal) with the participating Insurer(s).

To the best of our knowledge and after having made reasonable inquiries, we hereby state that all of the declarations contained in this document are accurate and that the organization/corporation is in compliance with the provisions of its abuse prevention plan, as stated in this Abuse Prevention Declaration.

1. _____
Name of Executive Director, Minister or Children's Ministry Director (PLEASE PRINT)

_____
Title

_____
Signature   Date

2. _____
Name of Chairman or President of the Board (PLEASE PRINT)

_____
Title

_____
Signature   Date

BILLETING CHECKLIST

Appendix 38

Host Church Requirements

- Provide sleeping accommodations for either boys or girls, but not both.
- Ensure that youth are billeted in groups of three preferably, but no less than two per home.
- Provide homes that can ensure sleeping/dressing quarters that are distinctly and physically separated from the sleeping/dressing quarters of household members of the opposite gender and from adult members of the billeting household.
- Provide accommodations for youth in homes supervised by parents for the duration of the stay.
- Provide homes that are safe for youth with physical challenges (food or pet allergies, physical limitations, etc.).
- Provide appropriate meals as required for the duration of the stay.
- Provide police records checks for all members of the billeting household who are 18 and older.
- Provide homes that can provide parental supervision throughout the duration of the stay that will ensure that the guidelines for youth at the event are followed.

Youth Guidelines/Expectations

- Youth will respect and follow the rules as outlined by the event organizers.
- Youth will respect the 11:00 pm curfew for bedtimes.
- Youth will respect the rules of the host family and abide by them.
- Youth will notify event leaders of any special needs of which the host family may need to be aware (food or pet allergies, physical conditions that require special attention, etc.).
- Youth will remain in their assigned sleeping accommodations for the duration of the evening.

PROVINCIAL ACTS ON CHILD ABUSE

Alberta	The Child, Youth and Family Enhancement Act
British Columbia	Child, Family and Community Service Act
Manitoba	Child and Family Services Act
New Brunswick	Family Services Act
Newfoundland and Labrador	Children and Youth Care and Protection Act
Northwest Territories	Child and Family Services Act
Nova Scotia	Children and Family Services Act
Nunavut	Child and Family Services Act
Ontario	Child, Youth, and Family Services Act
Prince Edward Island	Child Protection Act
Quebec	Youth Protection Act
Saskatchewan	Child and Family Services Act
Yukon	Child and Family Services Act

Source: Provincial and territorial child protection legislation and policy, Government of Canada. Located at:

https://www.canada.ca/en/public-health/services/publications/health-risks-safety/provincial-territorial-child-protection-legislation-policy-2018.html, (published 2018)

CONFIDENTIALITY AGREEMENT

Appendix 40

Note: It is recommended that a confidentiality statement be signed by all employees and volunteers - whether that clause is in their employment agreement or in a separate confidentiality agreement.

I understand that I will obtain or have access to sensitive and confidential information in my role as an [employee / volunteer] with church. That confidential information may include, without restriction, personal information regarding employees, volunteers, members, attendees, supporters or persons assisted by the church including information in relation to donations, personal or family matters, or obtained from background screening of prospective employees or volunteers. I agree to maintain strict confidentiality of all such confidential information and I will not disclose such information to anyone (including to employees, volunteers, members, attendees, supporters, persons assisted, or my spouse or family members) except authorized representatives of the church who need to know such information or as required by law. I understand and agree that confidentiality is very important in my role and critical to the effective functioning of the church. If I become aware that any confidential information was improperly disclosed, I will immediately advise [title] of the church.

Dated this _____ day of _____, 20____

Name _____

Signature _____

Witness Name _____

Signature _____

OFFENDER'S COVENANT
(Adapted from Smart Justice with permission)

Dear _____,
(name of Offender)

On behalf of the leadership of the church, I would like to welcome you to participate in the worship and congregational life of our church. We want you to know that we see you as a very important and valued part of God's family. In light of all that has taken place in your life there are some guidelines that we feel must be followed. These guidelines are not meant to be punitive but to ensure safety and peace of mind for the congregation and yourself.

- You must refrain from all contact with Children and Youth while attending church functions. This includes all verbal and written communication.

- You must not volunteer or agree to lead, chaperone or participate in events involving Children or Youth.

- You must not transport any Children or Youth as part of the ministry programs of the church.

- The Board will identify at least two "covenant partners", which at least one of them will accompany you if you leave the main congregation room or if you need to go the public washrooms.

- You are to avoid being in the building unsupervised at all times. This includes all Children and Youth ministry areas and washroom areas. When entering the church, you must use the most direct route to the sanctuary area and sit in an area that is visible to your covenant partners.

- You are to abide by any terms and conditions of probation as set out by the court.

- You are not to be in any poorly or unlit areas of the church property.

- You are welcome and encouraged to join one of our adult small groups. However you may not join a group that has minors present or in the home. The small gorup leader and the host family will be informed of your history and the covenant agreement in place.

- You are to avoid befriending families of the church with minors.

- At least twice per year you are requested to meet with the Board to discuss your adherence to these guidelines.

We are so grateful that you have made us aware of your situation. It shows us that there is a cooperative spirit and willingness for restoration and wholeness.

_____ Appendix 41

I, the undersigned, accept the following people as Covenant Partners. I agree to these Covenant Partners being made aware of the circumstances of my situation and the contents of this covenant.

_____
(Covenant Partner #1)

_____
(Covenant Partner #2)

_____
(Covenant Partner #3)

I have read and agree to abide by the conditions of this covenant.

I understand that any violation of this covenant may result in refusal of access to the church property or congregational gatherings may be restricted or prohibited.

I understand that this covenant will be reviewed every six months and will remain in effect for an indefinite period of time.

Offender's Signature: _____ Date: _____

Pastor's Signature: _____ Date: _____

Board Member's Signature: _____ Date: _____

TERMS OF REFERENCE FOR PLAN TO PROTECT® COMMITTEE

The purpose of this committee is to ensure that the Plan to Protect® Policies and Procedures are implemented throughout the church.

Goals:
- To stay abreast of best practices of abuse prevention and safety for our context;
- To coach and train department leaders on the necessary steps to ensure implementation of the policies and procedures;
- To screen and maintain the screening requirements of all Ministry Personnel (paid and unpaid) that will be placed in a Position of Trust;
- To provide orientation training and maintain the annual training requirements of all Ministry Personnel (paid and unpaid) that will be placed in a Position of Trust;
- In partnership with the administrative staff ensure the management of documentation is in order to protect the stakeholders of the church;
- To address questions and concerns that arise in relation to the Plan to Protect® policies;
- To conduct an annual audit of the policies and report back to the Board the findings of the audit; and
- To alert the Board of needed policy revisions, and potentially draft and recommend amendments to the policies;
- To prepare an annual report on the outcomes of the safeguarding initiatives of the church.

Committee Make-up:
- **Chair (1)** - call meetings, write annual report, meet with Board and staff as needed, assist with policy development and audits, in partnership with pastoral staff and administrative staff update and review forms, assist with trainings, and coach team members.
- **Board of Directors (1 or 2)** - liaison with Board and assist with serving Pastors and Chair in dealing with difficult issues that arise from opposition or screening.
- **Administrators (2)** - Volunteers or staff who have strong administrative skills or gifts (setting up the screening files, managing the master list of screened Ministry Personnel, processing police record checks)**
- **Screeners (2)** - Volunteers who have strong discernment gifts and/or experience in interviewing/screening staff (in partnership with pastoral staff, they conduct interviews, check references, etc.).
- **Members at Large (2)** – Individuals serving in departments that minister to the vulnerable sector i.e., children, youth, elderly, or special needs.
- **Trainers (2)** – Volunteers or paid staff who have strong communication skills and influence, willing to be certified as a trainer. Estimated 4-8 trainings per year.

Recommendations:

For the size of church we should have 1 trainer for every 100 volunteers

The committee will meet initially 2-3 times until the policy is approved by the Board.

Once the policy is approved, the team will meet quarterly. This is not the extent of their involvement as each role on the committee will have a portfolio which will require active involvement in either administration, screening or training.

SAMPLE JOB DESCRIPTION - PLAN TO PROTECT® ADMINISTRATOR

Appendix 43

We need to protect the vulnerable sector!

As a Plan to Protect Administrator/Leader you will be responsible to administer, implement and maintain a strong abuse prevention program for our organization.

Personnel Status: EMPLOYEE or VOLUNTEER

Term: Preference to candidates that will commit for a three-year term based on certification term

Report To:

Qualifications:

- Strong interpersonal and communication skills (both written and oral)
- Pleasant phone manner
- Plan to Protect® Administrator/Leader Course Level 1
- Plan to Protect® Administrator/Leader Course Level 2 – (Working Towards)

Responsibilities:

- Uphold the standard of protection and abuse prevention that Plan to Protect® recommends and reflects requirements of our Insurance Company.
- Demonstrate an understanding of the value and importance of abuse prevention and vulnerable sector protection and disseminate the importance down to Ministry Personnel.
- Understand the legal requirements for reporting and responding to abuse of Children and Vulnerable Adults and have the organization adhere to these, as outlined by Provincial Laws.
- Assist and support Ministry Personnel in reporting and responding to abuse.
- Assist with the development and maintenance of our Plan to Protect® Policy, adhering to the laws of the Province/State and Country, and reflect Insurance requirements, and ensure policy and amendments are approved by the Board.
- Identify and develop a strong recruitment and screening process for Ministry Personnel outlined by the policy.
    - Ensure a 6-month waiting period
    - Application
    - Interview
    - References
    - Police Records Check
- Work with Trainer and Department Heads to communicate needs of screening requirements.
- Schedule Hall Monitors in conjunction with department heads.
- Ensures information management system captures the fields necessary to track data needed for documentation management.
- Update personnel files when each component of the screening process is satisfied (including training attendance).
- Assure personnel are up to date and current with yearly training.
- Assure personnel are up to date and current with their Criminal Record Check.

- In consultation with leadership determine next steps for individuals that have red flags regarding:
  - Criminal Record Check that came back "Not – Clear"
    - i.e., attend to local Police Services
  - Unfavorable references
    - i.e., possible additional reference
  - Training Component incomplete
    - i.e., take online
- Ensuring documents are created, stored, and maintained properly and permanently.
- Maintain certification status with Plan to Protect® Administrator/Leader Certification Course.
- Annually submit budget proposal for administration needs.
- Prepare annual report to membership of the numbers of those who have been screened and approved to be in a Position of Trust with the vulnerable and provide supporting documentation need for annual audit.
- Work with the Board to schedule annual audit (Audits are to be done by individuals not directly involved in abuse prevention).
- Stay current with Plan to Protect® offerings of Special Interest Webinars, legislation updates, insurance requirements and best practices.
- Work in conjunction with leadership and department heads, in dealing with disciplinary action.
- Supports the crisis response team as needed.

Contact:

SAMPLE JOB DESCRIPTION - PLAN TO PROTECT® TRAIN THE TRAINER

We need to protect the vulnerable sector!

As a Plan to Protect® Trainer you will be responsible for training our volunteers and staff on abuse prevention and vulnerable sector protection.

Personnel Status: EMPLOYEE or VOLUNTEER

Term: Preference to candidates that will commit for a three-year term based on certification term

Report To:

Qualifications:

- Strong communication skills
- Experience in training and/or public speaking
- Plan to Protect® Train the Trainer Course Level 1
- Plan to Protect® Train the Trainer Course Level 2 – (Working Towards)

Responsibilities:

- Customize Plan to Protect® Orientation Training, including teaching notes, student notes and visual aid (i.e., PowerPoint) to reflect our policy, procedures and context.
- Customize Plan to Protect® Refresher Training, including teaching notes, student notes and visual aid (i.e., PowerPoint) to reflect our policy, procedures and context.
- Provide Plan to Protect® Orientation Training for Ministry Personnel who are new or have not taken the training before.
    - Determine with leadership how often the Orientation Training should be held; i.e, September, January, June
    - Determine with leadership how often Annual Refresher Training should be held; i.e., September, January, June
- Book training room for training events.
- Ensure LCD projector is available for training sessions.
- Work with Administrator/Leader and Department Heads to communicate and promote upcoming training events.
- Ensure photocopies of student notes are prepared in advance of Training Sessions.
- Ensure attendance is taken during each training event and pass on to Administrator/Leader.
- In consultation with leadership determine next steps for individuals that do not attend training sessions (i.e, suspend involvement, require on-line training).
- Stay current with Plan to Protect® offerings of Special Interest Webinars, legislation updates and best practices through newsletters and websites.
- Maintain Certification Status with Plan to Protect® Train the Trainer course (Level One and Level Two).
- Annually submit budget proposal for training needs.
- Annually update PowerPoints and Training notes as needed.
- Report annually the number of trainings held, and number of personnel trained during the course of the year.

Contact:

PLAN TO PROTECT® SERVICES

Plan to Protect® provides the HIGHEST STANDARD of abuse prevention and safeguarding. Our customized tools, training, policies and procedures help leaders, and their organizations meet that standard.

Our products and services include:
- Plan to Protect® A Safeguarding Guide for Children, Youth and Adults (Church Edition)
- Customized policies and procedures
- Risk Assessments
- Policy Audits
- Crisis Response Certification and Consulting
- Inquiries and Investigations
- Trauma Informed Consulting
- Memberships
- Certification training for Trainers and Administrators
- Onsite Orientation and Refresher Training
- Online Training at www.plantoprotectschool.com
- Speaker's Bureau providing
- Screening Services at www.plantoprotectscreening.com
- Resources

We have membership packages available for different sized budgets and needs. Members of Plan to Protect® enjoy wide access to our products and services.

The Plan to Protect® team is committed to providing the tools, training and momentum to help you achieve excellence in your programming. We can help make planning and implementation of abuse prevention a manageable task.

Whether you are looking for assistance writing abuse policies, a facilitator for on-site training, Criminal Record Checks, contract help implementing abuse prevention, or consulting services, Plan to Protect® provides all your safeguarding needs.

www.plantoprotect.com

BIBLIOGRAPHY

ONLINE RESOURCES

Bullying Canada. (https://www.bullyingcanada.ca)
A support service for youth, parents, coaches and teachers.

Cybertip.ca. (https://www.cybertip.ca/en)
Canada's national tip line for reporting the online sexual exploitation of children. Contains useful resources for child safety online.

Elder Abuse Prevention Ontario. (https://www.eapon.ca)
An organization providing support to seniors affected by abuse, fostering public awareness, delivering training, and community building.

Government of Alberta (n.d.). *Effective Supervision in Childcare Settings.*
Techniques that promote effective supervision practices and create safe care environments.

Hall, K. (n.d.). *Facing the Risk - Precious Cargo: Managing Transportation Risk for Churches and Charities.* **Robertson Hall Insurance.** (https://robertsonhall.com/pdf/ADVANTAGE%20-%20Precious%20Cargo.pdf)

Hall, K. (n.d.). *Charities and the Rental of their Facilities: An Insurance Perspective.* **Robertson Hall Insurance.** (https://robertsonhall.com/pdf/Outside%20User%20Groups.pdf)
How charitable organizations can be well prepared when renting their facilities.

National Centre on Sexual Behaviour in Youth. (https://ncsby.org/resources)
Resources pertaining to child abuse prevention, sexual health of youth and sex education.

Office of the Fire Marshal and Emergency Management of Ontario. (2016). *Fire Drills.* (https://www.mcscs.jus.gov.on.ca/sites/default/files/content/ofm/docs/TG-04-2016%20-%20Fire%20Drill%20Guideline.pdf)
Guidelines for fire drill planning.

ProtectKidsOnline.ca. (https://protectkidsonline.ca/app/en)
Helping parents/guardians stay on top of the digital world their children are engaging in. Information about the ever-changing online interests of young people, the potential risks they face and proactive strategies to help keep your child/adolescent safe while online.

Public Health Ontario. (2020). *Program Planning and Evaluation.* (https://www.publichealthontario.ca/en/health-topics/public-health-practice/program-planning-evaluation)
Information, resources and related links on the subject of effective health promotion program planning and evaluation.

Rembert, L. (2021). *Online Safety 101: How to Keep Your Kids Safe Online.* (https://privacycanada.net/online-esafety-guide-for-kids)
Parent guidelines, online predators, cyberbullying, personal information protection and tips.

Rennie, P. (2016). *Guide to Effective Practice in Mentoring for Children and Youth who are, or have been in Receipt of Child Protection Services.* (https://bigbrothersbigsisters.ca/wp-content/uploads/2018/02/YiC_BBBSC-Min_of_Youth_w_appendices_v0.3_lite.pdf)
Guide to recruiting, screening, and training mentors, as well as matching, monitoring and supporting mentors and mentees.

Robertson Hall Insurance INC. (2019). *Abuse Prevention Made Easy(er).* (https://robertsonhall.com/pdf/RH_Abuse_Prevention_Newsletter.pdf)
Seven-point Abuse Prevention Plan Checklist.

Samuelson-Glushko Canadian Internet Policy and Public Interest Clinic (CIPPIC). (n.d.). *Copyright and Privacy in Photograph.* (https://cippic.ca/en/FAQ/Photography_Law)
FAQ and resources on copyright and privacy in photography.

Save the Children International (n.d.). *Child Safe Programming Guidelines.* (https://www.end-violence.org/sites/default/files/paragraphs/download/SAVE%20THE%20CHILDREN%20Child%20Safe%20Programming%20Guidelines.pdf)
Guidance on how to implement child safe programming within the context of a safeguarding policy.

Toronto Public Health (2019). *Infection Prevention and Control in Child Care Centres: Requirements and Best Practices.* (https://www.toronto.ca/wp-content/uploads/2019/07/98cb-CCC-IPAC-RBP-Revised-2018-2019-AODA.pdf)

Volunteer Canada. (http://www.volunteercanada.ca)
A charity providing national leadership and expertise on volunteerism to increase the participation, quality and diversity of volunteer experiences.

BOOKS

Brown, B. (2012). *Daring Greatly: How the Courage to Be Vulnerable Transforms the Way We Live, Love, Parent, and Lead.* Penguin Books.

Cobble, J., Hammar, R. & Klipowicz, S. (2003). *Reducing the Risk II: Making your Church Safe from Sexual Abuse.* Church Law & Tax Report.

Deepak, R. (2014). *On Guard: Preventing and Responding to Child Abuse at Church.* Greensboro: New Growth Press.

McCoy, D. (2006). *The Manipulative Man: Identify His Behavior, Counter the Abuse, Regain Control.* Simon & Schuster.

Milfred Minatrea, (2004). *Shaped by God's Heart, The Passion and Practices of Missional Churches.* San Francisco: JosseyBass.

Roblin-Lee, D. (2018). *Who is the Predator: Warning Signs.* Bydesign Media.

Walker, T. & Spears, P. (2013). *The Inspired Caregiver: Finding Joy While Caring for Those You Love.* Createspace Independent Publishing Platform.

Zarra, E. (1997). *It Should Never Happen Here: A Guide for Minimizing the Risk of Child Abuse in Ministry.* Baker Publishing Group.

LEGISLATION, CONVENTIONS AND GOVERNMENT POLICIES

Canadian Human Rights Act (R.S.C., 1985, c. H-6).
https://laws-lois.justice.gc.ca/eng/acts/h-6

Office of the Privacy Commissioner of Canada (2020). *PIPEDA Fair Information Principle 5 – Limiting Use, Disclosure, and Retention.*
https://www.priv.gc.ca/en/privacy-topics/privacy-laws-in-canada/the-personal-information-protection-and-electronic-documents-act-pipeda/p_principle/principles/p_use

Ontario Human Rights Commission (2015). *Defences and Exceptions. Policy on preventing discrimination based on creed.*
http://www.ohrc.on.ca/en/policy-preventing-discrimination-based-creed/8-defences-and-exceptions

Personal Information Protection Act (SA 2003, c. P-6.5).
https://www.qp.alberta.ca/documents/Acts/P06P5.pdf

Personal Information Protection and Electronic Documents Act (S.C. 2000, c. 5).
https://laws-lois.justice.gc.ca/ENG/ACTS/P-8.6/page-1.html

UN Convention on the Rights on the Child (1989).
https://www.ohchr.org/en/professionalinterest/pages/crc.aspx

www.ingramcontent.com/pod-product-compliance
Lightning Source LLC
Chambersburg PA
CBHW080533300426
44111CB00017B/2704